977.2 O
Owens, Robert M. (Robert Martin), 1974-
Mr. Jefferson's hammer
30049002704527

MAR 2012

DISCARD

MR. JEFFERSON'S HAMMER

D0143982

Piqua Public Library
116 West High Street
Piqua, Ohio 45356

D90

Mr. Jefferson's Hammer

WILLIAM HENRY HARRISON
AND THE ORIGINS OF
AMERICAN INDIAN POLICY

ROBERT M. OWENS

977.2 O
Owens, Robert M. (Robert Martin), 1974-
Mr. Jefferson's hammer
30049002704527

Piqua Public Library
116 West High Street
Piqua, Ohio 45356

University of Oklahoma Press : Norman

Library of Congress Cataloging-in-Publication Data

Owens, Robert M. (Robert Martin), 1974–
   Mr. Jefferson's hammer : William Henry Harrison and the origins of American Indian policy / Robert M. Owens.
   p. cm.
   Includes bibliographical references and index.
   ISBN: 978-0-8061-3842-8 (cloth)
   ISBN: 978-0-8061-4198-5 (paper)
   1. Harrison, William Henry, 1773–1841.   2. Governors—Indiana—Biography. 3. Generals—United States—Biography.   4. Indiana—History—19th century. 5. Frontier and pioneer life—Indiana.   6. Harrison, William Henry, 1773–1841— Relations with Indians.   7. Indians of North America—Indiana—Government relations—History—19th century.   8. Jefferson, Thomas, 1743–1826.   9. United States—Territorial expansion.   10. Presidents—United States—Biography. I. Title.
   E392.O94   2007
   977.2'03092—dc22

                                                                        2006039092

The paper in this book meets the guidelines for permanence and durability of the Committee on Production Guidelines for Book Longevity of the Council on Library Resources, Inc.

Copyright © 2007 by the University of Oklahoma Press, Norman, Publishing Division of the University. Manufactured in the U.S.A. Paperback published 2011.

All rights reserved. No part of this publication may be reproduced, stored in a retrieval system, or transmitted, in any form or by any means, electronic, mechanical, photocopying, recording, or otherwise—except as permitted under Section 107 or 108 of the United States Copyright Act—without the prior written permission of the University of Oklahoma Press.

For my grandfathers:
C. Ralph Owens (1907–1979)
Pfc. James M. Bell, U.S. Army, World War II (1915–1978)

MAR 2012

Contents

Illustrations

Preface and Acknowledgments

In writing this study of Harrison, I had certain advantages that previous researchers on this topic did not have. The simplest is timing. A tremendous historiography of the Northwest, including the works listed in this preface, already existed to build upon. Further, it was pure luck on my part that editor Douglas Clanin and the Indiana Historical Society (IHS) published, in 1999, the most comprehensive collection of Harrison documents from his frontier days. *The Papers of William Henry Harrison 1800–1815* (microfilm) provides vastly more material on Harrison than previously available in any one place. It offers roughly three times what Logan Esarey's 1922 print edition of Harrison's *Messages and Letters* (2 vols.) contains, and all in an easily readable and footnoted format. The present book is therefore the first to take full advantage of this tremendous resource, as well as more traditional archival manuscripts. I imagine that part of the reason we have waited so long for a more detailed study of Harrison is the widely scattered nature of the documents so laboriously collected by the IHS.

Like most first-time authors, I have many people to thank. Visits to Indianapolis always proved fruitful, largely because of the fine collections and helpful staffs of the Indiana Historical Society and the Indiana State Library. I am grateful as well to Brian Spangle of the McGrady-Brockman House and the Grouseland Foundation in Vincennes. Dr. James Holmberg and the staff of the Filson Historical Society in Louisville—who have had the wisdom to keep their old card catalog—were tremendously helpful. They were also kind enough to make me a Filson Fellow while I was finishing my dissertation. The Illinois State

Historical Society in Springfield also honored me with a King V. Hostick Award and allowed me access to what is now called the Abraham Lincoln Presidential Library. Thanks as well to the *Journal of the Early Republic* and the *Journal of Illinois History* for allowing me to republish parts of articles I wrote for them (cited in the Bibliography).

I am grateful to the editorial staff and anonymous readers of the University of Oklahoma Press, whose suggestions and criticisms greatly strengthened this work.

Throughout my life, I have had great teachers. Thanks to professor emeritus Donald S. Detwiler of Southern Illinois University at Carbondale, my unofficial undergraduate adviser. I owe a great debt as well to Fred Hoxie, Swanlund Professor of History at the University of Illinois, Urbana-Champaign, who read innumerable early drafts of this work and provided invaluable insight and advice. Part of that advice constituted introducing me to Helen Hornbeck Tanner at the Newberry Library. Helen remains a walking treasure trove of Great Lakes history and has always been generous with her support. Andrew Cayton, Distinguished Professor at Miami University, encouraged me from the earliest stages of this project. Dr. John Hoffmann not only provided me with my best job in graduate school—archivist for the Illinois Historical Survey—but was also extraordinarily gracious in sharing his knowledge of research methods and Midwestern history.

My thanks also to Michael F. Conlin, associate professor of history at Eastern Washington University, my colleague, sometime RA, and always friend. I am grateful as well to my colleagues here at Wichita State University for their support and encouragement and to Professor Andrejs Plakans and the History Department at Iowa State University, who gave me my first real job.

Thanks to Jon Stewart and *The Daily Show.* (You can't read microfilm all the time.)

Above all others, I wish to thank my adviser, Daniel C. Littlefield, now Carolina Professor of History at the University of South Carolina, Columbia, for his unyielding support. I would not have finished without him.

Finally, I must thank my family for tolerating my scholarly eccentricities and genuinely trying to understand just what I was babbling about.

Introduction

On June 22, 1807, the HMS *Leopard* came alongside the USS *Chesapeake* and ordered her to allow a boarding party to search for Royal Navy deserters. Much to Americans' irritation, British men-of-war had been stopping American ships to look for absconded sailors, or to impress needed men of any nationality, for decades. But this was an American warship, not a merchant ship, and in U.S. territorial waters no less. Further, Britain and America were at peace and had been for twenty-four years. Those facts meant little to the British captain. The *Chesapeake* was harboring deserters from the Royal Navy and had not yet installed her heavy guns. Those facts meant little to the American captain. When the *Chesapeake* refused the request, the *Leopard* fired, killing three Americans and wounding several more. British tars then boarded the American ship, removed accused deserters, and left the *Chesapeake* to limp back into port.[1]

The *Chesapeake-Leopard* Affair, as it came to be known, was an outrageous international incident, immediately protested by the American government. Great Britain, in no hurry to widen its list of enemies in its mortal struggle with Napoleonic France—the primary reason for impressing sailors in the first place—tried to minimize the affair without relinquishing the practice of press gangs. President Thomas Jefferson, hating Britain but despising public expense even more, also sought to avoid war. Eventually, diplomats prevented a further escalation of hostilities. For many Americans, however, the affair confirmed what they had long suspected and vociferously maintained: Britain was their implacable foe and would never respect American rights unless U.S.

military victories clubbed it into doing so. One such American was William Henry Harrison.

As the governor of Indiana Territory, at that time a frontier outpost, Harrison viewed any potential fight with Britain and its nearby Canadian territories with keen interest. As the son of a hero of the American Revolution, he entertained a lifelong suspicion of British motives, policy, and even morality. As the ranking government official in his territory, the first among Indiana's social elite, the commander-in-chief of the territorial militia, and an unabashed patriot, Harrison felt compelled to speak out on the issue. His first great opportunity to do so in a public forum came when he addressed the territory's general assembly that August.

Governor Harrison first vented his outrage over the Royal Navy's general practice of abusing America's rights as a neutral shipper and impressing American sailors. The *Chesapeake-Leopard* Affair he found particularly egregious. He railed at the insult to national honor, the "disgraceful" episode in which a British officer had given such mortifying orders to members of the U.S. Navy. It was an example of British "tyranny," he intoned, and, God willing, such tyrants would be smote by virtuous and free Americans. These statements do not necessarily attract the casual reader's eye. Obviously, an American official would denounce such an act by a foreign power, and one would expect him to alloy his words with affirmations of his own patriotism. Yet something else the governor said might give one pause.

He noted that open war might break out as a result—not an unreasonable assumption—and that he and his frontier neighbors would be "peculiarly interested" in the conflict. Then he added, "[F]or who does not know that the tomahawk and scalping knife of the savage are always employed as the instruments of British vengeance." Why mention the Indians? The Shawnees had no navy. The Delawares never impressed American sailors. He continued, "At this moment . . . I sincerely believe [British] agents are organizing a combination amongst the Indians within our limits, for the purpose of assassination and murder."[2] Harrison's speech to the assembly reveals his Western career in microcosm: patriotism, Anglophobia, saber-rattling posturing, and a smidge of political opportunism to boot.

Upon closer examination, linking British and Indian interests was not only common but also reflexive for men of William Henry Harrison's generation. The vast majority of Americans, both public officials and private citizens, took it as a given that Great Britain was the ultimate source for any "Indian trouble." Many Indians had sided with His Majesty during the American Revolution, and British agents had indeed encouraged Indian resistance to American expansion in the 1780s and early 1790s. What Harrison and like-minded Americans seemed unable or unwilling to admit, however, was that they themselves were the primary sources of unrest among their Indian neighbors. A rapacious American hunger for Indian lands, the swift destruction of resources on which Indians depended, and a string of treaties broken largely by Americans fueled far more anti-U.S. anger than the British Indian Department. By the late eighteenth century and certainly by the early nineteenth century, no intelligent Indian needed a British (or Spanish) agent to point out that America's citizenry and government posed a threat to Natives' way of life.

William Henry Harrison and most other Americans, especially on the frontier, tended to blame Britain not just for Indian troubles but for almost any ill afflicting the United States. Whether the issue was economic, social, or, in the case of slavery, both, it proved far easier to attribute American problems to British interference rather than look within one's own soul.

The paradox, however, was the degree to which Americans, for generations prior to the Revolution, had admired and emulated British culture and society. At the triumphant conclusion of the Seven Years' War, American colonists had ecstatically celebrated their part in the victory over France. Colonial leaders were proud of their status as citizens of the empire. And yet, when they felt their rights as Englishmen were threatened, they rebelled in an attempt to restore them. Or, as Fred Anderson put it, "[M]en . . . who otherwise would have liked nothing better than to pursue honor, wealth, and power within the British imperial framework" were forced to confront issues of local rule versus distant sovereignty. Their defense of local autonomy spurred them to seek independence, and "Americans who would have been imperialists in any case became Revolutionaries first."[3] They fought against the Empire because parliamentary rule was cramping their imperial style. That unstable cocktail of admiring British tradition and hating British rule always lay just beneath the surface for Americans in the early Republic.

To explore that issue, I chose to write a cultural biography of William Henry Harrison. To most, he would not be the obvious choice. As one manuscript referee noted, he has often been characterized as a "bland functionary." Henry Clay was a far greater statesman, Andrew Jackson a far greater warrior, and Thomas Jefferson easily a far greater scholar. But Harrison was on the ground in question, and his decisions, foolish or wise, had immediate impact. He exercised tremendous authority over a vast area and was empowered to negotiate with numerous Native American peoples. He held extraordinary military and civil power for much of his tenure as Indiana's governor.

Harrison's lineage and upbringing were typical for American leaders of his era. His life and career span a period of intense tumult and change in U.S. history. He was a Virginia gentleman who sought his fortune in the emerging West, with mixed results. He was a former soldier who built his subsequent political career on his service during the War of 1812. He was a husband and father who sought to secure his own livelihood and standard of living, not always successfully. Warts and all, William Henry Harrison was quintessentially American.

Harrison occupies an odd niche in American history. Most Americans know him, if at all, as the hapless president who died after only one month in office. My generation might remember an episode of *The Simpsons* that memorialized him for just that fact. For historians specializing in the nineteenth century, the fact that he was the first president to die in office and that his death led to a wave of hand-wringing and soul-searching among numerous ministers across the nation seems mildly interesting. For most Americans, his true impact remains unnoticed or misunderstood. The decisions Harrison and his contemporaries—allies and opponents—made in the decade prior to 1812 had a profound impact on the history of the Midwest and laid the groundwork for American expansion into the Far West as well. To this day we live with the echoes of Harrison's proclamations, the boundaries of his treaties, and the ramifications of his actions.[4]

Aside from his background, Harrison's duties as frontier official and Indian agent make him important to remember as well. To understand Americans in the early nineteenth century, one must acknowledge the almost fanatical reverence most held for the Revolutionary generation. Doing so requires some background information, especially regarding early American thinking.

With the Peace of Paris in 1783, Americans embarked on what (for them) was a bold adventure and a grand sociological experiment. Having inherited, on paper at least, the vast territory from the Appalachian Mountains to the Mississippi River, the United States also sought to determine how to administer and exploit this windfall. In a broader sense, Americans—in 1783 and for succeeding decades—also had to figure out how they would govern themselves.

It was the American Revolution that posed but did not answer the question. Many of the greatest leaders of the Revolution embodied the resulting ambiguity. The most prominent and pronounced was the Virginian Thomas Jefferson, who wrote of man's inalienable right to "life, liberty, and the pursuit of happiness" with the same hand he used to write bills of sale for his slaves. The years of Jefferson's presidency (1801–1809) coincided with the most crucial years of Harrison's governorship in Indiana Territory.

As Peter S. Onuf and Leonard J. Sadosky have argued, "[I]t was the sustained struggle against sinister foes"—the British, their Indian allies, rebellious slaves, and seemingly monarchical Federalists—"that gave Jeffersonian republicanism its sometimes hysterical tone and its widespread popular appeal." Jefferson and his followers, while lacking a truly coherent political ideology, nevertheless shared beliefs that "served as a lens through which they saw the world and provided the tools with which, for better or worse, they reshaped it."[5]

In the short term at least, this worldview worked well enough, especially against outsiders not directly empowered by the political process. The situation became considerably more convoluted when Republicans fought among themselves or against other Americans who claimed an equal share of Revolutionary heritage. Then the logic could become tortured.

While Americans in the first decade of the nineteenth century were often divided on other issues, their opinion of proper Indian policy was nearly unanimous. Jefferson, like George Washington, Ben Franklin, and many other Revolutionary leaders, had long coveted Western lands. The land hunger of these prominent speculators was matched by many ordinary Americans who hoped to buy or squat upon such lands. They saw opportunity in the "unused" space west of the Appalachians. The key component of William Henry Harrison's popularity would be his success in securing cheap land cessions.

America's Revolutionary generation accepted unquestioningly that Anglo-American society was the best, and therefore the only, model to emulate. Indians' cultures and societies were therefore backward. While Natives themselves had natural rights, their way of life did not, and Indians had to change for "their own good." In the late nineteenth century this attitude was summed up as a desire to "kill the Indian but save the man."

Disdain for Indian cultures combined with a distrust of the Indians' British allies in the minds of most Americans. Because the Revolution had been divine, its opponents had to be devilish. Mercy Otis Warren's history of the American Revolution serves as a good example of this simplistic dichotomy.[6] Even more graphic was the media storm associated with the murder of Jane McCrea (see chapters 1 and 5). American politics, Indian policy, and debates about slavery all grew largely from an intense patriotic and anti-British sentiment. Britain's continued close relationship with Indian tribes in the Great Lakes region only exacerbated Americans' distrust of them. Years later Americans on the frontier, like William Henry Harrison and the people of Indiana Territory, still struggled with the meanings and repercussions of those fears.

This is not the first biography of Harrison. A number of campaign-driven pieces written during his post-1815 political career offer more insight into nineteenth-century political mythology than into the facts of Harrison's life. Even his twentieth-century biographers tended to fall in love with "Old Tippecanoe." Aside from tone—I do not see it as my duty to paint Harrison as a hero or a villain—I differ from the older biographies by showing comparatively little interest in Harrison's genealogy. The fact that he was descended from Puritans strikes me as more interesting than significant. Nor do I spend much time on Harrison's role during the War of 1812 or his subsequent career in national politics. While those phases of his life are much better known,[7] it was during his years in Indiana that he had a much greater impact on American history.

A number of post-1815 campaign biographies were written by Harrison partisans. Of those, Moses Dawson's *A Historical Narrative of the Civil and Military Services of Major-General William Henry Harrison, and a Vindication of His Character and Conduct as a Statesman, a Citizen, and a Soldier* (Cincinnati, 1824) is probably the best, although still to be used with caution. In the twentieth century, Dorothy Burne Goebel's dissertation, *William Henry Harrison: A Political Biography* (Indianapolis, 1926), offered, for its time, a very respectable treatment.

Freeman Cleaves's *Old Tippecanoe: William Henry Harrison and His Time* (New York, 1939) probably remains the most thorough Harrison biography to date, but it is also one of the more fawning. Reading Cleaves, one gets the impression that Tecumseh and other Native American chiefs were silly for not immediately selling the governor their lands and committing cultural suicide.

After Cleaves, Harrison's territorial years drifted without serious biographical study until Andrew Cayton's *Frontier Indiana* (Bloomington, 1996), wherein the author offers insightful chapters on Harrison and territorial Indiana through the point of view of the governor's wife, Anna Symmes Harrison, his chief political rival, Jonathan Jennings, and his former rival-turned-reluctant ally, Chief Little Turtle.

Professor Robert Gray Gunderson, author of the classic study of the 1840 presidential election, *The Log-Cabin Campaign* (Lexington, 1957), was working on what no doubt would have been the definitive Harrison biography. Professor Gunderson's death robbed us of such a work, although he did publish a thoughtful preliminary study, "William Henry Harrison: Apprentice in Arms," in the *Northwest Ohio Quarterly* (Winter 1993).

Some excellent secondary works in the past few decades have discussed Harrison's role in the Northwest. Eugene Berwanger's *The Frontier Against Slavery* (Urbana, 1967) and Nicole Etcheson's *The Emerging Midwest: Upland Southerners and the Political Culture of the Old Northwest, 1787–1861* (Bloomington, 1996) discuss many of the political and social debates Harrison and other American officials contended with north of the Ohio. Reginald Horsman's *Expansion and American Indian Policy, 1783–1812* (East

Lansing, 1967) and Richard White's magisterial *The Middle Ground: Indians, Empires, and Republics in the Great Lakes Region, 1650–1815* (Cambridge, 1991) both place Governor Harrison in context as the chief American negotiator with American Indian tribes in the region. Bernard Sheehan's *Seeds of Extinction: Jeffersonian Philanthropy and the American Indian* (Chapel Hill, 1973), Francis Paul Prucha's *The Great Father: The United States Government and the American Indians* (Lincoln, 1984), Anthony F. C. Wallace's *Jefferson and the Indians: The Tragic Fate of the First Americans* (Cambridge, Mass., 1999), and Peter S. Onuf's *Jefferson's Empire: The Language of American Nationhood* (Charlottesville, 2000) all examine, with slightly different conclusions, the Jeffersonian mind and its influence on Indian policy. All of these works stand quite well on their own.

Yet these very able books still left me with questions. Was Harrison a sincere Republican or just an opportunist? Why did he push so hard for extending slavery north of the Ohio? I was especially curious about Harrison and his role in U.S.-Indian affairs north of the Ohio River. Typically, secondary sources discussing Harrison's activities at Indian treaties would refer to him as a tough negotiator, a man who drove a hard bargain with Indians and purchased vast quantities of their land for a pittance. I did not dispute that this was so, but I wanted to know *how* he did it.

I am not the only one to ask these questions. In a 1975 review of Sheehan's *Seeds of Extinction*, William T. Hagan offered, "An analysis of Jefferson's relations with Governor William Henry Harrison of Indiana Territory would tell us more about Jefferson and his impact on the American Indian than we could ever learn from his correspondence with European intellectuals."[8] By academic standards at least, this book is not particularly late.

This is a cultural biography, making efforts to place Harrison within the context of his era. I argue that, rather than springing from internal passions of good or evil, his actions become readily understood, almost predictable, when one recognizes the man's worldview. To appreciate William Henry Harrison's thinking in Indiana during the early nineteenth century, one must understand the Virginia gentry of the eighteenth century.

MAPS

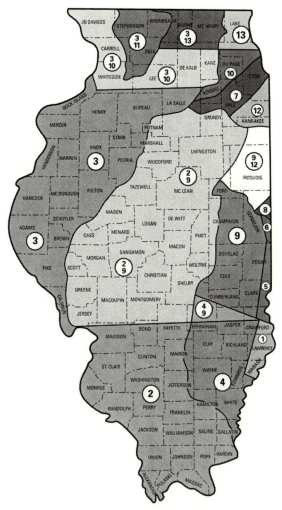

Indian land cessions in Illinois. Harrison's land cession treaties in Illinois were enormous and perhaps among his most corrupt. Subsequent commissioners negotiated redundant cessions just to be certain of the land title. Reproduced with permission from Robert M. Owens, "Jean Baptiste Ducoigne, the Kaskaskias, and the Limits of Thomas Jefferson's Friendship," *Journal of Illinois History* 5, no. 2 (Summer 2002): 109–36, map on 131.

1. June 7, 1803
2. August 13, 1803
3. November 3, 1804
4. December 30, 1805
5. September 30, 1809
6. June 4, 1816
7. August 24, 1816

8. October 2, 1818
9. July 30, 1819
10. July 29, 1829
11. September 15, 1832
12. October 20, 1832
13. September 26, 1833

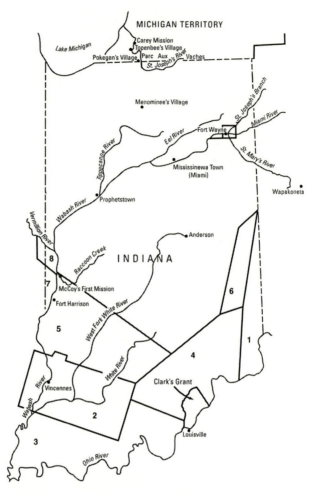

Indian land cessions in Indiana, 1795–1809. Harrison's treaties bought title to about half of what became the state of Indiana. Note how the Fort Wayne treaties of 1809 jut threateningly into Indian territory, which enraged Tecumseh and the Prophet. From George A. Schultz, *An Indian Canaan: Isaac McCoy and the Vision of an Indian State* (Norman: University of Oklahoma Press, 1972). Reproduced with permission of the publisher.

1. Treaty of Greenville, August 3, 1795
2. Treaty of Fort Wayne, June 3, 1803
3. Treaty with the Delawares, August 18, 1804
4. Treaty of Grouseland, August 21, 1805
5. Treaty of Fort Wayne, September 30, 1809
6. Treaty of Fort Wayne, September 30, 1809
7. Treaty of Fort Wayne, September 30, 1809; validated by Kickapoos at Fort Wayne, December 9, 1809
8. Treaty of Fort Wayne (Kickapoos), December 9, 1809

Northwest Territory. From George C. Pence and Nellie C. Armstrong, *Indiana Boundaries: Territory, State, and County* (Indianapolis: Indiana Historical Bureau, 1967). Reproduced with permission of the Indiana Historical Bureau.

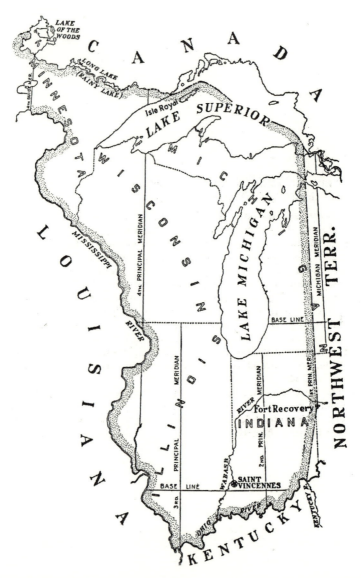

Indiana Territory 1. From George C. Pence and Nellie C. Armstrong, *Indiana Boundaries: Territory, State, and County* (Indianapolis: Indiana Historical Bureau, 1967). Reproduced with permission of the Indiana Historical Bureau.

Indiana Territory 3. From George C. Pence and Nellie C. Armstrong, *Indiana Boundaries: Territory, State, and County* (Indianapolis: Indiana Historical Bureau, 1967). Reproduced with permission of the Indiana Historical Bureau.

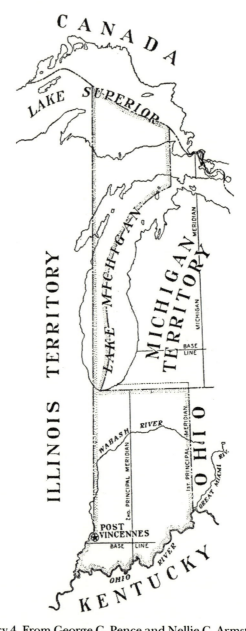

Indiana Territory 4. From George C. Pence and Nellie C. Armstrong, *Indiana Boundaries: Territory, State, and County* (Indianapolis: Indiana Historical Bureau, 1967). Reproduced with permission of the Indiana Historical Bureau.

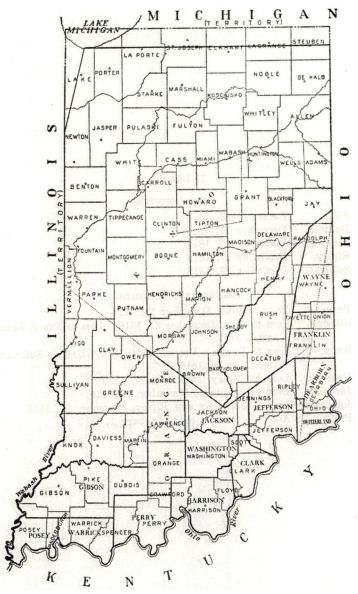

Indiana, 1816. Note how many of the counties bear the names of heroes from either the Revolutionary War or Harrison's generation. From George C. Pence and Nellie C. Armstrong, *Indiana Boundaries: Territory, State, and County* (Indianapolis: Indiana Historical Bureau, 1967). Reproduced with permission of the Indiana Historical Bureau.

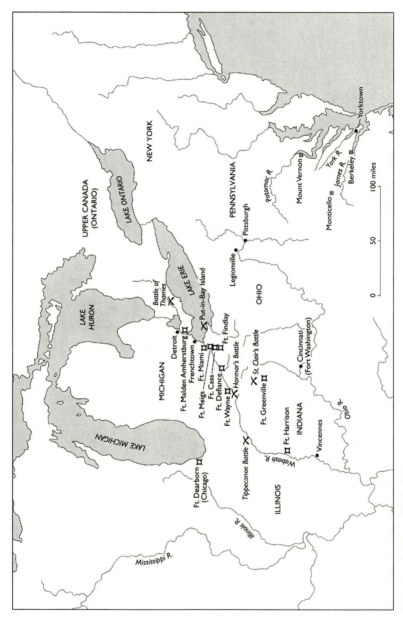

Harrison's West, 1791–1815.

MR. JEFFERSON'S HAMMER

CHAPTER 1

A Son of Virginia

William Henry Harrison was a son of Virginia. Twentieth-century historians referred to him as the scion of a wealthy Virginia family, largely to counter-balance the 1840s Whig campaign myth that he was a humble, hard cider–drinking Ohio farmer. It was a necessary revision, but emphasizing Harrison's privileged upbringing can be misleading. By the end of the eighteenth century the names of many of Virginia's leading families often carried more weight than their purses. William Henry may have been born with a silver spoon in his mouth, but it was no longer sterling.[1]

Financial difficulties aside, the Harrisons were rich in the capital of repute. An old Virginia family, with honorable roots in England, Harrison men were considered among the natural rulers of aristocratic society. Like the Lees, Randolphs, and Jeffersons, the Harrisons expected, received, and delighted in deference from the lower and middling classes. Usually, they lived up to expectations, exuding enough noblesse oblige to keep tenants, shopkeepers, even their slaves relatively content—or at least quiescent. Like other leading planter families, they tended to live above their means.

Few men in late-eighteenth-century Virginia commanded more respect than William Henry's father, Benjamin Harrison V (1726–91). The grand-son of Robert "King" Carter, one of Virginia's wealthiest planters, Benjamin Harrison attended—but did not graduate from—the College of William and Mary in Williamsburg. He married Elizabeth Bassett in 1748. He began his political career in 1749 with election to Virginia's colonial assembly, the House of Burgesses, where he served for the next quarter century. Harrison was one of nine burgesses who dominated the legislature from 1761 to

1774. He ranked with men like Richard Henry Lee, Peyton Randolph, and John Robinson as an unquestioned leader of the house.[2]

A boon to the careers of later generations of social and cultural historians, Benjamin Harrison's eighteenth-century Virginia displayed a classic social hierarchy based on race, class, and gender. In essence, well-born white men needed only to avoid long-term strife with those of their own class. Working-class and poor white men, women, Indians, and African Americans could not legally offer much trouble. The relatively crude system of patriarchy, or rule by adult males over their families, was ameliorated by a slightly subtler adaptation—paternalism.[3]

In this system, leading planters viewed anyone under their power, not just their offspring, as under their care. A great planter was typically a husband, father, master, and employer. As father figures they provided, or felt they provided, protection and sustenance to their symbolic children— employees, servants, and slaves. In return, these groups were expected to show deference and submit to the commands and whims of the male gentry. By 1720 or so, Virginia's leading families were nearly all related through intermarriage and were generally united in their economic goals and social values. The grandees, through direct or indirect influence over the legislature, had created a semi-idyllic world that, locally at least, was heavily tilted in their favor. Through their dominance of the House of Burgesses, the leading men of Virginia created a society in which they controlled politics, local taxation, firearms ownership, the courts, and even people's sex lives. They believed in liberty, but not equal amounts for every person. Some were not granted liberty at all. For Tidewater gentry, however, life could be very good. Indeed, a few of the greatest no doubt felt as though they were petty versions of the king himself.[4]

In the second half of the eighteenth century, the great planters of Virginia's Tidewater region became increasingly radicalized in their sociopolitical worldview. Although they seemed to have much to lose and little to gain from any change in the social order, these petty lords began to embrace what was variously known as Radical Country ideology, republicanism, Commonwealthman ideas, or Radical Whig ideology. This dissenting theory was basically a "bundle of ideas" circling around shared notions of what defined personal autonomy, civic virtue, and political corruption.[5] Indebtedness moved from the private to the public sphere and came to be seen as a moral failing. A man who mismanaged his finances might not live up to his word. In colonial Virginia especially, where hard money and written contracts were in relatively short supply, a man's personal honor was everything.[6]

As the great planters' lavish lifestyles and sloppy record keeping combined with a tightening of British mercantile and government reins on them, they slowly began to see the mother country as a threat to their personal liberty. Virginia's aristocrats became increasingly jealous of their property rights, even territorial. Their personal estates and sumptuous homes were increasingly seen as necessary refuges and evidence of manly independence.[7]

For most of the colony's existence, Virginia's gentry had placed themselves as middlemen between the mother country and the Old Dominion. They tried to serve the interests of Virginia, as they saw them. At the same time, they wanted to demonstrate their loyalty to the Crown and receive the plums of patronage in return. In the 1760s, however, as radicals like Patrick Henry raged, sentiment began to turn against Britain, or at least against British trade policies. The gentlemen planters in the end revealed that they were most loyal to their role as Virginia's leaders rather than to any king, and they adopted more radical steps themselves. Instead of denouncing Patrick Henry, Virginia's aristocrats rallied to his cause, then steered it to their preferred course.[8]

After mid-century, Virginia's great planters came to see themselves as inviolate and autonomous, and any challenge to supposed independence was viewed as the work of tyranny and an attempt to enslave them. In an odd way, Virginians' (and other Patriots') attempts to emulate their English planter idols made them even more likely to resist parliamentary supervision. They insisted upon enjoying what they felt were the "rights of Englishmen." Any attempt to limit a planter's "liberty," through regulation, taxation, or even collection of voluntary debts, was not only annoying but also wrong.[9] This ideology tended to minimize Anglo-Americans' responsibility for any wrongdoing, shifting the blame outward—a trend that still reverberates in American thought.

Although it is not necessary to delve into a biography of Benjamin Harrison, it is useful to note some similarities and differences between him and his seventh child and third son, William Henry, born at the family manor, Berkeley, on February 9, 1773. Benjamin Harrison was a large man, 6'4" in height and a fleshy 250 pounds. As an adult William Henry stood about 5'8" and weighed perhaps 100 pounds less.[10] Both men saw public service as a natural duty and an opportunity as well. Benjamin Harrison, in addition to his long service in the House of Burgesses, also represented Virginia as a delegate to the Continental Congress. While serving in the Second Continental Congress, Harrison shared a house in Philadelphia with fellow delegate George Washington, who later gave William Henry his first real job.

Benjamin Harrison had a conservative streak, and unlike Patrick Henry and others, he had to be pushed considerably by British policies before he advocated independence. The royal governor's threat to emancipate slaves was crucial for Harrison, as for many planters. By 1776, he was chairing the committee that approved the Declaration of Independence, and he became one of fifty-six Founders to sign the document. During the Revolutionary War, Harrison took the place of Thomas Jefferson, who resigned, in the national Congress. He also defeated Jefferson to become speaker of the House of Delegates (the new name for Virginia's representative body), and he then succeeded Jefferson as governor of Virginia.[11] The elder Harrison's career was often intertwined with that of Thomas Jefferson, and so it would be for his son.

While Harrison and Jefferson both served Virginia in numerous capacities during the war, both drew most of their fame from the Declaration of Independence—Jefferson for writing much of it, and Harrison for signing it. While the document had obvious importance in stating American political intent, it was equally important because it expressed many commonly held ideas. A document of rebellion, it contained few revolutionary thoughts. In some instances it was ridiculous, blaming the hereditary king for actions taken by an elected Parliament. What the Declaration did do, by specifying grievances, was serve as a rallying point for American Anglophobia, both in 1776 and for decades after. Britain's role in the impressment of American sailors into the Royal Navy, as well as in instigating Indian attacks on the United States, would still be sore points more than thirty years after the Declaration first spelled them out.

Thomas Jefferson was the principal author of the Declaration of Independence, or rather, he wrote down the complaints in a coherent form after borrowing most of the ideas from contemporary debates in the Continental Congress or from John Locke. He deserves credit for the eloquence, if not the substance, of the Declaration. For our purposes, two of the Revolutionaries' complaints bear particular importance: first, the charge that the Crown instigated Indian attacks on the American frontier; second, the accusation that George III was responsible for the slave trade.

The latter charge is rather interesting. Although it echoed a House of Burgesses petition of 1772,[12] it was largely Jefferson's creation. The Declaration committee, not wanting to bring up the thorny issue of slavery, deleted it from the final draft. Also, Jefferson's personal implication of the king was ludicrous and hypocritical. Nevertheless, the concept that it was the king of England who had allowed the "execrable commerce" to continue, who had "determined to keep open a market where MEN should be bought and sold,"[13] remained in some Americans' minds. It was no doubt easier for Americans, particularly slaveholders, to see a clearly repugnant institution from which they profited as the work of someone else, allowing them to enjoy the boons of the slave trade without the associated guilt.

In a similar vein, a passage cited George III as having "endeavoured to bring on the Inhabitants of our Frontier, the merciless Indian Savages, whose known Rule of Warfare, is an Undistinguished Destruction, of all Ages, Sexes and Conditions." That charge remained in the final draft because it weighed heavily on the committee member's minds, and there was some truth to it. The British had in fact enlisted American Indian allies to attack the rebels, and Indian war parties sometimes killed women, children, and the infirm. They sometimes adopted captives as well. The main problem with this charge was that it did not take into account Americans', including Virginians', role in antagonizing Indians.

In the seventeenth century, Virginia's record of relations with the Indians was, put gingerly, less than stellar. In the eighteenth century, the commonwealth led the charge regarding the land west of the Appalachians. Land acquisition had been a key force in shaping Virginia society since its beginning.[14] It was, after all, Virginia's 1754 expedition to the forks of the Ohio River, led by a disastrously inexperienced George Washington, that had touched off the French and Indian War. In 1763, the year that war officially ended, George III issued a royal proclamation forbidding colonists to settle west of the crest of the Appalachian Mountains. In the wake of the costly Indian war inspired by the Ottawa warrior Pontiac, the Proclamation of 1763 seemed sound policy. But speculators in western lands, including Washington and Benjamin Franklin—Pennsylvanians were also mad for western lands—were furious.[15]

The king had, in the speculators' view, frozen valuable assets that should have been theirs. A treaty with the Iroquois Indians at Fort Stanwix in 1768 supposedly ceded their claims to lands south of the Ohio River to Britain. The problem was that the Iroquois did not actually live there and never had. That region was claimed primarily by the Shawnees and Cherokees. In 1774 Virginia picked a fight with the Shawnees and forced them to cede their hunting grounds south of the Ohio—in essence, Kentucky. Virginians also saw an opportunity to trump Pennsylvania's claims to the Ohio Valley. The conflict was known as Lord Dunmore's War, named for Virginia's royal governor.[16]

When the Revolutionary War began, the Indians needed British arms and material aid to successfully attack the Americans. But the visceral motivation had been provided by generations of shady land deals and frontier thuggery. In blaming the king (whom Tom Paine called a "Royal Savage"[17]), the Declaration provided psychological succor to Revolutionaries—like the Tidewater speculators responsible for many land claims—who preferred not to see their own role in the suffering of their fellow citizens. As governor of Virginia, Benjamin Harrison himself admitted to being "shocked when I reflect on the unbounded thirst of our people after Lands they cannot cultivate, and the means they use to possess themselves of those that belong to others."[18] In retrospect, one might have asked Jefferson if the rapacious land acquisitions of generations of his fellow Virginians might have influenced those Indians who fought against them. One might also have asked if the brutal warfare practiced by Indians was noticeably different from that waged by frontiersmen.

With a few notable exceptions, such questions would have been anachronistic, to say the least. The Declaration of Independence, and the Patriot press in general, sought to motivate Anglo-Americans to choose sides in the struggle—an example of self-fashioning writ large. Accuracy and objectivity were not part of the equation.

When the Crown's Indian allies attacked Rebel forces, Americans were quick to point out, accurately, that the weapons they carried—especially the scalping knife and tomahawk—had been made and supplied by Britain. They ignored the fact that most American frontiersmen and militia carried and used identical implements in identical fashion. They glossed over the fact that while such knives had been commonly called "scalping knives," they also had a wide array of functions, many as innocuous as whittling or skinning game. The same implement carried by a Virginian might be called a belt-knife or a long knife. (Virginians, and later all Americans, were referred to by Ohio Valley Indians as "Long Knives" or "Big Knives.")[19] Unlike a war club, a steel tomahawk was valued in part because it was just as handy in building a campsite or gathering firewood as it was in combat. In the war of public opinion, Americans wisely zeroed in on the most dastardly interpretation of their foes' accoutrements.

Focusing on the king's Indian allies proved to be a stunningly effective, if perhaps curious, part of rebel propaganda. (Prior to the war, Indians had been a symbol of America and freedom—so much so that the Sons of Liberty had dressed as Mohawks for the Boston Tea Party.) Yet the American Revolution was, from the beginning, an odd sort of struggle. Typically, wars fought between foreign nations allow each party to rally its people around some patriotic standard, some sense of sameness—us versus the other.[20] But in a war of rebellion, essentially a civil war among British people, the inherent contradictions made such a distinction far more difficult. As Linda Colley noted, Americans needed to convince themselves that the Loyalists and "the British were cruel *and therefore alien.*" Such a task was far more difficult for Great Britain. How could one drum up undying hatred for Americans when the point of the war was to reincorporate them into the empire?[21] Partly from luck and partly from necessity, the American rebels soon took a commanding lead in the propaganda war against the Loyalists and British imperialism.

The most notorious example of such a propaganda victory resulted from a July 1777 crime, the murder of Jane McCrea. At first glance, the incident seemed to hold little interest for American Revolutionaries. McCrea, from a Patriot family but betrothed to a Loyalist officer, was killed during a phase of British General John Burgoyne's campaign in upstate New York. Apparently, she and her party were attacked by some of Burgoyne's Indian allies in a case of mistaken identity—another example of the confusion inherent in a civil war. From there the facts become hazy. She may have been killed at the first firing, but the version Americans trumpeted was that she had been tomahawked to death by Indians quarreling over who would get to ransom her. Her scalped body was later discovered, and some reports said she was found naked.[22]

Patriots seized upon what was one family's tragedy and hyped it into a psychological missile to hurl at the British cause: "In the ensuing propaganda storm, all that mattered was that an innocent civilian had been killed and mutilated by Indians in British pay." American printers relentlessly insisted, despite paltry evidence, that McCrea was found naked, thus implying that she had been raped by the warriors. (They might have taken her clothes as plunder, but it is highly unlikely that they would have assaulted her sexually. Most American Indian men, in the seventeenth and eighteenth centuries at least, considered any sexual contact with women captives as taboo. If the woman were adopted into one's family, then sex, even if consensual, would be considered retroactively incestuous. And rape was considered a particularly heinous crime, even against enemies. For many tribes, rape was automatically considered a capital crime, while murder was not.)[23]

Americans hyped the cruelty of McCrea's murder as inhumane, an act they themselves could never have committed. And for the rest of the war, that brush was used to broadly paint the British and Indians as one and the same—aliens, others, savages. Yet just two years before, when a "Patriot" at Concord had bashed in the head of a wounded British soldier with an ax, it was the Redcoats who decried their enemies' inhumanity. As the Regulars retreated back to Boston, false rumors ran wild that their savage American cousins were scalping wounded Redcoats. (Indians themselves sometimes identified far more with the British and could consider Americans the other as well—see chapter 4.)[24] Such conflation of British and American Indian warriors did not end with the Peace of Paris, nor did invocations of Jane McCrea's murder. That aspect of the Revolution would continue long after 1783.

With Benjamin Harrison gone for long periods in the House of Delegates or in Congress, William Henry was without a father, and Elizabeth Harrison and her elder sons had to run the plantation. In January 1781 a British army led by the infamous traitor Benedict Arnold invaded Virginia. Elizabeth gathered her youngest children and fled Berkeley. When the Harrisons returned, they found the house intact, but their portraits, clothes, and personal effects had been burned. The invaders had also taken away forty slaves—about a third of Berkeley's total—and all the livestock had been stolen or destroyed.[25]

Decades later, it is said, William Henry recalled that an English nobleman visiting Virginia after the war remarked that while the local mansions were as fine as English ones on the outside, they lacked the portraits and fine decor of English mansions. Benjamin Harrison reportedly replied, "I can account for my paintings and decorations, sir—your soldiers burned them in my back yard."[26] The exchange between Harrison and the Englishman may have been apocryphal—even the finest Virginian mansions paled in comparison to English ones—but it does illustrate the popular anti-British sentiment that lingered in Virginia and the country long after the war had ended. Eighteenth-century gentlemen on both sides of the Atlantic saw their property as sacred, and few acts brought more offense than an attack on one's property. Perhaps the only British measure Virginians found more execrable than assaults on their property was the recruitment of American Indian allies to attack their frontiers.

The position of wartime governor of Virginia was a thankless, sometimes dangerous job, and by 1781 Thomas Jefferson was happy to be rid of the burden. Seeing Virginia through to the end of the war was the task of the next governor, Benjamin Harrison. Elected to three one-year terms during the period 1781–84, Harrison wrestled with numerous issues. British merchants, under flags of truce, remained in Yorktown after Cornwallis's surrender. Some may have feared that such sutlers would act as British spies, but the underlying reasons for distrusting them may have been more banal. Even before the war, many Southern planters had resented the British merchants to whom they were often indebted. Such debts were more the result of the planters' lavish lifestyles than of British avarice. In January 1782, Robert Morris of Philadelphia notified

Governor Harrison that the British merchants in Yorktown had not yet been paid for goods purchased by Americans after Cornwallis's surrender. Harrison wanted them out anyway. In February, the governor ordered the merchants to settle their affairs and leave for New York. When a few stragglers still remained in May 1782, he ordered the local militia commander "to direct all British merchants there to proceed without delay to Hampton to take ship."[27] Years later, territorial governor William Henry Harrison would seek to implement President Jefferson's orders that British traders, and their corrosive influence, be expelled from American soil.

Although annoyed by British merchants, Benjamin Harrison's years as governor were especially focused on the West. As late as March 1783, some feared yet another round of Indian attacks on the Virginia frontier. In a letter to Colonel Arthur Campbell, in charge of defending Washington County, Governor Harrison revealed some opinions that were later shared by his youngest son. Harrison denied Campbell's request to build additional fortifications on the frontier, as they were too costly and did little good: "[F]atal experience has shown us that they never yet have been of service, but rather [are a] cloak to Idleness, the Garrisons Spending their time within the Walls when they should have been in the woods looking after the enemy." The sentence also contained implicit skepticism regarding a militia's effectiveness. Despite the widespread fear of further combat on the frontier, Harrison could sense a coming peace settlement with Britain and predicted a relatively quiet summer ahead. The Indians were "far too prudent to continue the War unsupported by the English."[28] In his own career as an Indian-fighting governor, William Henry would wrestle with the defensive value of militias. In practice he depended on them, although he would have preferred regular troops. He and his father would have been of the same mind regarding the cause of Indian wars, however—British influence.

The war ended none too soon for the Harrisons. Like many families they needed to try to recover their financial and psychological losses. Although now an ardent Patriot, Benjamin Harrison sought to speed reconciliation by relaxing legal measures against Loyalists who had not actually fought in the war. One of the final key events of Benjamin Harrison's tenure as governor was Virginia's cession of its western land claims to the United States. Coincidentally, that act would later enable William Henry to become secretary of the Northwest Territory.[29] While the Commonwealth of Virginia no longer declared dominion over the Ohio Valley, individual Virginians would continue to covet the region and its potential wealth for years to come.

Within a decade of the Revolution's end, Virginia was not only the most populous state in the Union but had nearly as many people as the next two largest states combined. Rather than leading to dominance, however, this proved a push-factor for migrants from the state. Most of Virginia's best farmland was already occupied by the late eighteenth century. While the era from 1770 to 1820 might appear to be Virginia's golden age—four of the first five U.S. presidents were Virginians—the state was already in decline prior to the Revolution. Soil erosion and agricultural overuse were devastating the land's value. The Berkeley plantation's falling productivity mirrored that of the state. By the time William Henry Harrison was born, it was difficult to maintain one's finances in Virginia. For his generation, fortunes would have to be made elsewhere.[30]

The decline in the quality of Virginia's soil coincided with Virginians, and Americans generally, looking to the West for a new start. Prior to the Revolution, the trans-Appalachian region was usually referred to as the "backcountry" or "back parts." As David Hackett Fischer and James C. Kelly noted, "The fact that colonists thought of it as the 'back' rather than 'front' of their world tells us which way they were facing." But by the eve of the nineteenth century, new attitudes were emerging. The concept of "the West" as a destination, rather than simply a direction, emerged. In Virginia especially, migration to allegedly better lands had been common from its founding. Lord Dunmore, on the eve of the Revolution, had complained about Virginians' "wandering" tendency. By the end of the Revolutionary War, Virginians had a number of reasons to look to the West.[31]

Despite the turmoil of the war years, William Henry Harrison seems to have had a happy childhood. Like other sons of the Virginia gentry, he would have spent ample time hunting, riding, and fishing, as well as listening to glorious tales of the Revolution from his father, eldest brother, Captain Benjamin Harrison VI, and their assorted cronies. And while British depredations, not to mention his father's freewheeling spending, had damaged the family fortune, William Henry was still relatively well-off. Further, the Peace of Paris did not signal the end of his father's importance to Virginia. He returned to the state legislature and later opposed the ratification of the U.S. Constitution, seeing it as a threat to what another generation would call states' rights.[32]

While attending William and Mary was something of a tradition for Harrison men, Benjamin sent his youngest son to Hampden-Sydney College, a small Presbyterian school. William Henry attended the school for perhaps three years (1787–90). As evidenced in his later correspondence, the youth spent considerable energy there reading classical histories in Latin, being particularly enamored with Julius Caesar and Roman military history. Also shown by subsequent correspondence, he appears to have learned a smattering of French as well.[33] In his senior year he left, perhaps withdrawn by his father because of the religious revival that came over the school in the late 1780s. Although they had some Puritan roots, the Harrisons were now Episcopalians, and Benjamin V was not of an evangelical bent. Virginia's eighteenth-century elite in general had viewed revivalists with suspicion, judging them as threats to the existing social order. In 1790, after a short stint at an academy in Southampton, William Henry went to Richmond, home of his eldest brother, Benjamin VI, to study medicine under a Dr. Leiper.[34]

While in Richmond, William Henry allegedly joined a Quaker abolitionist society that promoted gradual emancipation. Dorothy Burne Goebel surmised that this led to Benjamin, Sr., sending his son to Philadelphia, as the elder Harrison was "a violent opponent of any scheme of negro emancipation." If this were so, however, Philadelphia seems an odd choice—akin today to sending an addicted gambler to Las Vegas. Somewhat more plausible is the argument that Philadelphia had the best medical training available in the United States and was also the home of an old friend, Robert Morris—"Financier of the Revolution"—who could keep an eye on young William Henry. Whatever his father's motivation, William Henry's medical education proved short-lived. He had barely arrived in Philadelphia when he received word that his father had died on April 24, 1791. William Henry lingered with Morris and his family for a few months before making a fateful decision. Taking the advice of Governor Richard Henry Lee, a distant cousin, the eighteen-year-old

Harrison decided to ask for a commission as an ensign in the army. He would forsake the lancet for the sword.[35]

Just why William Henry chose the army over medicine is not clear. Perhaps medicine was his father's dream for him rather than his own. Perhaps he despaired over having enough money to finish school with his father now gone. Goebel suggests that a recent jilting by a young Philadelphia woman, Sarah Cutler, may have influenced Harrison to leave town. Whatever the reason, subsequent events show that Harrison made the correct decision. He loved military life, and it would give him a key background for his subsequent political career.[36]

Governor Lee personally presented William Henry's application to President Washington and Secretary of War Henry Knox. In March 1791, Congress had allowed for an increase in the military—despite a habitual fear of a standing army—and Washington "had no reason to reject the request of the son of an old friend." The president signed the commission on August 16, 1791.[37] Actually, Washington might have found reason had he chosen to reject the application: Harrison was asking to become a member of the officer corps despite being only eighteen and having no formal military training. He was a gentleman, however, and in the eighteenth and nineteenth centuries that was often enough. Besides, the army needed men at this juncture.

With the Peace of Paris in 1783, Britain had ceded the lands between the Mississippi River and the Appalachian Mountains to the United States. Much of the U.S. claim to that land drew from the western campaigns of Virginia General George Rogers Clark, who famously captured British outposts in the Ohio Valley in 1777 and 1778.[38] Americans were optimistic that this vast region, with its spectacular potential for agricultural wealth, would be quickly and painlessly settled. This naive view ignored the military reality, for although Britain had given up those lands, the Native people who actually lived on them had not. Though unrepresented and betrayed at the treaty negotiations, these Indians were largely undefeated and preferred to resist any incursions into their territory. Americans at first behaved as arrogant conquerors, trying to dictate how Indian lands would be divided and used. Indian land seemed part of "the fruits of Independence."[39] But as the body count continued to rise through the 1780s and with no end in sight, American leaders took a different view. While they still insisted that Indian lands would eventually belong to the United States, they recognized Indians' rights to their lands. Specifically, they decided to buy lands from the Indians—claiming sole right of preemption rather than initial ownership—which seemed both more humane and more cost-effective than conquest.[40]

On paper, the American occupation of the Ohio Valley was proceeding smoothly, but in practice the Indians were neither impressed by American laws nor swayed by American overtures. Undaunted, they continued to rack up military victories against American armies, militia, and civilians. They also received arms, supplies, and encouragement from British agents. While Britain had agreed in 1783 to abandon its forts in the Great Lakes region, in practice it held onto them to keep a hand in the lucrative fur trade with the Indians. Besides, the British countered, the Americans had yet to live up to their promise to compensate Loyalists ruined in the Revolution. Unbowed and feeling confident with British material support, the Ohio Valley Indians refused to sell any of their lands.[41]

The Washington administration, the first under the new U.S. Constitution, found itself in the odd situation of wanting to peacefully purchase Indian lands but needing a solid military victory to force Indians to the treaty table. Unfortunately for the Americans, such victories were hard to come by. A 1790 expedition under General Josiah Harmar was thrashed, and in 1791 the army under General Arthur St. Clair, the Northwest Territory's governor, was nearly annihilated. It was the remnants of St. Clair's shattered force, which had lost 630 men killed—the worst American defeat ever at the hands of Indians—that gave young Ensign Harrison his first image of war in the Northwest.[42]

Fortunately for Harrison, he had arrived at Fort Washington (now Cincinnati) too late to join St. Clair's disaster. He had spent several weeks on recruiting duty in Philadelphia before making the long journey west. He arrived in time to view what was left of St. Clair's army, however. The coarse, physically and psychologically shattered men must have shocked the proper young man from Berkeley. Nor were the accommodations close to what he had grown accustomed to. Berkeley may have been run down, but Fort Washington was rustic beyond what Harrison could have imagined. Built in 1789, the fort was composed of log blockhouses surrounded by a rectangular wooden palisade ten to sixteen feet high: "[T]he blockhouses were each about twenty feet square . . . and about one hundred and eighty feet intervened on each side, between the four block-houses situated at the angles of the fort." Each wall featured a wooden barracks, and at least one well had been dug within the fort's walls.[43]

Being so young, having been commissioned without a scintilla of military experience or training, and showing little interest in drinking, gambling, dueling, or other common frontier pursuits, Ensign Harrison was not immediately popular at Fort Washington. Abstemious and studious, he habitually read military manuals, Cicero, and the like. He seemed to have little in common with his fellow officers. Over time, though, his intense work ethic and dedication gained him acceptance and even some respect from his more weather-beaten colleagues. Harrison's superiors came to think quite highly of him.[44]

Arthur St. Clair, eventually cleared of wrongdoing by the nation's first congressional investigation, soon left the army and returned to his job as governor of the Northwest Territory.[45] He was replaced by Brigadier General James Wilkinson of Virginia. An officer during the Revolution, Wilkinson had made a name for himself in the district, and then state, of Kentucky. While the frontier offered opportunities for advancement to those of industry and luck, Wilkinson preferred to seek his fame and fortune through intrigue, deceit, treachery, and the graves of better men's reputations. He was pretty good at it, too. Wilkinson had quietly defamed George Rogers Clark in the mid-1780s. He ruined the legendary Virginian, deliberately sabotaging Clark's 1786 Indian campaign by delaying vital supplies and encouraging sedition within the militia. He also spread rumors that Clark was an alcoholic and advanced his own career in the process. Wilkinson was secretly on the payroll of the Spanish government, which knew him as "Agent 13." For $2,000 a year, Wilkinson pledged to try to effect a revolt in Kentucky and add it to Spain's colonial holdings. He had also flirted with the British about adding Kentucky to George III's territory, in what was later referred to as the British Conspiracy of 1788. Wilkinson stayed on Spain's payroll until 1807 and remained dishonest, traitorous, and completely untrustworthy for the rest of his life.[46]

Interestingly, Wilkinson and Harrison seem to have gotten along well. Regardless of his amorality, Wilkinson was quite the charmer, and while he had sabotaged the careers of men he found threatening, he did not do so with Harrison. Perhaps the ensign's youth insulated him from Wilkinson's jealousy. At any rate, Wilkinson obviously thought well enough of Harrison to protect him when youthful zeal and a rash sense of duty got the ensign in trouble.

Drunkenness was a frequent occurrence on the frontier generally, and after St. Clair's defeat, it became a particular problem in the army. Wilkinson sought to clamp down on the problem by issuing a general order that any soldier found intoxicated outside the walls of Fort Washington would summarily receive fifty stripes on the back. Ensign Harrison, on patrol duty, encountered an intoxicated civilian ordnance worker and "promptly executed Wilkinson's order, applying the prescribed fifty lashes to the offender and ten to the offender's protesting friend."[47]

Indeed, throughout his life, Harrison's correspondence showed little sympathy for, or patience with, drunkards.[48] Predictably, the two workers were outraged by what they saw as "this arbitrary military justice" and sought legal redress against Harrison. General Wilkinson initially prevented the local deputy from taking Harrison into custody. When that could no longer be avoided, he took up a letter-writing campaign—news of the affair eventually reached President Washington—to ensure that the one night Harrison had spent in a civilian jail would be the extent of his punishment. Wilkinson assured the civilian authorities that he had admonished Harrison about the incident, but he declined "to offer further violence to the feelings" of his young ensign, "one of the best disposed, & most promising Young Gentlemen in the Army."[49]

The affair proved no lasting detriment to Harrison's army career; during the ruckus he was actually promoted to lieutenant. Nor did Wilkinson hold a grudge against the rash but "promising" officer, ordering Harrison to lead the escort taking his beloved wife, Ann, back to Philadelphia. The only long-term problem Harrison (although he could not have realized it at the time) would have to overcome was the impression he had made on one of the civilian authorities. Judge John Cleves Symmes would later (against his better judgment) become Harrison's father-in-law.[50]

En route to Philadelphia, Harrison and Mrs. Wilkinson stopped in Pittsburgh, where he reported to General "Mad Anthony" Wayne, who had been tapped to lead a new expedition against the Ohio Indians should negotiations fail. In the aftermath of St. Clair's defeat, while Ohio Valley Indians were hawkish for war with the United States, a number of American leaders, out of pragmatism, took the dove's stance. In January 1792, President Washington asked his cabinet for advice. Secretary of State Thomas Jefferson, Secretary of the Treasury Alexander Hamilton, Secretary of War Henry Knox, and Attorney General Edmund Randolph were all, for once, in agreement. They saw another military campaign as both too expensive and too risky.

Jefferson in particular felt it would be cheaper to sway the Indians with "presents" than to mount another military campaign. Senator Benjamin Hawkins of North Carolina gave one of the more thoughtful responses to the Ohio Valley problem in a letter to President Washington. Hawkins had experience negotiating Indian treaties and would later become President Jefferson's principal Indian agent south of the Ohio. Hawkins noted that after 1783, "[W]e seem to have forgotten altogether the rights of the Indians. They were treated as tenants at will, we seized on their lands and made a division of the same . . . alloted certain portions to the indians for hunting grounds, and did not even think of offering them compensation." Hawkins's argument was based more on justice than expediency, and he urged the president to make sincere efforts to secure a peace with the Indians through diplomacy, not combat.[51]

Americans on the frontier felt the horror and disappointment brought on by St. Clair's disaster even more strongly. Yet those who lived nearest to the Indians, those most likely to suffer war parties, rarely considered a diplomatic solution—at least not without a military victory to cow the "haughty" Indians. Most agreed with the sentiments of Kentuckian judge John Steele, writing to Arthur Campbell back in Virginia, who allowed that "[t]he defeat of the Army is truly alarming." He further noted that "to Vanquish the enemy flushed with Success as they now are, will require a powerfull Army, and a judicious Commander." Yet, he concluded, it had to be done.[52]

George Rogers Clark, unfairly discredited but still keenly aware of the situation in his neighborhood, echoed Steele's sentiments. "[T]he Indians are spreading Fire and the tomahawk through the frontier with out much resistance and I believe will continue to do so," he lamented. Eastern politicians, he argued, knew little of the real situation and lacked his knowledge of how to conduct Indian affairs: "It is a pity that the Blood and Treasure of the people should be so lavished when one Campaign properly directed would put a final end to the war and a well directed line of conduct after such event should take place might establish a Harmony between us and the Indians that might exist for many years." Suing for peace would only embolden the Indians, Clark insisted, and would likely even add numbers to their ranks. They would soon make demands so great that it would be "dishonourable" to meet them. "So much for the publick," Clark bitterly concluded.[53] During his years as governor and Indian commissioner, William Henry Harrison would often adopt a similarly aggressive attitude.

The more accommodating strategies advanced by Jefferson and others should not be mistaken for capitulation, however. It would have been extraordinarily difficult for Americans to imagine giving up on the Ohio lands under any circumstances in the 1790s. Aside from thinking that they had won the lands during the war, there was the related problem of how the impoverished nation would compensate its veterans—the living heroes of their glorious struggle. Enlistment bonuses and wages were long overdue, and selling the Ohio lands seemed the easiest revenue stream. Virginia had given awards from the Ohio country even more directly—by offering land grants as bonuses to those in the service. A great swath of what would eventually become Ohio was designated as the Virginia Military District. George Rogers Clark and the veterans of his campaigns had been awarded lands just north of what became Louisville, in what is now Clark County, Indiana. The U.S. promise to honor those land grants to its soldiers had been one of the stipulations Virginia insisted upon before ceding its claims to the region in 1784.[54]

Washington did make overtures to peace and he did send emissaries, although he harbored no illusions as to their efficacy. The president made offers of peace while he prepared for war. Although many wise and experienced counselors saw no feasible military solution, Washington, like Clark, felt that to suffer such "dishonourable" defeats damaged the standing of not just the army but the country as well. Unable to secure Senate confirmation of "Light Horse Harry" Lee and disappointed when General Benjamin Lincoln declined his invitation, Washington named Anthony Wayne, yet another veteran of the Revolution, to lead the next expedition against the Ohio Indians.[55] The choice was crucially important to U.S. territorial growth and to the professional growth of Lieutenant Harrison.

Wayne, who was forty-eight years old at the time, took the job, but only on the condition that he be named commander-in-chief of the entire U.S. Army and be allowed to run the campaign on his own terms. Most important, Wayne wanted the time to train his men adequately and to decide for himself when to engage the Indians.[56] Wayne began training his men almost immediately, in part because they needed it and in part to keep them busy while he waited for the outcome of negotiations with the Indians' confederation. The negotiations did not go well.

Two separate American emissaries, accompanied by servants, set out in late May 1792 to meet with representatives of the Indian confederacy, hoping to arrange a truce. Warriors of the confederacy murdered all the emissaries and their parties. The next American negotiator, Rufus Putnam, reinterpreted his orders en route to negotiate instead with some tribes already friendly toward the United States. With more chagrin than humor, Putnam wrote the secretary of war with the hope that the circumstances "will render my conduct excusable, at least, if not commendable." The council at Vincennes resulted in a treaty the Senate rejected as going too far in its assertion of Indian land rights.[57]

On the surface the treaty accomplished nothing, although it did bring one key ally back to the Americans. Serving the Wea Indians as interpreter at the council was William Wells, the son of a prominent Kentucky family who had been captured as a boy and adopted by the Miamis. Wells, renamed Apekonit ("wild carrot"), learned a great deal about Indian customs, became a trusted Miami warrior, and married the daughter of the Miami warrior Little Turtle. He fought against the armies of both Harmar and St. Clair, but a chance encounter with one of his brothers, a captain serving at Fort Knox (Vincennes), helped convince him to return to the Americans. In so doing, he risked likely torture and death if recaptured by the Miamis, but Wells was a brave and enterprising man. He performed innumerable vital services for the American cause, not the least of which was leading the Americans to the place where the confederation's warriors had buried St. Clair's captured artillery. Denying cannon to the Indians would make stout forts practically impregnable to Indian attack.[58]

Indians opposed to American settlement in Ohio did grasp at least part of the Americans' dilemma regarding western lands. At an August 1793 conference, they even expressed sympathy for the land-hungry frontiersmen: "We know that these settlers are poor, or they would never have ventured to live in a country which have [sic] been in continual trouble ever since they crossed the Ohio." Such sympathy only went so far, though, as the warriors adamantly refused to part with "the lands on which we get sustenance for our women and children." Instead, they suggested that the Americans take the money for proposed land payments, plus the huge costs of outfitting an army to invade Ohio, and use it instead to compensate the settlers for their lands and improvements. Only then, they argued, could peace resume. If not, further discussion was pointless. It was a novel solution, but not one likely to sway President Washington or the poor settlers who equated land with liberty and sovereignty. Besides, it was not just the settlers who were poor; surveying and selling the western lands seemed the most viable option for replenishing the impoverished national treasury.[59]

While negotiations foundered, Wayne and his officers continued to drill their troops relentlessly, even to the point of conducting mock battles with soldiers dressed as Indians. Historians have traditionally viewed Wayne's army, which Henry Knox dubbed the "Legion," as a machine-like instrument of superbly disciplined patriotism. Wayne worked the men hard and trained them well, and by the standards of the day the Legion was well disciplined. But it was a constant struggle. As late as October 1793, Wayne had to testily admonish his officers to enforce a general order that forbade the firing of guns in camp. Contrary to legend, most men in the Legion had not willingly volunteered, and many had been recruited in an unsavory fashion, including the use of liquor and unpaid enlistment bonuses. The only newspaper in the territory, the *Centinel of the North-Western Territory*, featured ads offering rewards for the return of deserters nearly every week from 1793 to 1795. Wayne also complained that smallpox and venereal disease ran rampant among the new recruits.[60]

Food, for both officers and enlisted men, was considered to be poor in quality, as attested to by a petition from the Legion's officers—including William Henry Harrison—protesting the awful rations. General Wayne endorsed the petition and sent it to President Washington, much to the president's displeasure.

Despite the shared discomforts of frontier living as well as Americans' democratic rhetoric, a social chasm still separated the rank and file from the officers, and transgressors faced a backlash. Most of the rules and physical punishments in the Legion, typical for the time, were directed toward the enlisted men. On January 24, 1794, Wayne forbade sutlers from selling alcohol to his enlisted men and noncommissioned officers. The rule did not mention officers, who were supposed to be above such behavior. Yet the next month, Wayne had Captain John Cummings dismissed from the service for going to a Cincinnati pub and associating (drunkenly) with "private soldiers," which constituted "ungentlemanly behavior."[61]

No one accused Lieutenant Harrison of ungentlemanly behavior. The straight-laced young officer continued to rise in others' estimation. Tangible reward had come in June 1793, when General Wayne appointed the twenty-year-old Harrison as one of his aides-de-camp. Although he remained a lieutenant, the post garnered considerable prestige, not to mention more pay. Instead of the standard $26 per month, Harrison now earned $64 per month in pay, four rations daily, and $12 monthly for forage (roughly $1,400 per month in 2004 dollars).[62] Decades later he was still complaining that the raise did not cover his expenses—the requisite fast horses were pricey—but Harrison's professional star was obviously rising.[63]

Wayne had wanted to move against the Indian confederacy in 1793, but a number of delays, particularly in supply, prevented him from doing so. Wayne refused to make St. Clair's mistake of beginning a campaign too late in the season. When, in the spring of 1794, the Legion marched forward, it was because Wayne felt the army was ready. In the interim, Lord Dorchester, the governor general of Canada, told a delegation from the Six Nations that a war with the Americans was imminent and that tribes fighting the United States should expect military assistance.[64]

Wayne knew that a great deal rode on his success or failure. The potential financial and psychological loss, not to mention the widows, that would result from another defeat by the Indians weighed heavily on the general. Despite the old sobriquet, "Mad Anthony" would not be caught in a rash and costly mistake. Whether marching or stationary, the army always had ample scouts and pickets. Wayne was particularly fortunate to have William Wells and his company of spies, many of whom, like Wells, were former Indian captives and knew the languages and customs of their former kin. True to the Legion's namesake, Wayne always fortified his camps before bedding down for the night. Embarking at dawn, marching ten to twelve miles a day, and then building breastworks was fatiguing, yet Wayne's army managed about twice as many miles a day as had St. Clair, who, disastrously, never bothered to fortify his camps. The draining pace of Wayne's march was just one of the complaints leveled by his second-in-command, General Wilkinson.[65]

Wilkinson, in addition to seeing Wayne as his chief rival for fortune and fame, also argued that Wayne's tactics were too conservative. Wilkinson wanted his mounted Kentuckians to play a more dynamic role, sweeping ahead to strike at Indian camps and villages. A number of the younger officers such as future explorer William Clark, who apparently did not know how Wilkinson had destroyed his older brother's reputation, sided with Wilkinson. The army pressed forward methodically, and Wilkinson continued to sow discord.[66]

On August 19, 1794, Wayne, ever vigilant, ordered a strong camp built to guard the army's heavy baggage. The long-awaited contest took place the next day. The Battle of Fallen Timbers—so named because it took place at a spot where a cyclone had leveled a large patch of forest—was not, in a tactical sense, the pivotal battle Wayne had hoped for. Many of his opponents, riven by internal rivalries and disagreements, had already gone home. Of the Indian force—Delawares, Shawnees, Potawatomis, Miamis, Mingoes, Wyandots, and others—no more than four or five hundred diehards remained. The Shawnee warrior Tecumseh stood among them, about to engage in his first large-scale pitched battle with the Americans. The fallen trees that littered the site would, the warriors hoped, provide them with cover. Instead, Wayne's superiority in numbers—he had about fifteen hundred regulars and an equal number of mounted volunteers—and his disciplined troops, combined with his simplistic but proven advocacy of the bayonet charge to carry the day. The battle need not have ended the confederacy's resistance, as the Indians did not sustain enormous casualties, perhaps only forty men killed.[67] Ten of these, however, were chiefs. Wayne lost at least as many men, about forty men killed and eighty wounded. But politically, the Indian confederation's loss at Fallen Timbers and its aftermath proved disastrous.[68]

The Indian warriors fell back to the British Fort Miami at the foot of the Maumee Rapids. The warriors thought the fort they were running to, well built and furnished with cannon and a decent garrison, would repulse Wayne's pursuing army or at least shelter them. The fort's commandant prudently (if not admirably) kept the doors of his fort shut and refused to do anything to antagonize Wayne into attacking him. Shielding Indians did not justify creating an international incident, especially when Britain was already at war with France. First stunned and then incensed, the Indians left the scene. While Tecumseh and other survivors of the battle might make expedient alliances with Great Britain in the future, they never forgot or completely forgave their *father's* failure on that day.[69]

William Henry Harrison's star shone as never before, however. During the battle he repeatedly rode through the thick of the fighting, relaying dispatches to and from his commanding general. Wayne was impressed and mentioned Harrison and the other aides-de-camp, Captains De Butts and Lewis, by name in his official account. Major Mills, another officer on the staff, singled Harrison out as having done the most dangerous riding while the other aides stayed by Wayne to keep him out of trouble. Lieutenant Thomas J. Underwood, recording secretary of the latter testimony, was moved to add that "if he [Harrison] continues a military man he will be a second Washington."[70] Aside from the hyperbole, one also detects an early guess that Harrison would not remain satisfied in the army. Regardless, the young lieutenant was beginning to accumulate some of the public recognition he so desperately craved and painstakingly cultivated.

Still, actual combat proved a sobering experience for the twenty-one-year-old. While he had made it through the battle unscathed, some of his friends had not been as lucky. Three months after Fallen Timbers, Harrison finally wrote to his brother Carter about the experience. Unlike George Washington, who had referred to the whizzing of bullets in his first firefight in 1754 as "charming," Harrison declined to brag about the experience. Instead, he tersely noted that Carter would have to consult the newspapers and Harrison's courier, Captain Samuel Tinseley, for an account of the battle. Harrison's only personal commentary revolved around his regret at the death of Major Edmondson, who had "behaved remarkably well." Mortally wounded, Edmondson had apparently lingered for hours "in the utmost agony," his body not found until well after the battle. Harrison had seen the major just moments before he received his mortal wound and had unsuccessfully "endeavoured to check his ardour." Reflecting perhaps survivor's guilt, Harrison further noted that he should have sent a detail sooner to recover the major's body. Instead, Harrison—displaying a trait he would retain throughout his public career—did his best to provide for the relatives of the fallen soldier, in this case Edmondson's young brother, a corporal in the Legion: "I take a good deal of pains to make him a good soldier by my advise [sic] & his situation comfortable by now & then advancing him small sums."[71]

Even though the Indian confederacy in the Ohio Valley had been broken, Harrison and the Americans had a bête noire on which to base their views of the region for the next two decades. What Wayne found after the battle only strengthened the American conviction that British intrigue was the root cause of Indian wars. The Legion captured British muskets and equipment on the battlefield. Jean Baptiste Ducoigne, chief of the Kaskaskia tribe and an American ally, confirmed the suspicion that a few British rangers and Canadian militia had taken part as combatants. An American deserter captured months later even alleged that General Wilkinson had sent him to inform the British that he would be at the head of the army when it reached Fort Miamis and would surrender to them. This last accusation was not followed up, however.[72]

British involvement in the confederacy's war against the United States backfired terribly. Field agents' promises gave the Indians unrealistic expectations that were cruelly dashed. Few Indians ever fully trusted the British again. Further, the use of His Majesty's material, employees, and troops confirmed beyond a doubt what Americans had suspected about Britain's Indian Department and Indian militancy. Britain's involvement in Indian warfare colored British-American relations for years afterward and tended to poison any attempt at rational negotiation. Even long after the War of 1812 ended, Americans—on the frontier and in the highest levels of government—convinced themselves that British agitation, rather than American land hunger, had been the root cause of all Indian troubles.

That assumption fit nicely into Americans' tendency to attribute all of their misfortunes, and even their flaws, to the taint of Britain.

The Fallen Timbers campaign held great significance because it represented the concerted effort of both the Revolutionary generation—Washington, Wayne, and Knox—and the next generation of American expansionists, such as William Clark and William Henry Harrison. It showed that while differences and squabbles might arise—the older men were Federalists, the younger became Republicans—both groups remained committed to expansion, land acquisition, and the conviction that British influence in any form was corrupting and dangerous.

Wayne's victory at Fallen Timbers did not immediately end the Indian threat on the Ohio frontier.[73] His men suffered a number of deadly attacks in the weeks and months after the battle. The attacks were reduced in scale, probably carried out by small groups of warriors bent on revenge, but they were unnerving just the same. Still, as the months wore on, an increasing number of former militants began to seek peace with the Americans, something that pleased Wayne immensely. Wayne's most significant victory was yet to come, however.

Wayne called for the belligerent tribes to meet him at his fort at Greenville (Ohio) in June 1795. Perhaps considering itself lucky to have finally defeated the confederacy in battle, the government felt ready to negotiate as well. Secretary of War Thomas Pickering made it clear to General Wayne that the cession of southern and eastern Ohio, "from the mouth of the Cuyahoga to the mouth of the Great Miami," was the sine qua non for peace. (Pickering's predecessor, Henry Knox, had hoped that St. Clair's expedition would yield cessions giving the United States title all the way to the Mississippi.) The government's decision to secure the acquired lands with a minimum of friction, with the ultimate goal being fast, easy, and (especially) cheap settlement, further moderated the treaty's proceedings. Only a lasting peace could secure the benefits of a cession. While Wayne must insist on taking the land, Pickering instructed, he was to carry himself diplomatically in doing so.[74]

Wayne's negotiations with the Indians after Fallen Timbers had a huge impact on William Henry Harrison and on U.S.-Indian relations in general. Wayne's methods would prove to be a template for future councils. The treaty that unfolded at Greenville was in many ways more of a negotiated settlement than subsequent U.S.-Indian treaties proved to be. The confederacy's warriors had lost a battle, but they were still numerous and capable of waging a protracted, bloody, and costly war. Wayne needed to convince, not command, the chiefs to sign. Still, Wayne held most, if not all, of the cards. As Reginald Horsman noted, "[T]here was no negotiation in the real sense of the word."[75] It was therefore an eye-opening experience for any future commissioner plenipotentiary of Indian affairs in attendance.

Although he called for a mid-June council, Wayne found hungry Indians at his door in May and ordered his officers to issue them rations. Other tribes were tardy in arriving—some, like the Sauks and Foxes, never did show up—so the council did not begin in earnest until mid-July. As shown by the surviving quartermaster's receipts, many signed by Lieutenant Harrison, the army continued issuing large quantities of food and liquor to the Indians in attendance. The generous pantry, while a concession to Indian protocol, also displayed the wealth and power of the United States. Additionally, the Legion took steps—some intentional, some not—to entertain and awe the Indian delegations. Wayne ordered frequent military parades to show off his troops, blending entertainment with intimidation. Such was also the case on June 24, when the soldiers' makeshift fireworks factory—in preparation for the Fourth of July—accidentally went up, nearly taking the main powder magazine with it. The next day in council, Wayne had to reassure his Indian guests that no incendiary mischief had been meant for them, as "they had been much alarmed."[76]

In addition to the hearty pantry, Wayne also had $25,000 worth of trade goods[77] (not including numerous kegs of Madeira and liquor) to facilitate the proceedings. While the Indians would welcome, and even expect, such gifts, they came at a cost. Secretary of War Pickering had ordered that the gifts be distributed only when his terms for land cessions were met. By allowing the Indian delegations to camp within his redoubts, Wayne was creating a symbol for future relations with the Indians. The fort sheltered them, yet its guns could instantly turn on them if need be.[78]

The Reverend David Barrow, a Baptist minister originally from Virginia, attended the council and noted, "Mr. William Henry Harrison, Carter Harrison's brother, introduced me to the general." Wayne, the

Reverend observed, "seems to be full of eyes. . . . I found him very clever."[79] Wayne announced that the negotiations would be based on the 1789 Fort Harmar Treaty, in which the Iroquois had relinquished their tenuous claims to the Ohio Valley. Using the permission of tribes that did not even live in a potential cession was a tried-and-true, if amoral, technique with Indian treaties—the Iroquois had long performed the same function for their English allies regarding the Ohio Valley. Wayne's announcement drew immediate protest from Little Turtle of the Miamis, who decried the sale of lands by tribes that did not live on them. Wayne opted to adjourn for the day without responding.[80]

The next day Wayne reiterated the Americans' position that they had already paid for the lands in question twice, at the Treaties of Fort McIntosh and Fort Harmar. Only the "justice and liberality" of the United States led it to pay for the same lands yet a third time. He argued that the fact that both France and Britain had held forts in the area constituted circumstantial evidence that the lands had previously been sold to them. Little Turtle flatly rejected this argument. Wayne then read aloud copies of the Treaty of Paris (1783) and John Jay's new treaty with England (1794) to drive home the point of Britain's former ownership of the Ohio country. Jay's Treaty proved crucial to Wayne's case, especially the clause wherein the British promised to honor their 1783 pledge to evacuate their forts in American territory. This revelation—apparently Wayne's reading was the first time most Indians had heard of Jay's Treaty—confirmed the suspicions warriors had formed after Fallen Timbers. The British military support requisite for holding off the Americans would not come. To lessen the blow, Wayne ordered a double liquor ration for all. Little Turtle seethed.[81]

Wayne delivered the Greenville Treaty to the Indian delegations on July 27. By July 29, many of those present had agreed to, or at least accepted, the American terms. Little Turtle delivered a rebuttal speech in which he denied that France or Britain had ever purchased any Ohio lands. He also proposed a compromise, in which the new boundary would extend no farther than Fort Recovery. In so doing, Little Turtle was offering up Shawnee, not Miami, lands. Wayne pronounced that Little Turtle and the Miamis were contrary to the wishes of the rest of the Indians and stated that an eight thousand dollar annuity would amply compensate the tribes for the lands taken. On August 3, representatives

from all tribes present signed the treaty. Little Turtle refused, but Chief
Richardville signed for the Miamis. The son of a Miami female chief and
a French trader, Richardville had received a Canadian education. His
status as the nephew of the Miami chief Pacane entitled him, by Miami
custom, to hereditary chieftainship. Richardville had been a village chief
for about ten years prior to Greenville. The treaty would not be the last
time he squared off against Little Turtle.[82]

Wayne distributed the presents and annuities, and Tarhe of the
Wyandots declared that the United States was now father to the Indians.
On August 10, Wayne bid the 1,130 Indians present farewell. In a private
council on August 12, Little Turtle, having reconsidered his position,
promised to abide by the treaty and became one of the last to sign.[83]

The treaty allotted one thousand dollars per annum in trade goods
(minus the cost of shipping) each to the Wyandots, Delawares, Shawnees,
Miamis, Ottawas, Chippewas, and Potawatomis. The Kickapoos, Weas,
Eel Rivers, Piankeshaws, and Kaskaskias—the latter of whom had never
opposed the United States and had not participated at Fallen Timbers—
would each receive five hundred dollars worth of goods (again, minus
shipping) per annum. In keeping with the stated goal of "civilizing" the
Indians, any tribe could substitute farm implements or livestock for part of
its annuity. Article VII allowed Indians to continue to hunt on lands ceded
to the United States provided they did not become troublesome. In Article
VIII the Indians agreed to protect the licensed traders among them.[84]

At first glance, the treaty seemed to offer something to all sides. It
ended twenty years of often horrific warfare in the Great Lakes/Ohio
Valley region and for the most part maintained peace for more than
fifteen years after its signing. While the tribes had made a considerable
land cession, they received compensation for it, as well as formal acknowledgment of their title to lands. A great many Indians from several nations
attended the council, and ninety chiefs—many of them fairly prominent—
marked the treaty. The chiefs represented an interesting cross-section of
Indian leaders. Civil chiefs, like Richardville of the Miamis and Red Pole
of the Shawnees, signed, as well as great warriors like Little Turtle and the
Shawnees Black Hoof (also a civil chief) and Blue Jacket. These warriors
had long since proven their courage. Yet after Fallen Timbers, Jay's Treaty,
and Greenville, many prominent leaders felt continued war with the

United States was a losing proposition. Black Hoof in particular believed that becoming Anglo-American–style yeomen farmers was the only pragmatic course for Indian survival.[85] Certainly, Greenville drew genuine Indian leaders who, to the extent possible, could speak for their peoples.

Many aspects of the treaty did not bode well for the Indians, however. Little Turtle had obviously not wanted to sign, but he did anyway. Although he clearly saw the dangers inherent in accepting the treaty, the fear of losing influence and prestige among his people by not associating himself with the powerful Americans compelled him to mark it. He never opposed the United States so openly or fundamentally again. Wayne's council had brought the confederacy's greatest war leaders into the fold by playing chiefs against each other. The general gained influence over Chief Blue Jacket by more direct (although secret) means: he hired him. In partial compensation for siding with the pacifist Wyandots against Little Turtle, Wayne ordered that "a decent house" be built for the Shawnee chief at government expense. True, as Richard White has pointed out, the treaty was not simply a case of Wayne manipulating Indians. For example, Blue Jacket manipulated Wayne into officially acknowledging him as a chief. In the end, though, this served the greater goal of Wayne and the Americans. The turmoil and division engendered by power struggles among and between the tribes only made the United States more powerful. As chiefs fought each other for the scraps their father threw them, they made it easier for him to divide and conquer.[86]

Although it appeared that Wayne negotiated with a confederation, "in reality he negotiated with quarreling and embittered groups of villagers." Villages sent separate delegations to Greenville, and they openly disagreed as to their rights and claims. While both Red Pole and Tarhe had asserted that Indians owned the lands in common—a gift from the Great Spirit—the vast body of Indians were so divided that they asked Wayne to supervise the division of their lands.[87]

Annuities were a new wrinkle in U.S.–Indian treaties, designed to secure Indians' dependence on the Americans. In accepting the annuities, Indians ushered in other disturbing side effects of the treaty. Annuities "formally institutionalized federal influence within tribal government" and "gave the Americans a permanent lever within a tribal power structure." As chiefs and peoples scrambled for American payments, they became less likely (or less able) to combine against the United States. By not selling out one's allies, one risked missing out on valuable trade goods. A chief's authority among his own people rested to a great extent on his ability to be generous to them in distributing gifts. Often they did not wish to cede lands and their people opposed cessions, but the chiefs could not act as chiefs without the presents and annuities land cessions brought. The Potawatomis and Kaskaskias, for example, had no real claims to the territory ceded at Greenville. The Kaskaskias, in fact, do not even appear to have attended formally.[88] They all agreed to accept annuities for the cession, however.

Granted, they would have seemed foolish turning down what looked like free gifts, but in signing on they reinforced an ominous precedent. It became increasingly acceptable to pay one tribe for another's lands. This had been a standard treaty tactic for European-Indian treaties in the past. The English found the Iroquois particularly helpful in this capacity, and the Americans had continued in this vein with the Iroquois at Fort Stanwix. Little Turtle had suggested that the United States take only southern Ohio—an area inhabited by Shawnees, not the Miamis. Wayne and the Americans declined this offer, not on principle but merely because the area was too small.

Adding to these bad omens, a plague struck the Potawatomis who had attended the council, killing sixty. The Shawnee chief Red Pole also died from disease soon after the council. Many Indians saw such deaths as the work of witchcraft, either by Americans or other Indians, and the loss of these leaders undermined Indian political capabilities. Finally, the treaty also reserved numerous plots of land for the United States, including old grants made by Indians to the French, which became contentious later.[89]

Greenville held great significance for the Americans, both symbolically and legally. It had not been enough to simply gain Indians' marks on the treaty. They wanted Indians' open acknowledgment of American sovereignty and a retroactive endorsement of the righteousness of the American cause. U.S. officials sought public reassurance that the twenty years' investment in blood and treasure had been well spent. To their own satisfaction at least, the Americans succeeded in that task.[90]

"Carter Harrison's brother" and the other secretaries spent the rest of the month making copies of the treaty, as well as recording the proceedings.

This was typical of the rather dull tasks Harrison was assigned after Fallen
Timbers, as when he had to run Wayne's proclamations to the territorial
newspaper. The secretaries' labors were considerable, but they were
undeniably successful in both recording and disseminating information.
By September 1795, even the hated British Indian agent Alexander
McKee had a copy of the treaty.[91]

Twenty years of brutal warfare had profoundly affected Americans on
the frontier. Their subsequent relief at Wayne's military and diplomatic
victories is illustrated by some remarkable notices in William Maxwell's
Centinel of the North-Western Territory, published in Cincinnati. In May
1794, when the Indian confederacy seemed unbeatable and Americans
along the Ohio suffered repeated attacks, the *Centinel* began running an
ad from six local men who, in true American fashion, blended commerce,
"public good," and competition. They offered a bounty of $136 to the
first subscriber who brought in ten Indian scalps "taken" between April 18
and Christmas Day, 1794. The scalps had to be taken (although presumably it would have been easy to cheat) from within these boundaries:
"beginning on the Ohio ten miles above the mouth of the little Miami,
on a direct line thence northwardly, the same distance from the said
Miami, until it shall extend twenty five miles above where *Harmar's trace*
first crosses the said Miami, thence southwardly, keeping the distance of
ten miles from the said great Miami, to the Ohio, thence up the middle
of the said river Ohio, to the beginning."[92]

The ad further stipulated that the second subscriber to bring in ten
Indian scalps would receive $117. The next week the *Centinel* added that
two Indians had stolen a horse from Columbia, and a posse from nearby
Nelson's Station had killed one of them. The *Centinel* listed the posse's
names and dubbed them "heroes." It also noted that by killing and scalping
the Indian and retrieving the horse, the men had accrued "nineteen
pounds [£?] of plunder" and were awarded a bounty. Editor Maxwell
further declared that such actions were needed to suppress the Indians:
"Should their example be followed, those yellow gentry would be cautious how they paid us visits, and our property and persons [would be] in
a great measure protected."[93]

Yet American officials drew a clear distinction between hostile Indians and
friendly ones, between times of war and times of peace. On September 8,

1794, not a month after the victory at Fallen Timbers, drunken rowdies from Cincinnati harassed and threw stones at a party of Choctaw Indians in their vicinity. The Choctaws, natives of Mississippi and Louisiana, were there because they had fought alongside Wayne's army against the Indian confederacy. The crowd dispersed when armed American guards arrived to protect the Choctaw camp, but the rowdies returned the next morning as soon as the guards were dismissed. Again they surrounded the Choctaws and threatened their lives. The infuriated secretary of the Northwest Territory, Winthrop Sargent, publicly castigated the citizenry for acts "repugnant to the statutes of the Territory, subversive of every moral obligation, and disgraceful to a people pretending to the smallest degree of civilization." Blaming the outrage as much on alcohol as bigotry, Sargent proclaimed a crackdown on liquor distributors.[94]

Sargent's reaction to indiscriminate Indian hating (in the same newspaper that had run the scalp bounty ad a few months before) is striking, although perhaps predictable, given that he was defending important (and potentially dangerous) military allies. More telling was Cincinnati's reaction to its former enemies following the Treaty of Greenville. In March 1796, one Daniel McKean stole a horse from Indians on Clear Creek, a tributary of the Great Miami River. (It was almost certainly a village of Shawnees, arguably the most adamant members of the Indian confederacy in the late war.) It was not the Shawnees but white settlers on Clear Creek who obtained a warrant, followed McKean across the Ohio into Kentucky, and apprehended him on suspicion of horse theft. Even before his trial, "[T]he horse was restored to its proper owner." It is noteworthy that ordinary American settlers rather than government officials led this particular charge.

While settlers held a dim view of horse thieves in general, two years prior, McKean's feat against an Indian would have likely won him free drinks at the nearest tavern. Instead, he faced a jury of his peers: "The prisoner's guilt was clearly proved. Verdict, GUILTY." Not only did the court order McKean to pay his Indian victim a one dollar fine, but he was also paraded shirtless through the main streets of Cincinnati while receiving thirty-nine lashes on his back and wearing a hat affixed with the sign "I STOLE A HORSE FROM INDIANS." Lest this less-than-subtle message miss its mark, *Centinel* editor Maxwell drove the point home. It was hoped that McKean's treatment would serve as "a wholesome caution to others. Many an innocent person, many a worthy family has fallen under the scalping knife of the incensed Savage where the guilty depredator himself should rather have been the victim." Neither the territory nor the country could afford the waste in money and blood brought on by lawless frontier thugs, and the citizenry trusted the legal system to protect them from Indian anger as well as protecting the Indians from crimes: "[T]hose who in future shall wantonly injure and irritate the Indians may expect to suffer that just and severe punishment which justice and sound policy demand."[95]

The transition from vigilantes killing Indian horse thieves to vigilantes returning stolen horses to Indians, neatly bookending the Greenville Treaty, is startling. It would be too much to say that the treaty had ended or precluded animosity between Indians and whites. Nor did it restore a balance of power on the frontier: despite what Greenville said, only Americans were allowed to punish Americans. But clearly a shift in thinking had occurred. Although it is difficult to imagine a scenario in which Americans—with or without the U.S. government's help—would not eventually overrun the Ohio Valley, military campaigns and para-military warfare were not inevitable. Dispossession of the Ohio Valley Indians would by definition be a shameful chapter for future generations, but it could have been far more gradual and peaceful than it turned out to be.[96] After Greenville, most Indians and Americans, leaders and common folk alike, would try to keep the peace. It would take considerable and repeated blunders, based in fear, impatience, and greed, to bring about Indian Removal as it actually unfolded.

William Henry Harrison learned a great deal during his first four years in the army. He saw firsthand how and how not to organize a military campaign. He met numerous men, Indian and white, who would later prove crucial to his own efforts at administering Indian affairs. And as proven by subsequent events, Harrison paid keen attention to Wayne's use of threats, spies, bribes, and presents in negotiating the Greenville Treaty.[97]

William Henry Harrison was a son of Virginia, and he shared many of the common traits of those uncommon men. He had a presumptuous confidence in his abilities and felt entitled to leadership in particular. He was ambitious both financially and socially, for the two were generally linked. He also felt enough of a sense of noblesse oblige to take his public service as seriously as he did his private goals, although that could bring about conflicts of interest. Also in the tradition of his forbears and peers, Harrison would display what we see as hypocrisy, or at least a lack of self-reflection, regarding the political and social issues of his day. Finally, he would follow a well-worn planter's trail in tending to live beyond his means. As dedicated as he was to the nation his father and others had struggled to create, Harrison's career in public service would be as much a search for a steady paycheck as anything else.

CHAPTER 2

Rustic Gentility

In the mid-1790s, Harrison's life was taking off, both personally and professionally. A young man trying to move up the social scale needed a wife of suitable character and background. And, equally important, life in the frontier army could be lonely for a single man. William Henry realized his difficult position in courting eligible young ladies—he had the pedigree but not the purse to pursue the prettiest girls from the leading families. Initially and understandably, Harrison tried to persuade himself that his character and good breeding might compensate for his humble finances. Given the circumstances, a few misfires were to be expected.

Among Harrison's first loves was "Miss M" of Philadelphia, most likely Hetty Morris, the daughter of Harrison's benefactor Robert Morris. Although Morris later lost much of his fortune and part of his reputation in a financial scandal, in the early 1790s his clan was among the new nation's wealthiest and most prestigious. Apparently, William Henry was smitten by Miss M. In a late 1794 missive to his brother Carter, Harrison lamented that he might not be able to visit Philadelphia that winter. But if he could, he insisted, he would make his "addresses to Miss M—without any apprehension of encountering *vexation Mortification Chagrin* or *Discomfort.*" It was not confidence in success, he noted, that stilled any apprehensions, but the soldierly knowledge that there was "no Dishonor in a *well meant & well conducted* enterprise, even if it should fail in its object."[1]

William Henry reassured himself that the young lady's high character would preclude any "Disgust" on her part at his proposal, and he further asserted that he knew of no one who would be disgusted by his overtures. Still, he tacitly admitted that it would be "humiliating" to him if that were the case. As to his meager salary's influence on his courtship, William Henry offered that Miss M's kin was "a family who must consider me their equal in every thing but fortune." As long as he wore the uniform of the U.S. Army, he continued, he would not "Dishonour [it] by owning myself inferior to any person."

Having, to his own satisfaction at least, explained to Carter why Miss M should have him, William Henry then described why she was the only one for him: "Since *you wont* let me Court Miss M—you must find out Some other Lady for me equal in charms and accomplishments." In the smitten lieutenant's view, Carter's task was nearly impossible, even if he included women with only one-third Miss M's charms. The young Virginian swore that he would desist only if convinced that another man could make her happier than he could.[2]

William Henry did love Miss M "ardently," and he seems, in his youth, to have thought that would be enough. The fact that Carter disapproved of his efforts suggests that the older Harrison was more realistic about the courtship. Carter was apparently prophetic as well, for we hear no more about Miss M in Harrison's future correspondence and note that Hetty Morris married the younger brother of John Marshall in the spring of 1795.[3]

Any chance for Harrison to court Miss M had been dashed by his military duties, which tied him to his post. The work included transcribing preliminary peace treaties with the Indians at Greenville in the first months of 1795. But after the Greenville Treaty's conclusion, Harrison let his official duties assist him in his private pursuits. When Harrison had finished his secretarial work for General Wayne, he borrowed three hundred dollars from Dr. Charles Brown, an army surgeon friend, and led a pack train of supplies to North Bend, Ohio. Normally, this would have been a boring assignment, but Harrison was eager for the opportunity because he had personal business there. North Bend, outside of Cincinnati, was home to Judge John Cleves Symmes, and Symmes was the father of a dark-eyed lass named Anna.

In the spring of 1795, Harrison—perhaps having heard of Hetty Morris's looming nuptials—had met Anna in Lexington, Kentucky, when she was visiting her sister Betsey and brother-in-law, Peyton Short. Harrison now meant to ask Judge Symmes for his daughter's hand. The judge said no. Later accounts say that Judge Symmes liked Harrison but did not think the man's financial prospects were good enough for his daughter. He may indeed have thought that, or perhaps he remembered Harrison's scrape with the law when he whipped the ordnance worker in 1793.[4] Subsequent events would prove that the two men had key differences regarding social and political issues, especially slavery. William Henry Harrison would conduct business affairs for Judge Symmes for the rest of the latter's life and even after, but their relationship seems to have been more cordial than close.

Although Symmes's own finances were perpetually in disarray, he was justified in seeing Harrison as a weak suitor for Anna. He knew about the importance of marrying well, as much of the judge's own social standing came from his having married Susan Livingston, of the powerful New York family.[5] Harrison had himself admitted that "my sword is almost my only patrimony." His situation was compounded by the fact that his small salary was coupled with a poor business sense. When his mother died in 1793, William Henry had inherited about three thousand acres of the Berkeley tract, as well as a few slaves. In March 1793, William Henry sold all his valuable Tidewater lands to his brother Benjamin, Jr., for an old bond note worth one thousand pounds in Virginia currency from one of Ben's cronies, as well as five hundred pounds in bonds and a one-eighth interest in a shaky Kentucky land company, also run by Ben's friends. Benjamin pledged to ensure that the bonds would be paid off, although William Henry had to know that, in eighteenth-century Virginia's planter society, there were no such guarantees. In effect, he gave away his three thousand–acre birthright for a handful of promises.[6]

Rebuffed by Symmes, the son of Virginia's aristocracy showed (for the moment) a distinct lack of respect for patriarchy and schemed with Anna to elope. Unlike his unrequited ardor for Miss M, Harrison found that Anna returned his sentiment. They set their forbidden wedding day for November 25, 1795, when the judge would be away on business. Apparently, few in the North Bend area feared Judge Symmes's wrath. William Henry and Anna married at the home of Stephen Wood, the Northwest Territory's treasurer and local justice of the peace, who happened to be one of Judge Symmes's tenants.[7] After the ceremony, the Harrisons rode to Fort Washington in Cincinnati. Harrison had to face his reluctant father-in-law two weeks later at a farewell dinner in honor of

General Wayne, who was moving to Philadelphia. The judge could not have been happy to see Harrison but managed to hold his temper in check.

General Wayne had given his aide-de-camp his blessing for the wedding and consented to let Harrison stay behind at Fort Washington so he could remain near his bride. Harrison was soon given command of Fort Washington when its commanding officer took a furlough. But Lieutenant Harrison was upset that he had not yet been promoted to captain, and in July 1796 he asked Wayne that he be allowed to resign as the general's aide, noting that he would soon retire from the army. Wayne politely declined to accept the resignation. Harrison was anxious about more than the promotion. He also wanted to spend more time on business ventures Judge Symmes had offered him—apparently the judge remained convinced that Harrison would need help in providing for Anna. Harrison also worried about his time and his income because of "the delicate situation of Mrs. Harrison's health at present." Anna was in fact about seven months pregnant with their first child. Betsey Bassett Harrison, named for William Henry's mother, was born September 29, 1796. Harrison soon purchased 160 acres from Judge Symmes at North Bend, Ohio, and then bought a four-room cabin on the land.[8]

William Henry and Anna were soon very busy, although the same was not true for Harrison's troops. After Greenville, the army had considerably fewer duties—in the Ohio Valley at least—which was just as well. The dissension and hostility within the officer corps, centered on the Wayne-Wilkinson feud, continued unabated. Wilkinson, who had ruined better men than himself before, might have succeeded in permanently besmirching Anthony Wayne's reputation. But on December 15, 1796, Wayne, ever the master tactician, outflanked Wilkinson by dying.[9] One of Harrison's champions was now gone, and life in the army seemed less fulfilling than ever. He was not alone in that sentiment.

While the post-Greenville peace gladdened the hearts of many frontier families and Eastern politicians, it left the army rather bored. The officers in particular lamented the peace, as they had little hope of promotion without combat. Further, once the Indian threat had subsided, the War Department tended to ignore the troops. The old problems of poor food and inadequate equipment, not to mention stalled pay, grew worse. General Wilkinson considered leaving the army, and William Henry

Harrison, despite a 1797 promotion to captain, resigned his commission in the spring of 1798.[10]

William Henry agreed with Judge Symmes about an army captain's pay. Part owner of a distillery, Harrison found his business interests were not well supplemented by his salary. Consistent with his family's station and history, Harrison sought to augment both his financial and social capital with a career in public service. He took an appointment as register at the government land office in Cincinnati in the spring of 1798, and later he became a justice of the peace, but he quickly campaigned for an even more important position. He received a considerable boost when his friend Winthrop Sargent recommended him to Timothy Pickering, now the secretary of state, for Sargent's old job as territorial secretary. Sargent offered that Harrison was "a Young Gentleman of Virginia, and of Education, son to a former Governour of that name, long in the family of General Wayne, in a Confidential Character, and who for seven years I believe has sustained a fair, indeed unblemished reputation as a Military Officer."[11]

Harrison, already showing a knack for high-level lobbying and politicking, then wrote to Congressman Robert Goodloe Harper of South Carolina:

> The appointment of Colo. Sargent . . . will of course make a vacancy in the Secretaryship . . . to obtain this is the object of my wishes. . . . I have been seven years a soldier during which period my exertions to render service to my country have been unceasing. . . . I have in no small degree enjoyed the confidence and friendship of all three Commanders in Chief and almost of all my superior officers. . . . My friend Colo Nevill (who was here a few days ago) informed me that he had engaged Mr. Ross of the Senate in my interest—and that yourself and General Morgan of the lower House had promised your assistance.[12]

At age twenty-five, Harrison became secretary of the Northwest Territory.

For young William Henry Harrison, the quest for financial independence ran deeper than a simple need to put food on the table or even material greed. He wanted, he *needed*, to be among the sociopolitical elite. Given his background, anything less would have constituted failure in his eyes and in the eyes of others as well. Thinking of himself as a gentleman was not enough; it was paramount that this son of a Signer be *seen* as a gentleman. As Rhys Isaac noted, "The defining characteristics of gentility are elusive." The first step was making the claim itself, publicly, and having the claim accepted. Gentility was difficult to define, yet it was readily identified upon viewing. Gentility was composed of a web of various factors, and if a man was lacking in one area, excelling in another could compensate.[13]

In Harrison's case, he lacked the great wealth one normally associated with the gentry. But he could carry himself as a gentleman. Appropriate demeanor, dress, manners, and conversational style were essential. If one could combine such "traits—especially if accompanied by a familiarity with the sources of the sacred, Classical, or legal learning—[it] gave a *presumption of gentility.*" William Henry was no theologian, and his interpretation of the laws during his years as governor shows that his legal education was also lacking. But he had read Cicero and Caesar and was not shy about letting people know it. However, the benchmark of a true gentleman was personal financial independence. In Harrison's native Virginia, a society based on unfree labor, "the customary English valuation of manly independence was carried to very great heights."[14]

A gentleman, as William Henry understood it, was free from worry over his daily subsistence. Gentlemen did not have to subject themselves to other men, sacrificing honor and dignity, just to satisfy material desires. Of course, Harrison would never be completely independent, as he had to rely on government superiors—especially the president—for his job. But he made every effort to insulate himself through his image and standing with his neighbors. A gentleman also had a "disposition to undertake important responsibilities in the community at large," often pro bono.[15]

When Harrison agreed to sit on the board of the newly created Vincennes University, it was not for the salary, as there was none. Nor was there any financial compensation for serving as president of the "Vincennes Society for the encouragement of Agriculture and the Useful Arts." Years later he donated a sizable portion of his award from a successful slander suit to orphans of the War of 1812. These were acts the leading men of society would graciously undertake as a way of serving their community and in turn garnering social capital. To serve the community in such fashion would have been among the easiest decisions Harrison made in his public life. He truly did believe in furthering education and agriculture, and helping to do so would add to his reputation fairly painlessly.[16]

During his public career, Harrison did indulge in what were essentially charitable acts, both to build his reputation among the citizenry and to make himself feel more like a gentleman. The bottom line, however, demanded that he accrue wealth to secure his station, and he tried to do so in a manner befitting his heritage. One of his many for-profit ventures was offering horses for stud service. While secretary of the Northwest Territory, Harrison placed newspaper ads for "The High Blooded Horse, FEARNAUGHT." Sired by the famous Virginia horse of the same name, Fearnaught would cover mares at a rate of "two dollars the single leap" or $3.25 for the entire season. In placing the ad, Harrison was not simply trying to make easy money (though presumably Fearnaught would be doing most of the work). The breeding and racing of fine horses in the Ohio Valley was, as it had been in Virginia, largely a blue-blooded activity. In announcing himself publicly as a man who knew horseflesh, William Henry was advertising himself as a gentleman. When he noted that Fearnaught's colts had been judged "at least equal [to] those of any other horse in the country," he was also implying that he himself was the equal of (or better than) other men.[17]

William Henry Harrison was not the only one who hoped the path to fortune led through the Ohio Valley. In many ways, the U.S. government was also banking on the region. Anglo-Americans—Virginians in particular—had coveted the obviously fertile soil since at least the mid-eighteenth century.[18] In the 1780s, Congress began passing a series of ordinances to organize the lands north of the Ohio, both for land sales and settlement. The fact that the local Indians were unbowed and spirited in their defense did not figure into the debate until the 1790s, leading ultimately to Wayne's campaign. The laws passed from 1784–87 established that the lands of the Ohio country would be surveyed in a rectangular grid pattern and publicly auctioned in an orderly fashion.

Such scientific rationalism imposed upon nature bore the imprint of one of the principal authors of the Ordinance of 1784, Thomas Jefferson.

It was doubtless a huge improvement over the old European-style sur-veying by metes and bounds, which caused considerable confusion with land titles. Congress had also established that Indians had a right to compensation for their lands but that Americans had the sole right of preemption—the lands would be sold only to the United States. Finally, these public lands would be sold at public auction only in sections of one square mile, or 640 acres squared, at a minimum of a dollar per acre. Thus any prospective land buyer could expect to pay at least $640 within one year—equivalent to $12,500 today[19]—and often considerably more, a steep investment for most working farmers.

The members of Congress wanted it that way, though. The tremendous bounty of the land made them fear that lazy men might fill up the area, living as the Indians were thought to and not improving the land prop-erly. Such haphazard settlement would retard the civilization of the Ohio region and make it susceptible to foreign invasion and insurrection. Instead, Congress wanted the high price of investment to encourage only stouthearted, hardworking farmers—New Englanders were considered the ideal model—to settle the region. As Eric Hinderaker noted, Congress's goal was "to impose an ordered liberty on western settlers." Congress was not bothered by what we would see as an oxymoronic "imposed liberty," but in practice the high prices tended to keep government land sales low, and speculators gobbled up much of the good land.[20]

While the Ordinances of 1784 and 1785 had dealt primarily with land sales, the Ordinance of 1787, better known as the Northwest Ordinance, created the blueprint by which the Ohio country might achieve state-hood. The land would eventually comprise three–five states, which, after passing through a territorial phase, would enter the Union on an equal footing with the thirteen founding states. When a region's population reached five thousand, it might advance to the second grade of territorial government, which meant gaining an elected legislature to complement its appointed governor and governor's council, as well as the right to send a nonvoting representative to Congress. When a territory reached a population of sixty thousand and had adopted an acceptably repub-lican constitution, it could apply for full statehood. The Northwest Ordinance stated that maintaining peaceful relations with the Indians was a definite goal, although a clause authorizing "just wars" would be used considerably in the early 1790s. Public education would be supported, and habeas corpus was in effect. The last provision, Article VI, was adopted with little debate but would eventually prove the most controversial: "There shall be neither Slavery nor involuntary Servitude in the territory."[21]

Initially, the laws passed to facilitate settling the Ohio country had little effect, as prior to 1795 the Indians there made it a dangerous place for newcomers. But even after the peace established at Greenville, government lands in the region sold slowly. The Land Law of 1796 did not help, as it raised the minimum price of land to $2 per acre, meaning a prospective buyer needed at least $1,280 within a year of purchase. The government also faced stiff competition from Judge Symmes, who sold excellent Ohio lands from his own grant at half the government's price. (Unfortunately, many of his clients later regretted their decision, as Symmes was a more skillful promoter than a diligent clerk.) In the first year after passage of the Land Law, only about 49,000 acres, mostly along the Ohio River, had been sold—far less than anticipated.[22] If the federal government hoped to sell its valuable western lands, bringing in much-needed revenue and securing America's hold on the West, a more skilled negotiation of frontier needs and high-level politics was required. As it happened, an able candidate was in the midst of his frontier apprenticeship.

From his appointment on June 26, 1798, until October 1799, William Henry Harrison served as secretary of the Northwest Territory. His annual salary was $1,200. Much of the time he acted as the de facto governor when Governor St. Clair was at home in Pennsylvania. Sometimes this involved making weighty decisions, as in the spring of 1799, when Harrison opted to pardon convicted murderer John Bradley. Harrison did so in part because of popular sympathy for the man, who apparently had killed either in self-defense or by accident. Harrison also stated that, given the enormity of the consequences, he preferred to "err in favour of life."[23]

Even far less crucial experiences proved valuable. As Harrison continued to learn about the territory and its people, he also continued to become acquainted with the leading men in the country. On October 3, 1799, Harrison won election as the territory's delegate to Congress by narrowly defeating Governor St. Clair's son.[24] Nathaniel Massie and the other

Northwest Territory legislators felt Harrison should be allowed to vote in
Congress, although Congress demurred. In this close election, Harrison's
support was derived mainly from a group of Virginians, a pattern that
would recur throughout his political career. This Virginia group included
Edward Tiffin, Tiffin's brother-in-law Thomas Worthington (later a U.S.
senator from Ohio), and Nathaniel Massie. They were also allied with Harrison's land-speculating father-in-law, Judge Symmes from New Jersey.[25]

With Harrison's political résumé and connections,[26] it is not surprising
that he quickly settled into the Congress and made an impact, despite the
fact that he was not a voting member. Harrison was already well attuned
to the political and military needs of American settlers in the Northwest
when he read a petition from Solomon Sibley of Wayne County, part of
what later became Michigan. Sibley's petition, written between late 1799
and early 1800, listed the wishes of Detroit-area settlers. They wanted the
government to ensure proper land titles for them, promote public education, deliver the mail, and appoint a federal judge for Detroit. Sibley's
petition also asked for a clear demarcation between Indian and American
landholdings and the fixing of American land titles. One portion of the
petition seemed particularly prescient. It asked for the rapid sale of Great
Lakes real estate already purchased from the Indians: "Such a measure
would secure the Interest of the U. States on the lakes, by enabling
that part of the U States to defend itself against their Indian neighbours,
should a war take place."[27]

Sibley's petition struck a chord with Harrison, as it combined his two
primary public interests: land acquisition and national defense. He
addressed the latter issue on the floor of the House in January 1800,
about a month shy of his twenty-seventh birthday. Reflecting the coming
wave of Jeffersonian Republican sentiment, many in Congress sought to
reduce the size of the standing army, for reasons both financial and
philosophical. Young Harrison, a former army captain, strongly opposed
such a move, which he felt would be "disastrous." Although Jeffersonians
relied greatly on militias for defense, Harrison argued that they lacked the
necessary discipline to stand against "the military tactics of a Bonaparte."
He further asserted that while he had seen militias perform bravely in
the Indian wars, their desire to return home quickly made them untrustworthy for something as critical as frontier defense. Only when backed by

numbers of regular troops, he insisted, could they be useful.[28] Congress reduced the army anyway.

Harrison also served on the committee charged with evaluating whether to divide the Northwest Territory along the Great Miami River, allowing what became Ohio to separate into its own territory. Many, like Harrison, felt the region was sufficiently populated to justify the move and large enough geographically to be unwieldy for a single territorial government. Further, many American citizens had crossed to the Spanish side of the Mississippi for a more certain government. (Some had also crossed out of a fear that the Northwest Ordinance would emancipate their slaves.) Using a fraction that became habitual in public discourse, Harrison assured Congress that "nine-tenths" of the citizenry agreed with him on the need for dividing the territory.[29]

He was, however, opposed by the Northwest Territory's governor, Arthur St. Clair. The conservative St. Clair objected primarily out of concern that any acceleration in the statehood process might bring more Jeffersonians into the national political process. Further, St. Clair feared division would move the territorial capital to Chillicothe, away from his home in Cincinnati, and he relied on his Federalist friends in the House and Senate to block the measure.[30]

The debate over dividing the Northwest Territory resulted from a Federalist-Republican schism over the future of westward expansion. Most Americans had been in favor of opening the Ohio Valley lands for public auction. But by 1800, as they realized that their hold on the government was slipping, Federalists like St. Clair tried to stymie the incorporation of new states into the Union. Jeffersonian Republicans, on the other hand, were eager not only to create new states but to acquire more territory as well. They assumed, drawing on contemporary European political theory, that continual expansion was the only hope for the survival of the republic. Otherwise, Americans would settle in congested urban areas and opt for industry rather than agriculture, and the social and moral decay so prevalent in Europe would rapidly set in. Social decay was inevitable, but the Jeffersonians hoped to postpone it as long as possible. This view was typical for Americans in the early Republic, and the domestic policies of the Jefferson, Madison, and Monroe administrations were all centered on territorial expansion. Indeed, from the 1790s to the 1830s, American nationalism "thrived at the expense of . . . the continent's other inhabitants."[31]

Federalists succeeded in stifling the Jeffersonians until May 1800, when Congress divided the Northwest into two territories—Ohio and Indiana, the latter including the lands that became Illinois, Michigan, Wisconsin, and part of Minnesota. Harrison was at the forefront of the debate and, despite his nonvoting status, remained conspicuously committed to division. He had also made his presence known in other respects.

Equal in importance to his work in securing the division of the Northwest Territory were Harrison's efforts regarding land acquisition statutes. Harrison chaired the House committee charged with examining the existing land laws, despite his youth and the presence of much more senior members, like Albert Gallatin of Pennsylvania, on the committee. Harrison was the primary champion of what became the Land Law of 1800, sometimes known as the Harrison Land Law. Always eager to encourage western land settlement, Harrison's Land Law made it easier for settlers to purchase government lands. It established four land sale offices, allowed half of all public lands to be sold in half-sections of 320 acres, and allowed for payments to be spread out over four years. The fact that many in Congress realized the need for a revised land law helped Harrison's cause. Still, there were dissenters.[32]

Federalists in Congress, including Roger Griswold of Connecticut and Henry Lee of Virginia, opposed the measure, arguing that the extra surveying involved would be too costly and that squatters might be difficult to remove from federal lands. But Harrison, joined by leading Republicans like Gallatin, argued that western land sales would pay for themselves and reap even greater benefits. Reducing the size of the required purchase would encourage actual settlers rather than just land speculators "and of course increase the price of the purchase." Eventually, Congress passed a version of Harrison's bill. Harrison had hoped for an even more liberal land law—allowing all the land to be purchased in half-sections and free of interest—but he could rest assured that his efforts had both aided prospective settlers and furthered the cause of American expansion. The young Virginian had proven to be adept at politicking in the elite levels of the House and Senate—both of which initially had considerable opposition to his measures for division and the Land Law. Well-bred and well connected, Harrison was a man for other politicians to take notice of. He also made a name for himself among the land-hungry residents of the Ohio Valley.[33]

In addition to the two major pieces of legislation Harrison helped shepherd through Congress, he also did his best to help his constituents who petitioned the government for relief. He delivered a report favoring congressional land grants and confirmation of land patents to the settlers of Vincennes and the Illinois country.[34] Harrison's committee recommended presidential recognition of a four-square-mile tract of land held by Isaac Zane on the Mad River. Zane, a former captive of the Wyandots, had taken considerable risks to warn the Americans of impending Indian attacks in the 1790s, and Harrison felt he deserved to be rewarded.[35]

Reminiscent of his patronage of Corporal Edmondson back in his Legion days, Harrison also did his best to help the widow of a former comrade in arms. In May the House reported unfavorably on a bill to aid Ann Elliot, the widow of one of Anthony Wayne's wagon drivers. Robert Elliot had been killed by an Indian sniper in October 1794.[36] Harrison could not vote, but he did succeed in getting the House to delay its decision until December 1800. Belatedly, in the spring of 1805, both houses of Congress passed "[a]n act for the relief of the widow and orphan children of Robert Elliot." Harrison would continue his efforts on behalf of veterans and their dependents when he held more powerful office.[37]

Typical of politicians of his day, William Henry Harrison had few qualms about blurring the line between the public good and personal gain. Given his aristocratic upbringing, he may not have even comprehended such a line. A good example of this occurred in February 1800, when he read "a memorial of sundry inhabitants of the Little Miami, purchasers of lands from John Cleves Symmes, praying a confirmation thereof." Clearly, securing confirmation of these land titles would benefit both the settlers and his father-in-law, the beleaguered Judge Symmes, whose poor record keeping had resulted in many conflicting claims within his grant.[38]

While the division of the Northwest Territory and the Harrison Land Law were in the best interest of promoting American settlement in the Ohio Valley and therefore in the country's best interest, they offered plums for the scion of Berkeley as well. The new posts necessitated by these laws had to be filled, and Harrison made a point to recommend his friends. He tried to get James Findlay of Cincinnati appointed receiver of monies (at the new land office) in Cincinnati, and Harrison himself had his eye on being the register of the land office there. In fact, Harrison was under the impression that he had this new job when word reached him of an entirely different appointment.[39]

Harrison's last official act as the Northwest Territory's delegate to Congress was the publication, in the Cincinnati-based *Western Spy*, of a circular to his constituents. A typical document for congressmen of the era, it detailed his accomplishments while in the House and offered the people of the Northwest—soon to be Ohio—Territory a preview of coming legislative issues, including the suspension of new enlistments for the army. While he opposed the measure in his heart, Harrison put the best face on it in print, noting that by not enlarging the army, Congress was probably saving the taxpayers "one million of dollars."[40]

Unbeknownst to the delegate from the Northwest, on May 12, 1800, President Adams had nominated him to serve as governor of the newly created Indiana Territory. The Senate confirmed the nomination the next day. Much was made during Harrison's later public career about his first appointment having been made by John Adams, as ties to a staunch Federalist soon became a liability in American politics. As a presidential candidate in the 1830s and 1840, Harrison asserted that it was his avowed Republicanism that had spurred Adams to make the appointment in an effort to remove Harrison from the capital.[41]

The argument strains credulity. As is readily seen in Harrison's speeches in Congress, he did not seem to rest firmly in either political camp at this point: his championing of the Harrison Land Law and the Division Bill were favored by many Republicans, but his ardent support for a standing army and criticism of the militia's effectiveness had a Federalist bent. Like his father's generation of Virginia Burgesses, he was more attuned to elite politics than to any particular party. His father had opposed ratification of the U.S. Constitution, yet some of his chief early benefactors, including Light Horse Harry Lee and Anthony Wayne, had been among the staunchest partisans of Federalism. A more reasonable assessment would be that Adams simply felt Harrison was the right man for the job: experienced with the region, yet young and vigorous enough to do a good job. In 1840, Harrison would write that he was initially reluctant to accept the honor, holding out for several weeks. By his own correspondence, however, four weeks later he had taken steps to allow him to draw on the Bank of the United States for his governor's salary.[42]

Governor of Indiana was easily the highest office Harrison could expect to hold at his age, and it offered a decent annual salary—two thousand dollars, including eight hundred for being Indian affairs commissioner—and considerable power and influence. But it would necessitate uprooting his family yet again and leaving the seat of national government for the relative wilds of Indiana. The capital would soon shift to the unglamorous Washington, D.C., but for an ambitious young politician like Harrison, a move from the eastern center of government to the western periphery must have looked like a huge backward step for his career. Yet he must have sensed that his star would shine brightest in the more sparsely populated West, where he had been casting his lot, consciously or not, since becoming a teenage ensign in the army. Also, remaining a congressional delegate was no longer a serious option—it did not pay well enough.

Harrison continued to show some political instincts. He accepted the appointment by Adams only after receiving private assurances from the Jeffersonians that he would not be cast aside when the Republicans swept into office with the fall elections.[43] He was indeed retained by the new president, Thomas Jefferson, and the two men maintained a synergistic relationship throughout Jefferson's presidency.

Harrison needed a steady new source of income in part because his family continued to grow. Two children had been born while he was still serving at Fort Washington in Cincinnati, Betsey Bassett and John Cleves Symmes Harrison, and Anna was well into a third pregnancy.[44] William Henry was aggressive with his investments, but so far he had little to show for them. Harrison's 1793 land sale to his brother Benjamin had been risky and ill advised, but at least it was the action of a young man with no dependents. Now responsible for Anna and the children, William Henry sought a reliable salary as a public servant.[45]

It might seem crude to continually refer, as this book does, to Harrison's repeated efforts to accrue wealth. One should not infer that he was interested solely in money or that he did not truly believe in public service. But aside from basic material needs, Harrison's quest for cash also served very real and pressing social needs. While it is unclear in the 1790s whether Harrison was a Federalist or a Republican, he had definitely been raised to embrace small "r" republicanism. Poverty, Harrison felt, could cripple a man's liberty just as completely as a tyrannical king. For a Virginia gentleman in the West, a secure source of funds was not just pleasurable but an absolutely necessary bulwark to one's freedom and true independence.[46] Furthermore, no self-respecting gentleman planter (especially one who hoped to maintain repute among his neighbors) could afford not to entertain with generous hospitality any guests who might call. But yes, steady income would also make things easier at home.

William Henry's marriage to Anna Symmes was evidence of the social shift taking place in American society at the time. Based largely on romantic notions, the nuptials occurred without the consent of the bride's father, as discussed earlier.[47] Anna loved William Henry, although she may have also welcomed the marriage as a way to avoid her clingy, sometimes controlling father. Better to live under a patriarch of one's own choosing, she may have thought. Harrison probably fell in love with Anna quickly as well—his previous failed attempts at courtship betrayed no fear of commitment on his part. Whatever William Henry's thought process, it was a marriage of choice rather than convenience.

Anna and William Henry must have been relieved at their domestic happiness. It was definitely an amorous marriage, something William Henry revealed in writings to his friend Nathaniel Massie in Chillicothe, Ohio, when Harrison was in Philadelphia with the Congress. Harrison congratulated Massie on his recent marriage, and his envy of a husband who was near his wife was unmistakable: "Before this reaches you, you will no doubt have exchanged the solitary life of a batchelor for the soft silken bands of Hymen in other words—I suppose at this very hour (for it is eleven oClock PM) you are locked in the arms of the charming Susan—what a repast for a susseptable [sic] mind! feast my dear Sir with a Keen appetite but recollect that one too many now may deprive you of a great many here after."[48]

The oblique reference to pregnancy's disruption of marital relations was not the only potential burden married people assumed. Harrison could only fret and hope for the best when Anna had the children inoculated for smallpox, for example. Not having seen Anna or the children for weeks, in July 1800 William Henry met them in Richmond while waiting for Anna to give birth. They named their new daughter Lucy Singleton Harrison.[49]

The Harrisons spent the summer and part of the fall in Virginia, both to allow Anna adequate recovery time from childbirth and perhaps because Harrison was not exceptionally eager to start his new career as territorial governor. In 1801 the entire Indiana Territory had only about 6,500 non-Indians. Judge Symmes had visited Vincennes, now the territory's capital, back in 1790 and been singularly unimpressed. Starting out in Indiana meant starting from scratch. The Harrisons had few other options, though.[50]

Several weeks after Lucy Singleton's birth the Harrisons set out for the West, making a detour to their old home outside Cincinnati, Ohio, to pick up some of Anna's things. By keelboat they continued down the Ohio, where they spent Christmas with the family of Anna's brother-in-law, Peyton Short of Lexington, Kentucky. After Christmas, Harrison and one or two of his slaves from Berkeley headed west, arriving in Vincennes in early January 1801. Anna and the children would come later, when weather permitted.[51]

When William Henry Harrison arrived in Vincennes, he found the framework of a territorial government coming together, cobbled in part from existing forms and in part from scratch. Vincennes and the immediate area had about seven hundred residents, mainly old settlers from the French era, a few of their slaves, and some Americans who had ventured forth in the years after the Revolution. As prescribed in the Ordinance of 1787, Indiana's government during the first territorial stage consisted of an appointed governor, a secretary, and three territorial judges. Harrison did not arrive in Vincennes until January 10, 1801, so for the first six months of the territory's existence, Secretary John Gibson was its sole government official.[52]

Born in 1740, Gibson was said to have received a good education, at least by frontier standards. At eighteen he served in General Forbes's successful expedition against Fort Duquesne, and after the Peace of Paris (1763) he took up the Indian trade at Fort Pitt, the previous site of Fort Duquesne and future site of Pittsburgh. Not long afterward Gibson was taken captive by Indians, probably Shawnees, and adopted. Gibson made good use of his time among the Indians, learning the languages and customs of the Ohio Valley tribes. But when the opportunity arose, he escaped back to Fort Pitt and later served Virginia in Lord Dunmore's War against the Ohio Indians in 1774. When the Revolution broke out, Gibson raised a Patriot regiment, with himself as its colonel, and served honorably throughout the war. He then returned to the Indian trade and became a general in the Pennsylvania militia. His skill as an interpreter permitted him to help find others suitable to translate during negotiations with the Indians in 1793. With the creation of Indiana Territory in May 1800, Gibson was appointed territorial secretary. He arrived in Vincennes that July.[53]

Assisting the governor and Secretary Gibson were judges Henry Vanderburgh, William Clarke, and John Griffin. At their initial meeting, Harrison's first order of business was to administer the oath of office to Judge Clarke. Clarke returned the favor by swearing in the new governor, who then administered the oath to Secretary Gibson and Judges Griffin and Vanderburgh.[54]

After service in the Continental Army, Vanderburgh had moved from New York to Vincennes. Little evidence exists of his legal training, which was probably rather informal, "but his services seem to have been satisfactory." Judge Griffin came from Virginia and was "of some elegant accomplishments and fond of social pleasures, a man of no great force, and an intriguer." His legal education is also unknown. In 1806 he left Indiana for a judicial appointment in Michigan Territory. Little is known of William Clarke, whose appointment ended abruptly with his death on November 11, 1802. Harrison and the judges could adopt laws from those of existing states but had no power to draft legislation of their own.[55]

Thus the four men who initially held all legislative control of what would become Indiana, Illinois, Michigan, and Wisconsin had little apparent legal education, and it is perhaps fortunate that they were not empowered to draft their own laws. Still, they were well esteemed and had records of at least competent public service. Soon after Harrison's arrival the four men set about laying a legal framework for the territory's basic operations. The first law they adopted, published January 19, 1801, was from the Pennsylvania code and dealt with the regulation of county levies.

The next day they adopted, from the Kentucky code, "A Law to regulate the practice of the General court upon Appeals and Writs of Error, and for other purposes." The balance of the laws adopted prior to Clarke's death concerned civil servants' salaries, the courts, and the like, and were all adopted from the codes of Virginia, Kentucky, or Pennsylvania.[56]

In addition to getting his professional house in order, Harrison needed to find a suitable home, particularly for Anna and the children's arrival. When Harrison first came to Vincennes in January 1801, he had no place to stay and knew almost no one. Francis Vigo, an old trader who had aided George Rogers Clark in the conquest of Vincennes during the Revolution, offered the new governor and his family the run of his handsome, nearly completed new home. Harrison gladly accepted, although he insisted that he and his family would use only one room on the ground floor. The governor also purchased a three hundred–acre farm from the trader. Vigo's hospitality was alloyed by good sense. Despite building the new home, he had been in considerable financial trouble since the Revolution and had nearly been ruined by debt in the 1780s. Making a friend of the most politically powerful man between Ohio and the Mississippi River was politically and financially astute, as well as neighborly.[57]

Harrison was forced to return to Kentucky in March, having received word that Anna's sister Maria Short had died. He visited with his mourning wife in March and into April, then returned to Vincennes. Anna and the children arrived in May. Harrison was preoccupied while in Kentucky, but he did take the time to write one William McIntosh, attorney for the powerful Detroit fur trader John Askin. In buying land from Francis Vigo, Harrison had unwittingly purchased acreage the indebted Vigo had included in his mortgage. Harrison asked McIntosh to tell Askin that he would pay for the lands in question in two installments by January 1803 and assured him that Askin and company should accept this offer, as they were unlikely to get anything from the financially strapped Vigo: "I wish you could get Authority from this Company to release any other land which I may purchase from Vigo—& the payments of which to be made to them." Relations between Harrison and McIntosh, a former member of the British Army, were cordial at this point. Harrison soon appointed him both the treasurer of Indiana Territory and a militia officer.[58]

Although bereft at the loss of her beloved sister, Anna no doubt took comfort in having the family together again. Even a cursory glance at her surviving correspondence shows that family and religion were the primary foci of her life. The Harrisons quickly resumed enlarging their family. As Andrew Cayton noted, Anna bore children at almost perfectly spaced two-year intervals until 1814, giving birth to ten live children. Only the last, James Findlay Harrison, died in infancy. The frequent pregnancies often left Anna in frail health, as the majority of Harrison's references to her in correspondence note. Still, the Harrisons were justifiably proud of their brood, living in a society where children were seen as credits rather than debits. But it would have been awkward, socially and physically, to have kept such a rapidly expanding group in Francis Vigo's parlor.[59]

Despite the Vigos' generosity and his own apprehensions about not being reappointed, Harrison needed his own place, and he soon commissioned what would be the grandest home in the territory: Grouseland. Harrison began building it in 1802 and did not finish the home until 1804. Although not an architect, Harrison obviously spent considerable time on the design. The entire structure speaks of permanence and, by territorial Indiana standards, opulence. In addition to conspicuous consumption, Grouseland offered the young governor exceptional practicality, both for his growing family and his professional needs. A brick house (said to be the first in Vincennes) resting on a stone foundation, Grouseland was built to last, with few expenses spared. The bricks alone cost the governor four hundred acres of land, worth perhaps a thousand dollars.[60]

Beautifully restored by the Knox County Daughters of the American Revolution,[61] Grouseland remains impressive today. The basement walls are roughly two feet thick, and the solid brick walls of the home are at least a foot thick. Good bricks were not easy to obtain, but Harrison had them specially baked at a location about five miles north of Vincennes. The layout is something of a bridge between the early-eighteenth-century planters' homes and those of the post-Revolutionary generation. In spatial terms, it allows for large, communal gatherings with numerous visitors, treated with ceremony and grand hospitality, like the old planters' homes. Yet it also has separate spaces intended to allow for more privacy—an increasingly common feature as the American celebration of the individual took hold.[62]

The home has two stories, insulated with a combination of clay and straw, both for heat retention and, as the museum captions note, for primitive soundproofing between floors. The first floor featured a large dining room and a council room, separated by a hall. Harrison could have used these two rooms to entertain important guests and conduct business. The upstairs featured bedrooms for the Harrisons, their children, and their guests. Servants, except those directly watching the children, would have quartered in outbuildings no longer extant.

By its very appearance, a great planter's house conveyed authority. Grouseland, built in the Federal style and somewhat resembling the mansion at Berkeley, did just that. It was also a stout, defendable place for a frontier governor to fort up if necessary, and the design was well planned and carefully laid out. About 150 yards east of the Wabash River, Grouseland was built on the high bank to avoid spring floods. The thick brick walls would have been impervious to anything but cannon fire, while the fine English glass windows featured heavy shutters for defense and provided well-placed firing ports.[63] The basement held a warming kitchen—actual cooking was done in an outbuilding to prevent a potentially catastrophic fire in the home's interior. The basement also featured a small well, in case a siege ensued. In its majesty and military efficiency, Grouseland parallels Johnson Manor, the custom-built home of another frontier gentleman who negotiated Indian treaties, British superintendent of Indian affairs Sir William Johnson.

As intended, Grouseland served as an imposing, impressive site for Indian council negotiations, most notably the Grouseland Treaty of 1809. With its completion, Harrison became the "cliché" of "the independent Virginian lodged in his plantation fortress." Despite a close call in 1810, when a melee nearly broke out between Harrison and the Shawnee Chief Tecumseh, Grouseland never saw actual combat. There was one instance in 1806, however, when a bullet flew through the dining room window as the governor was walking with his infant son John Scott in his arms. Just who fired the shot remains a mystery.[64]

The Harrisons would perhaps have mixed emotions about their home's current surroundings. Long gone is the original majestic walnut grove where Harrison had his tense encounter with Tecumseh. About one hundred yards from the south-facing front porch, along subsequently built railroad tracks, lies the ugly brick building of a heating oil company. As a proponent of higher education, the governor would no doubt be pleased, however, that the rear of his home is now only 150 yards from Vincennes University.

The longer Harrison lived in Indiana, the more favorably impressed he was. His letters to friends, like James Findlay and Jonathan Dayton, bragged about the fertility of the land. As he noted to Dayton, "[T]he face of the country is highly beautiful—Extensive plains, Groves & rivers are intermixed in the most pleasing variety—& form Some of the finest prospects in the World."[65] Harrison was just one of a vast multitude who coveted the fine farmlands of Indiana Territory.

A great part of the challenge of being Indiana's governor was the attached role of serving as the U.S. commissioner plenipotentiary to the Indian tribes north of the Ohio River. Basically, this meant that Harrison was the head U.S. negotiator with local Indian tribes. A later commission would make Harrison the Americans' chief land cession negotiator with Indians in the Ohio Valley.

It seemed only natural to citizens of the early Republic that Indian affairs be placed under the War Department. Harrison therefore answered directly to the secretary of war, Henry Dearborn, and the president, Thomas Jefferson. Dearborn had served ably, if not brilliantly, as a lieutenant colonel in the Revolution and represented the district of Maine in the House of Representatives. He had little administrative experience or ability, but he was honest and a hard worker. His appointment as secretary of war stemmed largely from his unwavering adherence to Jeffersonian principles, which included reducing military expenditures. Jefferson did not worry about Dearborn charting his own ideological course.[66]

Jefferson, Dearborn, and Harrison agreed that America's national honor dictated that the United States should avoid conquest on the Spanish model and that Indians should receive fair and just treatment. As Dearborn wrote Harrison in early 1802:

> It is the ardent wish of the President of the United States, as well as from a principle of humanity, as from duty and sound policy, that all prudent means in our power should be unremittingly pursued for carrying into effect the benevolent views of congress relative to the Indian nations within the jurisdiction of the United States. . . . [The

U.S. should help Indians] by encouraging and gradually introducing the arts of husbandry and domestic manufactures among them.[67]

At the same time, the men were also ardent nationalists and expansionists, and when fair treatment of the Indians clashed with the needs of expansion, expansion usually won out. However, Jefferson in particular seemed to have convinced himself that this would ultimately benefit Indians as well as Americans. Their old ways could not be maintained, he reasoned, in the face of the sweeping prairie fire that was American land hunger. As Anthony F. C. Wallace noted, "All that a humane, educated, and politically powerful white man could do in the social milieu of the time was save as many brands as possible from the burning."[68] The contradiction with Jefferson was that he often fanned the flames himself.

In addition to a governor, the territories had Indian agents, appointed by the president, who took their orders from the secretary of war. The agents were also responsible to the territory's superintendent of Indian affairs (the governor). The system did not always function smoothly. Agents might receive contradictory or incompatible instructions from the secretary of war and the territorial governor. Even if both superiors were in agreement, their physical distance from the agency might render their instructions too tardy or poorly informed to be practical. Finally, some agents, like William Wells at Fort Wayne, suffered under allegations that financial or familial motives clouded their judgment.[69]

Initially, however, Harrison's primary concern regarding the Indians was their deplorable condition in his own neighborhood. In an oft-cited letter to Secretary of War Dearborn, Harrison openly lamented the state of the Indians living in and around Vincennes. He detailed the poverty, poor health, and deadly knife fights among the Indians (most likely Weas), which he directly linked to alcohol abuse among them: "Whether some thing ought not to be done to prevent the reproach which will attach to the American Character by the exterpation [sic] of so many human beings, I beg leave most respectfully to submit to the Consideration of the President."[70]

Not waiting for a reply, five days later Harrison issued a proclamation banning liquor sales to Indians in and around Vincennes. The next month, citing the complaints of several Indian chiefs, he forbade traders from following Indians to their hunting camps and stated that trade should only be conducted in towns, where presumably the proclamation could be enforced. He further promised to seize unlicensed traders and their wares. It was a good idea, but Indiana could not muster even a fraction of the resources needed for such a policing effort. Indeed, the effort was compromised at all levels. Several months after signing these proclamations, Harrison discovered that Secretary Gibson, whose talents were never bureaucratic, had failed to send them to all the Indian agents. The alcohol trade proved especially difficult to stop because the supply of whiskey on the frontier was exceeded only by the demand for it among Indians, as well as whites. Interestingly, Governor Harrison's own effort in the distilling business failed.[71]

Indian chiefs complained to the governor about alcohol, yet some peddled it themselves. They also noted white hunters' tendency to wantonly destroy game animals—although, spurred by the fur trade, some Indians did so as well. By far the biggest Indian-related problem Harrison faced in the early days was convincing the tribes that the United States would provide them with justice when whites murdered Indians. He noted that "these Injuries the Indians have hitherto born[e] with astonishing patience," yet he feared that "should the United States be at war with any of the European nations who are known to the Indians," 90 percent of them would likely attack the United States "[u]nless some means are made use of to conciliate them."[72]

For reasons of human decency, law and order, and national security, Harrison had to hunt down and punish Indian killers. Unfortunately, he was having better luck executing Indians who murdered whites, as he bragged to a friend in November 1801: "We have, indeed, a few days ago executed an Indian for the Murder of a white man—this is Considered by the Neighbouring Spanish government a very bold Step—they, poor devils, would not dare to punish an Indian for any thing—and so Confident were they that our apprehensions of—Indian hostilities were so great as theirs that the Governor of Upper Louisiana offered to bet that the Indian would be pardoned after condemnation."[73]

These were arrogant words from a young man with far less Indian affairs experience than his Spanish counterparts. Executing Indians was a delicate proposition, particularly for a man who had gone on record as secretary of the Northwest Territory saying he preferred to "err in favour of life." Regarding fair play, Indians could legitimately complain that all suspected murderers were tried by white American juries; such juries rarely convicted whites and usually convicted Indians. Equally important, most Ohio Valley Indian tribes rarely enforced capital punishment against their own. While war captives could expect to be tortured to death, civil crimes, even murder, were usually settled by the perpetrator's family assuaging the grief of the victim's family with ritualized gift giving. Indians viewed hangings as unduly cruel and were loath to give up accused murderers. In the years after Greenville, most of the tribes north of the Ohio River tried to comply with American requests, but the lopsided administration of such justice made it difficult for chiefs to do so. Recognizing this, the secretary of war suggested offering generous rewards to Indians who turned state's evidence and to chiefs who helped bring in their accused tribesmen.[74]

When Harrison arrived in Vincennes, the Delaware Indians were extremely upset over unpunished murders, particularly those committed a few years earlier by brothers John and Martin Williams. In 1798 the two had slain three Delawares, including a woman, who were peacefully hunting near the Ohio River. It was a robbery homicide, committed for "about fifty dollars worth of property and the trifling equipage belonging to the Camp of a Savage." The act was rendered even more despicable because it was achieved by a ruse for fear of the courage and prowess of one of the Delawares, warrior Jim Gilloway. The Williams brothers became special objects of prosecution, and President Jefferson, through Secretary of War Dearborn, ordered Harrison to "use every means in your power for apprehending and bringing [them] to justice."[75]

On February 23, 1802, Harrison appointed Davis Floyd of Clarke County to go to Kentucky, where the Williams brothers were hiding, and demand the extradition of Martin Williams, John Williams, and their accomplice, John Crutchelow. In April, Harrison notified Secretary Dearborn that John Williams had been captured. Unfortunately, Williams escaped from the Knox County jail on May 4, 1802, most likely with the help of "some Villain or Villains." The next day Harrison issued a proclamation, offering a three hundred dollar reward for the apprehension of John Williams and one hundred dollars for information leading to his accomplices. Predictably, the citizens of Kentucky were at least as reluctant as those of Indiana to surrender an Indian killer to justice, and the U.S. district judge in Kentucky dragged his feet on the matter, sticking to the minutia of procedure.[76] This would not be the last time an obviously guilty white man escaped justice for murdering an Indian.

The failure to secure justice for Indians, aside from bringing embarrassment, took on more ominous tones with the specter of British influence. Harrison never forgot the British arms and advisers he had encountered at Fallen Timbers. Like most Americans, he saw British intrigue at the heart of nearly any trouble the United States faced. In December 1801, when he learned that the British superintendent of Indian affairs, Thomas McKee, had circulated a speech to Indians living within the territory, Harrison took notice. (Harrison's letter does not specify what McKee's talk entailed.) Secretary Dearborn followed suit, and within the month, both believed McKee and his agents were up to no good.[77] Their suspicions of McKee's motives were not unreasonable. However, the old tendency—left over from the Revolution—of seeing British and Indian interests as one and the same blinded Harrison, Dearborn, and others. American officials overlooked the fact that most Northwestern Indians held little enthusiasm for British promises in 1801.

While Harrison and Dearborn feared Britain might stir up Indian resentment against them, they were oblivious to the fact that their own policies largely fostered that resentment. For American officials during Thomas Jefferson's presidency, Indian land cessions were both official policy and the key to personal advancement. In February 1802, Harrison offered the secretary of war his opinion that "the obvious construction of the treaty of Greenville will be found to be much more extensive than is generally imagined." Taking the hint, in June Secretary Dearborn wrote to Harrison concerning the disposition of the Vincennes tract, a land cession that had been mentioned in the Greenville Treaty but never delineated. Dearborn wanted to know how large the local Indians, the Kickapoos and Piankeshaws, would make this cession. He directed Harrison to hold a council with Little Turtle of the Miamis and two or three other chiefs and assured the governor that he would receive an extra three dollars per day for expenses while the party surveyed the tract's boundaries. As Vincennes was his home, the governor took a keen interest in the tract's size.[78]

Harrison argued that because of Indian cessions to the now defunct Wabash and Illinois land companies (acquired from the French) and a clause in Article IV of the Greenville Treaty that gave the Americans Vincennes and all of the old French claims, the United States actually had rights to lands 12 leagues (36 miles) north and 30 leagues (90 miles) to the west of the White River. He did this despite the fact that Congress had already nullified the Wabash and Illinois Company cessions twice. While Harrison saw the U.S. claims to this land as indisputable, "it would be extremely impolitic," he reasoned, to demand all of it from the Indians. If, however, the width of the tract were reduced to 10 to 12 leagues (30 to 36 miles) on each side of the White River, the Indians would certainly agree to it.[79]

As a cost-cutting measure, Harrison called for a preliminary council of Weas, Potawatomis, Eel Rivers, Piankeshaws, and Kickapoos to be held immediately after the 1802 annuities from the Greenville Treaty had been distributed that August. Therefore, the Indians would not expect any further goods, except a few special gifts for the chiefs. Accordingly, on August 6, Dearborn ordered fifteen silver medals and $1,500 in silver to be sent to the governor for the chiefs. He probably wondered if these gifts would suffice, as in late June he had written Harrison that "[t]here can be no doubt but some evil minded person or persons have been attempting to deceive and mislead the Indians by false representations relative to the views and intentions of our Government towards them."[80]

Presiding over his first Indian treaty council that August, Harrison addressed the assemblage, speaking against the dangers of violence and alcohol and assuring them that President Jefferson had their best interests at heart. The speech failed to impress his Native audience, and negotiations dragged into September. Most of those present seemed unwilling to cede the tract. Harrison concluded that someone, probably the British, had poisoned the chiefs' minds. Many of the Indians present felt the Piankeshaws had such a small claim that any decision they made should not be binding on the others. This exclusion would disrupt what would become one of Harrison's key negotiating tactics—the inclusion of tribes that had little claim to an area, which would increase the likelihood that they would agree to sell it. The bulk of the chiefs present flatly rejected the additional land claim and added that the Great Spirit was already angry with them for ceding lands and that they did not wish to offend him further. Whereas Harrison had asserted a claim to well over one million acres, most chiefs insisted that the tract given to the French was no more than eight thousand acres.[81]

Desperate to secure some success, Harrison sought Native allies. He enlisted the help of Little Turtle (who was receiving a $150 private annuity from the United States) and Turtle's son-in-law, the Indian agent and interpreter William Wells. Little Turtle had achieved fame as a young war captain, and the bear claw necklace he wore, as well as his victories in battle over Generals Harmar and St. Clair, said much for his personal courage and skill. But in his later years, especially after Fallen Timbers, Little Turtle increasingly preferred the treaty council to the warpath. He was the last prominent chief to mark the Greenville Treaty in 1795, and he managed to help secure an unusually large annuity for the Miamis. He met President Washington in Philadelphia in 1796 and met President Adams there in 1797. Now about age fifty-six and troubled by gout, Little Turtle advocated accommodating, rather than fighting, the Americans. Literally and figuratively, he was increasingly comfortable in white men's clothing. For his part, after fighting as a Miami against Harmar and St. Clair, Wells returned to the Americans (although he retained his Miami wife and close ties to the tribe) and served as a scout and spy for General Wayne before and after Fallen Timbers.[82]

The Miami confederacy provides a good example of the realities of tribal existence in the Northwest in the early nineteenth century. Formerly six closely related bands, the Miami confederacy now consisted of the Piankeshaws, Weas, Eel Rivers, and those who lived on the Mississinewa River. The more numerous Mississinewas were considered the leaders of the Miami confederacy, and a hereditary civil chief from the Mississinewas would, in theory, be the confederacy's principal chief. However, the Miamis, with Little Turtle as their main spokesman, had secured additional annuities at the Greenville Treaty by maintaining that the Eel Rivers, Weas, and Piankeshaws were separate tribes from the Mississinewas or Miamis proper. This distinction served the Miami confederacy well in 1795, although it would prove divisive and costly for them later.[83]

To these relatively recent allies of the United States, Harrison added Chief Ducoigne of the Kaskaskias, who had been unwavering in his pro-American stance since the Revolution. Although until recently he had politely complained about American encroachments, Ducoigne felt his tiny tribe's only prudent course was to acquiesce to the United States and hope for the best. Lapoussier, a Wea chief, took a different view, probably because his land was in question. He noted that while most of the chiefs who had marked the Greenville Treaty were dead (recall that a great many had died of diseases they probably picked up at the council), the Weas would honor the treaty. However, he also complained about Indians killed in the streets of Vincennes and a Wea child kidnapped by whites on the Ohio River. And he insisted that his people had only "lent" land to the French and British. With finality he stated, "We wish to be at a distance."[84]

Harrison, Little Turtle, Ducoigne, and Wells succeeded in cajoling the assembled chiefs into agreeing that Little Turtle and Richardville of the Miamis and Topenebee and Winamac of the Potawatomis (although Potawatomi claims to the area would be difficult to establish) would serve as their representatives when a final version of the treaty was drawn up the next year. Harrison knew that dealing with four pliable chiefs would be far simpler than arguing with numerous independent ones. While the chiefs at Vincennes reluctantly agreed, their people were furious, as were the chiefs of tribes not invited to the council. Buckongahelas, the elder war chief of the Delawares (among the uninvited), dictated a letter of protest to President Jefferson. Secretary of War Dearborn wrote to Harrison that he had heard complaints from the Miamis and Delawares concerning unfair tactics "for obtaining the assent of some of the Chiefs to the proposed boundaries."[85]

The Indians' complaints had little effect. Since at least August 1802, Jefferson had sought to firm up American control of the Ohio and Mississippi riverbanks.[86] Securing the large interpretation of the Vincennes tract was an important first step and required quickly extinguishing Native title to the lands. To do so, Jefferson gave Harrison a free hand.

The president assured Dearborn that "it seems absolutely necessary, after giving Governor Harrison our general ideas[,] to leave matters very much to his discretion."[87] In February 1803, Jefferson would write a stunningly blunt letter on Indian affairs that would give Governor Harrison rather specific ideas to utilize at his discretion.

As it would turn out, Harrison's implementation of Jefferson's Indian policies was one of the least controversial aspects of his career as Indiana governor. Regardless of region, most Americans felt Indians lived an outmoded lifestyle and that unless they adopted Anglo-American ways, they were surely headed for extinction. Such a view was inherently self-serving but also perfectly common. The issue of slavery, however, was a different matter.

CHAPTER 3

Indiana and Its Governor Take Shape, 1803–1804

Given Harrison's Virginia planter background and the labor shortage in Indiana Territory, it is not surprising that his first major public initiative as governor was to bring more slaves to the area. What does surprise is how in later years, when the issue was clearly an albatross around the governor's neck, he remained doggedly pro-slavery. A literal reading of Article VI of the Northwest Ordinance leaves the impression that slavery was banned north of the Ohio. Yet from its birth this article was creatively interpreted by many, including Northwest Territory governor Arthur St. Clair, as merely prohibiting future importations. It was said not to be retroactive, which was welcome news to the old settlers of the area— Frenchmen along the Mississippi and Virginians along the Ohio—who had held slaves for years. In this interpretation, they could hold on to their slaves and their progeny indefinitely.

Yet others remained uneasy about Article VI. Illinoisans had been petitioning Congress since the 1780s for clear confirmation of their human property, and some called for a repeal or at least a suspension of Article VI. Their fears about its use for eventual emancipation were well-founded, in part because of the mixed response of government officials. At least two of the territorial judges appointed for the Northwest, George Turner and Harrison's father-in-law, Judge Symmes, freed slaves citing Article VI. Turner, for this and other political considerations, was forced to resign. But although he had been neutralized, the threat of emancipation loomed. Governor St. Clair and others protested that many good settlers had left or bypassed the Northwest for Spanish territory across the Mississippi, largely because they feared Article VI.[1]

Governor Harrison's stance was unambiguous. When he arrived in Vincennes in January 1801, he was accompanied by at least one black slave, presumably part of his inheritance. Once in Indiana, Harrison quickly fell in with the pro-slavery faction—old French settlers, well-established traders and farmers in the Illinois country, and recent slave-owning immigrants from Kentucky and Virginia. He soon became a large landowner, and like most Virginian men of his generation and station, he did not intend to work his lands himself. He was also drawn by the fact that the pro-slavery group initially seemed the most financially and socially influential faction in the region.[2]

There was more to it, however. Aside from the crudely material benefits (or supposed benefits) of owning slaves, having slaves would have meant something more to a man like William Henry Harrison. His main reason for going west and seeking to better his lot was to gain the material and social standing that he felt, by birth, should have been his. It would not have been enough to simply know in his own heart that he was the son of an important family. He needed to openly display not only his own worth but his power as well. For the society into which he was born, to be a man of note was to have control over others. For Virginians certainly, the greatest and most direct demonstration of that power was being a master to slaves.[3] Thus to be a truly independent man, he had to rule others. This helps explain why, as we shall see, Harrison would cling grimly to the idea of expanding slavery in Indiana long after doing so was clearly hurting his popularity.

In the fall of 1802, Harrison toured the Illinois country, asking residents to petition him to call a convention to consider formally establishing slavery in the territory. He was well received, no doubt, because Illinoisans had been petitioning for slavery since 1788. In November 1802, Harrison sent a proclamation to Congress stating that "a very large majority of the Citizens" favored a repeal of Article VI of the Ordinance of 1787 and that a convention would be held to decide the territory's stance. On Christmas Day, the Vincennes Convention, with Harrison serving as convention president and delegate from Knox County, voted to suspend Article VI for ten years, pending congressional approval.[4]

The petition to Congress soon followed, stating that Article VI had "prevented the Country from populating and been the reason of driving many valuable Citizens possessing Slaves to the Spanish side of the Mississippi." Considerable evidence suggests that Article VI had in fact encouraged some migration to Spanish Louisiana. Yet the petition, and Harrison's championing of it, carried powerful irony. In Virginia's House of Burgesses in 1772, Benjamin Harrison sat on a committee that called for George III to end the African slave trade. It was, the committee said, a "Trade of great Inhumanity," which also posed a security risk for whites. Further, "[I]t greatly retards the Settlement of the Colonies, with more useful Inhabitants." The general assembly agreed and passed a resolution petitioning the king to end the African slave trade, although not slavery itself. As with most correspondence from America, the petition was ignored.[5] Thirty years later William Henry, who so greatly revered his father's generation—especially the representatives from Virginia—in effect argued that they had erred in passing the resolution.

The Indiana petitioners asked for a ten-year suspension of Article VI, which would then be reinstated, but the slaves from the ten-year window (and their progeny) would remain enslaved. On the same day, convention president Harrison sent a letter to the speaker of the U.S. House of Representatives relating the convention's desire to suspend Article VI.[6]

The convention was forced to wait until March 2, 1803, for the report of John Randolph of Virginia, Roger Griswold of Connecticut, Robert Williams of North Carolina, William Hoge of Pennsylvania, and L. R. Morris of Vermont. Led by Randolph, the committee determined that suspending Article VI would be "highly dangerous and inexpedient" and that Indiana's settlers "would at no distant day find ample remuneration for a temporary privation of labor and immigration" in maintaining a free society.[7]

Still hoping for a favorable reaction from Congress, Harrison and his judges set the table for Article VI's suspension with two laws they adopted in 1803. "A Law in addition to a law intitled a law to regulate the practice of the General Court upon appeals and Writs of Error, and other purposes," adopted from the Virginia and Kentucky codes and published September 20, 1803, denied "negroes, mulattos, and Indians" the right to testify against whites in court. It also took pains to define race: "Every person other than a negro, of whose grand fathers or grand mothers any one is, or shall have been a negro, altho' all his other progenitors, except that descending from a negro, shall have been white persons, shall be deemed a mulatto, and so every such person who shall have one fourth part or more of negro blood shall in like manner be deemed a mulatto."[8]

The next law adopted, also from the Virginia code, was "A Law concerning Servants." While this law did state that "[a]ll negroes and mulattoes . . . who shall come into this territory under contract to serve another in any trade or occupation, shall *be compelled* [italics mine] to perform such contract specifically during the term thereof," it did offer black servants some rights and protection.[9]

The law required masters to adequately feed, clothe, and house their servants and also to allow them to keep any money or goods they earned. A master "guilty of injurious demeanor towards his servant" was to be "redressed on motion" by the local county court (although punishments were ill defined), and county courts were to "at all times receive the complaints of servants being citizens of the United States of America." (The law would not, in all likelihood, have considered blacks slaves to be citizens.) Yet servants could be whipped and jailed for refusal to work and were to be whipped in cases "where free persons are punishable by fine" or for running away. Granted, the rationale at the time was that servants lacked the funds to make fines a viable form of coercion, and they could only be punished physically. But undeniably, servants, especially non-whites, were subject to far more legal violence than others. The law also denied blacks, mulattos, and Indians the right to purchase white servants, and if any did so, the white servant was to be immediately freed.[10]

In the fall of 1803, the governor learned that his old friend Thomas Worthington had been elected to serve as one of the first senators from the new state of Ohio. The news pleased Harrison greatly, both for Worthington's success and for the opportunities that might arise with another westerner in the Senate. Although troubled by a painful eye infection, the governor wrote to congratulate his good friend and then presumptuously lectured him on how new senators should not make long speeches. Clearly, Harrison wished for Worthington's success and equated it with recognition for the rest of the Ohio Valley. It was intensely hypocritical, though, for one who had made speeches in the House as a twenty-six-year-old nonvoting member to try to muzzle an elected senator.

Harrison followed that faux pas with a patronizing depiction of Worthington's stance on introducing slaves into Indiana. Although the senator had pledged, through Harrison's friend Benjamin Parke, to support all of the governor's other initiatives—such as not dividing the territory—he criticized Worthington's decision against slavery: "I am Sorry you are So Much opposed to this measure—but more So on account of the opinion you have given that the Consent of the State of Ohio is necessary before we Can have Slaves in this territory[.] You Certainly did not Consider this Subject Sufficiently or you would not have given Such an opinion." Actually, Worthington had given the matter some thought, which was why he freed the slaves he had brought to Ohio from Virginia, then hired them to work his fields.[11]

The Northwest Ordinance, Harrison's argument continued, did not require the "Mutual Consent" of all the states and territories north of the Ohio to any alteration in the articles of the ordinance—in this case Article VI—unless the new law directly affected all the parties. Harrison contended that the territories and states north of the Ohio, and the United States as a whole, would not be directly affected by suspending or repealing Article VI for Indiana: "[O]n a question like the present . . . the state of Ohio has no More interest or Concern than the State of Kentucky[,] Vermont or Any other State in the Union."[12] That was poppycock; Ohio shared a border with Indiana. The governor might as well have argued that Francis Vigo should show no concern if Harrison set his parlor afire.

On December 15, 1803, the pro-slavery petition was referred to Congressmen Caesar Rodney of Delaware (later the attorney general for Presidents Jefferson and Madison), John Boyle of Kentucky, and James Rhea of Tennessee. This all-southern, all-Republican committee made its report in favor of the petition to the entire House on February 17, 1804, provided that no foreign-born slaves were introduced and that the children of slaves introduced would be freed at age twenty-five (men) or twenty-one (women).[13] Benjamin Parke, Indiana's delegate to Congress, apparently believed the House of Representatives would eagerly repeal Article VI and that President Jefferson was "decidedly in favor" of such a repeal. Congress took no action on the committee's recommendations, however.[14]

Jefferson's reasoning often seems inscrutable and contradictory, but it is doubtful that he would have strongly favored increased slavery in the

Northwest. He had first proposed a delayed ban on slavery in all western territories in 1784, and for all his ambivalence regarding slavery, he did not seem to actively want it to spread. More characteristically, his political philosophy and desire to avoid conflict would have led him to defer to local authorities on such an issue. While Jefferson's distaste for slavery in the abstract prevented him from encouraging its spread, a lack of moral courage prevented him from decisively discouraging it. Delegate Parke's read on Jefferson appears to have been wishful thinking, an interpretation bolstered by the fact that he incorrectly gauged congressional sentiment as well.

The slavery debate took a curious turn in the spring. On April 6, 1804, Harrison issued a proclamation forbidding the "nefarious and inhuman design" of kidnapping "colored indentured servants" and selling them into slavery outside the territory. Harrison issued the proclamation to stop one Simon Vannorsdell, acting as agent for the heirs of John and Elizabeth Kuykendall. Vannorsdell was attempting to take two black servants, George and Peggy (who had been brought to Indiana from Virginia by the Kuykendall family), out of the territory, "with a design as is supposed of selling them for slaves contrary to the law and dignity of the United States."

The Northwest Ordinance had been creatively interpreted as non-retroactive toward slaves already held, but it seemed to ban bringing more slaves in. This was the obvious construction of the law—why else would Harrison and others campaign so hard for Article VI's suspension? Yet it seems the idea of selling indentured servants, even black ones who had so recently been slaves, into slavery struck Harrison as abhorrent. Or perhaps he simply wanted to avoid a precedent that could strip Indiana of its black servants. A court order stopped Vannorsdell from taking George and Peggy, and a writ of habeas corpus temporarily freed them from him. Governor Harrison and lawyer John Rice Jones took out a bond, pledging that they would ensure that George was present at the September court session, or they would forfeit two hundred dollars and one hundred dollars, respectively.[15]

Vannorsdell tried again to take George and Betty into custody, and again a writ of habeas corpus freed them. At the September 1804 session, Governor Harrison was joined by Attorney General Washington Johnston and trader John Johnston in the surety bonds for George and Peggy, Harrison standing for six hundred dollars and the Johnstons for three hundred dollars each. The case was held over until the June 1805 court session. Perhaps tiring of the process or fearful that his luck was running out, prior to the June session George indentured himself to Governor Harrison for eleven years. Faced with an obstinate territorial governor, Vannorsdell gave up on George. Peggy was released by the court the following year, and she then sued Vannorsdell for lost wages.[16]

George's indenture to Harrison drew criticism from at least one of the governor's political enemies, who charged that George had been duped out of his freedom.[17] The charge is interesting, although it is difficult to imagine Harrison going to so much trouble against a respectable family from his home state just to secure one servant for himself. It would have been far simpler to ignore the case and get another servant. While eleven years was a long indenture for an ostensibly free man, it was undeniably a better situation than George could have expected had he been sold into slavery in the South. Finally, if Harrison and his cronies went to such lengths to defraud the Kuykendalls of rightful property, then why did they allow Peggy to go free?

Peggy's suit for lost wages dragged on for two years, and she eventually lost in court. It was decided that Peggy was neither a criminal nor a slave and that legally she could not be detained, although there were qualifications to the decision. The ruling of judges Thomas T. Davis and Henry Vanderburgh stated that "this order is not to impair the right that the defendant [Vannorsdell] or any other person shall have to the said negro girl Peggy, provided he, Vannorsdell, or any other person, can prove said negro Peggy to be a slave. Nor shall this order impair the right of said Peggy to her freedom, provided the said Peggy shall establish her right to the same." The judges were so uncertain of their decision that they intentionally chose to keep it from being final.[18] The status of black servants in the territory was becoming increasingly blurry. Before long, however, the lines of the slavery debate in Indiana would crystallize.

Harrison repeatedly argued that allowing the importation of slaves to Indiana would improve the quality of life for American citizens there and help spur the settlement and development of the territory. While trying to effect this change for what he saw as the public good, he also tried to further his own private holdings. Notably, his efforts in both arenas later drew harsh criticism from opponents.

Like his Virginia gentry forebears, William Henry Harrison saw land as the most noble and reliable source of wealth. Virginia's Tidewater elite viewed vast landholdings and numerous slaves as the keys to a man's independence. Having sold his Tidewater lands to his brother for a relative pittance, he hoped to secure vast amounts of fertile western lands, which would provide both wealth and prestige. He realized that he particularly needed the former, as he also shared the Virginia planter's tendency to live beyond his means.[19] Rather than constrict his spending, Harrison did his best to improve his finances through aggressive investments. He engaged in a veritable orgy of land sales and purchases from the late 1790s well into 1812.

Sources on Harrison's early land dealings are scattered, and the available records are not always complete; sometimes acreage is left out, sometimes the exact price is omitted. From the most complete compilation of his records currently available—the 1999 Indiana Historical Society microfilm edition of his papers—some patterns do emerge. From 1801 to 1803, Harrison purchased at least 3,718 acres of land, mostly in Indiana and especially in his new home of Knox County. In so doing, he spent at least $7,113. At the same time, he sold at least 1,102 acres, mostly land outside of Indiana—lands he had previously purchased in Ohio and New Jersey lands owned by his wife. These sales brought in at least $2,917.50. While admittedly incomplete, the data strongly suggest that Harrison was continuing to cast his lot with the West and cutting ties to the eastern seaboard. They also demonstrate that he was either unconcerned with accumulating early debts, or his lack of business acumen made it difficult to avoid them. By early 1803 he owed his wife's brother-in-law Peyton Short—no financial wiz himself—$3,200.[20]

Harrison's appetite for land speculation seems comparable to Thomas Jefferson's appetite for books, although presumably the land had a better chance of appreciating in value. Indeed, through August 1812, Harrison paid more than $28,000 for land while taking in perhaps $22,000 for land he sold. Many other Americans shared William Henry Harrison's lust for land, and he was not alone in investing more than he seemed to have. What set Harrison apart were his prominence and political influence, which allowed him to rely as much on sociopolitical capital as he did on specie. His conduct seemed consistent with a general pattern of western lands purchasing by government officials, such as his father-in-law, Judge Symmes. There was assuredly a "close connection between administrators and the land business [that] would continue . . . and would often cast a doubt on the integrity and impartiality of the administration of the public lands."[21] Governor Harrison's desire to accumulate land personally was mirrored by his drive to acquire Indian lands for the United States.

Harrison had little difficulty getting his way in pro-slavery matters or anything else because he was the most powerful among the small group of men entrusted with the territory's governance. He had their support, as well as that of many other elite men of the territory. Harrison had deliberately cultivated men such as the Welsh-born lawyer John Rice Jones of the Illinois country and two Virginians, both named Shadrach Bond,[22] who now made their homes in Illinois as well. Judge Henry Vanderburgh and Francis Vigo, the elder statesman of Vincennes, were also Harrison's friends. The governor had been bred to elite politicking, and his personality and pedigree gave him considerable clout, as shown by his remarkable influence while a territorial delegate to Congress. Yet he knew the day would come when Indiana reached its second grade, and he would have to contend with a territorial legislature, the lower house of which would be popularly elected. Understandably, it was not a day he looked forward to. The older French inhabitants of Indiana Territory had not known representative self-government and did not actively seek it. But as more Americans came into the territory, popular sentiment for democratizing measures rose.

The first years in Indiana treated the Harrison family well. For the most part, William Henry enjoyed a two-year honeymoon as Indiana's governor. From 1801 to 1803, he managed to ingratiate himself with the right people, and he did not antagonize anyone who seemed important. As will be discussed in chapter 4, he did anger some Indians with his heavy-handed treaty negotiating style. In 1802 and 1803, the Indians of Indiana seemed more objects of pity than reasons for concern, however. Nor did many in the territory seem to be protesting the governor's pro-slavery overtures. Work on Grouseland continued to progress in 1803 and 1804. In parallel fashion, in those years Governor Harrison laid the foundation for the rest of his tenure as Indiana's chief executive—years that would prove far more eventful and chaotic.

The truest test of a public servant's character and will come with the pressures of office, and the years 1803–1804 saw the genesis of the first true crises of Governor Harrison's career. Jeffersonian foreign policy bled into domestic concerns with Indian affairs, and Harrison leaped readily into the breech to fulfill the president's wishes and secure his own livelihood. These years also saw the first murmurs of discord within the territory, as citizens began to question just how much power their appointed governor should wield. And in the first months of 1803, the continuing ripple effect of the war in Europe was felt keenly in the United States, particularly regarding the West.

The rise of Napoleon and a rumored transfer of Louisiana Territory from relatively weak Spain to aggressive France made Americans suddenly uneasy about their western border. To protect the nation, the Mississippi needed to serve as a staunch line of defense, which would only come, President Jefferson concluded, with a sizable white population along the river. To secure this, in February 1803 the president wrote Governor Harrison a frank and private letter regarding his course of action:

> Our system is to live in perpetual peace with the Indians, to cultivate an affectionate attachment from them, by everything just and liberal which we can do for them within the bounds of reason, and by giving them effectual protection against wrongs from our own people. The decrease of game rendering their subsistence by hunting insufficient, we wish to draw them to agriculture, spinning and weaving. . . . When they withdraw themselves to the culture of a small piece of land, they will perceive how useless to them are their extensive forests, and will be willing to pare them off from time to time in exchange for necessaries for their farms and families. To promote this disposition to exchange lands, which they have to spare and we want, we shall push our trading uses, and be glad to see them run in debt, because we observe that when these debts get beyond what the individuals can pay, they become willing to lop them off by a cession of lands.

Jefferson also instructed Harrison to keep these plans secret, as it would be best for the Indians if they did not foresee their future.[23]

The letter was strikingly devious, not to mention self-serving. It was practically, if not intentionally, malevolent. As Peter S. Onuf has noted, "The inexorable progress of civilization—self-evidently a good thing— absolved Americans of agency or moral responsibility for the displacement of indigenous peoples; in stark contrast, the Indians did face choices and were responsible for their own fate." Further, "White settlers' land hunger [in Jefferson's mind] thus was not a threat but a resource Indians should exploit." Jefferson was definitely manipulative as a "Great Father" to the Indians, although perhaps no more so than he had been with his own children.[24]

For Americans generally, the assumption was that Indians were fated to disappear unless they adopted Anglo-American ways. It was a convenient concept—removing the United States from any possible blame for what would surely be the ultimate result. Like the conflation of Indian war parties with British armies, this view was something of a holdover from the Revolution. Yet unlike such othering propaganda, the presumption of American cultural superiority may have been less consciously manufactured. Ethnocentrism is a common (perhaps even natural) feature of human societies. Americans' ethnocentrism was largely a by-product of their veneration of the Revolutionary generation. They interpreted "their economic progress as testimony to the soundness of the revolution they had inherited."[25]

That progress, in turn, they attributed to the Founders' wisdom in choosing democratic institutions. Americans in the decades after 1783 saw so many new "improvements"—farms, buildings, and inventions— "that it was possible to think of the United States as having implanted itself on a blank canvas, flourishing because of its good sense in adopting democratic ways." The United States, thanks to the success of the Revolution, "made possible the creation of a distinctive American society that honored individual initiative, institutional restraint, and popular public participation." While such a simplified causal analysis does not satisfy a historian, "the connection between prosperity and democracy sealed the American imagination against a critical stance towards either, a portentous development."[26] It was the early Republic's version of the Puritans' "City upon a Hill," or what later generations would call the concept of

"American Exceptionalism." Wearing such cultural blinders made it easier for Anglo-Americans to run roughshod over Native cultures. "Inferior" cultures had no right to stand in the way of "progress."

In 1803 Jefferson launched Governor Harrison on an intense campaign to extinguish Indian land titles. While Jefferson was clearly the architect of his own Indian policy, he knew he needed a strong foreman on-site. Less than a month before he sent his Indian affairs instructions, the president nominated Harrison for another term as Indiana governor and a new commission for negotiating land treaties with Indians north of the Ohio River. He was easily confirmed for both. Clearly, Jefferson saw Harrison as the right man to push his Indian policy, and he would not be disappointed. As his first priority that spring, Harrison sought to get the various tribes to recognize the validity of his August 1802 "quasi-treaty" regarding the Vincennes tract. Most Indians, however, denounced the proposed cession. Harrison continued to suspect British intrigue among the Indians. Sympathetic to this view, if less fully convinced, Secretary Dearborn told the governor to find out if there actually were traders acting as foreign agents and causing trouble among the Indians. If so, he was to have the unlicensed traders arrested and the licensed ones "unlicensed" and deported.[27]

Most of the leading chiefs, probably fearing the ire of their people, said they would refuse to attend Harrison's council scheduled for June 1803. No doubt with Jefferson's letter in mind, the governor resorted to strong-arm tactics and announced that he would distribute the Greenville Treaty annuities only to those tribes attending the conference. While this was probably not a life-threatening situation for all the tribes, they certainly wanted their annuities, and their chiefs would have difficulty acting like chiefs with no goods to distribute. Most gave in and attended.[28]

The council at Fort Wayne saw few smiles. At one point the Delaware war chief Buckongahelas—who had distrusted the Americans since the Revolution and treated with them only reluctantly—angrily interrupted Harrison. The chief declared that the lands in question belonged to the Delawares through the gift of the Piankeshaws and that the Vincennes council of 1802 was not binding on anyone. The Shawnees were even more vehement in their disapproval of the council. When Harrison (undiplomatically) threatened to withdraw his protection from them, their delegation became so enraged that they stormed out—a stunning breech of Indian protocol.

The Shawnees later returned and proposed that the chiefs journey to Washington to meet directly with President Jefferson. However, through pressure applied by Harrison, Little Turtle, and the Potawatomis—the latter "entirely devoted to the Governor"—those present finally relented. The chiefs representing the Delawares (Buckongahelas, Hockingpomska, and Kechkawhanund), Shawnees (Black Hoof, Neahmemsieeh, and Methawanasice), and Potawatomis (Five Medals, an elderly chief from the Fort Wayne area) signed for themselves rather than allow Little Turtle, Richardville, Topenebee, and Winamac to sign for them. Only the Miamis and the smaller tribes—the Weas, Eel Rivers, Piankeshaws, and Kaskaskias—allowed the designated representatives to sign for them. Records of the proceedings did not survive, but "a judicious distribution of presents or a threat of withholding the annuities from tribes that would not sign may have accelerated the proceedings."[29]

Certainly, Little Turtle, Richardville, Topenebee, and Winamac hoped siding with the governor would benefit themselves and their peoples. In all likelihood, the other chiefs gave in because they feared Harrison's picked chiefs would usurp them in the governor's eye, costing them annuities. They also signed to assert their independence of Harrison's four chiefs and possibly to gain his favor. These men were all understandably jealous of their positions and guarded their influence vigorously.[30]

The Treaty with the Delawares, etc., signed at Fort Wayne on June 7, 1803, concluded the business begun in 1802 and gave the United States the 1.152 million acres (1,800 square miles) surrounding Vincennes, despite the insistence by the tribes involved that the French cession had comprised no more than 8,000 acres (12.5 square miles). Although Harrison had initially stated that the United States should seek only 30–36 miles of land on either side of the White River, the treaty as signed gave the United States almost twice as much territory. Because it was now considered part of the original Greenville Treaty, the United States paid no additional annuities for the land, other than "a quantity of salt not exceeding one hundred and fifty bushels" to be divided yearly among the tribes.[31]

The Vincennes cession proved important for several reasons: it was Governor Harrison's first Indian treaty and thus the beginning of a career in Indian land acquisition that remains singular. The cession, and the high-pressure tactics used to engineer it, demonstrated the acceleration of Jefferson's manifest Indian policy—to purchase as much Indian land along the Mississippi and Ohio rivers as possible so as to settle the area with white Americans who would provide a bulwark against possible Spanish or French invasion from Louisiana.[32] The treaty served as a model for future negotiations with Indians, and it also showed how the previous decade had treated many once-imposing Ohio Valley tribes.

Whereas members of the Miami confederacy had served as leaders in the Indian resistance movement of the early 1790s, they and their most famous war chief, Little Turtle, now sought desperately to maintain some leverage in dealing with the U.S. government. The Shawnees' breaching of council decorum and veiled threats now rang hollow, whereas before they had been the Ohio Valley tribe most feared by the Americans. For Ducoigne and the Kaskaskias (the Illinois confederacy had been in decline for a century), continued raids both by other tribes and by white frontiersmen had so reduced them that they could no longer even try to maintain their landholdings. The Kaskaskias became completely dependent on the United States for protection and were willing to facilitate selling lands to the government. Now it was their turn to cede.

The August 13, 1803, treaty with the Kaskaskias proved a coup for the United States. The Kaskaskias, estimated by Harrison to number perhaps thirty souls, signed away nearly 8 million acres of southern Illinois.[33] Harrison had noted the previous March that the Kaskaskias eagerly sought U.S. protection, and the threat of their "extirpation by the Potawatomis"[34] served as a key incentive for them to do so. In the treaty, the United States promised to protect them from all enemies, as it would U.S. citizens, provided that the Kaskaskias did not make war on anyone. Their annuity doubled to a thousand dollars. Reflecting the civilizing goal, Chief Ducoigne received a new house with a fenced-in field, and the predominantly Catholic Indians were given funds for a church[35] and a salary for a priest for seven years. They got to keep 350 acres for themselves, although this was merely confirmation of their land grant by act of Congress in 1791. They could also pick a 1,280-acre reservation for themselves within the ceded lands.[36]

Article IV spelled out the relinquishing of their independence, as the United States reserved the right to divide the annuity among the several Kaskaskia families. Doing so reduced Chief Ducoigne's prestige by preempting his right to distribute goods, as a chief would normally do. Dividing the annuities by family would eventually save the government money because when a family died out, the government was no longer obliged to pay them—something President Jefferson would point out in 1804. Six Kaskaskias (about one-fifth of their total number, by Harrison's reckoning) marked the treaty.[37]

Jefferson and Harrison hoped Ducoigne and the Kaskaskias, having relinquished the vast bulk of their lands and independence for monetary and material rewards, would inspire other chiefs to make large cessions to the United States. Yet the cession seems to have had the opposite effect on Ducoigne's neighbors. As Reginald Horsman noted, the "Kaskaskias were, in fact, a decimated and impotent tribe; indeed there was considerable doubt as to their rightful claim to all the land they had ceded." This might partially explain why tribes like the western Potawatomis and the Kickapoos of the prairie sought vengeance against the Kaskaskias.[38]

Jefferson's enthusiasm for the 1803 cession may have represented a fundamental shift in his thinking regarding Indian lands. In 1796 he had written that he hoped the Kaskaskias would remain "undisturbed" on their lands. By February 1803 he was writing his infamous private letter to Governor Harrison explicitly calling for the rapid purchase of Indian lands in the Mississippi Valley by any means necessary. Whatever cerebral gymnastics Jefferson may or may not have performed to get to this point, the end result was that the Indiana governor understood that he now had a mandate to acquire Indian lands. Some Indians recognized this shift in tone all too clearly. Harrison wrote Dearborn on August 23, 1803, that "[i]n relation to the treaties[,] the indians continues [sic] to be constantly intoxicated."[39]

It bears mentioning that William Henry Harrison, like Thomas Jefferson and other leading American officials, did not hate Indians per se. They were certainly ravenous, often patronizing, and even unethical when it came to buying up Indian lands. Unlike their views of blacks, though, they did not draw the strictest of racial lines with Indians. They were more than willing to help Indians who cooperated at treaty negotiations and who were acculturated enough not to threaten the Jeffersonian goal of "civilization." Harrison's opinion of Captain Hendrick Aupaumut serves as a good example of this worldview. Aupaumut, a Mahican, had fought alongside the Americans during the Revolution and was present at the Vincennes cession council. As Harrison noted, Aupaumut "has done me Much Service by recommending to the Indians to adopt the plans which were proposed to them."[40] Like Chief Ducoigne, Captain Aupaumut deserved to be taken care of.

Harrison asked the U.S. Indian agent at Detroit, Henry Jouett, to look after Aupaumut and his men when they arrived there and to help them gain passage on Lake Erie by public ship to Ontario, as they were making their way back east. Citing further evidence of Aupaumut's worthiness, Harrison asserted that "Captn. Hendrick has received a good english education & you will find him deserving yr. attentions."[41]

That was the Jeffersonian view of Indians: if they were not threatening, and if they acknowledged the superiority of Anglo-American cultural practices, Indians were worth saving. But the moment they resisted the Great Father's teachings or demands, they ceased to be wayward children and instead became the Other.

President Jefferson's stated (if private) reason for unleashing Harrison on such rapid land purchases stemmed directly from his fears of Napoleon occupying Louisiana. In a tremendous stroke of luck for the United States, however, Napoleon, who had since given up his North American dreams, sold the entire territory to American commissioners on April 30, 1803. The Senate ratified the treaty in October, and the United States took formal possession on December 20, 1803. The fear of French expansionism no doubt influenced both Jefferson and Harrison, and the treaties of 1803 must be seen in the context of looming military and diplomatic catastrophe. Yet after this threat ended, the rapid acquisition of Indian lands did not.[42]

The Louisiana Purchase immediately drew praise for Jefferson's administration, and it certainly was a tremendous bargain. For Harrison, it offered the excuse to strike up correspondence with William Clark, an old comrade in arms from their days in General Wayne's Legion. Clark was now near St. Louis, preparing for his great transcontinental trek with Meriwether Lewis. Harrison wrote Clark in November 1803, thanking him for the map the two explorers had sent and noting that he had made a copy of it: "I beg of you to let me know from Cahokia whether I can do anything for you in yr. absence." He was thankful for their offer to send word occasionally, and he passed on some information of his own. The previous evening's mail conveyed that the Senate had in fact voted in favor of the Louisiana Purchase.[43]

Although it was a boon to the country, Louisiana did bring additional responsibility for Indiana's governor. In March 1804, Congress divided the Louisiana Purchase into the Territory of Orleans and the District of Louisiana, and the latter became part of Indiana. The move was never intended to be permanent, as Indiana Territory, in square miles if not population, was already huge. Accordingly, Governor Harrison could not, and did not try to, micro-manage Louisiana. Harrison did have some knowledge of the territory, as he corresponded with its lieutenant governor, Charles De Hault Delassus. When Spain transferred Louisiana back to France, Harrison had even offered to shelter Delassus's father, should the old gentleman flee to the United States. Still, it was something of a chore for Harrison to gather the information President Jefferson so eagerly sought.[44] In June 1804 he wrote the president a detailed account of his findings.

Upper Louisiana, Harrison noted, contained 7,876 whites and 1,497 blacks. For simplicity's sake, he suggested dividing the territory into five districts, in nearly the same fashion as the Spanish had. For clarity, they should be called "counties," as the entire region was a district. He could not say with certainty how many militia Louisiana could muster, but he guessed it to be about a fifth of the number of able-bodied men in each of the counties. Harrison went on to make his suggestions to the president for improving Louisiana's existing militia system. Currently, there were no groups larger than a company and no officers ranking above captain.

Harrison never missed an opportunity to offer his views on military matters: "This arrangement ought in my opinion no longer to exist. The prospect of promotion is one of the greatest inducements to men of enterprise to accept Military appointments & the most effectual stimulus

to urge them to a prompt & faithful discharge of their duties." Harrison
believed the most heavily populated counties should have a colonel commanding two battalions, while a major might lead the counties with one
battalion. Finally, for military commandant he recommended Pierre
Delassus de Luziere, "an old gentleman of the greatest respectability and
of considerable talents" who was now in a "destitute Condition." True,
de Luziere had been an adherent of "the former Despotic Government
of France," but Harrison felt he was "now in Sentiment an American
Republican." Jefferson agreed with the governor regarding the drawing
of the counties but said nothing about the militia or de Luziere.[45]

Harrison then set aside the Louisiana questions for a time, as he had
pressing matters closer to home. Although initially a success, the 1804
treaty with the Delawares would become troublesome for him. In this
treaty, signed August 18, the Delawares relinquished their claims to the
lands between the Wabash and Ohio rivers. Over the next ten years they
were to receive $3,000, plus $1,500 worth of instruction and materials
for teaching them the "agricultural and domestic arts" over the next
five years. The fact that Delaware women had been excellent farmers
for centuries was not mentioned. In the treaty Harrison also stated that
the Delawares were the sole owners of the great tract between the Ohio
and White rivers and were seriously considering a move to join relatives
west of the Mississippi. The Delawares, in fact, had been pushed west
from Pennsylvania since the seventeenth century and did not own the
tract. They lived there by permission of the Miami confederacy.

Despite what he had said, Harrison knew this well before the treaty.
He had mentioned in a May 12, 1804, letter to the president that the
United States should quickly secure a land cession from the Delawares
before they left. The Delawares, Harrison noted, were far less attached to
the land than other tribes, such as the Piankeshaws, "who Set a higher
value on [it] from their ancestors having resided on [it] for Many
generations." The treaty itself acknowledged that this situation was likely
to cause trouble, as Article V noted that the Piankeshaws had "obstinately
persisted in refusing to recognize" Delaware ownership of the tract. If the
Piankeshaws could not be made to agree to Delaware ownership in a subsequent treaty, the Delaware treaty would be null and void.[46]

On August 17, nine days after the Delawares signed the treaty, the Piankeshaws acknowledged the Delawares' "ownership" of the disputed tract and agreed to its sale to the United States. They also acquiesced in the Vincennes tract purchase of 1803. In return, they received $700 in cash and $2,000 more to be delivered over the next ten years.[47] On paper, then, everything appeared settled—neatly and legally. Yet Harrison would spend a considerable part of 1805 explaining himself concerning the Delawares' cession.

By September 1804, Harrison was well into his second three-year term as Indiana's governor. He seemed to wear his public responsibilities well, although he was finding that his duties did impede his socializing. He complained to his friend James Findlay of Cincinnati that he had not had time to pay him a visit, although he extended an offer for Findlay to come to Vincennes. Finances continued to be a problem: the governor noted that he had to reject a $1,600 offer to sell land to his brother-in-law Peyton Short, as the tract in question was worth considerably more. He also had to ask his brother (probably Carter) for help with paying Findlay and other creditors in Ohio, which must have been at least somewhat embarrassing. And Anna, well into the third trimester of her fifth pregnancy, could not have been happy with him for scheduling a trip out of town.[48]

In October 1804, Harrison left for several weeks to personally visit St. Louis, where he set up the rudiments of territorial government for Louisiana. While en route, he missed by a day or two the birth of his third son, John Scott Harrison, named after the Harrisons' favorite doctor who had supervised the birth. Angry wife not withstanding, the trip was productive for the governor. Harrison's relatively hands-off style pleased the settlers of Louisiana, who had wanted their own territory all along. In part, the Louisianans feared the anti-slavery provision of the Northwest Ordinance might somehow extend to them. They were happy when Congress created the Louisiana Territory in July 1805. The citizens of St. Louis sent a polite resolution of thanks to Governor Harrison and the judges of Indiana for their "just and impartial administration" during an "arduous public service."[49]

Harrison was equally relieved to be rid of the extra duties. Having to deal with Louisiana had made him responsible for Indian affairs involving many of the most powerful tribes in the West, who did not seek American interference. It was difficult enough, Harrison found out, to keep the western tribes from warring against each other—part of Jefferson's Indian policy. It proved more difficult still to keep the tribes of his own neighborhood from crossing the Mississippi to attack old enemies, particularly the powerful Osages of present-day Missouri. In April 1804 the Delaware war chief Buckongahelas summed up the feeling of many Ohio Valley tribes regarding the Osages: "You have endeavoured by your Speech to persuade us from going to War with the Osages—If you Knew the injuries that we have Sustained and the many provocations and insults we have received from that nation You would not We think, then, Say My children don't go to war."[50] Keeping peace among the Indians and avoiding collateral American casualties continued to be a headache for the governor. As it turned out, though, many of his Indian troubles would be largely of his own making.

Before leaving St. Louis, Harrison concluded one more important piece of business in November 1804. In addition to securing title to the lands along the Mississippi River, Harrison anxiously sought to bring Indian tribes into the treaty system as a way of establishing both peace and control. The 1804 treaty with the Sauks and Foxes accomplished both goals in stunning fashion. Yet as with many of his other treaties, the full ramifications did not surface until long after the treaty's conclusion.

In February 1802, Harrison wrote Secretary Dearborn that the Sauks, "a considerable nation who reside between the Illinois River and the Mississippi," by some error had not attended the Greenville Treaty council in 1795. (More likely, they deliberately avoided the treaty to avoid American interference.) The Sauks and their close relatives, the Foxes, or Mesquakies, in fact occupied lands straddling the Mississippi, bounded by the Wisconsin River on the north and the Missouri on the south—the middle of present Illinois to the east and the watershed between the Des Moines and Missouri rivers to the west.[51] Harrison implored, "They are now extremely desirous to be put on a footing with the other tribes, and receive an annual present, and it appears reasonable that they should." Harrison had an additional motive for treating with the Sauks: "I have reasons to believe that several white persons and negroes taken during the wars are still in the possession of those people, particularly the son of a Mr. Tanner of Kentucky who is extremely desirous to recover him." Harrison proposed inviting the Sauks to his Indian council that summer, but they apparently declined. It was not until 1804 that Harrison got his chance to bring the Sauks and Foxes to council.[52]

In the interim, tension between the United States and the Sauks and Foxes had increased considerably. First, the Sauks and Foxes were angered by the Kaskaskias' large cession in August 1803—the former felt they and the Kickapoos had some claim to the lands ceded. Discontent continued in the wake of the Louisiana Purchase. Not only did it bring dozens of new tribes within American jurisdiction, but the new territory also contained a number of groups who regularly made war on one another. Wars could defend or take hunting grounds vital to the fur trade. In August 1804, when U.S. Army officers stopped a party of three hundred Sauks and Foxes intent on raiding the Osages, the Sauks and Foxes perceived that the Americans were favoring the Osages, their nearest competitors in the fur trade.[53] American policy was not so much to favor the Osages but to break the cycle of tribal warfare that disrupted trade and put settlers at risk.[54]

Americans also encroached on Sauk and Fox hunting grounds in what is now Missouri. Jealousy of the Osages and anger toward the Americans burst forth later that month when Sauk hunters murdered four Americans on the Cuivre River. Returning to their homes, the hunters tauntingly threw the scalps in front of their shocked and agitated village chiefs.[55]

Greatly alarmed by the murders, the Sauk civil chiefs denounced them, and the four southernmost bands removed across the Des Moines River in fear of retaliation. Both the Sauks and Foxes had quasi-executive councils, usually about a dozen senior chiefs, who devised policy regarding the fur trade, the disposition of hunting lands, and diplomacy. In September 1804 the Sauk council sent two chiefs to St. Louis to condemn the murders and to ask what compensation the United States required. They added that they hoped the innocent would not be punished along with the guilty. American officials responded by demanding the Sauks give up the murderers, with a thinly veiled threat of war if they did not do so. They also "invited" the Sauks to attend a treaty council with Governor Harrison to decide how the guilty would be delivered. Accordingly, a small delegation led by Quashquame, the chief of a Sauk village (probably

home to at least one of the murderers), set out for St. Louis in late
October: "Quashquame and the others were acting, as the party responsible for the murder, under charge from the Sauk nation as a whole to
settle the matter of the murder before the Americans launched a war.
They brought with them one of the murderers for trial and possible punishment by the Americans."[56]

The Sauk delegation met with the Americans on November 3, 1804.
The Sauk council had charged Quashquame with settling the issue of
the murders and laying the foundation for peaceful relations with the
United States. He bore no authorization regarding land cessions. His
counterpart, Governor Harrison, was not only authorized but actually
ordered to seek lands from the Sauks.[57] From this disparity began one
of Harrison's most controversial treaties.

Quashquame, Pashipaho, Layouvois or Laiyuwa, Outchequaha, and
Hahshequaxhiqua (at least one of whom was a Mesquakie) marked the
treaty of November 3, 1804. The treaty promised the Sauks and Foxes the
protection of the United States, as well as the sum of $2,234.50 and an
annuity of $1,000. It stated, as the Greenville Treaty had, "that for injuries
done by individuals no private revenge or retaliation shall take place,"
but the issue would be taken before the U.S. government for a proper
redress of grievances. Also echoing Greenville, the treaty promised to
remove any whites who squatted on Sauk or Fox lands. These provisions
pleased all concerned. Two additional provisions, however, soon proved
devastating for the Sauks and Foxes.[58]

Article II noted the general boundary between the United States and
the Sauks and Foxes:

> Beginning at a point on the Missouri River opposite to the mouth of
> the Gasconade River Thence in a direct course so as to strike the
> river Jeffreon at the distance of thirty Miles from its mouth and
> down the said Jeffreon to the Mississippi, Thence up the Mississippi
> to the mouth of the Ouisconsing [Wisconsin] river And up the
> same to a point which shall be thirty six miles in a direct line from
> the mouth of the said River, Thence by a direct line to the point
> where the Fox river (a branch of the Illinois) leaves the small lake
> called Sakaegan, Thence down the Fox River to the Illinois river
> And down the same to the Mississippi.

The Sauks and Foxes, the article continued, "do hereby cede and relinquish forever to the United States, all the lands included within the above-described boundary." The language seems perfectly clear—the Sauks and Foxes agreed to cede, forever, a huge territory to the United States. But Article VII read, "As long as the lands which are now ceded to the United States remain their property, the Indians belonging to the said tribes, shall enjoy the privilege of living and hunting upon them." The Greenville Treaty allowed Indians to continue to hunt in ceded territory *until* Americans settled it. Article VII's wording seems to give the Sauks and Foxes perpetual use of the lands, however.[59]

The Sauk and Fox delegation likely did not understand the ambiguously worded treaty as a cession of most of their land. The delegation may have seen the treaty as a symbolic transfer of ownership, not unlike those utilized previously with European powers. Spain, France, and Britain had claimed to rule vast territories, yet they did little to interfere with Indians' sovereignty within those territories: "The interpretation of the cession as an empty gesture could very easily occur to Indians unfamiliar with the public land system of the United States (by which such land is alienated to private individuals) but familiar with their own allotment system (by which the tribal council retained the right of disposition of the hunting lands year after year)." This interpretation gains strength when one considers the rather small monetary compensation agreed to. The Sauks and Foxes combined brought an estimated $60,000 worth of furs to St. Louis in 1804 alone. They would not have given away so much of their valuable hunting territory for a relative pittance.[60]

As the Sauk leader Black Hawk would remark years later, "I find that, by that treaty, all our country, east of the Mississippi, and south of the Jeffreon, was ceded to the United States for *one thousand dollars* a year! I will leave it to the people of the United States to say, whether our nation was properly represented in this treaty? or whether we received a fair compensation." In contrast, Black Hawk noted, "we were sorry to lose our Spanish father, who had always treated us with great friendship."[61]

Because the alleged murderer who had surrendered was later pardoned, an unwritten deal was probably made to free the prisoner. The Indian delegates may also have been intimidated into the land cession, fearing both a war and execution of the prisoner if they refused.[62] Black Hawk later charged that the Americans got the Sauk and Fox delegation drunk and tricked them into the cession. While this is possible, it seems unlikely. This accusation first came about long after the treaty, leveled "by Quashquame at a time when he was sorely pressed to explain away the treaty as a thing for which he was not to blame."[63] The wording of Article VII could easily have been misinterpreted by the Indian delegation, sober or not, and the Americans, seeing a willingness to mark the treaty, would not have probed too deeply to ensure that Quashquame and the others really understood it. Finally, at this point in his career, Harrison was making sincere efforts to keep alcohol away from his treaty councils, and Quashquame's and Black Hawk's accusations do not fit the governor's modus operandi.

The Sauk and Fox councils soon learned that Harrison and the Americans interpreted the treaty as giving away Sauk and Fox lands, which seemed cruelly ludicrous to them. Both tribes had an extensive, time-honored protocol that would have made land sales possible, and none of the requirements had been met. There had been no official invitation to treat, no subsequent announcement to the nation as a whole, no tribal council to discuss the proposed cession, no ratification with wampum, and no opportunity for the women of the tribe to caucus and express their views. The last was especially important in a practical sense, for women were the primary farmers of the Sauks and Foxes (and of most tribes east of the Mississippi) and had to be consulted when land was at stake. Further, the eastern boundary described in the cession exceeded the lands claimed by the Sauks and Foxes. In fact, it exceeded Secretary of War Dearborn's instructions, which told Harrison to seek the lands south of the Illinois River in Illinois and a "considerable" session on the other side—not mentioning anything west of the Mississippi.[64] When seeking land cessions, erring on the side of aggressiveness would become Harrison's pattern.

The president was pleased with the treaty and betrayed no misgivings concerning its validity or boundaries. In his December 31, 1804, address to the Senate, Jefferson noted, "This cession giving us a perfect title to such a breadth of country on the Eastern side of the Missisipi [sic], with a command of the Quisconsing [Wisconsin], strengthens our means of retaining exclusive commerce with the Indians on the Western side of the Missisipi: a right indispensable to the policy of governing those Indians by Commerce rather than by Arms." The latter point provides superb insight into Jeffersonian Indian policy. He wanted to "govern" the Indians, but preferably not by force—a gesture at once both controlling and benevolent, or the very definition of paternalism. He would conquer with blankets rather than bullets, but it was conquest just the same. "Exclusive commerce" refers primarily to reducing the influence of British traders whom Jefferson and Harrison were convinced had agitated Indians against the United States. The idea of controlling territory and people through "Commerce rather than by Arms" displays Jefferson's tendency to oversimplify complex phenomena and seems to foreshadow his disastrous embargo against foreign trade in 1808. Curiously, Jefferson did not mention the sizable portion of Missouri also included in the treaty.[65]

Although they certainly saw the sale as invalid, the Sauk and Fox tribal councils proceeded to view the cession as an accomplished fact; they felt resisting it would put them at war with the United States. Instead, they sought a redress of their grievances through diplomacy, as several Sauk and Fox chiefs did at the 1805 council in St. Louis. With Harrison and the Americans maintaining the validity of the cession, it became increasingly difficult for the chiefs to restrain their angry younger warriors.[66]

Misfortunes continued to follow the Sauks in the wake of the treaty. Having handed over one of the alleged murderers, they nevertheless hoped for his release. The man did receive a pardon from President Jefferson, but it arrived in St. Louis about a week after the prisoner was shot while trying to escape. Historians, lacking much evidence, have jumped to the conclusion that the prisoner was in fact executed by soldiers and that the alleged escape was a cover-up. However, correspondence from Pierre Chouteau and other officials during the weeks in question makes it clear that the prisoner did escape with what turned out to be a mortal wound. The Americans later found his body about seven miles from the fort, all the while thinking he had successfully escaped.[67]

The Louisiana-Missouri Territory's governor was Anthony Wayne's old rival, General James Wilkinson. Wilkinson had the unenviable task of explaining the unfortunate sequence of events to a Sauk and Fox delegation, which included the dead man's brother, in the summer of 1805.

Wilkinson finessed the situation, explaining that the man's death, coming after the president had pardoned him, simply meant the Great Spirit had intended for the murderer to die for "Spilling the Blood of his White Brethren, without Provocation." Wilkinson gave the pardon slip to the deceased's brother, bidding him to keep it both to remember his brother and as a warning against "Bad Deeds." The notoriously dishonest Wilkinson assured Secretary Dearborn that the Sauk man "received the paper with Evedent Marks of Pleasure." That winter Governor Wilkinson sent a stern letter to the Sauks chastising them for their continued attacks on Americans using the Missouri River.[68]

No further major developments occurred among the Sauks, Foxes, and the United States during Harrison's tenure as governor. His treaties, however, would help bring new trouble three decades later.

Among white Americans in Indiana, Governor Harrison's Indian treaties were probably the most popular aspect of his years in office. Most Americans wanted to take Indian lands quickly and cheaply, and throughout his tenure Harrison proved exceptionally adept at getting such cessions, on paper at least. Harrison's pro-slavery sentiment was just beginning to create a stir in 1803 and 1804, as anti-slavery settlers continued to filter into the territory and settlers of the Illinois country began to resent the distant government of Vincennes. Harrison's first great public relations headache, however, came with the territory's move to the second grade of government. In 1801, as discussed previously, Harrison had opposed attempts to bring on that grade, for he feared losing influence to the requisite elected legislature. By 1804–1805, though, he favored a quick move to the second territorial grade and an equally swift election of the lower house so he could stack both houses of the legislature in his favor before a growing anti-slavery element could overwhelm him at the polls.[69]

On August 4, 1804, Harrison called for a plebiscite on the issue of advancing to the second grade of government, to be held on September 11, only five weeks away. While technically legal, the move was rightly criticized at the time as contrary to the promotion of democracy. Harrison deliberately left little time to spread the word about the vote or any pertinent issues, and only four hundred men in the entire territory voted. Wayne County[70] did not get word in time to hold a vote. The majority of the votes cast (largely from Harrison's Knox County) favored the move to the second grade, but apparently many men in the eastern and western parts of the territory, who did not have sufficient notice to vote, disapproved of so rapid an election.[71]

The elected assembly was also to make a list of ten nominations for men to serve in the Legislative Council, the territorial legislature's upper house, from which President Jefferson was to pick five. Jefferson, however, not knowing any of the individuals, let Harrison pick them, cautioning him not to choose "dishonest men, federalists, or land-jobbers." Harrison took care not to broadcast this to his fellow citizens.[72] Thus between the swift election, geared to benefit the governor's supporters, and President Jefferson's hands-off approach, Harrison effectively carried the territorial legislature in his pocket until the next election.

The sudden move to the second territorial grade greatly disturbed some of the Illinois country's leading citizens, including Robert Morrison of the trading firm of Bryan and Morrison. Those along the Mississippi River felt increasingly isolated from the center of government in Vincennes, over a hundred miles away, and viewed most of Governor Harrison's political moves with suspicion. Illinoisans had few business links to Vincennes and found the journey across marshes (in the winter) or a virtual prairie desert (in the summer) unduly taxing.[73] Morrison, in Kaskaskia, wrote to his brother Joseph in Philadelphia on December 31, 1805. His disgust was palpable:

Dear Joseph,

The Citizens of the Illinois Country have now from experience become universally satisfied that a division of the Indiana Territory, is indispensable and inseparable from their happiness. That a connexion with the settlements on the Wabash at Vincennes and those east of them in this Territory, is in fact a connexion with those who have different views and interests, from the people of the Illinois, and that the former will never cease to embarrass the Situation of the latter.[74]

One of his greatest complaints was about the election of Benjamin Parke as the territory's delegate to Congress. When Governor Harrison recommended his close friend Parke to President Jefferson, he declared Parke "a man of the Most unblemished Morals & of the purest Republican principles."[75]

Robert Morrison did not agree, contending that Parke was elected solely "to promote the interest of G. Harrison, and oppose the division of the Territory as the constitutional agent, as far as his feeble abilities would admit." He contended that Harrison's influence had led to Parke's election as representative for Knox County in the territorial legislature, which is probable. Wayne and St. Clair counties declined to send delegates, protesting that the legislature (and hence the second grade) had been improperly formed. The Knox County representatives, and one from Randolph County, "whose insignificancy rather calls for a commiseration than a censure!" made nominations for the Legislative Council.

When the representatives from Clark and Dearborn counties arrived, they were told, Morrison asserted, that since they had arrived late, they could take their seats only if they approved the nominations for the Legislative Council. (Had Morrison known that President Jefferson had let Harrison choose his own council, he would have been even more incensed.) The representative from Clark County, "being a man of integrity and talents," nearly resigned on the spot but was persuaded to take his seat: "This I hope will be considered as a Sufficient a Pology [sic] for Sending P.[arke] to Congress, When you reflect that, he himself was one of the three that Sent him."[76]

The legislature, Morrison continued, then passed laws blatantly violating the Ordinance of 1787—creating a court of chancery[77] and "a law authorising the indinturing of Servants for an Unusual length of time," the Act concerning Introduction. The greatest offense to Morrison, however, stemmed from the legislature's attempt to pass a resolution asking Congress to modify the ordinance to make dividing the territory more difficult. This resolution would have passed if not for the opposition of the representatives from St. Clair and Clark counties, Morrison asserted. He concluded the letter by adding that his correspondence had often been "intercepted" from the Kaskaskia mail, so he had sent it through Cahokia. Morrison wrote to Joseph again on February 6, 1806, detailing his hope that Illinois would be separated from Indiana and asking him to use any political clout he could muster with Congress to do so. If they could not "obtain a division of this Territory," he noted, "the House of Bryan and Morrison will have a tax of at least $700 Dollars per-annum to pay, John Edgar the like sum, all to Support the Second grade of government, without deriving one solitary advantage from it."[78]

Morrison's commentary must be viewed in context—many of the traders who were prominent in the Illinois country prior to Harrison's appointment, like Morrison's family, became bitter enemies of the governor. This was the case less for philosophical reasons—they all favored slavery—than out of a struggle for political patronage and economic advantage. For his part, Harrison saw these wealthy traders who protested the move to the second grade of government as "land Jobbers." "[T]hese gentry," Harrison wrote to Jefferson, "(Some of whom own upwards of 100,000 acres of land) [and] frightened at the Idea of having a land tax[,] did not hesitate to spread any falsehood that was likely to defeat the Measure."[79]

For a time at least, Harrison's preemptive strike in forming the legislature managed to safeguard the pro-slavery agenda and his prerogative. Yet the grumbling about the quick plebiscite over territorial status paled in comparison to the demands for a division of the territory. Starting in 1804, the counties in the Illinois country, fearful of the growing number of anti-slavery settlers moving into Indiana's eastern counties and troubled by being so distant from the capital, sought to create their own territory.

Harrison vehemently opposed division. The Illinois counties sent a number of petitions to Congress asking for both a repeal of the anti-slavery Article VI of the Northwest Ordinance and a division of the territory. While Congress seemed sympathetic to these pleas, it did nothing. Perhaps its members feared the possible political ramifications an overt pro-slavery move might bring or northern competition for southern plantations. At any rate, after 1808 the Illinoisans would give up petitioning for slavery and simply ask to be separated from the rest of Indiana.[80]

While Morrison's letters had been private, the rumblings against Governor Harrison were becoming increasingly public. The most convenient medium of political exchange available was the local newspaper. Indiana's first paper was the *Indiana Gazette* (1804–1806), edited by Elihu Stout. Stout realized that one of the paper's primary functions was to disseminate political information and opinions. He therefore felt it proper to lay down some ground rules in issue number 2, August 7, 1804:

To the public:

The political complection of the paper shall be truly republican; but it never shall be prostituted to party—Essays of any political

complection, couched in decent language[,] shall find a ready inser-
tion—but the Editor pledges himself that the column at the Gazette,
shall never be tarnished with matter that can offend the eye of
decency, or raise a blush upon the cheek of modesty and virtue.[81]

Perhaps predictably, Stout's noble rhetoric collapsed within the month.
The soot and linseed oil of the printer's ink soon became a surrogate for
personal political venom. The August 28, 1804, issue featured Benjamin
Parke's diatribe against William McIntosh: "Circumstances have recently
occurred, which authorise me in pronouncing and publishing WILLIAM
M'INTOSH, an arrant knave: a profligate villain: a dastardly cheat: a per-
fidious rascal: an impertinent puppy: an absolute liar: and a mean,
cowardly poltroon." Those words were all key triggers for bringing about
a duel (see chapter 6).

Benjamin Parke, a transplanted Virginian, served Indiana as a lawyer,
then a judge, and then as the territory's delegate to Congress. His job
there was to push the pro-slavery agenda and to oppose any move to
divide the territory. He proved one of Governor Harrison's staunchest
allies, and the governor twisted arms to make Parke the congressional
delegate. Harrison, typical of political leaders of his era, generally preferred to let his supporters do the political mudslinging, and Parke did so
with gusto. The personal attack on McIntosh resulted from his having
written an editorial opposing the Harrison clique's move to the second
grade of territorial government.

While Indiana's first press proved short-lived—destroyed by a fire in
1806—popular political debate in Indiana did not. The Gazette, reborn
as the Vincennes Western Sun (also edited by Stout), continued to serve as
an outlet for political views and personal spleen.[82]

William Henry Harrison spent part of Christmas Day, 1804, writing to
his closest friend in the Senate, Thomas Worthington of Ohio. In part,
the letter was that of one old friend to another. Harrison thanked
Worthington for the senator's previous efforts on his behalf. And he
passed on two pieces of family news that had become common occur-
rences: Anna was not well, but she had, on October 3, given birth to yet
another child (John Scott Harrison), giving them three boys and two
girls. In the main, though, the letter was one long wish list, and Harrison
hoped Worthington would play Santa.

Referring to his temporary administration of Louisiana, the governor complained that Congress had made him "perform the duties of two governments" while only paying him for one. Harrison's tour of Louisiana—actually, he does not seem to have traveled past St. Louis—had gone better than expected. He found the people there more loyal to the United States than anticipated and flattered himself, perhaps justly, that they were even more so after his visit. Still, they were not ready to enter the Union, and Harrison hoped Congress would make them "pass a probationship" before joining.

The governor further noted that Indiana had passed to the second grade of government, despite the strong opposition of Judge Vanderburgh and the "Scotchman" William McIntosh (who was rapidly morphing from friend to foe) in Vincennes and by John Edgar and the Morrisons in the Illinois country. Engaging in some careful spin control, Harrison mentioned that the settlers of Detroit had not voted. Although they claimed they had not had enough notice, Harrison offered that in fact they had not participated because they wanted nothing to do with Indiana. Despite having chosen the time for the plebiscite for the second grade, the governor complained that he would probably not have enough time to nominate men for the governor's council. He asked Worthington to see to it, either through a rider or a separate law, to allow the president to make his selections while the Senate was in recess. If not, Indiana would be delayed in sending a territorial delegate to Congress. The governor was very eager to get a pro-slavery delegate to the capital as soon as possible.

The governor hoped the principal officers in the territory, himself in particular, would receive a raise. Harrison, who by this time was pouring money into Grouseland's construction, complained that if the salaries of territorial judges were raised to $1,200, they would be earning as much as he did for being governor: "It is true that I receive $800 as Super-intendant of Indian affairs (Making in the whole $2000) but God Knows that I richly earn the 800—& so will any man who performs his duty & has the Superintendance of 10 or 12 Indian Tribes."

Harrison had not forgotten how the old-boy politics of Congress worked and begged Senator Worthington to lobby for him, especially with the more tight-fisted House of Representatives: "Those from Whose friendship I Should expect assistance in that House are—Messrs. [John W.] Eppes.

[Thomas] Newton[,] [John] Clopton[,] [Joseph H.] Nicholson[,] & Eliot [James Elliott]—I have Written to Eppes—Newton is An old School Mate— If you think proper you May Speak to them upon My subject."[83]

Despite his many complaints, William Henry Harrison had much to be thankful for as 1804 drew to a close. His family continued to grow, with five children and counting, and his house was coming along. The swift move to the second grade of government would soon prove to have been a political masterstroke that would give him a pliant legislature with which to pursue his agenda. He had good reason to hope that Indiana's pro-slavery petitions would receive favorable treatment in Congress. He did not even bother Worthington on the subject in this letter. And he had negotiated several Indian land cession treaties that, from the American perspective, were wildly successful in securing huge tracts of land for pennies per acre. What he did not anticipate was how the hubris shown in these years would come back to haunt him later.

CHAPTER 4

1805

The Pivotal Year

In 1805, William Henry Harrison truly came into his own as Indiana's chief executive and the U.S. Indian commissioner. Indiana's sudden advance to the second grade of government, combined with President Jefferson's indifference to territorial politics, left Harrison with a rubber-stamp legislature and essentially no organized opposition. Jefferson's reappointments of Harrison and the private instructions, as discussed in chapter 3, had given him unprecedented power to conduct Indian councils as he saw fit. Harrison, now fully confident in his support at both the local and national levels of government, imposed his will on the issues of slavery and Indian affairs. In the short term at least, his actions were successful.

The Ordinance of 1787 had promised both that Indians north of the Ohio would be treated justly and that the territory would be worked by free men, not slaves. The ordinance had already taken a beating on both counts. By 1805, Governor Harrison and his like-minded legislature were ready to abuse it further still. Although the issue of Louisiana's ownership (as far as Americans were concerned) had long been determined, 1805 saw yet another round of Indian land cession treaties, negotiated with increasing forcefulness by the governor. As Thomas Jefferson's Indian policy was incomparably illustrated in his February 27, 1803, letter to Governor Harrison, so Harrison's efforts in 1805 were exemplified by his August 26 letter to the secretary of war. Regarding Chief Little Turtle of the Miamis, the governor wrote Dearborn that "[i]n pursuance of the President's directions, I have promised the Turtle fifty dollars, per annum, in addition to his pension; and I have, also, directed Captain Wells to purchase a negro man for him in Kentucky, and draw on you for the amount."[1] The story of how the governor came to write such a letter encapsulates the problem of Jeffersonian Indian affairs and of a territorial executive working unchecked.

The letter illustrated Harrison's adoption of a cynically pragmatic attitude toward public life. He resorted to bribing Little Turtle with cash and a slave because he needed the chief's help in pushing through an additional treaty with his Indian neighbors. In such a policy, Harrison had more than tacit approval for his actions: he was actually following orders. In 1804 Secretary of War Dearborn had stated that "pecuniary advances," that is, bribes, were acceptable means for securing cessions, formalizing a tactic that had already seen considerable use. President Jefferson had in fact authorized a bribe—"a liberality," he called it—for Little Turtle, to secure his compliance.[2]

The fact that Little Turtle's bribe was part cash and part man was apparently an agreement he reached with the governor. Jefferson had not specified what gift the chief should receive. The choice of a slave also demonstrates the reaction of Governor Harrison and the pro-slavery faction to Congress's reluctance to legalize slavery in Indiana. Tired of wading through the proper channels, they had taken matters into their own hands, drafting and passing "An Act concerning the Introduction of Negroes and Mulattoes into this Territory." This law stated that it was now legal to bring bondsmen from slave states into Indiana and convert them to indentured servants. The law put no limit on the length of indenture, and the children of these "servants" would inherit their parents' status for a term of years as well. Governor Harrison signed the act the same day he wrote Secretary Dearborn about his bribe for Little Turtle. Unlike many other laws he signed, this one was to take effect immediately.

Tellingly, the 1805 land cession treaties were the direct result of Indian complaints about how unjust the previous treaties had been. In March 1805 the Delaware war chiefs Buckongahelas and Hockingpomskon sent a letter to William Wells, the Indian agent at Fort Wayne, protesting the 1804 Delaware Treaty. They argued vehemently that they had not intended to sell any land and lacked the authority to do so anyway. Furthermore, doing so would be "contrary to the articles of the Treaty of Greenville," presumably because that treaty had relinquished American claims to further lands north of the Ohio River. The Delawares asked Wells to write a letter to the president describing the "unlegal" purchase and asking him to prevent white settlement in the tract. Both Buckongahelas and Hockingpomskon had marked the 1804 treaty.[3]

Billy Patterson, a young métis Delaware and nephew of Chief Tetepachsit, wrote Wells on April 5 that Harrison had claimed he was present when the Miamis gave all the White River lands to the Delawares. Harrison had then stated that the road from Vincennes to the Falls of the Ohio should be the future boundary between the Delawares and the Piankeshaws and asked them to sign a paper in agreement to the latter point. They signed it. Patterson stated, "Friend and Brother! [Y]ou may judge how our chiefs felt when they returned home and found that the Governor had been shutting up their eyes and stopping their Ears with his good words and got them to sign a Deed for their lands without their knowledge." (The Delawares later assassinated Patterson because they considered him too pro-American.) The chiefs swore that they had not sold any lands to Harrison at Vincennes the previous summer. One historian has stated that the Delaware chiefs did know what they had signed and were simply ashamed afterward—a plausible argument. According to the Moravian missionaries living on the White River at the time, though, the returning Delaware chiefs made no mention of a land sale. In January 1805 the chiefs sent a messenger to the Moravians asking them to translate the 1804 treaty, lending at least some support to the idea that they were not sure what they had signed.[4]

In response to these grievances, Wells wrote a letter to President Jefferson for Little Turtle. He complained of Harrison's tactics and the unrest they were causing among the Indians. He charged that Harrison had given legal title to landless Indians and then purchased the land they occupied for a song and that he undermined the authority of recognized chiefs by treating with lesser ones, even creating new chiefs. These charges were all true enough. But then Wells strongly hinted that the Miamis might, if foreign aid could be had, fight the United States to hold onto their lands. Wells, walking the tightrope between his adopted people and his American employers, had slipped, and there was no net. The letter was forwarded to Secretary of War Dearborn rather than the president, and Dearborn became Wells's "inveterate enemy."[5] Wells lost credibility with his superiors, and the Miamis' negotiating position declined while Governor Harrison's strengthened correspondingly.

Although relations between the Delawares and the United States appeared to be deteriorating rapidly, President Jefferson had boundless blind optimism concerning Indian affairs, so long as the Americans continued to acquire lands cheaply. In May 1805, while the Delawares howled in protest, the president gushed that "the general approbation given to our measures respecting the Indians, shews that they are in union with the sentiments of the great body of our nation, & that there is no danger of a departure from them." This was also the point at which he suggested bribing Little Turtle.[6]

On May 24, Dearborn wrote to Harrison, directing him to meet with the Delaware chiefs, as well as some principal chiefs of the Miamis and Potawatomis. Harrison was ordered to satisfy them that the treaty had been both open and fair, and he was to publicly scold the Delaware chiefs who "have made false or improper representations of your conduct." The next month, because of rumors that the Ohio Valley Indians were joining forces against the United States, Dearborn instructed Harrison to determine if the Indians were allying against him and to take any "prudent measure" necessary to counteract them if they were. As was often the case with Harrison, "prudent measures" equaled more treaties and cessions.[7] In his next treaty council, Harrison firmly established a divide-and-conquer treaty system in which the tribes' only hope for further annuities—or even of continuing to receive those they were already legally entitled to—lay in aligning themselves with the governor against their neighbors in future treaties.

While Governor Harrison was directly in charge of Ohio Valley Indian councils, a systemic problem, based in a faith in American exceptionalism, infected Jeffersonian Indian affairs from the top down. While an empiricist in so many facets of his life, when it came to Indian policy, and race relations generally, Thomas Jefferson carefully selected data that would not jar his predetermined conclusions. Regarding western lands, his thinking came from the Virginia plantation rather than a Parisian salon. Americans needed, he felt, to keep acquiring Indian lands quickly and cheaply. Therefore, doing so by any means was beneficial not only to Americans but also for Indians. Indians' cultures, by definition, had to be inferior to Americans' cultures. By dispossessing Indians and forcing them to live like white Americans, Jefferson could tell himself he was doing them a favor.[8] Undeniably, Governor Harrison was the near-perfect instrument for carrying out Jefferson's goals.

Harrison's June 30, 1805, address to the Indiana General Assembly clearly spelled out the Jeffersonian Indian policy he intended to implement. Harrison was referring to the Indians in the Louisiana Purchase lands, "[t]hese children of nature," but his speech accurately described his views of Ohio Valley Indian matters as well. For white (male) Americans, the Louisiana Purchase had "secured the happiness of unborn millions who will bless the moment of their emancipation, and the generous policy which procured for them the rights of men." It also aided the current generation by removing the "need" to war against the tribes there. By ending Indians' contact with troublesome foreign agents "and forcing them to procure from our selves their arms and ammunition & such of the European manufactures as habit has rendered necessary," the United States ensured not only Indians' dependence and fealty but also "the means of ameliorating their own condition."[9]

The governor again drew a comparison between the United States and the nations of Europe, the latter having tried to effect "the utter extirpation of the unhappy people whose country they had usurped." The Americans, on the other hand, had passed laws to protect Indians and spent great sums for "agents employed to humanize their minds and to instruct them in such of the arts of civilized life as are adapted to their situation." Harrison did admit that it was American settlements that made Indians' hunting so precarious, although, true to form, he neglected to mention Indian women's farming skills. Providing for Indians' well-being, he insisted, "has been considered as a sacred duty." He reiterated the need to prevent alcohol sales to Indians and reminded the assembly that they were duty-bound by Article III of the Northwest Ordinance to do so (Article III promised the "utmost good faith" would be shown in Indian affairs and that laws to protect Indians would be passed): "The interests of your own constituents, the interests of the miserable Indians, and your own feelings" will suffice to see to the prohibition effort.[10]

Is it "to be admitted as a political axiom that the neighbourhood of a civilized nation is incompatible with the existence of savages? Are the blessings of our republican Government to be felt only by ourselves," the governor intoned? Should U.S. Indians share the fate of those to the south, destroyed by the Conquistadors? Anticipating the "white man's burden" of the Victorian era, Harrison offered: "It is with you Gentlemen, to divert from these children of nature the ruin that hangs over them; nor can I believe that the time will be considered mispent [sic] which is devoted to an object so consistent with the spirit of Christianity and with the principles of Republicanism."[11]

These statements simply ooze the post-Revolutionary paternalism that defined the early Republic. In his mind, and he was doubtless blessed with unanimous support in the legislature, Harrison had both carte blanche and a duty to negotiate Indian land cessions by any means necessary. He wasted little time in doing so.

At the Grouseland Treaty (named for Harrison's Vincennes home) with the Delawares, Potawatomis, Miamis, Eel Rivers, and Weas in August 1805, the governor conceded that the Delawares had never been the rightful owners of the White River tract. The Miamis, however, sanctioned the previous sale and sold their lands between the White River and the Ohio in return for a "permanent" annuity of $600 for themselves and $250 per annum each for their Eel River and Wea cousins. Harrison also acknowledged the Miamis' claim to the Wabash River watershed, a portion of which was occupied by the more militant Kickapoos, who were not invited to the council. The Potawatomis consented to the treaty for a $500 annuity for ten years. The governor also distributed $4,000 among the Indians present.[12]

Harrison's inclusion of the Potawatomis in this treaty seems curious. In the eighteenth and nineteenth centuries at least, the tribe does not seem to have lived at any time in southern Indiana. The argument that Indians held lands in common, made previously by Joseph Brant and later by Tecumseh, was one Harrison rejected outright. Secretary Dearborn had instructed the governor to include all tribes with a claim, but Harrison's reasons for including the Potawatomis were twofold: first, he clearly found Winamac, a pro-American Potawatomi, a willing treaty signer and an ally since the Vincennes Treaty negotiations of 1802–1803. Why would Winamac object to receiving annuities for lands his people did not own? Second, as a group the Potawatomis could be useful to the governor. They were the most populous tribe Harrison had to contend with and had a reputation for prowess in war. The governor would use the Potawatomis to threaten leverage against the Miamis at his 1809 treaty councils. Perhaps he did so, if somewhat more subtly, in 1805 as well? The next year, fearing a war with the Kickapoos and others, Dearborn advised Harrison that while he did not did believe the Kickapoos would attack, "It may be expedient to endeavor to have such an understanding with the Puttawattamies [sic], as will render them serviceable in case of any rupture with those other tribes."[13]

The 1805 treaty represented Harrison's use of bribery on both the personal and tribal levels. Little Turtle received more cash and a slave for his efforts, the Delawares got to keep annuities for lands they did not really own, the Potawatomis received annuities for lands many of them had probably never even seen, and the Miamis secured their claim to their Wabash lands.[14]

After December 30, 1805, Harrison negotiated no further treaties until 1809. He needed time to digest the new acquisitions and to contend with the problems they created. He also felt the need to defend his tactics—not just to Indian leaders but also to Secretary of War Dearborn and President Jefferson. He took considerable grief over the Delaware-Miami–White River tract affair, including embarrassing letters of complaint from Indians to his superiors—upon whom he was dependent for his office—and he wrote several defensive letters concerning it. In March 1805, for example, he wrote to the secretary of war that the charges leveled at him by Wells and Little Turtle were unfounded. He vigorously stated that he had issued no alcohol to Indians until after the treaties were concluded and that all conferences were public. No one signed a treaty until each article had been fully and repeatedly explained by interpreters, and sketches of each land tract were shown to the Indians, who obviously understood them and their implications.[15]

The governor's arguments were not wholly untenable. Apparently, Harrison did take steps to keep liquor away from his conferences. He did hold "public" conferences, although, having found smaller groups more pliable, he often did not invite all tribes involved. Whether he intentionally deceived the Delawares into signing the 1804 land cession remains open to debate—a question of Harrison's word against theirs. If we give Harrison the benefit of the doubt, the Delaware chiefs may have understood the ramifications of the treaty but gambled and signed anyway, miscalculating the extent to which their people and the Miamis would protest.

Given Harrison's record, however, this view seems an exceedingly kind interpretation. As outlined in Jefferson's private letter to Harrison in February 1803, official policy was to put land acquisition ahead of full disclosure when dealing with Indians. There seems little doubt that Harrison knew the 1804 Delaware treaty was invalid, which is why he did not want the Miamis there. Harrison's April 26, 1805, letter to the secretary of war does not mention that he had threatened to withhold the Greenville annuities of tribes that did not attend his next council.[16]

Furthermore, Harrison knew he was paying the Indians a mere pittance for their lands. Writing to Dearborn, Harrison noted that "knowledge of the value of land is fast gaining ground amongst the Indians, and, in the course of the negotiation, one of the chiefs observed, that he knew that a great part of the land was worth six dollars per acre." After the treaty with the Miamis in August 1805, he wrote to President Jefferson that to his best estimate he had promised about one cent per acre for the ceded lands: "This is much higher than I could have wished it to have been, but it was impossible to make it less." He stated that while he could not avoid guaranteeing the Miamis their remaining lands, he felt that after a few years, dividing (and presumably purchasing) the lands they held in common would be easy.[17]

Like many Jeffersonian policies, Harrison's Indian affairs were rife with double standards. In 1803 Jefferson himself had advised using traders to run Indians into debt to facilitate land cessions. Yet, writing to Secretary Dearborn in November 1805, Harrison opined that the United States needed to pass a law to save the Kaskaskias from local whites: "Designing persons are in the habit of getting them in debt and then threatening them with a suit unless they prevail upon me to assume payment." Several times circumstances forced Harrison to pay debts for Chief Ducoigne, which no doubt troubled the governor in many ways.[18] The next year the governor complained to Dearborn that no one should be allowed to trade with the Indians without a license. So much of the land the Indians still used for subsistence had been sold that they could fall prey to the "mercyless rapacity of the Traders."[19]

While Harrison's concerns for the Kaskaskias' well-being were well-founded, he need not have worried so much about his own job security, even after the Delaware and Miami protests against him. He was, if in his own sledgehammer way, merely applying Jefferson's manifest Indian policy. Jefferson wanted someone who could wrest cessions from the Indians quickly and cheaply, and clearly the governor was a shrewd and formidable negotiator with tribes that resisted the United States. The president needed an Indian commissioner loyal as a beagle and instead got one as aggressive as a pit bull. If Jefferson disapproved, he never said so.

While the United States worked largely under the assumption that its land purchases were mutually beneficial, and obviously so, many of the Indians involved begged to differ. Although Indians who resisted land cessions to the Americans were repeatedly dismissed as having been brainwashed by the British, they were in fact an indigenous phenomenon. Such Indians grew in number and militancy in the years after 1805. They followed Native revivalists who told of a rebirth of happiness for Indians that would accompany a return to traditional Indian values, which would include the cessation of land sales to the Americans. The most famous and influential of these Nativists was Tenskwatawa, the Shawnee Prophet. The Prophet, and later his brother Tecumseh, did not initially seek a war with the United States, but they were clear in asserting that further land cessions to the Americans were unacceptable.[20]

Harrison had at least some inkling of the anger created by his cession treaties. His August 8, 1806, letter to Surveyor General Jared Mansfield stated that Mansfield was correct not to run the boundary across the Embarrass fork of the White River. It had not been authorized yet and would also be imprudent because the Kickapoos and Sauks were looking for allies against the United States. The Prophet had a great many adherents among the Kickapoos in particular. Surveying the disputed boundary too early would only add warriors to the Prophet's cause. This movement coincided with increasing war tensions with Britain.[21]

In June 1806, Dearborn notified Harrison and Michigan Territory governor William Hull of a report from Captain John Whipple at Fort Wayne stating that the surrounding Indians had "hostile operations in view against the United States." Dearborn ordered the governors to investigate the Indians' disposition and report on the cause of their discontent.

That he even had to ask speaks volumes. On June 19, Agent William Wells informed Harrison that a French trader had told him of a plot by Ottawas, Chippewas, and Potawatomis against Detroit, Mackinac, and Chicago caused "by the intrigues of British agents and other mischief makers." This growing tension would nearly erupt in 1807 after the *Chesapeake-Leopard* Affair.[22]

While Indian land cessions and Anglophobia tended to unify white Indiana citizens, the issue of slavery proved confusing and divisive. Harrison's continued support of involuntary servitude in Indiana sparked the wrath of his most vocal and dangerous critic, John (Jean) Badollet. Born in Geneva in 1758, Badollet studied theology, eventually emigrating to the United States with his good friend and fellow Genevan, Albert Gallatin. From 1786 to 1788 they lived on a Pennsylvania farm and ran a store together. In 1788 Gallatin left to serve as a delegate on the commission formulating the Bill of Rights, launching himself upon a distinguished career in public service. By 1801, Gallatin was the secretary of the treasury, a position he held until 1813. Although they almost never saw each other after Gallatin left the farm, the two Swiss maintained a strong friendship and lively correspondence well into the 1830s. Gallatin, as one of President Jefferson's most respected cabinet members, could wield considerable influence; and Badollet frequently voiced his opinions, political and personal, to his old friend.[23]

Badollet remained in Pennsylvania until 1803. In what were perhaps the only known instances of Gallatin's cronyism, he appointed Badollet to survey roads northwest of the Ohio River and in 1804 secured his appointment as register of the new land office at Vincennes. The importance of the land office, as well as Badollet's political connections, made Badollet's friendship (or at least tolerance) very important to Harrison's ability to govern and to maintain his appointment. Initially, the two men got along well enough. Badollet was definitely impressed with Harrison, although he retained just enough suspicion to prophesy trouble. On May 18, 1805, he wrote Gallatin that:

> From the Governour I received every mark of attention that you had a right to expect from him. He is a man of fine & correct understanding, upright in his principles & conduct, a faithfull servant of the United States & highly entitled to confidence. His having been

a soldier for a long time, & his eyes having a side glance that fathoms you to the soul, render his company less agreeable to me, seem to repel familiarity & confidence, but it is perhaps my fault.[24]

As late as 1806, the same year he joined Harrison on the board of trustees of the proposed Vincennes University (like militia appointments, this was a privilege of social rank), Badollet still had kind words for the governor: "Making every allowance for the sallies of a man who is still young, & the foibles inticident [sic] to human nature, I consider the Governor as a man of true honour, of an unimpeachable honesty, and an excellent officer."[25] Badollet would soon retract all of these compliments and replace them with heated, pointed rebukes. Slavery put the two men on a collision course. Upon reaching the United States, Badollet had proven to be something of a free thinker and was viscerally opposed to slavery. He wrote Gallatin in late 1804 that he felt the introduction of slavery to Indiana was imminent "& that circumstance alone would prove sufficient to drive me from hence."[26] In fact, Badollet remained in Indiana, and his unwavering anti-slavery views led him into an exceptionally bitter dispute with the governor.

At least as early as 1805, the debate about bringing black slaves into the territory was becoming a political issue in Indiana. In a letter to President Jefferson in June 1805, Harrison remarked that "in all our elections the Contest lay between those who were in favor of adopting the second grade of Government & the admission of Negroes & those who were opposed to such measures." A little more than a month later Harrison approved an act that would intensify those issues in an unprecedented manner—"An Act concerning the Introduction of Negroes and Mulattoes into this Territory."[27]

The act stated that Negro and mulatto slaves ages 15 and up could be brought into the territory. The owners then had thirty days after their arrival to take the slaves before the local clerk of the court of common pleas to establish the term of indenture for the slave, who had now become an "indentured servant." If the slave refused this arrangement, the owner had sixty days to remove him or her from the territory, presumably to a slave state for sale. Owners who neglected to establish length of service before the court would lose their slaves, although where the slaves would then go is not stated. Negro and mulatto slaves under age

15 had to be registered following the same pattern, although such males could only be held until age 35 and females until age 32. The children of slaves-turned-servants could be held until age 30 (males) or 28 (females).[28]

The *Register of Negro Slaves 1805–1807,* now held in the McGrady-Brockman House in Vincennes, provides a fascinating glimpse at the 1805 act in practice. Fifty slaves' names are recorded, most with the owner's name, state of origin, sex, age (no mention of financial compensation for the indentured), and term of indenture listed.[29] The log lists twenty-four men, averaging 20 years of age, and twenty-six women, averaging 23.5 years of age. Most (fifteen men and fourteen women) came from Kentucky, with South Carolina and Tennessee finishing a distant second and third, respectively, and Georgia accounting for one woman only. Indentures for women averaged about 37 years, while those for men averaged about 27 years. (Typically, indentures for whites lasted 4–7 years.) The terms of indenture for the five children recorded as under 15 (four boys and a girl, ages 2–8) are not listed, presumably because they would be held until the ages prescribed in the 1805 Act concerning Introduction.

While a few slaves were able to secure relatively short indentures (10–15 years), four received terms of 90 to 99 years. Sixteen-year-old Jacob, for example, was brought from South Carolina by Eli Hawkins and given a 90-year indenture, "[f]rom and after the expiration of which said Term the said Jacob shall be free to all intents and Purposes." (Whether this last statement was a cruel joke or simply a rigid adherence to legal formality is unclear.) Two of the slaves listed, Isaac and Milly, both from Kentucky, are recorded as age 15½.[30] It seems doubtful that either would have been able to prove their ages if they were under 15. Would the clerk of the court of common pleas have taken their word over that of their respective owners? It is conceivable, although certainly not proven, that their masters could have knowingly misrepresented their ages and that Isaac and Millie would have been defenseless against such mendacity. Because of the 1803 law concerning court appeals, they could not testify against their masters in court. The fact that both were assigned hefty indentures (Isaac for 40 years and Milly for 70 years) far longer than 14-year-olds could have legally been held makes these transactions appear questionable.

But did the "indentured servitude" allowed by the 1803 and 1805 laws constitute slavery? This question is not easily answered. In the legal documents, "servant" sometimes appears to be synonymous with "slave," although "slave" seems always to denote blacks, mulattoes, or Indians. We think of a slave as someone bound to lifelong service of another, with this status passed on to the slave's children. "Servant" is a more ambiguous term. A servant could be a free person paid to help with domestic chores. A servant could also be a laborer bound to serve for several years or, as in Indiana and elsewhere,[31] a slave who was forced into a long-term service contract. Whites could also be bound to servitude or to serve apprenticeships, although for the latter they could only be held until age 21 (males) or 18 (females).[32] Rewards were offered for runaway white apprentices as well as slaves. The laws of 1803 and 1805 were explicitly aimed at blacks, however.

Black "servants" in Indiana, like black slaves in the slave states, were offered some protection, at least on paper. One of the provisions of the 1805 Act concerning Introduction stated that children of black servants who were abused by their masters would have recourse to a justice of the peace from outside the county to make redress. The 1803 Law concerning Servants had promised redress when a master was of "injurious demeanor towards his servant"[33] (although it was vague as to defining punishment) and, as previously mentioned, stated that courts would hear the complaints of servants who were citizens of the United States—a code for white servants.

In one case a master, James Trimble, received a court order not to "abuse or unreasonably chastise" his indentured servant Ann, "a Negro woman," in 1807.[34] It turned out that while the law held Trimble accountable, it was in fact his wife, Polly, who had attacked Ann, in the standard legal description of the time, "with force and arms to wit, with swords, knives, spades, shovels, tongues [fireplace tongs], sticks, staves, Horse whips, cow hides, Feet, Fists, hands, mouth & teeth." Ann's husband, Zachariah Rice, brought suit regarding the "outrages" against her. The assault was "against the Peace & dignity of the United States," and Rice asked for five hundred dollars to compensate the damage to his wife. The court, however, fined Polly only fifty cents and held her until she paid the fine and court costs.[35]

It may have been true that the labor assigned in Indiana was far less severe than that performed by slaves in West Indies sugar plantations or South Carolina rice fields. During the French period at least, black slaves in the area lived under a relatively relaxed system, allowing for marriages and baptism.[36] They worked as house servants for French settlers who were agricultural underachievers.[37] The high proportion (over 50 percent) of female slaves in the Knox County sample tentatively supports the notion that masters were looking for domestic laborers, but the small scope of the sample encourages caution. A Kentucky or South Carolina slaveholder would not suddenly relax his or her practices just by stepping foot in Indiana Territory. Besides, the dehumanization resulting from one person owning another, not workload, is the defining characteristic of slavery. In addition, Illinoisans imported some slaves to the saline works in what is now Gallatin County, Illinois, to perform the grueling work of making salt.[38]

In this sense, then, the laws of 1803 and 1805 constituted de facto slavery. True, the children of slaves brought into Indiana would not be held for life, but they would inherit their parents' status until they reached age 30 (males) or 28 (females),[39] terms that could conceivably last longer than their parents' indentures. No law subjected the children of white servants to inherited status. And what of these "indentures"? Were slaves taken to Indiana really voluntary laborers fulfilling a contract? As contemporary opponents pointed out, the idea that the indentures were voluntary was ludicrous. One petition to Congress later called Harrison's act concerning introduction "a Law which may properly be entitled 'A Law for the Establishment of disguised slavery in opposition to the National Will.'" It "was absurd to speak of the agreement between the master and a slave as a 'contract,' since slavery by its very nature made a person incapable of contracting."[40]

Slaves brought to Indiana had to accept a long-term indenture, yet they could hope that their children, after serving their own lengthy indentures, would eventually be free. Or slaves could refuse indenture and be sold back into lifelong slavery in the South, knowing the same fate would befall their children. It seems doubtful that 30-year-old Eve from Kentucky, contracted to serve Thomas Montgomery for 99 years,[41] would have relished the choice. While the 1805 Act concerning Introduction did not provide for perpetual bondage for the children of slaves brought into the territory, it did stipulate an inherited status of involuntary servitude and was therefore in blatant violation of both the letter and the intent of Article VI. Not only did Governor Harrison sign the act into law, but given his personal pro-slavery agitation and the composition of the legislature at the time, he must have been an integral force in its creation.

Interestingly, Governor Harrison was not among the owners listed in the *Register of Negro Slaves*. However, as mentioned, he had brought at least one or two slaves from Berkeley when he arrived in Indiana, and in 1801 he paid four hundred dollars for a runaway slave from Kentucky, whom he later freed. In May 1806, Harrison wrote Col. James Henry of New Jersey, mentioning that he would be happy to get "one or two negroes either male or female" and that "it would make no difference whether they are slaves for life or only serve a term of years." One year later he wrote Dr. Fredrick Ridgely of Woodford, Kentucky, that he was "totally at a loss [as to] what to do with Molly. Because I am yet uninformed whether she has been emancipated in Ky. & bound for 15 years or whether you have made a contract with her former master to have her set free in 15 years." Harrison worried over the thirty-day indenture registration deadline, Molly's possible refusal, and the dismal financial prospects of trying to sell "an Indentured Servant" back to Kentucky if she had already been indentured.[42]

While neither Congress nor President Jefferson felt compelled to complain about the Act concerning Introduction, anti-slavery citizens in Indiana Territory did not ignore or condone it. John Badollet proved the most virulent of such men. Just five days after Harrison signed the law, Badollet wrote Secretary of the Treasury Gallatin that introducing slavery was the "Hobby horse of the influential men here." He hoped Congress would disapprove of pro-slavery petitions, fearing "Shallow politicians, who to obtain a transitory good, are willing to entail on their country a permanent evil."[43]

Badollet was not alone in condemning slavery in Indiana. While pro-slavery settlers had been active in asking for Article VI's modification or repeal, a growing number of their neighbors, particularly in the eastern portions of the territory, argued just as strongly against a further introduction of slavery. A November 25, 1805, convention in Randolph and St. Clair counties blasted the 1805 Act concerning Introduction, stating the attendees' "hope that the General Government, after Guaranteeing to the people the privileges in [the Ordinance of 1787], will not pass unnoticed the Violation thereof By the late act of the Legislature of this Territory Authorizing the importation of Slaves, and involuntary servitude for a term of years."[44]

True, the conventioneers admitted, the act would give "a Spring to the Growth" of the Illinois country, yet they would never "Consent to a Violation of that ordinance, for this privilege of slavery." Only if Congress, not the territorial legislature, duly authorized a change in Article VI would the committee agree to such a measure.[45] The great debate over slavery in Indiana was just beginning.

In addition to the increasingly hostile tone of the slavery debate in Indiana, 1805 witnessed the public airing of the territory's, and the governor's, dirty laundry. As discussed in chapter 3, in late 1805 Robert Morrison had compiled a list of Governor Harrison's sins. Yet Morrison's complaints stayed in the family. The "Letters of Decius," on the other hand, railed about the governor not just to readers of his privately printed pamphlet but also to Secretary of State James Madison.

The first of the "Letters of Decius"[46] was sent to the Indiana legislature on May 10, 1805. "Decius" made some of the same charges Morrison would make—that Benjamin Parke was unworthy of serving as Indiana's congressional delegate and that he was the governor's picked man. Parke was definitely Harrison's picked man, although his résumé was certainly acceptable. Decius countered that Judge Thomas T. Davis was a far better choice. Decius left reason behind, however, when he declared that Governor Harrison did not want Indiana's population to increase, as that would dilute his power.[47] The available data clearly indicate that Harrison wanted Indiana settled, quickly and densely.

"Decius" was likely Isaac Darneille, a native of Maryland who had served as a U.S. attorney in the Northwest Territory in 1794–95. He later settled in Cahokia in the Illinois country. Illinois, home to the Morrison, Edgar, and Jones clans, was becoming a hotbed of anti-Harrison sentiment by 1805. Darneille himself was not without detractors. He seems to have done some philandering in Cahokia, as well as offending "Toby" while serving as U.S. attorney in the Northwest. A piece from the *Centinel of the North-Western Territory* reads as follows:

Advice to Mr.
Diminutive, paltry, petty Quibler,
Advocate of meanness, dirty scribbler,
Reasons what canst thou urge, all this winter
Nonsense so much to write? To plague the Printer?
I prithee now, thy foolish tricks give o'er,
Each piece of thine shows the blockhead more :
Let law thy study be, 'twill gain thee pelf,
Let S—— write his pesquinades himself.
            TOBY.[48]

Many of Darneille's attacks centered on the fact that Harrison was trying to use his powers to maintain himself in office. He also charged that Harrison had refused to confirm solid land claims—which he had the power to do—for men who were not his political friends. Confirmation of land titles was a huge issue for many Illinoisans, and if the charge were true, it could have constituted an abuse of authority by Harrison. However, a great many leading Illinoisans would later have their land claims disallowed by federally appointed commissioners Elijah Backus and Michael Jones for lack of proper records or in some cases outright fraud. Governor Harrison had no control over these men, and in fact they later invalidated four hundred acres of his own land claims for inadequate proof of ownership.[49]

As with many territorial political squabbles, Decius's complaints about Governor Harrison and his cronies smacked of a patronage "out's" jealousy toward the patronage "ins." The only truly noteworthy ones came in his sketch of charges sent to James Madison, written on December 1, 1805. Among these, Decius alleged that in March 1803, Harrison had misappropriated a detail of U.S. troops to burn lime for use on his farms, and they were left vulnerable to possible Indian attack while doing so. In August 1803, Harrison allowed "several of his favorites" to take superior quality cloth that had been sent for the Indians' annuities and replace it with cheaper calicoes. Harrison did not profit directly, but he had nevertheless violated his oath as Indian commissioner.[50]

If proven true, such charges could easily have cost Harrison his appointment. At least one territorial official, Michael Jones, register of the land office at Kaskaskia, warned Harrison that he might have to respond to Darneille's accusations "in due time." However, then and now, the charges were difficult to substantiate. Curiously, for both incidents Decius listed Secretary of Indiana John Gibson and Col. Francis Vigo as witnesses. Gibson seems to have gotten along well with the governor, and Vigo owed his militia appointment, as well as whatever financial solvency he could muster, to Harrison. It is doubtful that either would have testified against him, even had they seen the governor engaging in such acts.[51]

The indictments in "The Letters of Decius" were damning, if unproven. Darneille was later forced to recant the charges, although that in itself did not totally disqualify them.[52] Their format, rather than their veracity, was the most important issue. The political honeymoon Harrison had enjoyed during his first four years in office was officially over. After 1805, Indiana politics became increasingly contentious and nasty.

Amid all the other issues confronting Indiana in 1805, alcohol abuse, especially among Indians, continued unabated. There was no disputing the alcohol problem in the Ohio Valley. Drinking was prodigious on the frontier for most of the adult population and was not confined to Indians. With potable water and milk often unavailable or prohibitively expensive, whiskey seemed a practical choice to many Americans.[53] However, contemporary observers and subsequent historians seem to agree that alcohol abuse was greater among Indians than non-Indians. No medical data exist to suggest that North American Indians were or are more susceptible to alcoholism; they are not deficient in any alcohol-processing enzyme, for example. The frontier did produce a number of whites who had terrible drinking problems, including Simon Girty and George Rogers Clark. Peter Mancall has noted that alcoholism is more of a social-behavioral disorder than a disease in the biological sense. If such is the case, then sociocultural explanations of Indians' alcohol abuse, rather than genetic ones, must step forward.[54]

Indians appear to have consumed liquor for many of the same reasons frontier whites did: to escape, to celebrate, or to combat depression. Unlike their white neighbors, however, Indians sometimes also sought alcohol's aid in reaching a religious trance state, akin to South American

Indians' use of natural hallucinogens. Indians seemed more plagued by alcohol because of the often-dire circumstances of their physical and social upheavals. The era 1790–1830 was "a period of unprecedented change" in both Indian and white society. Change fostered an "underlying anxiety," which in turn encouraged heavy drinking, especially among Indians, the people most buffeted by lightning transitions.[55]

As tribal structures faltered in an era of rapid change, community and culture often failed to deliver succor to those caught in turmoil. When the Greenville Treaty removed warriors from prized hunting grounds— which it did gradually, not immediately—and reduced opportunities to wage war, it helped erode Indian men's warrior culture. Men stripped of traditional avenues to acclaim and status became bored and depressed and were more inclined to drink. Women who had to cope with male relatives' depression, not to mention their own declining standard of living and increased susceptibility to illness among their children, were also more inclined to drink. Increased reliance on the fur trade left Indians with less economic autonomy. With families to care for, whiskey was the last thing they needed to exchange for their furs.[56]

Even the Miamis, who had done relatively well as a people in the post-Greenville years, complained about the liquor trade and its debilitating effects. They asked for federal assistance in staunching the flow of whiskey to Indian villages. The government did take an unprecedented step to prohibit liquor within Indian country, tacking on a provision to the Trade and Intercourse Act of 1802. Supply and demand were so great, though, that neither national nor territorial legislation did much good. Tetepachsit, a Delaware chief, denounced the liquor traffic yet engaged in it himself.[57]

Tetepachsit's inconsistent (although common) policy on alcohol was lamented by Moravian missionaries who lived near his villages. Missionaries among the Indians reflected part of the greater goal of acculturating Indians through the "civilization" process. German Moravians, Pennsylvania Quakers, and other groups tried their hands at removing Indians' "superstitions." They preached that fulfillment lay not in drinking, fighting, and considerable leisure time but in a sober, laboring life, directed toward pleasing one, rather than many, deities. Understandably, the missionaries faced an uphill battle.

The Moravians, or Unity of the Brethren, were German Protestants (from Saxony) and pacifists who had worked to Christianize blacks and Natives in the Americas since 1732. They began trying to convert the Delaware Indians of Pennsylvania in the 1740s. The Moravians achieved notable success, yet they seemed to meet with tragedy as well. American militia under Col. David Williamson attacked their convert's town of Gnaddenhütten in 1782. They herded the Indian men and women into two separate houses and began bludgeoning them to death with a cooper's mallet. More than ninety innocent Delawares were murdered in cold blood. The Gnaddenhütten Massacre, as it came to be known, was a particularly bitter chapter in U.S.-Delaware relations, for it showed not only that ordinary Americans might perpetrate vicious murder but also that the government was powerless to prevent such acts or punish the guilty. The missionaries and surviving converts, under the Moravian leader David Zeisberger, lived briefly in Canada on the Thames River beginning in 1792 but soon returned to American soil.[58]

Zeisberger had considered establishing a mission on Indiana's White River, and in 1800, when the Delaware chief Hockingpomska invited the convert Delawares to Indiana, the missionaries saw an opportunity to join them. The fact that Hockingpomska had not actually invited the missionaries but merely wanted to consolidate the Delaware bands did not discourage them. In March 1801 Brother Abraham Luckenback, Brother Peter Kluge, and Kluge's wife, Sister Anna Maria Kluge, left Pennsylvania for the White River, traveling with thirteen Christianized Indians. They established a site near present Anderson, Indiana, twenty miles down the White River from the Delaware village of Wapicomekoke, near present Muncie.[59]

As the first Protestant missionaries in Indiana, the Moravians faced many obstacles in converting the Delawares, not the least of which was their own ethnocentrism. Turning Indian men into abstemious, pacifist farmers when their entire culture equated manliness with boldness in combat and skill in the hunt was difficult under ideal circumstances. Among the White River Delawares in the early 1800s, it was perfectly quixotic. Men frustrated by social forces largely beyond their control—loss of tribal lands, the decline of the fur trade, the prevalence of disease—could be expected to search for answers. But asking them to surrender their masculine identity in the process was asking too much.

Warriors probably clung all the more tenaciously to their pasts in the face of these woes, which partially explains the prevalence of drunken brawls. Similarly, Indian women would not have wanted to relinquish their role as the primary food producers for their communities. Indian women often performed tasks, especially horticultural ones, communally, whereas American women lived far more isolated lives. While Indian women engaged in considerable physical toil, they earned prestige and autonomy in doing so—much more in many respects than their white counterparts. And Native beliefs still had a powerful grip on the Delawares, in part because it was felt they could produce more immediate results than praying to the Christian God.

In October 1802 two women, a Nanticoke and a Mingo, living with the Delawares had come under suspicion of having transformed themselves into owls and bewitching the villagers, many of whom had recently died of disease. The Delawares, not wanting to bring Mingo anger on themselves, commissioned a Shawnee man to kill them, and the Shawnee willingly tomahawked the two women. With unintentional foreshadowing, the Moravians also noted that prior to the execution of the accused women, "some superstitious heathen came to the conclusion that perhaps the Christian Indians were the cause" of the epidemics.[60]

History, as well as tradition and cultural conservatism, confronted the Moravians. The Delawares, men and women, seemed never to tire of reminding the missionaries and potential converts of the Gnaddenhütten Massacre, which the brethren had been powerless to prevent. Some even charged that the brethren had deliberately set out to make the Indians "tame" so they might be more easily slaughtered. Bitterly, the missionaries noted that the unconverted Delawares referred to the Christianized ones as *gindower*, meaning "suckling." But for skeptical Delawares, the most damning indictment of the Moravians lay in the missionaries' inability to relieve their suffering. In April 1805, Mary, the wife of an Indian convert named Brother Jacob, summed up Delaware frustration. She noted that both she and her husband had consumption, adding, "The Word of God does not heal my body and that is what I want. My heathen friends told me to come to them, they would make me well."[61]

While a few dozen Delawares did convert to Christianity, the vast majority did not, in part because of growing competition from Native prophets. The increasingly gloomy Delaware situation made their villages fertile ground for revitalization movements. As early as November 1803, "heathen" Delawares spoke of visions in which eschewing non-European material culture and domesticated animals would lead to a return of abundant game animals. One of the most prolific visionaries was an older Delaware woman, baptized Beata. In February 1805 she related a vision of a recently deceased Delaware leader rising from the grave to lead them to prosperity. The Moravians dismissed Beata's vision as "[t]his foolish fable and gossip," without acknowledging that their own faith rested on a similar life-after-death scenario.[62]

Beata's visions became more elaborate and detailed. They critiqued old rituals and suggested new ones. They condemned a variety of sins, including "all evil, drinking, fornication, stealing, murder, and the like." She also claimed to know what each Indian was thinking and doing. Beata's visions and teachings, the Moravians lamented, "made the chiefs active at once. . . . For the present they do not want to hear anything at all except what they learn through the extravagant visions."[63] Unlike Anne Hutchinson nearly two centuries before, Beata did not live in a culture where male leaders automatically discounted women's visions.

Although President Jefferson, and most white Americans, believed women were practically slaves in Indian societies, the attention the Delawares paid to Beata's visions strongly suggests the contrary. For most tribes, Indian women provided the vast majority of their people's calories. Women butchered the animals and dressed the skins of the all-important fur-bearing animals the men brought in, which in turn served as a principal cash crop for necessary manufactured goods. Indian women built homes, made the clothing for both sexes, and were the primary force in child rearing. Because of their vital contributions, both symbolically and physically, their opinions on many issues carried considerable weight.

When Indian men wanted to go on the warpath, it was nearly impossible to do so without the women's consent. Without spare moccasins and dried corn for provisions—and women controlled both—any unsanctioned war party would have been footsore and hungry within a day or two. Among the Shawnees, for example, a women's council had to validate any proposal from male leaders to go to war. The women would not automatically honor such a request. The tightly knit community of the menstrual hut provided a sure head count of how many women in the village were with child. If too many women were pregnant, they would seek to veto a war in which too many husbands might be lost. Women commonly had established channels of power and influence within the tribe. Civil chief Jean Baptiste Richardville of the Miamis owed his rank in no small part to his mother's public declaration of his right to chieftainship. The fur trade had reinforced the sexual division of labor in Native communities—it did not skew the division in favor of one group or another.[64]

For the Indiana Territory, the most significant sociocultural event of 1805 was the beginning of a widespread Indian religious revitalization movement that would eventually challenge American expansionists and therefore the United States as a whole. Considering its importance, the movement began rather inauspiciously.

Lalawethika was a loser, by the standards of his Shawnee people and of most anyone living in Indiana in 1805. A pudgy, one-eyed alcoholic with few real skills, he routinely served as an embarrassment to his respectable family. Lalawethika's surviving brother, Tecumseh, seemed to embody all the positive ideals valued by his tribe: he was a great hunter, athlete, and warrior who showed kindness and consideration to less fortunate members of his community. Lalawethika was a failure in all these categories. He had fought at the Battle of Fallen Timbers alongside Tecumseh and another brother (who died), but no evidence suggests that Lalawethika distinguished himself. While Tecumseh spurned the Greenville Treaty council, Lalawethika probably attended, hoping for drinks and presents. When Thomas Jefferson thought about the supposedly gloomy destiny of Indians who declined to live like whites or when Kentuckians thought about how Indians lacked any human virtues worth considering, they probably thought about men like Lalawethika. He seemed to represent the worst-case scenario of post-1795 Indian life in Indiana.[65]

Tecumseh and his brother, together with a small band of Tecumseh's followers, had briefly lived in Ohio after the conclusion of the Greenville Treaty. In 1796 they moved to the Whitewater River in eastern Indiana and then to the White River, near their Delaware cousins who were there at the invitation of the Miamis. In 1804–1805 another wave of disease epidemics hit the villages on the White River, and Lalawethika, now a fledgling medicine man, tried to heal his neighbors. He had little success. In April 1805 he keeled over by his fireside and lay so still his relatives thought he was dead. When he finally stirred, Lalawethika announced he had witnessed the will of the Great Spirit and could lead the Indians out of their sufferings and into a new era of prosperity and happiness. He was Lalawethika no more, he said. Now he was Tenskwatawa, "He who opens the Door."[66]

The vision Tenskwatawa then related was not new. Much of it could have been borrowed from the visions of Beata, including elements of a Christian hell and the need to atone for sins to avoid such a fate. Also, like Beata, Tenskwatawa's visions were calculated to accrue power for the prophet. He insisted that he was the leader of the religious revival, with the power to judge which ceremonies were pleasing and which ones offensive to the Great Spirit. He even suggested new ceremonies. And, ominously for some, Tenskwatawa asserted that he had the ability to tell true spiritual leaders from false ones.[67]

Tenskwatawa, whom the Americans would soon call the Shawnee Prophet, vowed never to drink alcohol again and insisted that other Indians do the same. Alcohol "was poisoned and accursed," a tool of evil from the white man, and Indians who continued to drink it would end up in a fiery hell, tortured for all time. The Prophet sought to regain the assumed moral rectitude of his forbears and wanted all other Indians to join him. He condemned intertribal fighting, polygamy and adultery, and spousal abuse. He called on the Indians to abandon the manufactured goods of the fur traders—except guns, but only for defense—and to go back to the stone, bone, and wood tools they had previously used to hunt, farm, and kindle fires with. White men's clothing, domesticated animals, and marriages to white traders should all be spurned. Established shamans, who might protest or even challenge Tenskwatawa, were viewed with great suspicion.[68]

Building on the anti-American themes that had been circulating in the Delaware villages, the Prophet outlined the Great Spirit's order for the universe. While "the British, French, and Spanish had been made by the Master of Life, Weshemonetoo, and should be considered friends," Americans were the children of Matchemonetoo, the evil spirit. Weshemonetoo told the Prophet that the Americans "grew from the scum of the great Water when it was troubled by the Evil Spirit. And the froth was driven into the Woods by a strong wind. They are numerous but I hate them." If, and only if, Indians threw off the influence of the Americans could they return to a happy existence.[69]

As R. David Edmunds has noted, the Prophet seems to have borrowed some of the trappings for his teachings from Roman Catholicism—his string of rosary-like prayer beans and his insistence on the confession of past sins, for example.[70] Also, as with Christianity in general, Tenskwatawa saw the need to preach his gospel to a wide audience and to convert nonbelievers—a trait that does not appear to have been common among the region's Indians in previous eras. Many in the United States were also engaging in an intense period of religious revivalism at the time, the beginning stages of what historians call the Second Great Awakening.[71]

Nothing about the Prophet's proposed revitalization was especially original. The Delaware Prophet Neolin and Seneca Prophet Handsome Lake, not to mention Beata, all pre-dated Tenskwatawa. But several events beyond his control, combined with his genuine cunning and opportunism, made the Prophet's movement a major phenomenon and a force Americans had to fear and account for.

In June 1805, when the Prophet's movement was just gaining momentum, Buckongahelas, the grizzled Delaware war chief, died. Buckongahelas had participated in treaties with the Americans, but he had never trusted them and had never forgiven or forgotten the massacre at Gnaddenhütten. Nor had he warmed to the missionaries who sought to convert him. The Delawares loved Buckongahelas, and many refused to believe he had died of natural causes. They suspected witchcraft, and blame soon fell on Chief Tetepachsit. Tetepachsit was a fallen convert of the Moravians and had shown some friendship toward them and the Americans. These qualities, combined with most Delawares' grief over Buckongahelas's death and their general distrust of Americans and missionaries, doomed Tetepachsit. The Moravians justly feared for his life.[72]

In July 1805 the Delawares dismissed Tetepachsit from his position as civil chief. The dismissal may have been rooted in the chief's participation in land cession treaties with Governor Harrison. In the ensuing months, the Prophet's teaching became increasingly popular among the Delawares. In January 1806 the Moravians noted that Tenskwatawa was setting up a village at Greenville in western Ohio and that he had commanded his followers to observe strict temperance. Predictably, the missionaries loved that. They were far harsher regarding Beata's continued claims to religious enlightenment, particularly her assertion that she had swallowed the Good Spirit and therefore spoke only the word of God. "Such and similar blasphemous things met with favor among the poor blind heathen," Brother Kluge noted. It is unclear whether they objected strictly to Beata's message or if the fact that she was a woman influenced their dismay.[73]

The Moravians' partial approval of Tenskwatawa soon turned to horror when, in March 1806, the Delawares invited him to visit them at Wapicomekoke. This was no mere social call. The Prophet arrived on March 15 to honor his Delaware converts' request: he identified the witches among them. The Delawares formed a circle around the Prophet, and he named the guilty, including Tetepachsit, the war chief Hockingpomska, and Brother Joshua, a Mahican convert who had accompanied the Moravians to the White River: "The first prisoner whom the Prophet condemned was Caritas, or Anne Charity, an old woman and an avowed Christian. She had been raised among the Moravians in Ohio, survived the American Revolution, and adopted white modes of dress and manners." Accusing her of poisoning others and witchcraft, the Delawares tortured a confession out of her and then burned her to death.[74]

Tetepachsit had been taken and tortured even before the Prophet arrived to identify him, suggesting the religious fervor of the moment was not entirely divorced from political motivations. Tetepachsit was tortured until he confessed to spreading poison among the tribe. Given his participation in the liquor trade, the interesting (although impossible to answer) question is just how literal or metaphorical the answer was taken to be. He also named some co-conspirators, although later, when not being tortured, he recanted on all counts. His accusers seem to have had a predetermined verdict in mind. On March 17, 1806, they took him to the mission, where he had supposedly hidden his black magic bundle. None was found, but they tomahawked him anyway and "threw him half-alive into the fire," forcing the missionaries to watch. Brother Joshua, the Mahican convert, had been implicated by Tetepachsit, and the Prophet's followers killed him in like fashion the same day. The Prophet returned to Ohio, but the witch hunt continued for the Delawares.[75]

They also executed Tetepachsit's métis nephew, Billy Patterson, "a skilled gunsmith and a devout Christian" who had helped his uncle protest Governor Harrison's 1804 treaty with the Delawares. He denied any sorcery and carried himself with considerable bravery. He continued to pray at the stake as the fire consumed him. Then the witch hunters prepared to burn Tetepachsit's widow, also among the condemned, but her brother stepped in and removed her from their custody. He cursed the Prophet and dared anyone to harm his sister. Like chastened bullies, the witch hunters left her alone. Other Delawares took heart and intervened for their relatives. In this fashion the kin of Hockingpomska saved his life. According to Edmunds, "By mid-April 1806, the witch hunt among the Delawares was over."[76]

A movement of similar intent began among the Sandusky Wyandots, with four women accused of witchcraft and sentenced to death. But the influential Wyandot chief Tarhe, a signer of the Greenville Treaty, would have none of the Prophet's teachings or executions. Nor did he care to have an upstart—from another tribe, no less—challenge his authority. The old chief used his influence to secure the women's release. The Prophet's following was not large enough among the Wyandots to carry more weight than Tarhe did.[77] Conceivably, the Prophet's movement might have stopped there or at least slowed considerably, with his chief success remaining among the Delawares and a few of his own tribe. Fate, in the form of an absentminded territorial governor, intervened, however.

When Governor Harrison heard about the Delaware witch hunts and the Prophet's overtly anti-American preaching, he was immediately disgusted and alarmed. Aside from the brutality of the executions, Harrison doubtless recognized that all the accused had friendly ties to the United States. The normally cautious Harrison jumped in before looking. He fired off a remonstrative letter to the Delawares, expressing his sorrow at their bad behavior. He also sought to stamp out the Prophet's movement in its infancy and issued a challenge to Tenskwatawa: "If he is really a prophet, ask of him to cause the sun to stand still—the moon to alter its course—the rivers [to] cease to flow—or the dead to rise from their graves. If he does these things you may then believe that he has been sent from God." No doubt pleased with his foolproof plan to expose and humiliate the Prophet—the letter was also printed in the April 12, 1806, *Indiana Gazette*—Harrison had apparently forgotten about the solar eclipse predicted for June 16.

The Prophet, who was just as aware of the teams of astronomers in Indiana to view the eclipse as Harrison should have been, waited patiently. He did not try to raise the dead or stop any rivers, but in early June he informed his followers that he would soon bring about a Black Sun. The Black Sun was an ominous sign to the Shawnees in particular, who saw it as a harbinger of war. On the appropriate day and with great ceremony, the Prophet strode out and commanded the sun to darken just as the eclipse began. Then, as it began to wane, he ordered the sun to reappear. Recruiting for the Prophet picked up significantly, and Governor Harrison had to wipe the self-administered egg from his face.[78]

Contemporary Americans and subsequent historians often mistook the Prophet's message as anti-white. Rather, it was a cultural revitalization that took on increasingly anti-American, but not anti-British or anti-French, tones. The Prophet pursued some laudable social reforms, such as temperance, that Harrison himself approved of and had (from a distance) tried to encourage himself.[79]

The Black Sun incident displayed the Prophet's shrewdness, as well as Harrison's tendency to underestimate him. More important, it pointed to an interesting link between the two men that would play out over the next several years. While they hated and feared each other, they were nevertheless crucial to each other. Prior to 1805, Tenskwatawa was most notable for his nearly total failure, to Shawnee thinking, as a man. The encroachment of American settlers and culture had helped drive him to despair and debauchery. Yet from 1805 on he reinvented himself, using reform and resistance to the Americans as his raison d'être.

The Prophet's, and later his brother Tecumseh's, resistance to further land cessions obviously frustrated the governor, yet in a way it offered him a sense of purpose too. As with his continual and related struggle against perceived British influence, countering what he saw as the Prophet's disruptive and backward preaching would define Harrison's career as governor. He now had a boogey man to rally against. While Indiana's citizenry might have criticized Harrison over political, social, and even moral issues, few found fault with his Indian policy. They might not have always loved Harrison, but they never loved the Prophet. With an increasingly militant and threatening Indian movement so close to their homes, Indiana's settlers were glad to have a governor with such solid military credentials. This is not to suggest that either man consciously engineered or recognized the oddly reciprocal relationship, but it was there all the same.

In 1805 Governor Harrison consolidated his hold on Indian negotiations and local politics, particularly slavery. He also experienced his first harsh criticism on these fronts. Fellow citizens began to take issue with him over slavery and tried to discredit him with his superiors. Yet Harrison still saw local Indians, through the pernicious influence of the British, as the greatest threat to Indiana and the western United States generally. Harrison and many of his peers reflexively pointed to Britain as the root of all evil in the United States.[80] Thus it must have come as a shock when one of their own, a gentleman and Revolutionary War hero, attempted to throw the frontier and the expanding American empire into complete upheaval. Such was the paradox of Aaron Burr.

CHAPTER 5

Close Calls and Eerie Calm

1806–1809

Americans had lusted after the territory west of the Mississippi River for years. In the months prior to the Louisiana Purchase, rumors flew about Spain transferring the land to France, which only increased American anxiety and aggressiveness. There was therefore nothing unusual in William Henry Harrison's January 12, 1803, letter to his friend Jonathan Dayton, in which he offered: "The Conduct of Spaniards with respect to the post of New Orleans has excited Much indignation in this Territory— Nothing I believe would be More popular in the whole Western Country than the plan you Suggest of taking possession of the Island And town of Orleans before it gets into Stronger hands." Governor Harrison might have been embarrassed, however, if that passage had been publicly linked with his later assessment of "[m]y most intimate friend General Wilkinson," Aaron Burr's accomplice in high mischief.[1]

Harrison's association with the District of Louisiana had ended painlessly, but the vast territory to the west of the Mississippi and the temptations it offered also brought the governor some headaches. On May 22, 1805, Davis Floyd of Jeffersonville (directly across the Ohio River from Louisville, Kentucky) wrote to Governor Harrison. Floyd, a territorial representative from Clark County and a Harrison ally, had mixed news for the governor:

> You mention your expectation of seeing Colo. Burr at Vincennes. I fear you will be disappointed at presant Colo. Burr has gone to Frankfort from that he intends going to Nashville from that to New Orleans, tho to return as soon as possible, he says by the setting of

our Legislature, as I think he wishes to be at our first Session. It is said that he is to Supercede Govr. Claybourn [of the Mississippi Territory] tho' he never while here mentioned the Subject Genls. Wilkinson & Dayton are expected here every hour. they may pay You a visit probably.[2]

Since at least 1805, Aaron Burr, the prodigal former vice president from Jefferson's first term and killer (in a duel) of Alexander Hamilton, had been eyeing the West as a vehicle to power and glory. Historians still debate the extent of Burr's schemes. At the very least, he wanted to gather a private army to "liberate" Mexico and install himself as its emperor—an early version of the filibustering sentiment that became popular in the antebellum South. Some later charged he was really trying to detach the western sections of the United States to form a breakaway republic, again with himself as its leader. He had contacted British agents, including the British ambassador to the United States and, through him, Prime Minister William Pitt (the younger), for British naval aid in this endeavor. Pitt's death in January 1806 ended Burr's hopes for British aid, however, and he may have abandoned that part of the plot. Whether Burr's plans were merely criminal (the United States was not at war with Spain, Mexico's parent) or actually treasonous, we will never know. One thing is certain: he was up to no good.[3]

Burr's co-conspirator was General James Wilkinson, the military governor of the Louisiana-Missouri region and the highest-ranking officer in the U.S. Army. Wilkinson, it will be remembered, had met Harrison when both served in the army in the 1790s. Wilkinson had helped Harrison out of a potentially troubling legal situation, but Harrison's friendship with Wilkinson can only be attributed to the former's complete ignorance of the latter's true character. Besides, having governors as friends could be useful. After Wilkinson's appointment to take over Louisiana, Harrison wrote him in June 1805, congratulating him and recommending some of his friends—the Chouteau family, Charles De Hault Delassus, and others—for any plum positions Wilkinson might be filling.[4] Wilkinson, apparently in answer to Harrison's patronage letter, wrote back that September, using Aaron Burr as his courier, with a request of his own. He baldly asked Harrison to send Burr, who did not even live in Indiana, to Congress as Indiana's delegate, "where his talents and abilities are all important at the present moment. But . . . how is that to be done? By your fiat. Let Mr. [Benjamin] Parke [already Indiana's congressional delegate] adhere to his profession [he was a lawyer by trade]; convene your Solomons and let them return him—col. B[urr]— to Congress." Wilkinson added that, if need be, Burr would purchase, through Harrison, an estate in Indiana, which sounded like an invitation for Harrison to solicit a bribe.[5]

Say what one will about Wilkinson, he was not hindered by any sense of shame. The general was astute in sensing how much control Harrison held in Indiana in 1805—he could in fact have effected Burr's election as delegate had he chosen to do so. But Wilkinson overestimated Harrison's ruthlessness. True, he could absolutely punish political opponents or those he saw as personal liabilities. And, serving U.S. interests, he could be positively devious when it came to Indian affairs. But Benjamin Parke was perhaps Harrison's closest political friend in the territory, a fellow Virginian, and a loyal supporter. Plus, he had already been selected and was going to push the pro-slavery, anti-division agenda in Congress for the governor. If Harrison wrote a reply to Wilkinson, it does not survive. Burr was the governor's guest at Grouseland, but he later said he did not discuss the letter with Harrison.[6] Parke remained Indiana's congressional delegate, and the request from Wilkinson may have been Harrison's first inkling that Aaron Burr was not a man with whom to become too involved.

Burr spent much of 1805–1806 scouting the Ohio and Mississippi valleys, trying to gauge how much support he might receive for his enterprise. He wrote Harrison from Lexington, Kentucky, in October 1806, in an attempt to feel the governor out. Burr mentioned almost casually that Andrew Jackson, the general in command of the militia in western Tennessee, had put the militia on high alert. Burr suggested that Harrison do the same for Indiana, as "[a]ll reflecting men consider a war with Spain to be inevitable." The governor, Burr assumed, "would not be at ease as an idle spectator" if war broke out. "If it should be my lot to be employed, which there is reason to expect," he added, "it would be my highest gratification to be associated with you."[7]

Burr had convinced many, including General Jackson, that he was merely attacking the Spanish, of which Jackson approved, rather than trying to split the Union. Otherwise Jackson, one of American history's most rabid nationalists, might have called (literally) for Burr's head rather than accommodating him. If Jackson had known Burr was also dealing with the hated British, the results might have been truly gory. Burr, however, had fooled Jackson, who even went so far as to accept a private contract from Burr to build boats for him to float his proposed army down the Mississippi. But by luck or instinct or through the wise counsel of friends, Harrison did not warm to Burr. He complained in his November 4, 1806, address to the General Assembly that the militia was in a sorry state of preparedness—something he had mentioned previously—but he did not put the militia on high alert. Instead, the governor closed his address with a call to patriotism. He urged the assembly members to display and foster in their constituents "that ardent love of Country which is the parent of every noble action—Teach them to appreciate the felicity of their situation—The Citizens of a great And free Nation—The only republic on earth—the only Country where persecuted liberty Has found an assylum [sic]."[8] Burr had completely misread Harrison.

Realizing his mistake, in late November Burr, now in Louisville, tried to reassure the governor and negate the effects of the "various and extravagant reports" about his intentions and activities. He insisted that he had no wish to split the Union and baldly lied that he had no connections with any foreign governments, stating he had "never meditated" introducing any foreign influence into the United States or its territories. Burr continued that he "on the contrary should repel with indignation any Proposition or Measure having that tendency." He went on to assert that many of Harrison's close friends were part of his "extensive speculation" and that some of the "Principal officers" of the national government had been informed. If the situation had allowed for [another] face-to-face meeting, Burr added, Harrison's "active Support" would have been assured. Burr neglected to mention that *the* principal officer of government, President Jefferson, was already highly suspicious of the entire enterprise.

General Wilkinson had turned on Burr in November 1806, informing President Jefferson of the plot, largely (and with breathtaking mendacity) removing himself from wrongdoing. Jefferson's willingness to sustain the obviously tainted Wilkinson testified to his hatred and fear of Burr. Indeed, Jefferson's known antipathy toward Burr, and Harrison's need to stay in the president's good graces, might have accounted for Harrison's reluctance to join the scheme. The very next day, Secretary of State James Madison wrote to Harrison and the other western governors, sending them Jefferson's proclamation "in order to arrest an enterprize represented to be in preparation against the possessions of Spain." The circular did not mention Burr by name, and it did not need to.[9]

With the publication of Jefferson's circular, any rational chance for Burr's irrational plot ended. President Jefferson eventually had him tried for treason, although he could not be convicted, as Chief Justice John Marshall, presiding, held to the strictest interpretation of treason. Most of the general public in the East joined Jefferson in his shock and disgust at the acquittal, however, and Burr wisely left the United States for a time. In the West, opinions were more varied.[10] Some people were genuinely spooked by the whole affair.

Although not actually referred until 1808, the "Remonstrance to Congress by Inhabitants of Randolph and St. Clair Counties" was clearly written in response to Aaron Burr. While asking for a division of the territory, the inhabitants were primarily frightened for their lives:

> At this Critical Moment when your Petitioners have Strong Reasons to Believe that treasonable plans have been formed and put in Motion to separate the Union; When they see an Ambitious man at the head of a considerable force, about to shut up their Commercial Channels and Navigable Streams of the Western Country—When they Behold themselves on the Verge of a civil War and at the Threshold of Slavery and submission, they shudder at their Defenceless situation; without any Regular force,—without a well Organized Militia—equally unprepared for Attack and for Defence—Surrounded by Faithless Savages and threatened, perhaps, with Internal growing Treason against the Union.[11]

By January 1807, Harrison's friend and political ally Waller Taylor, visiting Louisville, reported that the state of Kentucky was confiscating horses purchased by Burr's supporters for the expedition. Meanwhile, Davis Floyd, territorial representative from Clark County, sheriff, and major of the county militia, had also been associated with Burr. Indicted for treason in Kentucky on November 3, 1806, by U.S. Attorney Joseph Hamilton Daveiss,

Floyd escaped back to Indiana to serve in the legislature. Subsequently, he asked Governor Harrison for a letter of recommendation.[12]

Harrison wrote Governor Robert Williams of Mississippi Territory that Floyd was a true patriot and merely "the dupe of the artful & mischievous" Burr. At some personal risk, Harrison noted, "I must Confess that the Solemnity of [Burr's] Declarations imposed for Some time on me as well as Major Floyd." He asked Williams to help Floyd, if he could do so consistent with his duty. In Indiana Floyd was indicted June 2, 1807, convicted on the 12th, and sentenced on June 13. He was sentenced to only three hours in jail and a ten dollar fine. According to the records, "The two judges were Thomas T. Davis, at whose home Floyd had met Burr, and Waller Taylor." Obviously, Judge Davis had an incentive not to press the matter too harshly. Judge Taylor, for his part, felt the need to write President Jefferson afterward to explain the rather light sentence. (Actually, given Burr's acquittal, a harsh conviction of his followers would have been odd.) Most of the evidence against Floyd came from his own confession, Taylor argued. Floyd had been convinced that he was acting in the interests of the United States, and a larger fine would needlessly hurt Floyd's family. Anyway, the territory had no suitable jail in which to hold him. The parade of lame excuses could not have pleased Jefferson.[13]

Apparently, the General Assembly did not hold the association with Burr against the representative from Clark County. Four days after his conviction, they elected Davis Floyd clerk of the territorial House of Representatives. Some people did not care to have a convicted Burrite holding office, however, and protested. Yet in the November 17, 1807, *Vincennes Western Sun*, General Washington Johnston and Luke Decker, both members of the assembly, offered a spirited defense of Floyd, who had merely been "deceived by Burr." It is interesting that Johnston was an anti-slavery man, while Decker was strongly pro-slavery and pro-Harrison. In spite of their different philosophies, both were willing to overlook Floyd's connections to Aaron Burr. The next week "Broken Blunderbuss" countered with a front-page editorial, bitterly denouncing Floyd's election as clerk, largely because of the Burr association.

As the slavery debate further intensified after 1807, Floyd, an anti-slavery man from an anti-slavery county, was suddenly abandoned and condemned by the Harrison faction. In July 1808, Governor Harrison stripped Floyd of both his commission as a major in the Clark County militia and his license to operate a ferry on the Ohio River—a lucrative trade. Harrison even mentioned Floyd in a letter to President Jefferson, declaring that Floyd was much deeper involved in the Burr Conspiracy than previously believed. Harrison, knowing exactly which buttons to push with the president, now asserted that Floyd had known about Burr's connections with the British.[14]

At "A Meeting of Citizens of Knox County," held at the Vincennes Court House on January 4, 1808, attendees passed several resolutions. The meeting was not simply a political maneuver by Harrison's supporters, as the governor's enemy William McIntosh was one of the men who drafted the resolutions, all of which were affirmed unanimously. They denounced Davis Floyd and "the Odium which has been cast upon the people of the Territory in consequence of that Appointment." While castigating Floyd, the citizens also felt it was "indecorous" to criticize his three judges or to make insinuations about their motives. The citizens recognized the right of their General Assembly to elect Floyd, but they strongly disapproved of the choice. They were especially upset that his election occurred after he had been convicted in Clark County and was under indictment in Virginia for treason. They added that the few citizens of Knox County who were approached by Burr and refused to join him were "highly honorable"—a statement perhaps designed to vindicate Harrison. The citizens of Knox County closed noting that they were, and always would be, "sincerely attached to the Constitution and Government of the United States." Floyd soon resigned the clerkship.[15]

For Indiana's political elites, a link to the Burr Conspiracy was less a cause for genuine moral concern or outrage than a convenient avenue for partisan attacks. William Prince, the first sheriff of Knox County and a Harrison supporter, had also been involved (although less deeply) with Burr. Elected to the Legislative Council in 1809,[16] Prince came under fire from the vehemently anti-slavery and anti-Harrison Dr. Elias McNamee. McNamee spearheaded a petition to the assembly calling for a purge of Burrites that, while it did not specifically name Prince, "had him in mind." Prince seems to have been even more popular in the assembly than Floyd, for a commission headed by General Washington Johnston found no cause for alarm in Prince's behavior or character. Revealingly, once the slavery issue was decided in late 1810, such attacks on old Burrites disappeared. Even Davis Floyd eventually returned to the governor's good graces. Harrison appointed him an emissary to the Delaware Indians in April 1812. Floyd succeeded in getting a Delaware pledge of neutrality and later served honorably in the War of 1812.[17] However, the period 1807–1808 was an especially dangerous time to have one's loyalty questioned.

The campaign against Burr's supporters, on the frontier anyway, seems cynical, and in many respects it was. Governor Harrison could overlook the indiscretion of Burrites or chastise them for it at his own choosing. Yet the delayed reaction against the Burrites on the frontier must be seen within the context of international events and patriotic sentiment. Davis Floyd received his light sentence for plotting with Burr a little more than a week before the *Chesapeake-Leopard* Affair of June 22, 1807. The incident, as discussed previously, involved a British warship, the *Leopard*, firing on an American warship, the *Chesapeake*, while in American waters in order to search for Royal Navy deserters. Three American sailors died in the exchange, the Royal Navy hanged another for desertion, and anti-British sentiment reached a fever pitch.[18]

Likewise, Indian Agent William Wells's June 19, 1807, missive to Harrison, alleging a British-inspired Indian assault on Detroit, Mackinac, and Chicago, also took on a retroactively sinister air.[19]

Although the United States and Britain had been officially at peace since 1783 and had reaffirmed that fact in 1794 with Jay's Treaty, the Americans' perceptions of Britain had not improved. Always lying just beneath the surface, Anglophobia may have even gotten worse in the twenty-four years since the Peace of Paris. Several currents collided to make this so. Britain's ongoing war with France and its irritating tendency to trod upon American maritime rights drew U.S. ire. While the latter directly hurt American merchants and sailors, indirectly it hurt Western farmers who sought access to European markets and the high prices American produce commanded as a result of the Napoleonic Wars. It was also irksome to American honor to swallow such insults. As would be seen in the War of 1812, Ohio Valley farmers, largely out of nationalism and wounded pride, were far more enthusiastic for the war than New England shippers more directly affected. The American Revolution had sought to establish that Anglo-Americans were the equals (or even the superiors) of their cousins in the British Isles. For Britain to treat Americans with such contempt, even before *Chesapeake-Leopard*, was not only galling but unsettling. It aggravated Americans' lingering self-doubts about their nation's legitimacy.

Further, the adulation heaped on the Revolutionary generation, while genuine, was also a constant reminder for the next generation of Americans that they themselves remained unproven. As Joyce Appleby argued, "The celebration of Revolutionary events that marked their childhood also made them conscious of not having fought in the war, or run the farm for an absent spouse or parent, or participated in a boycott, or hidden farm products from marauding British troops."[20] William Henry Harrison and his peers were continually eager to prove that they were worthy of their Revolutionary heritage.

Finally, while actual Indian-white warfare on the frontier and even random murders had fallen off drastically since the mid-1790s, the American preoccupation with Indians taking the warpath had not. As Harrison's generation had grown up with stories of Americans' Revolutionary War heroism, so had they also repeatedly imbibed tales of British and Indian perfidy. One graphic example was Jane McCrea. Her brutal demise, already the subject of poetry and sensational newspaper reports in the 1770s, was commemorated yet again in 1804 in a striking oil painting by John Vanderlyn. While the actual details of her death were sketchy, the painting itself seems to leave no doubt. Beautiful, fair-skinned, and helpless, McCrea is forced to the ground while two muscular and tawny warriors stand over her, one with his tomahawk arm cocked to strike. What is more, the pose of the scantily clad warriors over the kneeling woman strongly implies an imminent sexual violation as well.[21]

The murder also received another round of treatment in print when Mercy Otis Warren, the sister of one prominent Patriot and widow of another, wrote the first major American history of the Revolution. Published in Boston in 1805, Warren's *History of the Rise, Progress, and Termination of the American Revolution* became part of Americans' revisionist view of the war. It was aptly subtitled "Interspersed with Biographical, Political, and Moral Observations." Rather than a political-economic conflict or a civil war between Englishmen, for Warren the Revolution was a basic struggle of good against evil. She noted that McCrea had been murdered "in all the cold-blooded ferocity of savage manners." She implied that the Crown bore responsibility for having Indian auxiliaries, adding, "it was not always in the power of the most humane of British officers, to protect the innocent from the barbarity of their savage friends."[22]

Joel Barlow's epic *Columbiad* (1807) (for which Vanderlyn's painting was originally commissioned) described Indians driving an ax into Jane's face.[23] Such gory, explicit depictions of McCrea's death, backed by little or no real evidence, continued to inflame and (mis)inform Americans' vision of Indians. There was never even any agreement on what tribe the killers were from. Such imprecision actually aided expansionist rhetoric: McCrea was murdered by *the Indians*, therefore all *Indians* were guilty.

McCrea's death could have been a cautionary tale about the perils of siding with the monarch or allying oneself with Indians. In the new republic she was pressed into service to symbolize the possible fate of any white woman (or American civilization for that matter) if vigilance against Indian cruelty ever waned. At least one historian argued that Jane's death, and Americans' obsession with it, held great significance for gender roles in the early Republic. Aside from functioning as a bellows to inflame public opinion against Britons and Indians, it also reinforced American patriarchy. Jane, according to the legend, had gone against her Patriot father—in reality he had died in 1769—to side with her lover and the British. She fled the benevolent protection of her father and was then slaughtered by "savage" villains. Thus she became, in death and myth, "a national image of female vulnerability in an expanding republic."[24]

Patriotic men like Vanderlyn and Barlow, and even patriotic women like Mercy Warren, furthered and shaped the legend of Jane McCrea. In so doing, they effectually "rejected women's demands for a more serious role in both politics and culture and indicated a distrust of female power and sexuality which reasserted female dependence." The McCrea legend did double duty: it "reinforced notions of Indian savagery" and reiterated the "need" for paternalism in the early Republic. The tale of Jane McCrea continued as a favorite in American literature of the West well into the twentieth century.[25]

Americans, like most peoples throughout history, displayed a selective memory when it came to cruelty in acts of war. Particularly in the West, for decades afterward they remembered McCrea and also the infamous British colonel Henry Hamilton, the "hair buyer" who had supposedly paid Indians for American scalps during the Revolution. They rarely talked about Gnaddenhütten. Nor did they mention how their own hero, Virginian George Rogers Clark, had captive Indians tomahawked in front of Hamilton when Clark besieged Vincennes in 1779.[26]

The Washington, Adams, and Jefferson administrations repeatedly (and sincerely) insisted they did not want to destroy Indians in the manner of the Conquistadors. Yet it was equally true that any alarming incident, however physically isolated or chronologically distant, could easily lead Americans to fall back on the view of the British or American Indians as savages, the bloodthirsty Other. For Americans in the first decade of the nineteenth century, hostility toward Britain and its Indian allies was almost second nature. In this context at least, William Henry Harrison's reaction to a brief naval skirmish more than a thousand miles away seems almost restrained.

Addressing his territorial legislature on August 18, 1807, the governor seethed over Britain's abuse of neutral shipping rights and impressment of American sailors, not to mention the *Leopard*'s attack: "The blood rises to my cheek when I reflect on the humiliating, the disgraceful scene, of the crew of an American ship of war mustered on its own deck by a British Lieutenant, for the purpose of selecting the innocent victims of their own tyranny." The tomahawk and scalping knife always worked for British vengeance, he added, yet "[a] beneficent and discriminating providence will make us the objects of his peculiar care; another WASHINGTON will arise to lead our armies to victory and glory, and the TYRANTS of the world will be taught the useful lesson, that a nation of FREE MEN are not to be insulted with impunity!"[27]

Harrison, of course, viewed anyone resisting his acquisition of Indian lands, including the Indians, as trying to destroy Americans' rights as "FREE MEN"—freeholding being a particularly important right. Therefore he saw the Shawnee Prophet as "an engine set to work by the British for some bad purpose." The governor did not acknowledge that his treaties provided much of the engine's steam.[28]

In fairness to the governor, Indians also knew how to pass the buck. For different reasons, they could propagate the myth that British exhortation rather than Native motivation had led them to take the warpath. At peace councils between conflicts, Indians often asserted that the Crown's emissaries had encouraged them to fight, and they tried to leave the impression that they themselves would have preferred neutrality. Tecumseh later blamed the British for "raising the Tomahawk against the Americans and put[ting] it into our hands" and "inducing us to go to war."[29] All sides were guilty of misleading rhetoric on the issue.

Still, the Prophet obviously had nothing to do with the *Leopard's* aggression. But a paranoid conflation of the two separate threats was common at the time. Previously, President Jefferson had considered the Prophet's movement of little consequence, but in the wake of the *Chesapeake* affair, his old fears of a British-Indian alliance attacking the frontier resurfaced. Now, bribing the Prophet, or perhaps engineering his assassination by pro-American Indians, seemed perfectly legitimate.[30]

Jefferson never fully recovered from the British-inspired Indian attacks along Virginia's frontier during the Revolution, which he had railed about in the Declaration of Independence. It appears that, like most Americans, he did not want to forget, either. Fear provided not only a rationale but a sense of legitimacy as well. After *Chesapeake-Leopard*, Secretary Dearborn saw war with Britain as so imminent that he tried to commission spies to reconnoiter the British garrisons at Quebec and Montreal.[31]

In August 1807, William Wells, the controversial Indian agent at Fort Wayne, wrote to Harrison that "the British are at the bottom of all this Business and depend on it that if we have war with them that many of the Indian tribes will take an active part against us." The next month the governor again addressed the territorial assembly, announced that an Indian war was imminent, and proposed measures to keep Americans from supplying hostile Indians through neutral tribes. (Ironically, this sounds akin to a violation of neutral shipping rights.) Still, U.S. officials knew deep down that Americans themselves were at least partly responsible for frontier strife. Harrison had previously admitted to the assembly that much of the Indians' unrest sprang justly from Americans' inability to apprehend and punish Indian killers.[32]

The case of James Red, who had murdered a Delaware Indian in cold blood in 1805, illustrated the frustrating scenario. Harrison, realizing that lawless Americans threatened frontier peace, went to great lengths to secure a conviction. As the attorney general was away, the governor hired an eminent lawyer from St. Louis to prosecute Red. This attempt at justice for a dead Indian brought considerable criticism of Harrison from his fellow citizens. Secretary Dearborn, however, agreed with Harrison that Red must face justice. Every possible means should be taken to capture Red, Dearborn proclaimed, because it was "excessively mortifying that our good faith, should be so frequently called in question by the natives who have it in their power to make such proud comparisons in relation to good faith." Unfortunately, Red (probably with help from white neighbors) escaped and fled west. Harrison made repeated attempts to recapture him, even offering a three hundred dollar bounty, but Red escaped the governor for good. Harrison's August 1807 address again called for Red's capture to preserve peace. Yet neither Harrison nor Jefferson proved willing or capable of seeing that the overriding source of conflict was the rapid and ruthless acquisition of Indian lands.[33]

In September 1807 the secretary of war warned Governor Harrison, Governor William Hull of Michigan Territory, and Governor Thomas Kirker of Ohio that war with the Indians was imminent and directed them to organize and arm their militias. The War Department's chief clerk John Smith (writing for Dearborn) soon added a directive for Harrison and Hull. They were to meet with the various Indian tribes and tell them to remain neutral, upon threat of annihilation, if war with Britain came.[34]

In 1808, still feeling the war scare themselves, British officials in Canada sought an alliance with Tecumseh, the Prophet's militarily gifted brother, in case of war with the United States. The British realized that Indian allies would be essential in defending their undermanned Canadian frontier if such a war broke out. However, in 1808, Tecumseh was not looking for a military confrontation with the United States, nor did he relish the idea of teaming up with the Redcoats who had abandoned him after Fallen Timbers. He refused their offer. As much as the United States thought Indians could not properly decide for themselves where and how to live, Americans also failed to see Indians' capacity to decide when and with whom to ally themselves. In his address to the General Assembly on September 27, 1808, Harrison offered that "all the wars which have arison [sic] between ourselves & the aborigines, are justly

attributable to the prevalence of foreign influence amongst the latter."
Yet the Shawnee brothers did not seek a war with the powerful United
States; they only insisted that Americans stop purchasing Indian lands.[35]

For Harrison and many Republicans, perhaps the most damning
charge against Aaron Burr had been his association with the British. In
part this reflected the genuine, visceral distaste for Britain that Patriots of
his generation felt. Harrison's views mirrored Jefferson's—Anglophobia
that at times bordered on certifiable paranoia. Yet like Jefferson, Harrison
could also use his Anglophobia, and that of his countrymen, for his own
advantage. In the immediate aftermath of the Burr Conspiracy, an association with the plot could be seized upon or ignored, depending on
political expediency. But analyzing the motives of Harrison and his peers
after the *Chesapeake-Leopard* Affair becomes much more difficult, as their
fear and hatred of Britain seems to have been even more heartfelt than
previously. One thing is perfectly clear: the affair left those with obvious
ties to foreign nations increasingly vulnerable to xenophobic political
attacks and defamation.

William McIntosh, Scottish by birth, served in the British Army but had
lived in Vincennes since the Revolution. Originally a trader, he became
an attorney for the French *habitants* in their land claims cases, which
proved far more lucrative. One month after arriving in Vincennes,
Governor Harrison appointed McIntosh both a major in the Knox
County militia and treasurer of the territory. Yet a number of differences
arose between the two men. McIntosh had been a principal opponent of
the move to the second grade of government. The owner of considerable
acreage, perhaps McIntosh, like the Edgar-Morrison faction in Illinois,
feared the move would bring increased taxation. Further, McIntosh kept
appearing opposite Harrison in court. McIntosh was owed money by the
late Major John F. Hamtramck and had to sue the administrator of
Hamtramck's estate—Governor Harrison—to get his money. McIntosh's
brother Angus, the administrator of another estate, also had to sue
Harrison for payment due. And William McIntosh had also served as
John Askin's agent in the case against Harrison's oldest friend in Indiana,
Francis Vigo. Vigo characterized McIntosh as a "spiteful agent" and "a
man who seeks only to destroy me."[36]

For all these reasons, in the aftermath of the *Chesapeake-Leopard* Affair, Harrison used the most damaging rhetoric he could think of, characterizing McIntosh as a "Scotchman" and an "inveterate tory."[37] He did so to President Jefferson and to anyone else who would listen. The governor's partisans also attacked McIntosh, either openly or through inference, in the newspapers. "Shandy" offered an indirect attack in the September 12, 1807, *Vincennes Western Sun*. He accused Britain of infringing upon American rights generally and of trying to agitate the Indians against the United States. All those living within U.S. borders must be loyal, Shandy continued. If they could not be, then "[l]et them go to the nation they prefer to this," adding that no "disaffected miscreants" would be tolerated if war with Britain or the Indians broke out. One entry in the *Western World* of Frankfort, Kentucky, accused McIntosh (by name) of serving in the British Army during the Revolution and of obtaining lands by fraud. McIntosh had served in the king's army, and he did have hundreds of acres of land claims rejected, although in the latter respect he was not unlike Governor Harrison.[38]

Two weeks after Shandy's editorial, "Trim" (perhaps McIntosh himself) responded. He mocked Shandy as the tool of "the ignoble emperor [Harrison]" and a "nincompoop, alias the hon. Delegate of the Neediana territory." (Apparently Trim was convinced that Shandy was Benjamin Parke, the delegate to Congress.) Trim said President Jefferson was the "dispenser of offices" and therefore adored by Shandy as such, and he also pointed out (correctly, if not prudently) that three-fourths of America's trade was with Britain: "[B]y the credit they give to merchants, and these to farmers, lands are purchased, cleared, and improved, to the great . . . and visible prosperity of the United States."[39] This was all true, but it was not what most frontier Americans wanted to hear with war clouds gathering.

The increasingly tense climate made even the French habitants in Vincennes worry about the taint of Britain. They sent a memorial to President Jefferson, insisting that they had no knowledge of any British agents operating in their midst or in the Indian country but adding that they would report it immediately if one appeared. They voiced outrage at the *Leopard's* actions and reminded Jefferson of their support of the Americans during the Revolution. They denied any "partiality" toward France at the expense of the United States, and they also defended the character of McIntosh, their legal representative and the secretary of the memorial:

> We must be permitted to observe that the person [William McIntosh] pointed to by your Excellency has lived amongst us upwards of twenty years, has acquired a handsome Property, and has never to our Knowledge or belief attempted to weaken, but on the contrary has always, as on the present occasion[,] strengthened our Zeal in the common cause of our Country. It is therefore but an act of Justice to our own honor as well as so to him to declare, that we regard the means practiced to lessen him in the good opinion of his fellow citizens as repugnant to our Sense of the rights secured to every Citizen by the laws of our Country: as the accusations appear to us to be ill founded.[40]

Harrison forwarded the memorial to Washington, although he also included a testy defense of his own conduct. He insisted that he had not questioned the French residents' patriotism and that McIntosh had simply duped them into vindicating him. Jefferson responded to McIntosh, not Harrison, stating his complete confidence in the habitants' loyalty. The president assured McIntosh that he had never questioned their attachment to the United States, nor had Governor Harrison done so in any correspondence. All Jefferson asked was for "a return of a perfect good understanding with their governor" and the other civil authorities over them. He did not mention Harrison's accusations against McIntosh or address the latter's patriotism. He merely reiterated his confidence in the Vincennes habitants and closed with a "salute [to] them as well as yourself."[41] Jefferson wrote these words, of course, before McIntosh had stabbed Jefferson's cousin Thomas Randolph (see chapter 7).

When possible, Jefferson liked to avoid confrontations, both in his personal life and as president. When the European powers, especially Britain, drew Jefferson's ire for not respecting America's maritime rights, he shut down all of America's maritime commerce with foreign nations. The Embargo was designed to bloodlessly coerce Britain and France by withholding what Jefferson saw as America's indispensable trade. Instead, the Embargo wrecked the American economy while having little effect on the European belligerents. Americans on the frontier did not feel the commercial pinch as quickly or as acutely as those on the eastern seaboard, but they nevertheless experienced hardships and anxieties. Many saw war with Britain or perhaps France as imminent.

While some continued to plead for unity, others, particularly in the Illinois country, called for a division of the territory. They did so for a number of different reasons, and William Henry Harrison opposed them all. The Illinoisans, though, were accumulating political firepower and influence daily. John Messinger[42] was born in Massachusetts, moved to Vermont, and then migrated to Kentucky around 1801 with a group that included his father-in-law, Matthew Lyon. Lyon became a U.S. congressman from that state. Lyon and Harrison had, if from a distance, locked horns before, when the former campaigned against Harrison's reappointment as governor in 1802. In that year Messinger moved to the Illinois country to work as a surveyor and was elected to the territorial legislature in 1808. He maintained a frequent correspondence with Congressman Lyon.[43]

Writing to Lyon on October 17, 1808, Messinger noted his fear that Harrison would prevent the popular election of a territorial delegate to Congress unless he could install one of his political allies who would oppose division of the territory. While the "Majority of the lower House have hither to been in favour of a division . . . in the Council there are but three members[,] Mssrs. [John Rice] Jones, [Shadrach] Bond [Jr.], & [George] Fisher, two of which (Bond & Fisher) are opposed to a division & the only reason they can give is that the Governor does not wish for a division." While Bond and Fisher were from the Illinois country and knew the majority of their constituents favored division, they opposed it, as they were "Creatures of His Excellency." The governor's wishes, not those of the people, had "hitherto been represented," Messinger claimed, and he included copies of a pro-division resolution from the lower house for Lyon to send to the president, vice president, and speaker of the House. Messinger asked Lyon for his "utmost Exertions to get a division on some terms or other."[44]

Opposition to slavery, meanwhile, sprang from different wells. Some people, like John Badollet, opposed it primarily for moral reasons. Some worried that the proximity of slaves reduced the value and viability of free labor. Still others resisted what they saw as the aristocratic privilege slave owning represented. In the South especially, considerable tension existed between elite planters and the far more numerous yeoman class. Yeomen had been deferential socially, politically, and economically to the planter elite, but they resented them for it. For themselves, planters could not relax concerning such "grudging deference" or count on slave-less whites' continued allegiance to slavery. Planter elites might have seen slavery as essential for racial solidarity and white equality, but yeomen migrants to Indiana did not. They resented the ostentation of the slave-owning planters, and north of the Ohio they felt no need to defer to such men.[45] Thus while the patrician Harrison's attempts to reestablish a planter elite in Indiana were predictable and often welcomed by those with the means to join him, those of humbler economics might resent them out of jealousy, fear, or spite, even if blacks' natural rights did not sway them.

Anti-slavery sentiment was strongest in the East, particularly along the Ohio, while counties on the Wabash and to the west were more pro-slavery. Many settlers in the eastern counties had left Kentucky to get away from slavery, as John Badollet had argued. They lacked influence, however, because pro-slavery men dominated the territorial legislature and most government posts. In the 1807 General Assembly election, only one of the seven men elected, James Beggs of Clark County, was from an area with strong anti-slavery sentiment. The rest were from largely pro-slavery counties such as Knox, St. Clair, and Randolph.[46]

Illinoisans favored slavery and a division of the territory and had come to oppose Harrison in general. A major complaint was that despite President Jefferson having cautioned Harrison to mind geographic representation when making appointments, the bulk of appointments fell to men from east of the Wabash. To complicate the situation further, a third faction arose that opposed Harrison's powers of appointment and absolute veto and wanted more self-government. For example, Dearborn County in eastern Indiana had petitioned unsuccessfully in 1805 to be annexed to Ohio. Harrison now faced an anti-slavery faction (mostly the eastern counties), a pro-slavery, pro-division faction (mainly Illinois), and a pro–self-government faction (scattered), all of which opposed him personally.[47]

The rumbling resentment of the introduction of blacks into the territory that Harrison had noted in 1805 had become a roar by 1808–1809. In an effort to counteract the effects of Harrison and the pro-slavery legislature, anti-slavery forces fired their own paper barrage. A "Petition to Congress by the People of the Illinois Country," referred April 6, 1808, went after the governor directly. In part it read:

> Fourthly, That knowing all involuntary servitude to be forbidden in the Territory by the solemn Ordinance of 1787 he has sanctioned a Law permitting the Master of a slave who may be brought into the said Territory to apply to the Clerk of the Court and get said slave indented as a servant for any term of years he pleased, and providing that in case the slave should refuse to enter into indenture for the time required the master might take him back and dispose of him as he chose;—a Law which may Properly be entitled "A Law for the Establishment of disguised Slavery in opposition to the National will.[48]

The petition boasted 119 signatures. The Illinois country, with its long-time French residents, is generally seen by historians as having been a hotbed of pro-slavery sentiment within the Indiana Territory, making this petition all the more interesting. Its legitimacy may be questionable, though, as four men later sent a petition to Congress stating "we never did Signe A Petition in the year 1807 or 1808 Praying for A Division of the Indiana Territory and Exhibiting Several Charges aggainst [sic] Governor Harrison."[49]

Regardless of the four men's claims, the attacks continued. A petition to Indiana's territorial legislature from "sundry inhabitants" of the territory, dated October 19, 1808, blasted the "Act concerning Introduction" as violating the Northwest Ordinance, stated that the pro-slavery petitions were from a minority of settlers, and sought to correct the "general error" of easterners and anti-slavery southerners in thinking that Indiana was pro-slavery. The petitioners further stated that they were morally and financially opposed to the "corruption" of slavery. In drafting Article VI, they noted, Congress was "guided by an enlightened, humane and consistent policy, embracing not only the present, but future interests of this portion of the Union."[50]

By 1808, as the petitions suggest, the tide had turned against Harrison on the issue of slavery. Anti-slavery sentiment had strengthened even in the territorial legislature. John Badollet circulated a petition, referred to the legislature on October 14, 1808. It charged that the Introduction Act of 1805 was "in evasion if not in manifest violation" of the Northwest Ordinance and was approved by Governor Harrison, "the appointed guardian of that same Ordinance." A "sense of sacred duty" compelled the petitioners to condemn the act "in the most unequivocal manner." The petitioners took pains to mention that they did not "address [the assembly] as supplicants" but were seeking "the permanent prosperity, the happiness of this rising country." Slavery was, the petition charged, destroying the value of honest, free laborers in favor of slave owners and at the expense of poor men. Badollet also argued that slavery engendered a sense of "debility and fear" in a state and encouraged tyranny.[51]

Badollet's petition, as well as similar previous efforts, was gaining converts, as shown by the report of General Washington Johnson's committee of the territorial legislature, referred October 19, 1808, and printed in the *Vincennes Western Sun* on December 17, 1808.[52] The report is interesting for several reasons.

Slavery, it stated, was a "deformity not to be justified" in a country based on liberty, and those states that could safely do so "hastened to put an end to the horrid traffic." Other states had enacted laws to protect slaves and seek their gradual emancipation. Article VI had been Congress's obedience to "the impulse of justice and benevolence . . . to prevent the propagation of an evil which they could not totally eradicate." Yet the Act concerning the Introduction of negroes and Mulattos into Indiana, the report continued, blatantly violated "both the spirit and letter" of Article VI. The report also noted how ridiculous it was for a slave to be indentured, "parting with himself and receiving nothing." Slavery was morally wrong, the committee argued, and tolerating it for the purpose of "expediency" was unacceptable.[53]

The report then alluded back to the Land Ordinance of 1785, which had sought to populate the Northwest with reliable, middle-class farmers and anticipated the battle cry of antebellum Free Soilers: "The industrious will flock where industry is honorable and honored, and the man of an independent spirit where equity reigns, and where no proud nabob can cast on him a look of contempt." The report asserted that even "sordid England" was thoroughly embarrassed by slavery. The "good men" in the South were saying, "I tremble for my country when I reflect that God is just." The report obliquely acknowledged this quote from Jefferson's *Notes on the State of Virginia* as being from "a Real Friend of America."[54] Why then, the report continued, "must the Territory of Indiana take a retrograde step into barbarism and assimilate itself with Algiers and Morocco?" The reference to North Africa would have been particularly stinging, given the contemporary difficulties with the Barbary pirates.[55]

The committee members argued that extending slavery into Indiana— they did not acknowledge its preexisting status there—endangered "republican virtues" by encouraging slave owners to become physical and political tyrants. They suggested that slave owners instead migrate to the Territories of Mississippi, New Orleans, or Louisiana. Permitting slavery in Indiana, they insisted, would allow slave owners "a kind of monopoly" on future settlement, keeping "Eastern" and "Middle" states, as well as anti-slavery southerners, from forming states in other U.S. territories. The middle and eastern states were the "real strength of the Union," and opening them to slavery jeopardized domestic tranquility. The report concluded not only that the Indiana legislature should cease petitioning Congress for the modification of Article VI but that Indiana should also repeal the Act concerning Introduction and send a copy of the committee's findings to the speaker of the House.[56]

Johnston's resolution for repealing the Act concerning Introduction won over the lower house, and Harrison's picked men in the Legislative Council had to kill it. The increasingly vocal and numerous anti-slavery advocates had frightened the pro-slavery men of the Illinois country and driven them to continue petitioning for a division of the territory.[57]

The fall elections of 1808 afforded Harrison's enemies the opportunity to strike. The General Assembly forged a coalition between anti-slavery men from east of the Wabash and pro-slavery, pro-division men from Illinois. These strange bedfellows agreed on a division of the territory and free soil east of the Wabash—a nightmare for the governor. Harrison desperately tried to hold on to the council after Samuel Gwathmey, a staunch ally, resigned his seat to become the register of the land office at Jeffersonville.

The council was the governor's last line of defense against the General Assembly. Although it was illegal to hold a federally appointed office while sitting on the council, Harrison told Gwathmey to retain his seat. The governor managed to stall the lower house for a few days, but its members declared Gwathmey's seat vacant and nominated two men (including Charles Beggs, the anti-slavery leader from Clark County) for the post. Angrily, the governor and the council sought to censure the assembly, but the assembly in turn threatened to write to President Jefferson informing him that Harrison and the council were "in league" together. Harrison reluctantly accepted Gwathmey's resignation.[58]

The Gwathmey case appears illustrative of what Harrison's growing number of critics charged—that he was increasingly autocratic and willing to bend or break rules to maintain his prerogative as governor. Badollet accused Harrison of illegally stacking the legislature with appointees, a charge that, given his behavior with Gwathmey (and Jefferson's abdication of appointment power for the Legislative Council as a whole), had some merit. When Harrison apportioned the delegates for the entire legislature, Knox County (not the largest county but the most sympathetic to him) received five of the thirteen total appointments. As his opponents grew more numerous, Harrison did what he could to offset their numbers by placing his closest allies in positions of prominence, something not over-looked by his detractors.[59]

The case also demonstrates the struggle between Harrison's aristocratic, paternalistic tendencies and the increasingly participatory bent of American democracy in the early nineteenth century.[60] More anti-Harrison petitions followed, repeating the same basic charges of anti-republicanism and a violation of the anti-slavery clause of the Northwest Ordinance. Adding insult to insult, in 1809 one such petition came from the "Citizens of Harrison County."[61]

Messinger, Jones, and the other pro-division Illinoisans briefly allied with anti-slavery legislators from the eastern counties. On October 24, 1808, they elected a compromise candidate for territorial delegate to Congress, Jesse B. Thomas. Born in Maryland and reared in Kentucky, Thomas moved his law practice to Indiana in 1803. Dearborn County sent him to the legislature beginning in 1805, and he was elected speaker. Thomas's election as delegate proved how significantly Governor Harrison's political stock had fallen.

Thomas was strongly pro-slavery, but the eastern counties agreed to support him to rid themselves of the slavery-hungry Illinoisans. Thomas arrived in Washington in December 1808 and succeeded in convincing Congress to divide the territory. Division became official on March 1, 1809. Thomas had also been instructed by the Legislative Council to ask Congress to allow Indiana Territory to popularly elect both the Legislative

Council and the delegate to Congress—a sop to cries for democracy. Thomas performed this task as well, as seen in the Suffrage Act of February 27, 1809. Despite the fact that he had merely followed instructions, when he returned to the West Thomas found considerable hard feeling directed toward him from the Harrison party. Some of Harrison's supporters went so far as to publicly accuse Thomas of financial improprieties. In the *Vincennes Western Sun*, December 2, 1809, a James Dill placed a front-page editorial about Thomas:

> I take this method of reminding Judge Thomas, that although he is at more than arms length distance, and may feel himself secure on one score, yet he is not out of the reach of my pen; and that as soon as leisure serves, I shall prepare a complete history of the Judge, from the time of his Mercantile infamy until the period of his appointment on the Bench of the Illinois Territory—which shall be published for the benefit of those on whose lives and property he is appointed to decide.

Presumably, Thomas had accepted the judicial seat in Illinois with considerable relief.[62]

By mid-1809, Harrison's less numerous but still influential followers were known as the "Virginia Aristocrats," and their rivals touted themselves as the party of the people. Harrison's clique included men like Luke Decker, a Virginia planter and slave owner who had moved to the area in the early 1780s. He remained an ardent supporter of the governor throughout his tenure. Fellow Virginians Waller Taylor and Thomas Randolph, the latter a candidate for the territorial legislature, were also allied with Harrison.[63] John Badollet echoed the sentiment of many Hoosiers when he wrote Secretary Gallatin that, to avoid further political strife, the next governor should be from Pennsylvania or New York, with "no more Virginians."[64]

In Jeffersonian political climes, "aristocratic," connoting monarchist or even pro-British sympathies, was an intensely insulting term. As Nicole Etcheson noted, Harrison and other politicians took these charges very seriously and sought to dispel them as thoroughly as possible. The insult was especially acute when used publicly, as in the pages of the *Vincennes Western Sun*. In January 1809, "Citizen" wrote that "advocates of slavery" were really anti-Republican. The charge brought a vehement and sarcastic rebuttal from "Pop Gun":

[To the editor:] I wish you to let the Citizen's master piece of political composition, shine as far as the rays of the Sun—let it be published "from the house tops" in a "voice of thunder," so that the world may hear and understand it.—Let a special messenger be sent to the tombs of the departed patriots and heroes of '76 to inform them of the Citizen's new discovery of the meaning of the terms, Federalist and Republican, and injoin strict penitance for their political error.[65]

Pro-slavery men like "Pop-Gun" might allow their general morality to be questioned, but suffering an attack on their patriotism was viscerally and politically unthinkable.

Congress had granted the Illinoisans' request for division, but Harrison's opponents east of the Wabash continued to plague him, calling for greater democracy in Indiana. A petition from Clark County (with 258 signatures) asked Congress to allow them to elect local officials rather than suffer their appointment, for "the Executive may have an undue influence and prevent the wishes of the Majority from being known." A similar petition from the "Citizens of the Territory" (referred the same day) also complained that many men were denied the rights of American citizens, that is, the right to vote for local officials, while still having to pay taxes and serve in the militia.[66]

Whatever complaints some might have had about the militia, it was necessary. In the event of attack from foreign armies, Indians, or both, the militia would offer the territory's first line of defense. As the commander-in-chief of Indiana's militia and a former army captain, Harrison paid close attention to militia affairs. Frontier defense was a serious issue, even with the general peace established at Greenville in 1795. Still, arguably, Harrison would have fixated on the militia even if he had never served in the military or engaged in a single battle with Indians. Like a hunger for slaves, interest in the militia was another common trait among Virginia gentlemen.

By the mid-eighteenth century, Virginia's militia statute mimicked the gentry's ideal social order. The law was steeped in the notion of natural hierarchy. Only leading members of society held officer rank in the militia, and doing so was a considerable honor. While militia musters were infrequent, the honorifics of the officer class were not.[67] By definition, an officer was a gentleman. Francis Vigo was a debtor and therefore a potential subject of ridicule, but he was also William Henry Harrison's friend. Without fail, Governor Harrison's correspondence referred to the old man as "Col. Vigo."

Rhys Isaac has explained why members of the Virginia gentry were so preoccupied with the militia:

> The commitment of the leaders of this society to the militia and their roles in it . . . was in accord with a powerful current in eighteenth-century Anglo-American ideology. The arms-bearing English yeomanry and gentry were so closely associated with the farmer-soldiers of the venerated Roman Republic that Edward Gibbon could solemnly remark [in] his writing of the famous *Decline and Fall* that "the captain of Hampshire militia had not been useless to the historian of the Roman Empire." The internal pressures to which contemporary Virginia society was subject . . . ensured that such identification with the role of citizen as armed man was reinforced in the colony.[68]

By the mid-eighteenth century, Virginia was only periodically subject to Indian attacks, while slave revolts were a constant worry. In Indiana, there were never enough slaves to mount anything like a serious revolt, so the "Indian threat" replaced them in Harrison's mind.

The governor repeatedly prodded the General Assembly to hone and augment the militia's capabilities. In his July 29, 1805, address to the legislature he complained that the current militia law was too complex and needed revision. Yet, he continued, if the assembly members did this well, they would have nothing to fear in the event of an Indian war. The assembly responded by reviving and revising the militia law of 1799 (there was some question as to whether this law from the Northwest Territory was still in effect), approved December 5, 1806. However, it was after *Chesapeake-Leopard* that the assembly leaped to follow Harrison's admonitions.[69]

In his August 17, 1807, address to the assembly, Harrison warned the members that in times of war they must perfect the militia system and that they had not yet made good progress. He called for funds to pay for a staff officer in each county to drill the men. He complained about the lack of proper arms. Some men with ample resources shamelessly attended musters without a firearm or with one that was not serviceable. Some men practiced drill with sticks in lieu of muskets. While the governor felt public funds should provide arms for militiamen who could not afford them, he castigated those who could afford to bear arms and did not: "One of the

principal characteristics which distinguishes the citizens of a free government from the subjects of a despotic one is the right of keeping arms; and
that any American should neglect to avail himself of this valuable privilege
manifests a supineness which is highly censurable."[70]

The assembly, now stirred by events, responded in complete agreement with the governor, pledging to "endeavor to avert the great calamity
of immediately falling a sure prey to any and every savage or dastardly
foe; which would surely and inevitably be the case under our present
military or defensive arrangements." The result was the Militia Act of
1807, approved on September 17, 1807. It gave the governor practically
everything he wanted, including the exclusion of blacks from the militia.
While exempting judges of the territorial Supreme Court, the attorney
general, and licensed ministers of the gospel from militia duty, the law
set forth clear guidelines for the conduct of those on duty. Delinquencies
or dereliction of duty had a regular schedule of fines, from ten–one hundred dollars for militia colonels down to one–three dollars for privates.
Further, anyone heckling the militia when mustered could be confined
for up to six hours and fined up to four dollars. The governor could call
out the militia any time Indiana or any neighboring state was faced with
"an actual or threatened invasion"—an extraordinary amount of leeway.
Harrison now had the legal apparatus to enforce discipline and turn the
militia into a credible fighting force.[71]

Not sated with these wide-ranging powers, the governor decided to ask
for still more. In a subsequent address on September 27, 1808, he lectured
the assembly that "[t]he militia, at all times a subject of importance, is
peculiarly so at the present crisis, uncertain as we are at what moment its
services may be necessary. Constituting as it does the principal defence
of our rights and sovereignty, no labor or expense can be misapplied
which has a tendency to perfect its organization and discipline."[72]

One of the 1807 law's faults, he asserted, was that it lacked the means
to coerce officers to file regular reports. He recommended "a certain and
severe punishment to such officers, particularly the higher grades, as
shall neglect this important duty." Yet Harrison wrote these words at a
time when he felt Indian relations, especially with the Shawnee Prophet
and his followers, were improving. Only three weeks before, Harrison had
written Secretary of War Dearborn, noting the Prophet's efforts at social
reform, especially regarding alcohol: "Upon the whole Sir I am inclined

to think that the influence which the Prophet has acquired will prove rather advantageous than otherwise to the United States."[73] Why, then, did Harrison feel such urgency regarding the militia's preparedness?

Some citizens felt the governor held too much power regarding the militia and asked that the right to choose civil and militia officers be given to the voters. This criticism falls in line with the general complaint that Harrison was too concerned with his own prerogative. In fairness to him, though, Indian affairs could change quickly, and rumors of foreign intrigue and aggression still floated freely. He needed to be prepared for all contingencies. There was still another reason Harrison seemed so preoccupied with militia powers: he loved playing soldier and had ever since he was a teenage ensign. In April 1809, in the midst of yet another war scare with his Indian neighbors, Harrison wrote the new secretary of war, William Eustis: "As the two companies of militia are placed in a situation convenient to me I shall exert myself to improve the time that they may remain in service in teaching them such of the military evolutions as suits the service that they are likely to be employed in. Having spent seven years of my life in the army and very much attached to the profession this employment will be by no means unpleasant to me." For the Knox County militia, officered by Harrison's friends and allies—Francis Vigo was their colonel—the feeling was mutual. Citing Harrison's strenuous efforts on behalf of territorial defense, they sent a resolution to Congress on October 28, 1809, urging the president to reappoint the governor for another term.[74]

Despite the numerous petitions against Harrison after 1805 (and some in favor of him as well) and the venom of John Badollet and others, the governor's support at the federal level during both the Jefferson and Madison presidencies remained unshakeable. Petitions of support were helpful. But ultimately Harrison depended not on his neighbors but on the president for his job, and he was reappointed in December 1806 and again in December 1809. Perhaps in part this reflected a respect for Harrison's distinguished family's patriotism and service to Virginia and the nation. Perhaps Harrison's pro-slavery machinations did not upset, or even met with unspoken approval from, these Virginian presidents with conflicted views on the subject. More likely, though, it was Harrison's Indian policy that kept him in office and served as a life raft for his popularity both in Washington and the West.[75]

Portrait of Anthony Wayne. One of Harrison's early benefactors, Wayne taught him how to conduct both successful wilderness campaigns and Indian treaties. Harrison's rare failures in both areas usually resulted from not following Wayne's example. Courtesy of the Filson Historical Society.

Portrait of James Wilkinson. Immoral and often treacherous, Wilkinson nevertheless tried to shield Harrison from trouble in his early army career and later sought his aid in the Burr Conspiracy. Courtesy of the Filson Historical Society.

Rembrandt Peale's portrait of William Henry Harrison. The best likeness of the young governor, the portrait was altered (somewhat clumsily) after the War of 1812 by adding a military uniform and sword. Courtesy of the Grouseland Foundation, Inc.

Portrait of Anna Symmes Harrison. This portrait shows Harrison's beloved wife in her later years. Courtesy of the Cincinnati Historical Society.

LITTLE TURTLE.

Portrait of Little Turtle. The Miami chief's career is encompassed by his jewelry: the bear claw necklace symbolized his youth as a courageous warrior and hunter, while the peace medal represented the mature man who opted to negotiate with the United States to survive. Courtesy of the Indiana Historical Society.

TENS-QUA-TA-WA

or THE ONE THAT OPENS THE DOOR

Shawnese Prophet

Brother of Tecumthe

Painted for Gov. Lewis Cass by J. O. Lewis at Detroit 1823

Portrait of the Shawnee Prophet, 1824. Tecumseh's younger brother led a religious revival that sought to restore Indian spiritual power. Harrison saw him as "an engine set to work by the British." Courtesy of the Indiana Historical Society.

TECUMTHA.

Portrait of Tecumseh. Known as the LeDru-Lossing portrait of the chief, this is the closest to an authenticated portrait of Tecumseh that survives. Harrison admired the great chief as a rival, but he had no intention of letting him stop purchases of Indian land. Courtesy of the Indiana Historical Society.

Grouseland. Rescued and beautifully restored by the Knox County DAR and now maintained by the Grouseland Foundation, Inc., Governor Harrison's home projected his financial and social capital in a relative wilderness. Courtesy of the Grouseland Foundation, Inc.

Mary Adams's court case. As seen in this document, ca. 1805, the prefabricated legal forms of Indiana Territory needed adjustments in cases where men sued women. Note the scribbled changes, adding "s" to "he" and the like, especially in lines 11, 15, 21, 23; see Chapter 6. Knox County Court Files, Box 9, folder 703, McGrady-Brockman House, Vincennes, Indiana. Photo by author.

The Murder of Jane McCrea. What John Vanderlyn's 1804 painting lacked in subtlety and verifiable accuracy, it made up for with visceral impact. The image helped reinforce common American attitudes about Indians and, by extension, their British allies. Courtesy of the Wadsworth Atheneum Museum of Art, Hartford, Connecticut. Purchased by subscription.

The William Henry Harrison Monument, North Bend, Ohio. The late governor and president now rests just west of Cincinnati, in an impressive tomb overlooking the Ohio River. Photo by author.

CHAPTER 6

A Frontier Society

Indiana, 1800–1812

Indiana grew both demographically and economically during William Henry Harrison's tenure as governor. In 1800, what became Indiana Territory—initially including what would later become Indiana, Illinois, Michigan, and Wisconsin—had a non-Indian population of 6,550. In what became Illinois and Indiana there were 5,641 non-Indians, about half east and half west of the Wabash River. Following the separation of Illinois from Indiana in 1809, the Illinois country had about 11,000 non-Indians, and Indiana had about 17,000. The population of free blacks, black servants, and slaves had increased slightly but still remained a low single-digit percentage of the total population. By 1810, Indiana Territory had assumed the boundaries of the present state.[1]

The most dramatic change had come in the field of industry. Within Indiana Territory's borders—actually in the southern half, as the north remained Indian country—was a cotton mill producing $150 worth of cotton cloth annually, a nail machine producing 20,000 pounds of nails each year, 18 leather tanneries, and 28 distilleries producing 35,950 gallons of whiskey annually. Mills ground 40,900 bushels of wheat, and 14 sawmills produced 390,000 feet of lumber each year. Homemade goods were still of primary importance, though. The territory boasted 1,380 spinning wheels—Harrison's Grouseland housed two, as well as a loom. In their homes women produced 54,977 yards of cotton cloth, 92,740 yards of linen, and 19,378 yards of woolen products each year. Indiana had also attempted to enact one of President Jefferson's goals to promote health and civil order by developing only alternate lots in a township, leaving the others for parks and gardens and thereby, it was hoped, reducing the spread of infectious disease. The experiment, which Governor Harrison unsubtly christened Jeffersonville, was located on the Ohio River across from Louisville, Kentucky. Interestingly, the citizenry of Jeffersonville abandoned the alternating lots format in 1810, when Jefferson was no longer president.[2]

EVERYDAY LIFE IN EARLY INDIANA

As they do today, newspapers served as a source of information and entertainment in the early nineteenth century. In its first years, Indiana had to make do with only one local paper. Founded by Elihu Stout, the weekly *Indiana Gazette* began its run in the summer of 1804. A six-month subscription cost $2.50, with a one-year minimum. Subscribers had to pick up their papers—no delivery was included. Reflecting the cash-poor nature of a frontier society, Stout offered to take "BEEF, PORK, BACON, CORN, COTTON, WHISKEY, WHEAT, SUGAR, POTATOES, BUTTER, EGGS, CHICKENS, TOBACCO, TALLOW, FLOUR or OATS" in lieu of cash payment. Advertisements of modest length cost $1.50 and could be carried repeatedly for an additional 25 cents per week.[3]

To entertain subscribers, Stout featured a "Humor" column, from which came these "jokes": August 7, 1805, "An Irishman confessed he had stolen some Chocolate.—'And what did you do with it?' asked the confessor,— 'Father,' said he 'I made TEA of it.'" August 14, 1805, "A late advertiser for a house in some public part of the town, stipulates that it will be near either to a tinman's or blacksmith's shop—that the ringing of their hammers and anvils may drown the more unpleasant sound of his wife's tongue!"[4]

Astonishingly, the *Gazette*'s demise arose not from such painfully un-funny jokes but from a fire that destroyed the press in 1806. Undaunted, Stout rode to Kentucky, bought a new press, had it shipped up the Wabash to Vincennes, and founded the *Vincennes Western Sun*, serving again as editor. Although not always published regularly, the *Sun* became the closest thing to a regular newspaper most Hoosiers would see, and it remained the only paper printed in Indiana until after the War of 1812.[5]

The *Sun* ran ads for other reading material, including *The Real Principles of Roman Catholics in Reference to God & the Country* by Rev. Stephen Theodore Badin—which does not appear to have been a flattering account of the

Church—as well as bound copies of the laws of the territory, available for
$3.50. Like most American newspapers, the front page was usually devoted
to the latest news from the Napoleonic Wars or perhaps presidential
proclamations. In March 1808 the paper included a list of the books
available in the Vincennes Library. The library, open to subscribers only
and not the general public, was described as "a measure of public utility,
emanating from the most benevolent and patriotic motives." The library
featured 210 books, including Jefferson's *Notes on the State of Virginia*, volumes
of Shakespeare, and the published edition of Washington's *Letters.*[6]

The *Sun* further served as an organ for people, especially politicians,
to conspicuously display their patriotic fervor. The Fourth of July occasioned great parties sponsored by prominent men, and the numerous
toasts offered were printed in the next available issue of the *Sun.* Toasts
were usually polite and patriotic, honoring Washington, Jefferson, and
the other soldiers and statesmen of the Revolution. An 1807 party thrown
by Governor Harrison toasted, among others, "Our Indian neighbours—
may the benevolent design of our government to tame their savage
natures, be crowned with the success it merits," and "The people of the
U.S., the only free people upon the earth." By 1809 the tone was somewhat
less congenial, as one party featured a jibe at Harrison's chief political rival,
Jonathan Jennings: "Jonathan Jennings—may his want of talents be the sure
means to defeat the anti-republican schemes of his party." Another party
that same day was attended by a Delaware chief named Captain Bullitt,
who offered the much more cordial toast of "[h]ealth and prosperity to
the gentlemen present."[7]

Patriotic celebrations, especially in such public settings, carried deep
meaning. Americans born during the Revolutionary period and shortly
after had to navigate a world in some ways far different from what their
parents had known. Their generation had never been asked to renounce
loyalty to a sovereign, and their enthusiasm for Fourth of July picnics and
the like was terribly important, as such events made a point of reaffirming
their patriotic reverence for the founders.[8]

Beginning in late November 1809, the *Sun* began running an ad close
to many Americans' hearts. The ad lamented that no proper memorial
to the late President Washington had yet been erected: "How then, fellow
Countrymen, have ye permitted two whole years to pass since the noble

and natural resolution [of Congress to build such a monument] was everywhere, individually formed; and the traveller still to ask in vain,— Where is the National Monument, sacred to public and private virtue; to the manes of the illustrious **WASHINGTON**?"[9]

The ad chided Americans for their procrastination and suggested forming a committee to oversee the project, as no official design had been set. In a move both democratizing and patriotic (or xenophobic), the ad stipulated that none but American citizens should be allowed to donate funds, and not more than a dollar each—the price of one of the stones proposed to be used. The ad concluded, "A Book is opened at the house of Governor Harrison, where all who feel a veneration for the IMMORTAL HERO will voluntarily repair, and add one stone to the pile."[10] Washington's legacy belonged to all Americans, not just the wealthy. Not only did the ad affirm Harrison's own patriotism, but holding the subscription book at his home would allow him to keep tabs on those who were true patriots and those who were not.

As demonstrated by the *Western Sun*, patriotism infused almost all activities of frontier Americans in the early Republic. Fourth of July toasts and monuments to George Washington were obvious examples, but even a library's purpose was alloyed with "patriotic motives." Public good was largely synonymous with patriotism.

Indiana's citizens also sought to improve their children's educational opportunities. While the Ordinance of 1787 had made some provisions for the maintenance of public schools, the citizenry of Vincennes went further, founding Vincennes University in 1807. The university's board featured many of the leading men of Indiana, including Governor Harrison and his political enemies John Rice Jones and John Badollet. The university was to teach "Latin, Greek, French and English Languages, Mathematics, Natural Philosophy, Ancient and Modern History, Moral Philosophy, Logic, Rhetoric, and the Law of Nature and Nations." The four professors allotted were also to teach any Indian boys whose parents could be induced to send them there and to found a school for girls. Despite these admirable goals, funding remained a constant problem, and Vincennes University folded in 1824. (It was later revived.) The act to create a library company in 1806 had somewhat better luck, but the Vincennes Library remained small prior to 1812.[11]

Although growing in population, in the first decade of the nineteenth century Indiana remained a frontier area. Both Indiana and Illinois still offered a bounty on "wolf scalps," for example.[12] While they have disadvantages, frontiers also offer opportunities to those who might be stifled in more established communities. Men like William Henry Harrison, as discussed previously, left the original thirteen states for a fresh start in the West. To a lesser extent, the relative labor shortage on the frontier provided women with a sliver of economic opportunity. The Great Lakes–Ohio Valley region had a number of Indian women taking an active role in commerce, especially the fur trade. Occasionally, white women could break out of the purely domestic economic and social spheres they normally inhabited, to a degree. At least one trader wrote to Francis Vigo's wife rather than to Vigo regarding business. One woman, the widow Sally Lusk, succeeded in securing a license to operate a ferry on the Ohio River—a lucrative plum from Indiana's patriarchal governor.[13] But most women, regardless of social station, worked in their home or in the homes of others as servants.

Cash-poor societies are often financially unstable, and this was certainly true for Indiana. As described earlier, Governor Harrison himself had a difficult time avoiding debt, and the immense cost of building Grouseland did not help. In 1804 Harrison admitted to an old friend in Cincinnati that he was "engaged in building a large House which will I fear prove rather too expensive for my finances. However the trouble and three fourths of the expense will be at an end in a few days."[14]

Harrison correctly gauged that the home was too extravagant for his means, but he incorrectly predicted that the worst was over. By late 1804 he was complaining to his friend Senator Worthington about his low salary. He made the same complaint to President Jefferson in June 1805. Reining in his spending does not seem to have been considered. In December 1808, Harrison felt compelled to write Nathaniel Ewing, the receiver at the Vincennes land office, asking for a loan of a "few Hundred dollars." In August 1809 Harrison asked Secretary of the Treasury Albert Gallatin for additional compensation of $500 for having served capably as the superintendent of the U.S. saline works in what is now Gallatin County, Illinois. While Harrison felt undercompensated for this task, he also felt the need to assure the public that he had not personally profited from it, and he had its three lessees—James Morrison, Charles Wilkins, and Jonathan Taylor—sign an affidavit to that effect in 1809.[15]

Harrison had reason to complain about the salary. At the time of his appointment, it was worth a little less than $29,000 in 2004 dollars. The dollar fluctuated considerably in the decade before 1812: although he would not have known it, Harrison's peak buying power came in 1802, when his salary equated to nearly $34,000 in 2004 dollars. By 1812, inflation (Harrison did not receive a raise during his entire tenure as governor) had lowered it to the equivalent of just $27,000.[16] True, Harrison did not have to worry about annual income taxes. But other officeholders, such as the president, received a salary ($25,000) that, while some thought it low, would be on a par with that of his modern counterpart. And compared even to his best financial year, the governor of the vast frontier territory and commissioner plenipotentiary for Indian Affairs north of the Ohio River would be much better off today working for the Post Office.

Despite his efforts to secure help and reimbursements, Harrison's financial woes continued. The June 23, 1812, issue of the *Vincennes Western Sun* featured a list of all those whose lands were to be sold for nonpayment of taxes in 1810–1811. The list included the names of many prominent and respected Indiana citizens, including their governor, who had to part with eight hundred acres of land.[17] There was nothing unusual about Harrison's preoccupation with financial matters. And his nearly desperate need to *seem* well-off, to conspicuously consume, was especially common among Virginia's gentlemen planters and their offspring. Still, he was chronically short of cash. He had considerable company in that respect, as many fellow settlers, as well as their Indian neighbors, experienced financial troubles on the frontier.

Francis Vigo's debt to Detroit trader John Askin had become unmanageable by 1806, and Governor Harrison took it upon himself to intervene. Harrison asked William McIntosh, Askin's lawyer, to postpone the execution of Vigo's settlement, that is, to hold off confiscating his property. McIntosh, however, held to the strict letter of the law, saying he could not delay the settlement, although he stated his hope that "your laudable efforts for your Friend may be successful." He also promised the governor not to let any of Vigo's confiscated property be sold just yet. Harrison then wrote Askin and requested, as a personal favor, that Askin let Vigo pay off some of his debt with land rather than cash. Askin agreed, and Harrison wrote again in thanks, repeating his offer to be of service to Askin if the occasion arose.[18]

Harrison also tried to obtain work for old friends or those for whom he felt compassion. He wrote to surveyor Jared Mansfield on April 24, 1806, recommending "Old Soldier" Capt. John McKinney as deputy surveyor for the District of St. Charles. "Governor Greenup & other Respectable Characters in Kentucky" had spoken highly of McKinney, Harrison noted, "& I am persuaded that you will agree with me in the opinion that those who have suffered in the public service have a good claim to Such employments under Government as they are Capable of filling." The governor could also hinder one's career with a letter. Rufus Easton complained that Harrison had cost him a seat on the General Court of Louisiana with letters to Treasury Secretary Gallatin and Louisiana's governor, General James Wilkinson.[19] Part of Harrison's job, as he saw it, was to judge who needed his help and who did not.

With a sympathy born of both empathy and noblesse oblige, Harrison sought legislation to ease the lot of Indiana's poorer citizenry. In 1808 he criticized a tax on milk cows, stating that milk was a main food source for the poor. Similarly, he challenged a tax on workhorses as overly burdensome for working men.[20] The fact that he comprehended the regressive nature of such taxes was fairly enlightened for one of Harrison's social standing. It might also have reflected political pandering to the working class, as by 1808 his political situation had become increasingly tenuous. Harrison's concerns for the common man were consistent with his early political career, though, which had included the reform of land purchase laws. The governor wanted to remain in charge and felt he had a God-given right to do so. He also wanted to help less fortunate Americans, both out of a sense of public service and because making settlement easier aided his overall agenda of land acquisition.[21]

Grudgingly, old guard aristocrats like Governor Harrison allowed common free white men to have access to political decision making. The direct participation of others, though—free blacks, women, and American Indians—seemed unthinkable. Like most politicians in this era of paternalism, from the president on down, they were charged with protecting the common folk from themselves. Republican leaders championed the right of the male citizenry to speak to the government but often could not resist telling them what they ought to say. When it came to "the American fair," political leaders did not think twice about their presumptuousness.

Girls were to learn to read and write and master basic figuring, as well as manners and etiquette—skills they would need to be good mothers. Classical philosophy and languages, history, and the natural sciences, however, were strictly for males. When Harrison ally Isaac White wrote his will, he instructed that his son George "have a classical education; that he may be taught fencing and dancing; and that he may be sent one year to a Military School; and that after he be so taught, he be allowed a profession or occupation that he himself may choose. It is further my will that my daughters Harriet and Juliet have a good English education."[22]

Discerning just how this dynamic played out in Indiana Territory is difficult, as few women's diaries or letters survive from the period. We do have information on one Indiana woman who seems to have been a prototype of what historians later dubbed the Republican Mother: Anna Symmes Harrison, the governor's wife. By 1811 Anna and William Henry Harrison had eight children, including five sons of whom the governor was especially proud. They would eventually have ten children. Anna had servants and slaves at Grouseland, to be sure, but all available data suggest she took an active role in parenting and doted on her children. Her surviving letters focus exclusively on her family and her relatives—news about health, births, and similar topics—and make no direct commentary on contemporary politics or other social issues. She was fairly religious and faced life rather stoically. In 1808 she wrote to console her nephew on the loss of his mother, expressing her condolences and adding, "But we must as much as is possible for us, submit to the all wise Creator of things and endevour [sic] to make our selves suitable objects of his care for he has said that to those who love and fear him all things shall be ordered for their good."[23]

Without the benefit of much correspondence from women in Indiana, one resorts to court records, where women invariably appear. The court files from Harrison's Knox County provide a fascinating glimpse of Indiana's citizenry in their daily interactions and some interesting examples of how women moved in what was still largely a man's world.[24] Legally still the responsibility of their husbands and fathers—*feme covert*, or coverture—women occasionally acted for themselves in a wide variety of legal proceedings. One of the more common reasons women (and men) appeared in court was trespass on the case.[25]

In territorial Indiana at least, trespass on the case seems to have been a catchall complaint levied for a host of transgressions, the most common being nonpayment of a financial debt. Many people on the frontier fell to such a fate, and widows were especially at risk if their husbands died suddenly without their affairs in order.

While trespass on the case often meant a routine case of unpaid debt, it could also mean one involving other damages, including slander or even physical abuse. As Mary Beth Norton has asserted, whereas men had other options, women denied direct political rights could use slander and not much else to attack opponents. In a small community like territorial Indiana—as it had in eighteenth-century Virginia—one's reputation mattered a great deal in day-to-day transactions, both financial and social. Those without personal honor would be considered poor candidates for essential financial credit. Women felt the sting of slander and gossip directed at them but could give as much pain as they received in many instances.[26]

Nancy Lasley sued John Reed for $16—no reason given—in a case that stretched from February 1802 to August 1803. So many appeals were filed that after paying the sheriff, jury, crier, and others involved, the total cost came to $24.62, suggesting that Nancy's case and John's recalcitrance had more to do with personal enmity than with economics. Whatever the charge was, a jury decided John was innocent, and Nancy had to pay his court costs, although "in mercy &c.," John paid the jury fees.[27]

Slander could and did involve couples as well as individuals, as illustrated by the 1806 saga of Edmond and Rachel Rittenhouse versus Etheldred T. Bass and his wife, Catherine. Witness testimony asserted that both Basses had spoken "scandalous words" about Rachel, specifically that she stole "wool, cotton, linsy, stockings, and sugar." At the witness's suggestion of a compromise, Rittenhouse refused, saying the costs would "amount to the Value of a Cow." According to Justice of the Peace George Leech, "Said Rittenhouse's Wife appeared Very Desirous that her Husband Would

Dismiss the suit—and said she would not have her charracter [sic] tore to pieces in such a manner as it would be at court for the price of two or three Cows." Rittenhouse ended up settling out of court by paying Bass's court costs.[28] Both Rachel and Edmond Rittenhouse knew the alleged slander against her carried a financial as well as an emotional price tag. They did not initially agree as to which was more costly.

The July 1809 term saw the case of John Stork, on a charge of assault and battery against Baptiste Chevallier that April. In a demonstration of *feme covert,* John was actually in court because his wife, Catharine, had allegedly assaulted Chevallier. The all-male jury found Catharine innocent, however.[29]

Women were definitely making legal headway by the turn of the nineteenth century, but they still labored under the patriarchal yoke of coverture. When Thomas Chisley sued Mary Adams, for example, he did so because Mary had not paid him for fifty-two dollars worth of washing, ironing, goods, and merchandise his wife had provided. The court agreed that, strictly speaking, Adams owed the money to Thomas Chisley, not his wife. Yet on the pre-printed form, the clerk wrote "s" in front of "he" and "her" over each "him" in reference to Mary. The court was not accustomed to men suing women who were not serving as executrices of their husbands' estates but was willing to improvise when necessary.

In the end, women in early Indiana, although slowly edging their way into the legal process, had to rely on the patriarchal rule of law for protection. In March 1811 the court issued a summons for Isaac Decker. Susan Catt was suing Decker for trespass on the case in the amount of $500. Why? Despite Decker's repeated promises to marry Susan, he was "intending craftily and subtilly [sic] to deceive and defraud said Susan." He did not marry her but "did debauch the said Susan and get her with child." Decker then abandoned her and married another woman, "wherefore the said Susan saith she is injured and hath damage." The court agreed and ordered Decker to pay Susan $500.[30]

The problem confronting women in this scenario was that they were at the relative mercy of men who, reared in an era of patriarchy, were reluctant to release the reins of control. Governor Harrison certainly sought to protect (but also to control) what he saw as the weaker sex.

In 1807 Harrison addressed the General Assembly on a number of issues that directly affected women. He suggested an amendment to the marriage law of 1806 that would require marriage license applicants to post bond and security to ensure that they were not about to commit bigamy, so as to "save many unsuspecting females, from being made the victims of their credulity." Harrison's notion exemplified the best possible face of paternalism: he was legitimately trying to protect women, yet he was also implicitly insulting their faculties. The legislators did not follow this request, but they did pass a tough anti-bigamy law, with penalties of a $100–$500 fine and 100–300 lashes for convicted offenders. Harrison and the assembly also agreed to relax the guidelines for proving rape to make prosecuting offenders easier.[31]

Harrison was more patriarchal regarding divorce. It was an area where he and other patriotic men of his generation behaved more as throwbacks to their British heritage than as post-Revolutionary Americans. Prior to the Revolution, only the New England colonies allowed for "absolute divorce," that is, a legal separation that allowed each party to then marry another. After the war, every state legislature except South Carolina passed statutes allowing for some form of absolute divorce. While allowable grounds were "quite limited . . . public and legal recognition that there were circumstances justifying absolute divorce constituted an important break with past English practice." In the early Republic, divorce statutes proved the only major change in marital rights from the British system.[32]

But divorce was often very difficult and expensive to effect. As in Britain, some states left divorce to their legislative bodies rather than the courts, making divorce almost exclusively a privilege of the wealthy and connected. "No-fault" divorce did not yet exist—someone had to be legally proven guilty of wrongdoing. Rather than go through so much money and heartache, many unhappy spouses simply abandoned their betrothed for another.[33] The newspapers, particularly on the frontier, regularly featured "runaway-wife ads." An April 25, 1795, ad from one Zekiel Fuller was typical: "Notice, Is hereby given to all whom it may concern, that Elizabeth Fuller (my wife) has absented from my bed without any provication, and has since taken up with another man. This is therefore to forewarn all persons to trust her any thing upon my account, as I will pay no debts of her contracting."[34]

Such notices served two purposes: to protect the estranged husband from new debts racked up by his absented wife and, not unlike some runaway slave and servant ads, to publicly humiliate the offending party. Regarding the first purpose, wives were not legally responsible for their (living) husbands' debts and almost never took out corresponding ads when their husbands left. But a few absconded wives did feel the need to respond to the aspersions cast on their character. A Betsy Hendrickson told her side in a December 7, 1811, rebuttal ad:

> WHEREAS my man Henry Hendrickson, has paid me the compliment of putting my name in the public newspapers, I think it a duty I owe to myself to return the compliment—he has stated that I left his bed and board without just cause, which is a lie in two respects— first I can prove that he forced me away; secondly, I had occasion to go away if he had not sent me away. He, the said henry went away from his own country for reasons to dilicate [sic] for me to relate, took up his abode in this place, he sent for me to come to him sundry times, at length I come to him thro' much hardship, but alas, what did I find, his constant practice was hugging and kissing Dick Willey's wife—and if I am not mistaken, there is more that all will be tried to be proved. Much more ought to be published, which I must not—but I mean to have a hearing at court, then we shall see whether I am right or wrong.[35]

One son of a Virginia planter, Thomas Jefferson, had decided prior to the Revolution that women should have recourse to divorce. His main reservations lay in how property would be divided and whether women "beyond a certain age" would be able to remarry. Yet it was definitely a "remedy" for women.[36] Governor Harrison saw divorce in a considerably harsher light, even questioning its ethical propriety. When one was granted, he insisted that it only encouraged others to try to dissolve their marriages: "[T]he advantages which a few individuals may derive from the dissolution of this solemn contract, are too dearly purchased by its injurious effects upon the morals of the community. The scenes which are frequently exhibited in trials of this kind are shocking to humanity; the ties of consanguinity and nature are loosened." Children testified against parents, ties of affection were "destroyed," family secrets were revealed, and "human nature is exhibited in its worst colours."[37]

Harrison's points ring true enough, but the observation that divorce also weakens patriarchy is equally true. Harrison compared divorce rates in the virtuous Roman Republic to those in the decadent Roman Empire—he never tired of Classical analogies—and expressed his fear that easily available divorces would lead to frequent questions of rightful paternity. Harrison's concerns about paternity, even with legally married women, smacks of the patriarch's paranoia in his native Virginia, as discussed by Kathleen M. Brown.[38] One can also detect a subtle reference to contemporary views of republicanism. Harrison seemed to see the virtue of the Roman Republic as parallel to that of the young United States. Americans could expect to become like the wicked Roman (or British) Empire, "when their manners became corrupted by luxury [and] divorces were so common."[39]

For Americans in the early Republic, even when discussing ostensibly domestic issues like divorce laws, the overriding theme of Anglophobia lay just beneath the surface. The novel *Ameilia; or, the Faithless Briton*, published in Boston in 1798, was a cautionary tale about bigamy. The villain, a British army officer, deceived a virtuous young American girl into a fake marriage, then got her pregnant.[40] For Harrison and other Jeffersonian Americans, the potential taint of Britain and its threat to American morality and survival remained ever-present.

Harrison then mentioned the debate over divorce applications in his other favorite republic, Virginia, noting that until recently the state had seen only two applications for divorce, with one granted. Although the divorce granted had obvious merit, "it was nevertheless opposed by some of the most enlightened patriots of the state, upon the principle, that it was better for an individual *to suffer some inconvenience* [italics added], than that an example should be established, so injurious (as they supposed) to the morals of the community."[41]

The governor was rather behind the times on this score. The concept that marriages might legally end because of "gross violations of the marriage contract" was well established by the time of Indiana Territory's creation. Still, he thought the legislature was a far more suitable place than a courtroom to settle the issue. The legislature did not agree and passed no new law regarding divorce. Yet even Harrison did not deny the need for some mechanism to end a truly dreadful marriage.[42]

In 1808 Harrison and the assembly did pass a special act to grant a divorce to the unfortunate Catherine Moore, dissolving her union with a deadbeat husband who had "not only run through her property, and ill treated her, but likewise deserted her." The act further clarified that

Catherine's subsequent marriage, to the now deceased Robert K. Moore, with whom she had a son, was legal and the son legitimate.[43]

Governor Harrison's views on divorce reveal him as the product of his upbringing, in a time and place where men were honor-bound to protect women and children but not to actually listen to or consult with them. Protection in this context implied control as well. Harrison and the assembly were also just generally in favor of the institution of marriage. As in colonial Virginia and elsewhere, they saw it as having a calming, civilizing effect on men. Therefore, to encourage them to settle down, Harrison and the assembly subjected bachelors in the territory to a county tax.[44]

Still, Anna Harrison provides an interesting twist to the subject of patriarchy in the early Republic. Had she not rejected her father's decree, recall, she never would have married Lieutenant Harrison in the first place. Anna's marriage, as Andrew Cayton asserted, was a small act of defiance against traditional patriarchal prerogative.[45] Anna was a Patriot, not a rebel, however. She was a typical, conventional, free woman of her generation.

Stoic and accepting, Anna was not entirely meek. In addition to defying her father by marrying Lieutenant Harrison, she did not hesitate to scold the judge when he put off visiting the family at Vincennes: "I must write you a few lines . . . to make one more request and indeed Papa I know not how to take a denial[.] I well remember how very indulgent you ever were to me before I was Married and I cannot help thinking Papa that now you treat me unkindly not to comply with the many requests that I have made for you to visit us at this place."[46]

Like many men of his generation, Judge Symmes hated the idea of not being able to control his daughters. Still, he could not deny that they had grown into good people and that they were fine women of the Republic. In March 1808 he had written to his stubborn daughter in Vincennes, noting, "I pray God that all my Grandsons may prove to be valuable men, & all my Granddaughters, women of the first character for prudence and discretion, and copy after their dear mothers in modesty and industry."[47] In her own child rearing, Anna Harrison certainly succeeded.

Divorce was but one example of a private matter being seen as a public concern. For leaders in the early Republic, morals seemed tantamount to a public health issue. The Revolutionary generation had held this same view, feeling "that a republican polity required popular virtue for its stability and success."[48] In November 1806, Harrison railed against intemperance in Indiana, seeing it as a weakness of the soul and not just of the flesh: "The virtue of its Citizens is the only Support of a Republican Government—destroy this, and our country will become a prey to the first daring and ambitious Chief which it shall produce." Harrison may have been thinking of Aaron Burr when he delivered those lines.[49] Divorce and dis-unionism were not the only threats to American virtue for public officials to contend with.

Harrison's tenure as governor happened to fall in the midst of what was easily the most high-spirited generation in American history. In the period 1790 to 1830, Americans consumed about twice the amount of alcohol per capita each year as they do today, and alcohol was seen as a serious threat to one's ethics. In 1807 the Indiana General Assembly devoted an entire act to preventing "Vice and Immorality." The law set up a system of fines for violating the Sabbath, taking the Lord's name in vain, public drunkenness, cock fighting, gambling, and boxing. That same day the assembly had made "sodomy, or the infamous crime against nature," punishable by a $50–$500 fine *and* a 1–5-year prison term *and* a whipping of 100–500 stripes.[50] Governor Harrison and the legislature saw it as their duty to manage and safeguard public morality for the sake of the Republic. Allowing the United States to falter constituted negligence toward the living and sacrilege toward the dead.[51]

THE DUEL

While a quiet home life and security were common goals for Indiana's citizenry, the high proportion of restless, aggressive young men in the territory prior to the War of 1812 helped maintain an air of volatility. In addition to the violence still occasionally perpetrated by whites against Indians and, more rarely, vice versa, Indiana also saw mayhem among its own citizens. The most notable form of such violence was the duel.

Edward L. Ayers has written that dueling became prevalent in the United States during the American Revolution, when popularized by European officers serving in North America. Dueling took such strong root in America because it fed off of the older concept of honor, defined as "a system of values within which you have exactly as much worth as others confer upon you." In this ethos, only free white men could achieve honor—not women, children, or people of color—and even free white men had to actively defend their honor against all affronts. Attacking a man's honor was to say he was not really a man and was tantamount to assaulting him physically. In the South especially, the concept of honor encouraged men to rash and impetuous actions where prestige was concerned. Southerners were the first Americans to colonize Indiana, but honor was not exclusive to the South in the first decade of the nineteenth century. Much like the South, Indiana was a sparsely populated frontier setting where local reputations were all-important. "Honor and 'public opinion' came to seem synonymous" and were recognized by all social classes.[52]

Well-established men rarely colonized new places, and frontiers appealed to those with something to prove. The uncertain state of a man's social standing on the frontier and the prevalence of alcohol exacerbated the potentially dangerous situation created by the concept of public honor. When ambitious young men began to see dueling as a means to display their worth and courage, the situation invited short tempers and public challenges. Politics proved particularly dangerous, as men of middling pedigree sought to distance themselves from their peers to claim instant prestige.[53] William Henry Harrison detested dueling. He thought it was barbaric generally, and he probably saw it as the squabbling of lesser men trying to achieve what he felt was his birthright. But for other men, the duel constituted an obligation, an opportunity, or both.

At first glance a mindless explosion of ungoverned passions, dueling was—even in the very early nineteenth century—more ritual than brawl. As Ayers noted, only a few specific trigger words, especially insults, would bring one on. Many potential incidents ended without bloodshed or dishonor for either party, assuming the proper etiquette was followed. Questioning a man's honesty, patriotism, or courage would surely encourage a duel, provided the insult was obviously deliberate. This was almost universally understood in societies that practiced dueling. America's innovation proved to be the published insult, or "card," referring to another's misdeeds and low character. By putting his card in a newspaper, a man displayed to a wide audience the fact that he possessed honor and was ready to defend it publicly. Well-established men with high status in their communities rarely felt the need to go to such lengths—Governor

Harrison never did. But for a young newcomer hoping to climb the social ladder, a public challenge to his honor might, in an odd way, be welcomed for the opportunity it presented.[54]

The September 30, 1809, *Vincennes Western Sun* printed an early form of the dueling card regarding a dispute between Isaac White, Governor Harrison's appointee to administer the U.S. saltworks in what is now Gallatin County, Illinois, and one Adrian Davanport. When Governor Harrison appointed White, a fellow transplanted Virginian, it was a very lucrative act of patronage. Davanport had alleged "mal conduct" on White's part in running the saline works. The charge was serious, as the saltworks proved a very profitable business. White accumulated thousands of acres of prime land prior to his death, and he may have been illegally subleasing the works for profit. Or he may have simply been the victim of a patronage "out's" jealousy toward a patronage "in" with a high-paying job. At any rate, White found the charge serious enough to take the matter public, via the newspaper.[55]

White wrote of his fear that some of the *Sun*'s readers might have heard and even believed charges of fraud against him. He asserted that after failing to secure an investigation into his conduct to clear his name he sued Davanport, whom "I heard should have said a great many things, calculated to injure my character, and remove me from office." Yet when the two men met face-to-face, Davanport gave White a written statement about White's character that salved the latter's feelings. White asked for Davanport's statement to also be printed in the paper. Davanport described the dispute with White as "an unfortunate difference" and admitted that he might have made "some hasty expressions concerning him calculated to injure his character." Davanport only did so, he contended, because he surmised that White had treated him unfairly as the saltworks' agent. He did not back down completely on the idea that White was "prejudiced" against him: "But I have always said, and still say, that there is not a man within my knowledge, who is more to be depended on. And I do consider him to be a man of integrity."[56] That was good enough for White, and the two men, both captains in the militia, avoided unnecessary violence.

The money surrounding the salines continued to attract trouble for White, though. On May 25, 1811, he faced a Captain Butler, who "gave the first insult, and on my retorting he challenged me. I accepted it."

They met on an island in the Ohio River outside Shawneetown. The conditions of the duel were horse pistols at six paces. White had written his wife two days earlier stating that he did not expect to survive, and he sent his will with the letter. Butler, who either had not known or pretended to have forgotten the distance and weapons involved, protested that the duel would be murderous rather than honorable. White insisted that they proceed, but Butler left. White had maintained his honor and saved his own skin with his bravado. Understandably happy to be alive, White, now a colonel in the militia, nevertheless insisted on accompanying Governor Harrison's military expedition against the Shawnee Prophet a few months later.[57]

White and Butler had met just outside the territory's borders to avoid prosecution for dueling. Typically, Indiana duelists would cross the Ohio to Kentucky, and vice versa. The most famous Kentuckian to duel in Indiana was Henry Clay, then a member of the Kentucky House of Representatives. The up-and-coming legislator got into a heated dispute with fellow representative Humphrey Marshall in late 1808 over the passage of a resolution calling on the legislature to wear domestic manufactures beginning the next July. (It was not unusual for affairs of honor to stem from incidents that seemed trifling on the surface.) They published their respective cards on January 4, 1809, and met below Silver Creek near Jeffersonville, Indiana, on January 18. In the aftermath, the rules of the engagement and its results were also published.

They fired pistols at ten paces—three separate times. In the first two rounds, Marshall missed completely, while Clay managed only to graze his opponent's belly. With the third shot, Marshall hit Clay in the thigh, and Clay missed Marshall completely. Clay insisted on a fourth round, but the seconds felt his wound placed him at a disadvantage, and his request was denied. The account mentioned, as a point of honor, that both men had behaved coolly in the affair. Neither was chastised for not being able to hit the broad side of a barn. Assuming one survived a duel, courage was considered more important than skill.[58]

Despite the anti-dueling section of the 1807 "Vice and Immorality" statute signed by Governor Harrison and despite a large printed front-page address from the Anti-Dueling Association of Western New York in October 1809,[59] dueling continued in Indiana. Some quarrels, such as those of Isaac White, ended bloodlessly; others ended with nonmortal wounds, such as that of Clay and Marshall. But just as often they could leave one or both men dead. Hot-tempered young men, armed and often spoiling for a chance to prove their mettle, created a charged atmosphere. Sometimes the high emotions brought out by duels left their mark even after the principals had supposedly settled their differences. The inextricability of honor and politics compounded the problem.

Indiana politics became increasingly contentious after 1805. As both Joanne B. Freeman and Dan Monroe have observed, politicians in the early Republic considered themselves men of honor, whose careers hinged on their reputations for keeping their word. Thus, calling a politician a liar was a grave insult, one that had to be challenged immediately if the victim hoped to retain any standing.[60] Intense factionalism made Indiana's political scene an ideal breeding ground for such trouble.

The factions centered around Governor Harrison and his challengers and were often featured prominently in the pages of the *Western Sun*. One such feud pitted Rice Jones (son of John Rice Jones), a rising young Illinoisan and opponent of Governor Harrison, against the governor's partisans, including Illinoisan Shadrach Bond, Jr. (Bond later became the first governor of Illinois.) In the 1808 campaign for Randolph County representative, Rice Jones insulted his opponent, the pro-Harrison Bond. Bond, typical of frontier neo-gentlemen, challenged Jones to a duel. On the appointed day the antagonists met, but the cooler head of William Morrison, one of Jones's seconds, prevailed, and Bond and Jones retired without bloodshed. Jones won the election.

The encounter had nevertheless sparked a feud between Rice Jones and one of Bond's seconds, Dr. James Dunlap. In October 1808, Dunlap's card in the *Western Sun* mocked "little Ricey Jones" as a coward who had accidentally fired his pistol into the ground before the duel with Bond had even commenced. The doctor further charged that Jones had only agreed to reconcile after his opponent had drawn a bead on him. Dunlap's card concluded by mentioning that Bond had authorized him to publish his statement.[61]

Dr. Dunlap had publicly questioned Jones's honor and courage. He had, in effect, stated that Rice Jones was not really a man. In endorsing the card, Bond had done the same. Obviously, both men were still spoiling for a fight with Jones and wanted the entire community to know it. Jones, however, was not in a hurry to duel with either man. Jones's refusal to fight was too much for James Dunlap. On December 7, 1808, the doctor violated his Hippocratic oath, shooting Jones with a pistol in a Kaskaskia street. Jones died soon thereafter. Dunlap fled and was never brought to justice.[62]

Jones's allies saw his murder as an opportunity. Although Dunlap seems to have acted as much from personal as political motives, they accused Michael Jones—the land claims commissioner and a Harrison partisan—of inciting Dunlap to murder Rice Jones. The accusation was completely groundless, as opposed to the charges of land claims fraud the commissioner had gathered against John Rice Jones, John Edgar, and the Morrisons. A grand jury cleared Michael Jones in 1810, and he later won defamation suits against both John Edgar and William Morrison.[63]

By the end of the decade territorial politics had become increasingly contentious and dangerous. The code of honor made it nearly impossible for ambitious men to ignore the slight of a political rival. Harrison's enemy Elias McNamee swore before Judge Henry Vanderburgh that Thomas Randolph, a friend of the governor, had challenged him to a duel. By July, Randolph had reconsidered and was kind enough to note in the local newspaper that he no longer intended to kill McNamee. John Badollet nevertheless complained that Randolph could be seen regularly practicing his pistol marksmanship. Randolph then encountered William McIntosh, another Harrison political enemy, in the street and tried to beat McIntosh with a club. The Scotsman drew a dirk, however, and stabbed Randolph—a cousin of President Jefferson—so deeply that he remained near death for several weeks before recovering. In the aftermath, Badollet complained that most of the Vincennes gentry carried small daggers with them about town.[64]

Whites who saw Indians kill each other in drunken brawls in the streets expressed shock and dismay, yet white men could kill each other in an emotionless, premeditated ritual. Neither side appears to have caught the irony. William Henry Harrison saw both types of murder as disgusting but could not completely stop either of them. In some ways Harrison had more in common with the older Indian chiefs who had signed the Greenville Treaty and tried to abide by its rules than he did with many of his own citizens. The governor, the Miami Little Turtle, the ill-fated

Delaware Tetepachsit, and Black Hoof of the Shawnees were all trying to maintain what they saw as the traditional order of their societies (not to mention their own prerogative) against upstart challengers.

The Shawnee Prophet and other Native religious-political visionaries attempted to turn back the societal clock to a supposed golden era by returning to former cultural practices. Chiefs like Little Turtle and Black Hoof, on the other hand, were trying to negotiate what seemed like an inexorable wave of change. Governor Harrison tried, with varying degrees of cynicism, to hold back his own wave, in the form of new political challengers and the rising tide of democracy in his territory. Not that the Indian chiefs or the governor ever realized the link themselves. They allied only by coincidence, as when Harrison tried, albeit ham-fistedly, to rein in the Shawnee Prophet after his Delaware witch hunt.

Whereas the Treaty of Greenville had struck a blow against Ohio Valley Indians' pride and sense of, for lack of a better term, nationalism, the revitalization movements of the Prophet and others attempted to rekindle both ethnic pride and patriotism among Indians. In so doing, they set themselves on a collision course with the continuing nationalism of Americans who still actively revered the Revolution. Like President Jefferson, such Americans saw expanding settlements as one of the highest forms of patriotism. They also felt Anglophobia in almost every conceivable context. The Prophet and his followers saw their own traditions and cultures in a reverential light and reveled in past military glory; so did the Americans. Americans viewed land acquisition as the key to their economic and social well-being, while traditionalists like the Prophet saw land retention as a key to physical and cultural survival.

Indiana's territorial seal showed a buffalo bounding out of the way of an ax-wielding frontiersman clearing the land, light and progress pushing aside the benighted frontier. Such ethnocentric imagery was common in nineteenth-century America. Congress envisioned Indiana as a new beginning in the West. The territory was certainly that, yet those living in Indiana still had to contend with preexisting conditions not always of their own choosing. The decades of the late eighteenth and early nineteenth centuries saw a slow, general change within North American societies, punctuated by occasional revolutionary outbursts. Contemporaries and later historians saw numerous stark differences between the villages of

Indians and those of whites north of the Ohio. Yet they also held a great many similarities, more than either group might have readily admitted. All the peoples of early Indiana negotiated these dilemmas: violence, uncertain land titles, economic upheaval, challenges to established gender norms, burgeoning patriotism, ethnic pride, alcohol, and ecological change.

The general peace of Greenville severely curbed the old outlet of the warpath for both Indians and whites, although Americans were able to reap more benefits from the peace, in part because white juries were loath to protect Indians. The situation became more volatile with the increasing availability of alcohol on the frontier. Men in both Indian and American villages also saw public honor as important. For many whites, this might translate into harsh political tirades in the newspaper or even a duel. For many Indian men, retaining the identity of hunter and spurning that of farmer remained key to personal and public honor. Alcohol exacerbated social ills in all communities, but especially Indian ones.

So common ground existed between Americans and American Indians in Indiana Territory. A situation approaching harmony was not out of the question. But Americans, with Governor Harrison leading the charge, remained fixated not on common ground with Indians but on titles to Indian land. By 1811 the territory would be on the brink of open war.

CHAPTER 7

Dueling Visionaries

Politically, the loss of Illinois was a mixed bag for Governor Harrison. He had opposed separation with all his might, and now the external, if oblique, criticism further undermined his pro-slavery position. Treasury Secretary Albert Gallatin, who almost never referred to Indiana politics in his letters to John Badollet, stated, "[I]f you have had a share in preventing the establishment of slavery in Indiana, you will have done more good, to that part of the country at least, than commonly falls to the share of man." Gallatin's letter was a response to one from Badollet complaining of Harrison's "impudence" in attacking him for his anti-slavery views.[1]

Harrison did not know of this letter, but coincidentally he felt the need to write directly (and defensively) to Gallatin on August 29, 1809. Harrison defended his policies and moral fiber in a private letter to the treasury secretary. A series of editorials in the *Vincennes Western Sun* the previous March and April had mocked the pro-slavery position. The editorials were signed "A Farmer," revealed to be John Badollet. Badollet had also circulated his anti-slavery petition to all counties in Indiana in 1808 and submitted it to the legislature as well. Harrison took care to mention that Badollet had questioned his standing as a Republican and had attacked his pro-slavery ally Thomas Randolph, one of former president Jefferson's cousins. The governor, aware of Badollet's friendship with Gallatin, took great pains to couch his disapproval of Badollet's attacks in the most diplomatic terms. He further stated that any difference between himself and Badollet was a result of the influence of the "malicious & Mischievous" Nathaniel Ewing, Indiana's agent for completing roads and receiver of public monies. (Given that characterization, perhaps we should assume that Ewing did not loan the "few Hundred Dollars" Governor Harrison had asked him for in late 1808; see chapter 6.)[2]

Gallatin responded to Harrison less than a month later. With equal diplomacy, he restated his own strong anti-slavery sentiment, yet admitted that he differed in opinion from "many valuable friends." He also stated that even though no one had asked for his opinion, he favored Harrison's reappointment as governor. Gallatin downplayed—misleadingly—Badollet's criticism of Harrison, stating, "he has never written to me disrespectfully of you or against you." Given Badollet's frequent references to the corruption within Vincennes politics and his sarcastic references to "his most excellent Excellency" acting with the "the rage of a despot," Gallatin seems to have chosen to fib to the governor.[3]

More serious were the charges leveled against Harrison in 1809 by Badollet's brother-in-law, Dr. Elias McNamee, in a letter to the president of the Senate. McNamee, a Vincennes physician, served on the Vincennes University board of trustees with the governor and others. In addition to accusing Harrison of "official misconduct" and extortion of "hush money" in land speculation dealings, he also hammered away at Harrison's evasion of Article VI. Harrison was so "little governed" by the Northwest Ordinance that he not only approved the 1805 law concerning the introduction of Negroes and mulattoes, but the law had been "brought about by his intrigue & superior address, for it is now well ascertained that there was at that time, a decided majority in the Territory who were opposed to slavery." In so doing, McNamee contended, Harrison had violated his oath of office. He charged Harrison with having a conflict of interest regarding his post as superintendent of Indian Affairs and dissolving the House of Representatives and the Legislative Council (dissolving the latter was not among his specifically enumerated powers) over a dispute about bills concerning his control over the militia and slavery.[4]

The debate over slavery, and the entwined subject of territorial politics, raged not just in private correspondence and arguments but in public as well. By early 1809 a running war of words in the editorials of the *Western Sun* blurred the lines between free speech and outright libel. Pro-slavery men were accused of being not just "Federalists" and "aristocrats" but "tyrants" as well. Those who were anti-slavery were characterized as "scoundrels," hypocritical, and disloyal, not to mention unrealistic. As slavery already existed in the United States, the moral question was moot, pro-slavery editorialist "Slim Simon" argued. Further, the South needed an outlet for its surplus slaves—restating the diffusionist argument. As for the ethical question, Slim Simon asked, "Will you brand a minister of the gospel with a want of morality and religion because he possesses a slave?"[5]

Pro-slavery men held their own in newspaper editorials, but they were clearly losing ground to the anti-slavery settlers filling the territory. By August 1809, even Governor Harrison (if privately) had to admit that only his Knox County held a "slight Majority" still favoring the 1805 "Act concerning Introduction," while Indiana's other three counties were "almost unanimously against it."[6] Given such overwhelming popular sentiment, especially with the loss of the pro-slavery Illinoisans, the Act concerning Introduction's days in Indiana were numbered.

John Badollet continued his onslaught in his letters to Secretary Gallatin. He charged that he had been duped by the "Moral Cameleon" [sic] Harrison into believing the governor was a good man. Harrison had been the driving force behind the Act concerning Introduction, and prior to 1808 the territorial legislature had been "nothing better than the recorders of his edicts." He alleged that the governor and Judge Benjamin Parke had gone so far as to introduce a pro-slavery toast at a Fourth of July dinner and that he alone had mustered the courage to denounce it on the spot.[7]

Badollet further charged that Governor Harrison had responded to his anti-slavery petition in the territorial legislature with one of his own opposing division of the territory and "deceptive[ly]" adding a small pro-slavery paragraph of his own, trying to trick the legislature into endorsing it. Fortunately, the anti-slavery legislators defeated the measure. This might be an example of Badollet's gift for hyperbole—this "deceptive and dishonourable" attempt by the governor seems more like a legal (if somewhat pathetic) political maneuver.[8]

More valid was Badollet's assertion that Harrison had bribed anti-slavery men to change their opinions by giving them patronage appointments. Badollet singled out the appointment of General Washington Johnston as adjutant of the militia during an Indian scare, "although he knows as much about military affairs as I do about Pope's bulls," just to silence Johnston. Johnston did waffle publicly regarding slavery, and his training was legal, not military ("General Washington" was his name, not his rank, although he later served with distinction in the militia). Still, there was nothing illegal about Harrison's use of political patronage, and if Badollet found it morally reprehensible, one would have to agree that it was also perfectly common.

Badollet also charged that Harrison had told voters they should vote for the pro-slavery Thomas Randolph rather than the anti-slavery Jonathan Jennings in the Clark County legislative contest if they wanted to retain Harrison as their governor. Again, this seems like normal campaigning rather than political intrigue. Harrison had made a similar accusation against Badollet in his August 29, 1809, letter to Gallatin. The most notable result here was that Jennings beat Randolph in the election.[9] Clearly, the tide of political fortune had turned against Harrison and the pro-slavery clique.

The attacks continued into 1810. In a June 26 letter, Receiver of Public Monies Nathaniel Ewing wrote of grievances against Harrison to Secretary Gallatin. He sarcastically remarked that a "crime" he had committed against Harrison was opposing his stance on the admission of slavery, which had "been a darling plan of his ever since he has been governor of the territory."[10]

With the pro-slavery Illinois contingent now gone, it was only a matter of time before anti-slavery citizens fleeing Kentucky and the eastern states for Indiana would take over the legislature. On December 14, 1810, they passed "An Act to repeal the act entitled 'An act for the introduction of negroes and mulattoes into this territory,' and for other purposes." Besides repealing the introduction act, the new act threatened a thousand dollar fine for anyone trying to remove or assist in removing any blacks or mulattoes from the territory before first proving they had the legal right to do so before a judge of the court of common pleas. The act also repealed the 1807 "Act concerning servants of color," a continuation of 1803's "A Law concerning Servants." The new act did not, however, end indentures made previously, nor did it abolish slavery. It was only with the Indiana State Constitution of 1816 that slavery and involuntary servitude were officially outlawed, and even then the constitution was ignored for many years afterward, particularly in the western counties on the Wabash.[11]

Harrison, seeing little recourse, relented. The repeal of the indenture laws did not signal an end to discrimination against free blacks, however. On December 11, 1811, Harrison approved "An Act regulating the General Elections of the Indiana Territory," which denied the vote to all but free white men. (Even North Carolina and Tennessee permitted free blacks—legally, at least—to vote until the mid-1830s.) Such discrimination continued after Harrison moved on. Similar sentiment was expressed in a petition to Congress from the citizens of the Driftwood settlement (near the East Fork of the White River), referred February 13, 1813. The petitioners hoped to receive a land donation "to actuel Settlers [so that] People of Colour and Slaveholders may be debared from the Priveladges of Settling on the Lands so apropriated." In 1814 a "revenue" act placed a three dollar annual tax on all free black males ages twenty-one to fifty-five. These types of laws, consciously calculated to discourage the immigration and settlement of free blacks, were common north of the Ohio and west of the Mississippi. Free blacks were not allowed to vote in the Midwest or the West until after the Civil War.[12]

Anti-slavery sentiment was not necessarily pro–African American; in fact, it was often quite the contrary. Many whites opposed slavery simply because they did not want blacks around. In 1806, Indiana's Judge Thomas T. Davis had made an anti-slavery (and anti–African American) plea to U.S. attorney general John Breckenridge: "If you have any influence for God's sake dont [sic] let Congress introduce Slavery among us. I dispise the Colour & Situation & if Congress will let us alone we will in Two years become a state. But if they Humor the St. Vincennes party they will have the whole Territory in Confusion. Let us alone and we will do well."[13]

Aside from being instituted into the laws, "Negrophobia" (to use a nineteenth-century term) also prevailed in everyday encounters. The newspaper serves as a good example. An ad from the front page of the May 20, 1809, *Vincennes Western Sun* detailing proposals for the local mail service stated that "[n]o other than a free white person shall be employed to convey the mail." In fact, Congress prohibited blacks from carrying the U.S. mail in 1810. (Recall that the Militia Act of 1807 had also excluded blacks.) An August 11, 1809, ad in the *Western Sun* said that William McGowen had "Beef! Beef! Beef!" for sale and hoped to sell it to the citizenry, "(Indians and Negroes excepted)." In his oft-repeated ad,

McGowen also hoped "to meet with encouragement from every good American." The April 14, 1810, issue carried a notice for the auction of the estate of the late William Allen, including "Negroes, Horses, Cattle, & Beds." From 1807 to 1811 the *Western Sun* ran a number of ads offering rewards for runaway slaves, not just from Kentucky and Tennessee but from local masters as well.[14] Such was the dilemma of African Americans in the Indiana Territory—the only whites who wanted them there wanted them as slaves.

Pro-slavery sentiment in the North was not confined to Indiana. In 1800 only three states—Massachusetts, New Hampshire, and Vermont (which all had small slave populations to begin with)—had officially abolished slavery, but there were still over 36,000 slaves in the North. The other northern states (Pennsylvania, Connecticut, Rhode Island, New York, and New Jersey) had passed "gradual" abolition laws between 1780 and 1804. Basically, these laws stated that all slaves living at the law's passing would remain bound for life but that the children born to them would be freed after serving an "indenture" (up to twenty-eight years in some states) with the mother's master. New York did free all its slaves—over 20,000—in 1827, but in the other states slavery clung to life into the 1840s.[15]

Harrison and his pro-slavery allies had repeatedly argued that open suspension of Article VI was necessary to populate the territory, and in lieu of this they tried to establish loopholes that would encourage slave-holders to immigrate. Undeniably, Harrison's pro-slavery faction was successful in evading Article VI and allowing a legal basis for expanded slavery in Indiana. But few slaveholders took them up on it. According to a census of the territory in 1800, there were only 28 slaves in Knox County and 107 in Randolph County in the Illinois country. In other words, in 1800 slaves comprised about 2 percent of Indiana Territory's population. The 1810 census revealed a black population of 630 (only 237 of them were listed as slaves, although some others were surely indentured), with a white population of 23,890. Thus in 1810 the black population of the territory, even counting the "free" blacks, was still less than 3 percent of the non-native population. Granted, Indiana lost the pro-slavery Illinois country in 1809, but Illinois would still accumulate fewer than 1,000 slaves in the next decade. This growth was far outpaced by neighboring slave territories at the time. While Harrison's policies did increase the territory's slave population, the proportionate populations were almost unchanged. What is more, in 1810 Indiana was still woefully short of the 60,000 free inhabitants originally required for statehood in the Northwest Ordinance.[16]

Slave owners passed over Indiana and later Illinois for Missouri or Arkansas, despite Governor Harrison's having done everything within his power—and probably some things that legally were not to encourage their settlement. The looming threat of potential emancipation of their slaves, which slaveholders read in the Northwest Ordinance, led them to decide that settling in Indiana or Illinois was not worth the risk.[17] If not the governor, at least someone took Article VI seriously. Apparently, then, even had the proposed ten-year suspension of Article VI been granted, it would have been unlikely to sway many citizens.

Obviously, Harrison had few moral qualms about slavery, despite his youthful dalliance with an abolition society. Slave owning was part of his upbringing. Supporting slavery was personally and (at first) politically convenient for him. He later proved capable of waffling on the issue, though, as in his 1822 bid to become the U.S. congressman from Ohio. He declared to his anti-slavery constituents, "I have been the means of liberating many slaves, but never placed one in bondage"—a half-truth at best. He lost the election. By 1840, abolitionism was out of favor, and Harrison's handlers downplayed his role in the Quaker abolition society. His presidential inaugural address in 1841 asserted that Congress had no right to abolish slavery in Washington, D.C., without the consent of its residents.[18]

After the dramatic shift in personnel in the territorial legislature in 1810, Harrison's efforts regarding slavery in Indiana were relegated to the back burner. He may have been preoccupied with the Indians gathering at Prophetstown on the Tippecanoe and suspected British intrigue concerning them, as war clouds loomed before 1812. A look at the preponderance of correspondence dedicated to Indians in the closing years of the decade suggests this. Harrison might also have decided that Congress would not grant his wish or that the mounting political opposition to slavery made it more trouble than it was worth. Maybe it was a little of each.

In territorial Indiana, and the early Republic in general, both pro-slavery and anti-slavery sentiments were branches growing from the same ideological tree. Americans were justifiably proud of their Revolution, their

industry, and their political and social institutions. Americans enthusiastically celebrated the Declaration of Independence and an Enlightenment worldview that embraced Natural Rights theory. But whenever
natural rights proved inconvenient, as those of slaves did, many Americans looked to Great Britain for a culprit rather than face a painful mirror.
The right of the slave owner to his human property, rather than the slave's
right to his or her body, assumed the greatest importance. Or, as Stephen
Aron put it, it was "a world where hardheaded economics overruled soft-
hearted paternalism."[19] While most could publicly proclaim that slavery
was an evil institution in the abstract, few found the moral courage to end
it once they had profited from it.

While white men in the early Republic disagreed over whether slavery
was ethical or practical, whether their support or opposition was concrete
or abstract, the vast majority of them did agree on one thing: the Declaration of Independence was, in practice, for them and not for anyone else. A
great many do seem, like Jefferson, to have felt deep guilt concerning the
moral question of slavery, but in their concrete actions they tended to let
expediency guide their principles. Notably, both anti-slavery and pro-slavery
men blamed Britain, not themselves, for slavery's existence.

Anti-Harrison attacks by petitioners continued even after the introduction act's repeal in 1810, displaying that the governor's enemies opposed
more than slavery. The charismatic young lawyer Jonathan Jennings now
led the attack. Born in Pennsylvania and well educated, Jennings came to
Indiana to practice law and was soon admitted to the bar. The law did not
prove lucrative, however, so Jennings became a partner of *Vincennes
Western Sun* editor Elihu Stout in December 1807. The partnership lasted
just two weeks, as the political divide—Stout was strongly pro-Harrison—
proved too great. Jennings's fine penmanship won him the post of clerk of
the territorial assembly. In 1809, when Jesse B. Thomas stepped down as
Indiana's delegate to Congress to accept a judicial seat in Illinois, Jennings
ran to replace him.[20]

Jennings's main opponent was Virginian Thomas Randolph, the governor's ally. Randolph was the pro-slavery candidate, while Jennings ran
on the unambiguous platform of "No slavery in Indiana." Harrison
campaigned vigorously against Jennings's election. While Jennings
trounced his opponent in anti-slavery counties—in Dearborn County, for

example, the margin was 90 to 7 in Jennings's favor—the election overall was fairly close. Jennings received 428 votes, Randolph 402, and a third candidate, John Johnson, 81. John Badollet had been championing Jennings to members of the territorial legislature since at least 1808. Harrison had in turn protested to Treasury Secretary Gallatin that both William McIntosh and Badollet had told voters not to elect anyone who had confidence in the governor. Harrison was whining on this issue. Campaigning for a preferred candidate was not illegal.[21]

During the campaign Jennings had asserted, "Our territorial government is exercised by a 'glorious flirtation' too nearly allied to an aristocracy. Virtue is daily sacrificing at the shrine of ambition and intrigue, whilst honest men are exhibited to publick view as objects of detestation." He had billed himself as a defender of the "common man" and enemy of "privilege."

The contest did not end with Jennings's election. Randolph challenged the results, with the curious argument that Governor Harrison's proclamation calling for the election of a delegate was illegal. Jennings was put in the odd position of trying to uphold one of the governor's actions while Harrison held a fund-raising dinner to send Randolph to Washington to protest his proclamation before Congress. Jennings survived this strange affair, much to Harrison's discomfort.[22]

Jennings would lead a spirited, if unsuccessful, opposition. From 1810 to 1812 he labored to have Congress strip Harrison of his right to appoint local sheriffs, and he also fought to make the governor's appointees (except militia officers and justices of the peace) ineligible for service in the territorial assembly or the Legislative Council. He failed in these efforts. In January 1811, Jennings presented a petition from the Legislative Council and territorial assembly to move the territory's capital from Vincennes to the White River, something Harrison had long fought against. The petition died in committee. On January 20, 1811, Jennings presented a petition complaining of the governor's "arbitrary conduct" in vetoing bills to move the capital, and it also died in committee. The failure of these petitions actually supported the assertion of Jennings and others that Harrison was too well connected and privileged to serve democratically. The petitions died because of the influence of the governor's powerful friends in Washington, like Speaker of the House Henry Clay of Kentucky and Senator Thomas Worthington of Ohio.[23]

Some in Washington did consider limiting the power of territorial governors. While he was Indiana's delegate to Congress in 1808, Jesse B. Thomas noted that "[a] Bill was introduced (before my arrival) [he arrived December 1] by the delegate from the Mississippi Territory [George Poindexter] for repealing that part of the Ordinance [of 1787] which gives to the Territorial Governors the power of proroguing and dissolving the General Assembly." The proposal survived two readings in the House, then died in committee. Yet Thomas felt "[i]t will probably be revived again in the Senate and should that be the case it will pass into a Law." Poindexter had argued on November 16, 1808, that laws that "leave to the Governors of the Territories of the United States powers which are fitted but for the Sovereigns of Europe . . . should be spurned from the statute book." The Senate did not take up the matter, though, and there it ended.[24]

However the anti-Harrison petitions fared in Congress, the fact that they circulated and were signed tells us something about his political well-being in Indiana. One suggested that Harrison threatened "rights unsullied as they were handed to us by the patriots of Seventy Six," which, considering Harrison's family history, must have been highly insulting. In December 1811 Congress received two more such petitions by "Citizens of the Territory," with 208 signatures between them. Both petitions accused Harrison of interfering with legislative elections by "haranguing the Electors at the Polls" and sending "violent electioneering letters" to various counties, "which your petitioners Consider, when transacted by an Executive officer, to be hostile to the very principles of the American government and derogatory to our rights as free men."[25]

It would be very difficult to prove that these latter two petitions necessarily represented the thoughts of the majority of citizens in Indiana. Indeed, the strong similarity in the wording of the petitions might suggest that the same person or persons wrote them, although none of the signatures are redundant. What seems significant, however, is not the number of the governor's opponents but the fact that most petitions against him keyed in on recurring themes, especially that of his compromising the spirit of a republican form of government.

One could easily make too much of the petitions circulated by Harrison's adversaries during his time as governor. He held a powerful position in government, and powerful people tend to accrue enemies, whether they behave justly or not. Certainly, he typified a "spoils system" approach when making political appointments, but that was common in early-nineteenth-century politics, and as governor he was legally entitled to pick such officeholders. No doubt many who opposed Harrison drew as much on their discontent at being patronage "outs" as on moral-philosophical outrage for their inspiration.[26] Criticizing him for not voluntarily reducing his own powers would be unfair and unrealistic. What is noteworthy is how the opposition to Harrison coalesced around a desire for a renunciation of "privilege" and "aristocracy." (The capital needed to become a slave owner could fall under both those categories.) Resistance to Harrison actually *gained* momentum after the virtual end of the slavery issue.[27]

Nicole Etcheson has argued that a major factor in the political opposition to Harrison was the resistance of transplanted southerners in the Midwest to submit themselves to an aristocracy, even one dominated by other southerners. They resented his veto power, his arbitrary appointments, and his maneuvers, including gerrymandering when he apportioned representatives to the General Assembly to favor Knox County. Yet Harrison took great pains to insist that he was no despot. While he had most of the power, he realized that openly ignoring his countrymen's republican ideals would destroy any pretense of his legitimacy. He wanted, he needed, deference that was cheerful, not grudging.[28]

Viewing Harrison through the lenses of Jeffersonian political economy and paternalism reveals both the motivation and justification—in his mind, at least—for his actions. If Harrison had to bend laws or principles, if he favored friends for public posts or jealously guarded his own prerogative, he could rationalize it all. The governor was convinced that he understood what was in the public's best interest. If he had to drag them along, it was merely for their own good. While the Revolutionaries had championed a republican form of government and varying measures of democracy, only the most radical favored pure democracy, or what Harrison would have seen as mob rule. In his November 4, 1806, address to the General Assembly, Harrison offered:

> If you are not as completely independent Gentlemen in your legislative Capacity as you wish to be it must be recollected that the controle

which is exercised over you is only such as is indispensably necessary to preserve in our infancy a just and proper dependence upon the Parent Country and that even this controle is to be withdrawn so soon as our population shall have reached the number which is fixed by the Ordinance as necessary to entitle us to Independence.[29]

Governor Harrison paid lip service to democracy but explained that for the sake of stability, he remained in charge.

After the war scare of 1807–1808, tensions between Americans and Indians died down on the frontier, to the point where Harrison decided that the Prophet might actually be useful. Harrison even fed the Prophet's hungry followers from government stores in the hard winter of 1808–1809. War on the frontier might have been avoided. But Jefferson's last Indian policy directives as president called for securing the title to Kickapoo lands on the Mississippi to further hinder British traders from reaching Louisiana. Harrison would also purchase more lands on the Wabash, although the United States "had no immediate use for them. . . . In the last analysis, 'obtaining lands' needed for defense against invasion by British troops or traders took precedence over the policy of peace and civilization."[30]

Without doubt, Governor Harrison and most Americans needed little encouragement to seek land cessions. Accruing land was the foundation of American frontier society, and Indians were not the only ones treated unfairly. Daniel Boone had fought as hard as any American to help take lands away from Indians, only to see his claims pulled from under him by lawsuits.[31]

By August 1809, Harrison was claiming that Indiana's settlers were running out of land. Yet the entire territory (factoring in the loss of Illinois) had only 24,500 white settlers spread over several million acres. Harrison argued that the northernmost portion of the previous cessions, which formed the point of a triangle, was too narrow to form a new county: "The inhabitants are therefore obliged to attend the seat of Justice at Lawrenceburgh on the Ohio, to their great injury and inconvenience." Much more convincing is the argument that the loss of Illinois and Wisconsin reduced Indiana's population and slowed its march to statehood—something that irked Harrison tremendously. To amend this, Harrison negotiated a treaty at Grouseland that would have given the

United States another 300,000–400,000 acres and encouraged new settlement. Most of the chiefs present signed the treaty, but Harrison wrote that he "was obliged to have it expunged" because the Miamis protested so vehemently.

The governor, however, told the new secretary of war, William Eustis, that President Madison would have approved the proposed cession had he known the plight of Indiana's residents, and so Harrison would try again. Perhaps the abrogation of the treaty reflected Harrison's instructions from Washington that July. While he was to press for lands east of the Wabash, he was also "to prevent any further dissatisfaction" among the Indians by inviting all chiefs who felt they had a claim to a cession. With Harrison's decision to go after the expunged treaty again and to invite only some of the tribes with claims to its tracts, the young Madison administration might have seen that the governor was increasingly out of control. Yet Harrison continued unchecked.[32]

Harrison proceeded to Fort Wayne, arriving September 15, 1809,[33] to renew negotiations with the Delawares, Miamis, Eel Rivers, and Potawatomis. At the post named for his mentor, he lectured the chiefs on the benefits of ceding lands for annuities, which were all the more necessary since the Napoleonic Wars had stifled the European fur trade. He asserted that it was not the white settlers who had driven off game but the bad advice of the British traders who encouraged them to trade in skins—a statement he knew was only half true.

On the evening of September 23, the Miami chiefs requested liquor for their young men, and each tribe received two gallons. The request was granted exactly one month after Harrison had issued a proclamation forbidding the sale or distribution of liquor to Indians within a thirty-mile radius of Vincennes. Fort Wayne, however, was a long way from Vincennes. Later in the evening, the Potawatomi chief Winamac assured Harrison that the Indians would accept the treaty. The Potawatomis present certainly would, for Harrison had wisely invited only those from the St. Joseph River and Fort Dearborn areas because the western Potawatomi groups, like those following the warrior and prophet Main Poc, were fiercely anti-American. The next day, however, the Miamis declared that they would sell no land and that the Americans must stop encroaching on them by purchasing lands for less than their real value.[34]

Apparently, the break in Harrison's usual prohibition of liquor distribution during treaty negotiations did not help his cause, for the Miamis held out for another week before signing. For the council as a whole, Harrison proved able to set aside his beliefs concerning the immorality of giving alcohol to Indians. Whereas the fort issued fewer than 25 pints of whiskey in a normal month (in July it issued only 6 pints), between September and October the 1,390 Indians present consumed over 7,000 gills (about 218 gallons) of whiskey.[35]

The Miamis stated that they had heard Harrison had no presidential authority to pursue this cession but was doing so only to please his own settlers. The Potawatomis strenuously advocated the acceptance of the treaty, stating that they had acceded to treaties that benefited the Miamis, and now it was time for them to reciprocate.[36]

The next day, September 25, Harrison addressed the tribes in council. He made thinly veiled comments that the refusal to sell must be a result of British influence, and he reminded the warriors of Britain's failure to help them after Fallen Timbers: "Believe my Children the people upon the other side of the big water would desire nothing better than to set us once more to cut each others throats. Glad enough would they be to see us contending against each other in battle provided they were secured behind the walls of a strong fort."[37]

Harrison told the Miamis that they had always received justice from the United States and that this was both the first and last request their new father, President Madison, would make of them. Little Turtle responded, saying the Miamis did not agree with the Potawatomis and Delawares and needed more time to consult. The Miamis remained opposed in council the next day, and some of their warriors returned from Fort Malden, bringing gifts and advice from the British to avoid the treaty. They needed the gifts. Whether they needed the advice is debatable.[38]

The Miamis and Potawatomis continued to quarrel over the next several days, the former insisting that their lands should only be purchased by the acre and for two dollars an acre. The Miami chief Owl, who had supported Harrison in previous treaties, noted that the Weas were not present despite their claims to the land, and he repeatedly refused to sell land he did not occupy. Harrison then unleashed a two-hour speech in which he claimed that the Miamis had lost the land from

Pittsburgh to the Miami River because they associated with the British. He stated that Americans considered treaties to be solemn compacts, which their national honor would not allow them to break.

Using a very convenient form of logic, Harrison countered the Miami "per-acre" demand by saying that if the United States purchased land by the acre it would take only the best lands, leaving the poorer ones for the Indians. Large tract purchases allowed the Indians to receive payment for bad lands as well as good, so anyone suggesting selling by the acre was an enemy of both the Miamis and the United States. He announced that he was tired of waiting for an answer and that if they did not sign the treaty the next day, September 30, he would end the council. Because Harrison had not yet distributed that year's annuities, this was a serious threat, particularly for the hungry Potawatomis. Winamac rose to speak in favor of the governor and his treaty, and the disgusted Miamis broke protocol and left the council house.[39]

On the 30th, Harrison met with the Miami delegation, scolding them for their reluctance to sign the treaty. An Eel River chief named Katunga, or Charley, produced a copy of the 1805 Grouseland Treaty. Katunga had known Harrison since 1794, when he first made peace overtures to the Americans after Fallen Timbers. He pointed out the spot where the governor had promised to consider the Miamis owners of the Wabash lands. Why then did Harrison try to buy the land from others? Harrison answered that the Potawatomis had claimed more than he or the Miamis had expected but that he had no intention of putting anything in the treaty that recognized any new claims on their part. The entire compensation for this cession *could* go to the Miamis if they insisted, but that would needlessly insult the Potawatomis and Delawares. Harrison stated that he had always intended to word the treaty in a way showing that the Potawatomis and Delawares were merely allies of the Miamis and had no rights to Miami lands. As Harrison described it, "Every [Miami] countenance brightened at this declaration." They then leveled complaints against William Wells and Little Turtle. Harrison promised satisfaction for any claims against the two men and further stated that the Mississinewa civil chiefs (i.e., not Little Turtle, who was a war chief) represented the Miami nation.[40]

Harrison was immovable regarding the per-acre question, so the chiefs gave up. The Miamis, Potawatomis, and Delawares each got a $500 permanent annuity, while the Eel Rivers got one for $250. It was also stated that the treaty's acceptance hinged on the acceptance of the Weas and Kickapoos.[41]

That same day, Harrison concluded a supplementary treaty with the Miamis and Eel Rivers, providing them with further compensation for the cession. Because the Miamis had the greatest claim to the ceded lands, they would get $500 worth of domestic animals for each of the next three years and a blacksmith at Fort Wayne to repair their guns and tools. Further, if the Kickapoos accepted the first Fort Wayne treaty, the Miamis would receive an additional permanent annuity of $200, with $100 per annum to go to the Weas and Eel Rivers. Harrison spent the first three days of October doling out the 1809 annuities.[42]

Harrison had proven capable of overlooking his anti-liquor proclamation one month after issuing it, and one month after that he also proved capable of forgetting that he had (in spirit if not letter) broken his own rule. In late October 1809 he called the Weas to Vincennes to secure their acceptance of the Fort Wayne treaties. The governor invited the principal Wea leaders to Grouseland, noting with disappointment that while "he had shut up the liquor casks . . . some bad white men had disregarded his Proclamation & secretly furnished them with the means of intoxication." He was encouraged to find that they had sobered up by this point, however, and "hoped that they would not drink any more until the business on which he assembled them was finished. On the morrow he would explain to them the proceedings of the Council at Fort Wayne." On October 26, a treaty with the Weas secured their acceptance of the September 30 treaties for an extra $300 annuity and $1,500 in cash, with the understanding that they would receive an additional $100 annuity if the Kickapoos complied.[43]

Harrison feared that the Kickapoos, "very much under the influence of the Prophet," would prove much more resistant to the treaty and might hold out for eight to ten months before signing. That, of course, explains why they were not invited to the initial Fort Wayne Treaty but were saved until the last so their opposition would not just be in Harrison's face but in the faces of their neighbors as well. But just in case, Harrison bypassed the more obstinate Kickapoo chiefs, dealing with a small group of more amenable ones instead. They even agreed to a further cession above the Fort Wayne purchase, contingent upon Miami approval. For sanctioning the initial purchase, these Kickapoos got $800 in goods plus a $400 permanent annuity. For the additional tract, they were to receive $700 in goods and another $100 annuity. "The majority of the tribe violently opposed this treaty," however.[44]

The Fort Wayne treaties of 1809 represent the zenith of Harrison's negotiating style. They utilized all of his most effective tactics. The annuities promised by Wayne in 1795 allowed Harrison, by threatening to withhold them, to coerce chiefs into attending his councils. He then built upon his mentor's examples of bribery and exploitation of divisions among the Indians and took both to new heights. Both at the inter-tribal and intra-tribal levels, he masterfully and ruthlessly divided and conquered his opponents. The Potawatomis[45] and Delawares had little claim to the lands in question, as Harrison admitted to the Miamis. Yet he needed their presence because he knew they would agree to sell the Miami lands and would therefore pressure the Miamis to sell so that all might collect their annuities. Once Harrison had isolated the Miamis, he dissected them skillfully by exploiting the jealousy and resentment the civil chiefs harbored against Little Turtle. Little Turtle had thrust himself and the Miamis into a position of leadership through his skill and willingness to work with the Americans. Harrison, holding all the cards and dealing from the bottom of the deck, turned these qualities against both Little Turtle and the Miamis, stripping both the war chief and his confederacy of power simultaneously. An editorial in the *Vincennes Western Sun* summed it up coldly:

> The Little Turtle was one of the warmest advocates for the treaty from its commencement; and would have willingly signed it before the Mississiniway chiefs (who are the real heads of the Miamis) could be brought over. After the treaty he made an attempt to procure from the Indians a recommendation of a *friend* which failed altogether; this disgusted him so much that it is not improbable that he *may with some encouragement* endeavor to make the Indians dissatisfied with the treaty. But his opposition is of no consequence,—his influence is gone forever.[46]

Harrison alluded to his tactics in a November 3, 1809, letter to Secretary of War William Eustis. He noted Eustis's instructions "that the chiefs of all those tribes who have or pretend a right to these lands should be present," and so he had included the Potawatomis and Delawares. On the surface this might have seemed to favor the Indians, had it addressed all possible Indian claims. Yet Harrison himself had stated in 1805 that the Potawatomis and Delawares had no claims to the White River tract, whereas the Weas and Eel Rivers did. The latter two groups were not invited yet, for Harrison wisely preferred to attack the opposition piecemeal. He invited the Delawares and Potawatomis to use them against the Miamis. "The refusal of the Miamis," Harrison wrote, "to acknowledge the right of the Delawares to the country watered by the White River, at the Treaty of Grouseland, has from that time continued to rankle the minds of the latter and to produce a disposition which bordered on actual hostility." In other words, Harrison's previous treaty had driven a wedge between the Delawares and the Miamis, and the only way to reconcile the squabbling of such children would be for their benevolent father to remove the disputed toy, that is, the White River lands.[47]

Harrison saw the Potawatomis as particularly useful, noting, "The poverty and wretchedness of the Potawatomis made them extremely desirous of a treaty at which they expected to have their most pressing wants relieved." The Potawatomis were hungry. Because the governor had judiciously refused to distribute the tribes' rightful annuities until a successful treaty was negotiated, Winamac's Potawatomis were ready to sign practically anything. They anticipated the lion's share of annuities in return for supporting Harrison. In fact, the Potawatomis, whom Harrison referred to as a "numerous and warlike" people, threatened war if the Miamis did not sign the treaty. Since they constituted about half the Indians at the council, this was a serious threat. "To have excluded either [the Potawatomis or the Delawares] would have been extremely unpolitic [sic] on our part, as it would have entirely alienated the minds of those Tribes from us," Harrison declared. Yet it had not been considered "unpolitic" to wait until later to include the Weas, Eel Rivers, and Kickapoos.[48]

Harrison declined to invite them so he could keep them away from "bad advisors"—the British at relatively nearby Fort Malden. When the goods were doled out, the Potawatomis were so numerous that many would have left without a single gift. They protested loudly to the governor that even though they "were his most faithful children," they received fewer goods than the Miamis. Harrison agreed to give them $500 worth of goods in advance of their 1810 annuities, and in a letter to the secretary of war he recommended that to reward the Potawatomis' "zeal in favour of every means proposed by the Government," the goods should be simply a gift rather than being deducted from their coming annuities.[49]

The former president himself would have been challenged to offer a better example of Jeffersonian benevolence on the ground. Harrison's land purchases expanded existing rifts between tribes or opened up new ones, yet he argued that only further treaties would heal those wounds. In an era when surgeons bled patients to death, perhaps this made sense. Ruthless pragmatism led Harrison to include the Delawares and Potawatomis in these negotiations—not to ensure fair treatment for them, as mentioned, but to ensure the acquiescence of the Miamis. It was, of course, wholly consistent with the Jeffersonian reasoning that both Americans and Indians would ultimately be happier if Indians ceded their lands to the United States. Even without counting the additional cession by the Kickapoos, the Fort Wayne treaties would secure another 2.9 million acres for the United States. Harrison's treaties, through 1809, had secured title to almost 30 million acres of Indian lands.[50]

Regarding his recent Fort Wayne treaties, Harrison told the secretary of war that "the arrangement which has been made is just to all and is therfore [sic], I believe, satisfactory to all." Faithful to his treaties and negotiating style, Harrison's assessment also provides a blunt display of Jeffersonian Indian policy on the ground. Seeing American expansion as inevitable, he felt that, as Indian lands would be taken sooner or later, sooner seemed better. "More Good News for Indiana" was the caption of a December 9, 1809, newspaper column noting Harrison's latest treaties with the Kickapoos at Fort Wayne. A week later, General Washington Johnson, speaker of the Indiana House, took out an ad reading, "We feel highly gratified at the late extinguishments of Indian claim to a considerable tract of fertile country, as it will be one means of enabling the Territory to soon step into the Union, and assume the desirable office of self government, an office which the genius of liberty inspires every

American with a desire to assume." In all likelihood, a strong majority of Americans agreed.[51]

Another editorial asserted, "THE late treaty with the Indians has occasioned as much spleen and irritation amongst a *few* as it has pleasure and satisfaction with the people, generally." True, the editorialist continued, "some abandoned profligate, in the garb of an American," had tried to disrupt the treaty (again raising the specter of treason or British meddling in Indian affairs). But in the end, "The fact is the Indians were never so unanimous, or so well pleased with a treaty they had made, as with the late one." Only the agitation of enemies—the editorial singled out Harrison's rival Elias McNamee—could stir unrest over it now.[52]

John Badollet referred to similar comments being made about himself and Nathaniel Ewing by Harrison supporters after the treaty was concluded. Badollet assured Secretary Gallatin that he was personally in favor of Indian land purchases and actually complained that "Gen'l [John] Gibson and Col. [Francis] Vigo [both of whom were close friends of Harrison's] could purchase from the Indians more land in two hours than the Gov'r in ten years." Given Harrison's record regarding land purchases, the quote seems another example of Badollet's gift for exaggeration. It also helps to illustrate that, at least through 1809, even men of widely divergent opinions favored buying large tracts of Indian lands.[53]

One man did dare to challenge Harrison publicly on the issue. William McIntosh accused Harrison (accurately) of using the Potawatomis to threaten the Miamis at the council, and Harrison sued him for slander. He charged that McIntosh had "falsely maliciously openly and publicly spoke and uttered these other false feigned scandalous & approbrious words of the Said William H, to wit that he (meaning the plaintiff) defrauded the Indians in the purchase of their Lands & by which he (meaning the plaintiff) made them (meaning the Indians) enemies to the Government of the United States."[54] The accusation, though, raises an interesting question: If McIntosh really was a "Scotch Tory," why would he mind if Harrison alienated the Indians from the United States?

Ignoring the inconsistency of his own past charges against McIntosh and the fact that he had not acted in the best faith in the negotiations, Harrison pulled out all stops to win the case and obviously took the charge very seriously. He had both former Indian agent William Wells and Miami chief Jean Baptiste Richardville (who, as an Indian, should not have been able to legally testify against a white man in an Indiana court) serve as witnesses on his behalf. And the judge in the case was Harrison's appointee and friend, Waller Taylor. Predictably, Harrison won the case and a handsome settlement of $4,000 against McIntosh. He returned two-thirds of the settlement to the Scotsman and later donated the rest to orphans from the War of 1812. In this instance, public vindication, however suspect, was more important to Harrison than money.[55]

The rate at which the governor sought Indian lands raises the question of why he needed so much so fast. Obviously, it was not to please John Badollet. Harrison did occasionally speculate in land, including preemption rights on Indian lands. Yet the scale on which he sought to extinguish Native titles does not correspond with his personal gains from land sales, which were relatively minor. A better explanation comes from a December 24, 1810, letter to Secretary Eustis, in which Harrison advocated seeking still more land cessions (despite his promise at Fort Wayne that he would seek no additional lands): "For without such a further purchase Indiana cannot for many years become a member of the Union and I am heartily tired of living in a Territory."[56]

For once, the Madison administration said no to the ambitious young governor—he was neither to seek further cessions nor survey the 1809 lands, and he was to try to smooth the feathers he had ruffled at Fort Wayne. It was not because Madison objected to Harrison's treaty councils or the resulting land acquisitions, however. Engrossed in trying to secure West Florida for the United States, President Madison feared the complications a possible Indian war in the Northwest would bring. These words of caution came much too late, however. After Fort Wayne, Tecumseh called for a British-Indian alliance, and his new allies had to restrain him from launching a war on the United States.[57] Jeffersonian Indian policy, as implemented by Harrison, had turned the old fear of a British-Indian military alliance into a self-fulfilling prophecy. War on the frontier became merely a matter of time.

The assertion that Harrison's land purchases and Indian policy stemmed solely from personal ambition or malice toward the Indians does not survive close scrutiny.[58] In early 1809, the year that undoubtedly saw the governor's most rapacious and manipulative Indian councils, he pardoned Wappenuchkinewa, a Wea in the Knox County jail for stealing horses. The standard penalty for horse theft in Indiana Territory was death.[59]

The territorial Legislative Council's message to the governor on October 5, 1808, stated in part that "[t]he intelligence of the continuance of that harmony and good understanding with our Red Brethren, so much to be desired, is Calculated to inspire Pleasing reflections; The just & Philanthropic Policy which the General Government has observed towards this unenlightened race of men is highly appreciated, whilst in you is discovered the active agent who has given it effect."[60] While this may have been an example of the servile support of Harrison's picked men—they went on to praise Jefferson's soon-to-be disastrous Embargo in the same message—it also reflected a general, condescending sentiment toward Indians. While the motives were benevolent, the destructive results of such attitudes were equally undeniable.

When returning to Vincennes following the Fort Wayne treaties, Harrison stopped at the Miami chief Pacane's village, only to find that the previous night one of the chief's intoxicated men had mortally wounded another warrior. When the Miamis informed Harrison that they had not yet found the culprit, he advised that they should punish the man if he was found to have acted maliciously. If, however, the stabbing was accidental, they were to inform the governor and "he would assist to make up the matter with the friends of the deceased."[61] It had been some time since an American official in the area had made such an effort to "cover the dead." This incident demonstrates succinctly Harrison's pattern of Indian relations. Apparently oblivious to the U.S., and his own, role in the social disintegration visited upon the Ohio Valley Indians, Harrison twisted arms with one hand while offering fatherhood with the other.

So important were the land purchases to Harrison's plans—as governor, resident, and patriotic American—that they led him to engage in considerable mental gymnastics, as illustrated by the case of Agent William Wells. Harrison had first met Wells when they both served under General Wayne, the former as aide-de-camp and the latter as chief of scouts and spies. Harrison held Wells's contributions to Wayne's campaign in the highest esteem, later noting that he was "indispensable to the success of our operation." When Wells seemed to place Miami needs above those of the government (and Harrison) in 1804–1805, Harrison accused him of treason and intrigue. Secretary of War Dearborn fired Wells in January 1809, citing financial irregularities and openly questioning his loyalty to the United States.[62]

Yet when Harrison needed the support of Wells and Little Turtle for the Fort Wayne treaties in 1809, he gladly agreed to write letters of recommendation for Wells in return for the former agent's help in securing the treaty. Once the treaty was signed, Harrison again voiced misgivings about Wells's honesty and patriotism, hedging his political bets with left-handed compliments of Wells and praise for Wells's most vehement critic, John Johnston, who had taken Wells's post at Fort Wayne. Then, when Wells testified for Harrison against his "Scotch Tory" enemy William McIntosh in 1811, Harrison again declared that Wells was a fine American and even suggested that he be reinstated as an Indian subagent.[63] Hindsight being 20/20, Harrison would have helped Wells more by recommending him for a job somewhere in the East, far away from the gathering storm.

Part of the motivation for securing Indian lands was to force Indians to relinquish their independence and accept American sovereignty, thereby reducing British influence. In so doing, Harrison and the Americans felt they were safeguarding peace. Instead, rapid land acquisitions made the old British-Indian alliance viable once more.

CHAPTER 8

Return to Arms

While Governor Harrison, Thomas Jefferson, President James Madison, and most other Americans seemed oblivious to the inherent contradictions of the land acquisitions policy followed north of the Ohio River, a growing number of Indians saw them all too clearly. Tenskwatawa's movement gained both a new sense of urgency and greater significance after the full impact of Harrison's Fort Wayne treaties hit the region's Natives. After 1809, the Prophet's followers became increasingly militant and sought a British alliance against the Americans. Tenskwatawa's teachings became even more threatening to American plans because of the rise of the Prophet's older brother, Tecumseh.

Officials in Canada had tried to secure an alliance with the Shawnee brothers in 1808,[1] but Tecumseh refused, as he still hoped to avoid a frontier war with the Americans. The British, who recognized Tecumseh's importance well before Harrison did, had little choice but to accept his decision. However, after the Fort Wayne treaties, they had to restrain the enraged chief from launching his own war on the United States.[2]

Initially, Tecumseh drew little attention from American officials, and his reputation and influence were primarily based in his own community. As late as the summer of 1810, Fort Wayne Indian agent John Johnston still referred to him only as "the prophet's brother." Tecumseh soon eclipsed his brother and all others in the minds of government officials and later in the popular imagination. Tecumseh utilized his keen wits, rhetorical eloquence, and fierce passion to provide a formidable parry against American expansionists.[3]

Specifically, Tecumseh argued that the Great Spirit had given the land to all Indians, not just certain parcels to certain tribes. Therefore, no sale of Indian lands could be valid unless ratified by all Indians. Tecumseh held no illusions about the practicality of this argument; securing such a consensus was impossible, and that was the point. In his mind, the Americans had moved too far already and must push the Indians no further. Tecumseh forbade the surveying of the Fort Wayne cessions and boldly asserted that war would result if his demands went unheeded. To give his threats teeth, Tecumseh expanded on his brother's call for pan-Indian resistance and eventually tried to recruit most of the major tribes east of the Mississippi to his cause. His ambitious (although largely failed) efforts among the Southern tribes, including the numerous Creeks, Choctaws, and Cherokees, became the stuff of legend. The trip to recruit those tribes also left his incomplete confederacy vulnerable without his guidance.

William Henry Harrison admired Tecumseh almost as much as he detested the Prophet. In an oft-quoted letter to William Eustis from August 7, 1811, Harrison practically gushed about the chief, who was:

> [O]ne of those uncommon geniuses, which spring up occasionally to produce revolutions and overturn the established order of things. If it were not for the vicinity of the United States, he would perhaps be the founder of an Empire that would rival in glory that of Mexico or Peru. No difficulties deter him. His activity and industry supply the want of letters. for Four years he has been in constant motion. You see him today on the Wabash and in a short time you hear of him on the shores of Lake Erie or Michigan, or on the banks of the Mississippi and wherever he goes he makes an impression favorable to his purposes.[4]

The reaction was largely the product of the governor's ethnocentrism. He could understand much of what Tecumseh, a military-political leader trying to form a confederation, was doing, even if he opposed it. The Prophet, on the other hand, remained an odd, untrustworthy "witch doctor." Egocentrism played a role as well: the greater Harrison's enemies, the greater would be his triumph. Admiration and opportunism aside, Harrison saw Tecumseh as an obstacle to his public duty and a threat to his personal ambitions, and perhaps to his life as well. At a conference at Grouseland in 1810, "Carter Harrison's brother" and "the prophet's brother" nearly came to blows. As they stood in a walnut grove near the house, Tecumseh, with considerable justification, had cursed Harrison in Shawnee as being a liar. Secretary John Gibson and several attendees who spoke Shawnee became greatly alarmed, and a scramble for sidearms culminated with Harrison and Tecumseh squaring off face-to-face, a dress sword and a pipe tomahawk both raised to strike.[5]

But first Harrison and then Tecumseh regained their composure and avoided bloodshed. The council settled nothing, however. Both sides, representing competing nationalisms and ethnic pride, remained intractable. Tecumseh told Harrison he saw presidential intervention as the only chance for peace and hoped Madison would act. Ominously, the chief added, "he may sit still in his town and drink his wine, whilst you and I will have to fight it out."[6]

It is probably good for Harrison that no fuller record of these councils exists. Even from the scanty sources available, by any objective standard Tecumseh clearly dominated Harrison in these arguments. In addition to a litany of outrageous incidents, which he could recite with stunning accuracy and detail to bolster his assertions, Tecumseh was simply a better orator. While no fool, William Henry Harrison was no Daniel Webster either. Harrison's Virginia gentry background had favored erudition and eloquence, and he was definitely an educated man for his time. But against a man hailed as an uncommon master, even among a people known for their public speaking skills, Harrison had little chance. Had the councils been anything like fair debates, Tecumseh would have won. As an agent of the United States, though, Harrison—and all the American officers—saw the councils simply as paternalistic measures that would allow Indians to voice their concerns, which could then be ignored.

Tecumseh made one key strategic error, however, at his final conference with the governor in the summer of 1811. He made a point to mention that he would be gone to visit the Southern tribes and asked Harrison to make no mischief while he was gone. He had given the Prophet a similar admonishment. Harrison may not have been a visionary, but he was an opportunist, and he saw Tecumseh's absence as a chance to disperse the Prophet's followers.[7]

Prophetstown, located on the Tippecanoe River near modern Battleground, Indiana, was ground zero for Tenskwatawa's revival. At its peak, the well-ordered village housed about two hundred wigwams, each holding a family of perhaps four or five. Neighboring villages might supply hundreds more warriors. (Estimates of the warriors under his influence ranged from 650 to 3,000, the latter number sounding somewhat high.) The Prophet had moved there in 1808 at the invitation of the powerful and influential Potawatomi Main Poc, a war chief and religious visionary himself.[8] By the late summer of 1811, Harrison was again deeply suspicious of the defiant Shawnee brothers and their converts.

Secretary of War William Eustis tried to keep informed about the frontier situation, but as 1811 wore on he gave Harrison more and more leeway in deciding how best to handle the Prophet. Eustis did not covet a war in Indiana, but he did not want to take responsibility for hindering the citizens' ability to defend themselves either. He left that decision up to Harrison. The governor had already made up his mind. It was not so much that he wanted to fight as that he had decided a show of military force was the only way to bring about his goals of pacifying militant Indians and securing land. If the Prophet's followers could be cowed back into sensibility, as Harrison saw it, that would suffice. But, like his mentor Anthony Wayne in 1792, Harrison did not really believe diplomacy would work, and he wanted to be ready to make good on his promise of military action.

Harrison gathered an army of nearly 1,000 men, including 400 Indiana militia and 120 mounted Kentucky volunteers, 80 Indiana mounted riflemen, about 300 U.S. Army regulars under Colonel John Parker Boyd, and additional scouts. The regulars were key to Harrison's confidence, as he had probably not forgotten his speech to Congress in 1800 about militia effectiveness. Those concerns may also explain why Harrison refused additional militia volunteers from the Illinois Territory.

Many of the militia and Kentuckians in his army were eager for a fight—a combination of old hatreds and recent fears. Whereas Kentucky had nearly seceded from the United States back in the 1780s, Kentuckians by this point were rabid nationalists who sought to defend American honor by striking at the British and their Indian allies. By the fall of 1811, few Kentuckians argued with Congressman Richard Mentor Johnson's assertion that Britain's "infernal system has driven us to the brink of a second revolution, as important as the first. . . . We must now oppose the farther encroachments of Great Britain by war, or formally annul the Declaration of Independence, and acknowledge ourselves her devoted colonies."[9]

U.S. District Attorney Joseph Hamilton Daveiss practically begged to go along, and he led his Kentucky neighbors. Governor Harrison had declined former Salines agent Isaac White's request to bring the Illinois Territory's militia to the assemblage, but White insisted on going himself. White joined the Kentuckians, serving under Daveiss, his close friend and fellow Freemason.[10]

Part of the flaw in the argument that Harrison had single-handedly engineered an Indian war in 1811[11] lies in the widespread enthusiasm for the expedition, as evidenced by the actions of the many volunteers such as Daveiss and White. Most of Harrison's men simply wanted to preempt any action by the Indians and their British allies. William Clark, as governor of Missouri Territory, felt "the prophets party must be despursed[;] they do much harm." Robert Terry, one of the Kentucky volunteers, later explained that the "Shawnee Proffet . . . [and his followers] have been threatening us with ware & have carried matters to such lengths" that Harrison's expedition was necessary.[12]

A public gathering of the Vincennes citizenry in late July appointed a committee, composed mainly of Harrison's militia officer friends like Luke Decker and Francis Vigo. The attendees unanimously adopted the committee's resolutions stating that Harrison's actions to that point had staved off a "British scheme" and a massacre of Vincennes by Tecumseh and the Prophet, and they argued that "temporising measures" would not suffice against the Indians, "who are only to be controled [sic] by prompt and decisive measures." Many seem to have thought breaking up Prophetstown would be relatively easy. John Drummens, another Kentuckian, wrote his wife, Rebeca, in October 1811, stating that "the Governor says that he will insure every man safe home to his wife." In Drummens's case, it would be a promise broken.[13]

Some did view the campaign more skeptically. John Badollet remained Harrison's unyielding enemy and opposed the march to Prophetstown even more vehemently because his son Albert was part of Harrison's army. Badollet's naïveté regarding "the poor Tecumseh," and his continued insistence that the warriors at Prophetstown constituted no threat to the Americans, were no doubt in part the result of his hatred for

Harrison. Nor did he truly grasp what Tenskwatawa was trying to effect, later noting that the destruction of Prophetstown had spoiled "the fruits of the first rational attempts to reach the comforts of civilized life spontaneously made by the northern Indians."[14] Still, Badollet's apprehensions about Harrison's campaign were the genuine concerns of a civilian with a relative in the army, a situation to which Mrs. Lydia B. Bacon could relate.

Mrs. Bacon, the wife of Lieutenant Josiah Bacon, a quartermaster for the U.S. Fourth Regiment, accompanied her husband on his journey from Boston to Indiana. With the army moving north, she forted up in Vincennes with the wife of another officer. Bacon found her host pleasant enough, but the anxiety for her husband's safety and her own was inordinately taxing. Even when Lieutenant Bacon was nearby, she was reluctant to venture outside the fort's walls. When he left for the campaign, she felt even more vulnerable:

> Our situation was very much exposed while the Troops were absent, for every thing went that could carry a musket & left us Women & Children without even a guard, Mrs. W[hitlock] & myselfe had loaded Pistols at our bedside but I [have] some doubt if we should have been able to use them had we found it necessary, had the Indians known our situation a few of them could have Massacred the Inhabitants & burnt the Village.[15]

Harrison took his army into the disputed purchase lands, building Fort Harrison at what is now Terre Haute, Indiana. Warriors sent by the Prophet responded by shooting and wounding one of the fort's sentries. Like his father three decades before, Harrison knew building forts was not enough in an Indian war. He saw the attack, coming on the heels of several isolated but disturbing murders in Illinois and Indiana, as a pretext to march on Prophetstown. There he would confront the Prophet, asking for a parley and demanding that he turn over the Indians who had attacked American settlers and soldiers. If the Prophet refused, and Harrison was certain he would, the governor would attack and destroy Prophetstown, scattering Tenskwatawa's adherents. He sought to provoke a battle to avoid a war. In so doing, Harrison felt he could nip the pro-British, anti-American Nativist movement in the bud.[16]

Even with such an overtly hostile act as marching into Indian territory—Prophetstown was far north of even the latest, disputed land cessions—Harrison saw himself as performing his paternalistic duty. The Prophet's movement was backward and heavily corrupted by British influence. Harrison's primary concern was for the welfare of the citizens of his and neighboring territories, and he also wanted to safeguard old and future land purchases. But he also thought of himself as a father administering much-needed correction to his Indian children, and he would not spare the rod and spoil the child. His thinking in this regard fit well with former president Jefferson's, who had repeatedly stated his friendship for the Indians and yet also evidenced a determination to crush those who resisted American aims.

Harrison reached a suitable campsite about a mile north and west of Prophetstown, along Burnett's Creek in what is now Battleground, Indiana, on November 6, 1811. He agreed to meet the Prophet the following day, but he fully expected that the negotiations would fail and that his troops would attack the village the night of the seventh. Harrison's order of march had been careful and orderly, testament to Anthony Wayne's influence and also to Harrison's love for reading Roman campaign histories. As he was in "Indian country," he ordered his men to sleep fully dressed with their arms at their sides, lying in battle lines. Unlike Wayne and the Legion's namesake, though, he curiously did not fortify his camp but left only pickets, partially silhouetted by the great campfires that blazed against the cold drizzle.[17]

The Prophet's followers were already alarmed and under no illusion that they would be attacked in the next day or two. They had partially fortified their camp and prevailed upon Tenskwatawa to ignore Tecumseh's warning and to launch a surprise attack on Harrison in the predawn hours of November 7. Perhaps wanting to cloak himself in some military glory of his own or simply unable to withstand the pressure to act, the Prophet relented to the hawks in his camp. He consulted with the spirits and determined that the best hope would be to send in a party to murder Harrison in his tent. He assured his followers that he would cast spells on the Americans to make them blind and crazy and to protect the warriors on their sacred mission. The attacking force of perhaps five hundred Indians crept very close to the camp until a sentry fired on them, spoiling the surprise. The battle then became pitched and intense. In addition to being outnumbered, the warriors were also low on ammunition.[18]

Harrison always rose early when on campaign, and he was nearly dressed when the attack began at 4:30 A.M. He survived assassination in part because his usual light gray horse had run off, and he mounted another. His aide, Colonel Abraham Owen, riding a white horse, was shot down by warriors who probably mistook him for Harrison. A hot firefight ensued. Some evidence, from the journal of volunteer John Tipton, for example, indicates that the Americans may have suffered some "friendly fire" casualties—"[our men] manye times mixed among the indians so that we Could not tell them indians and our men apart"—but eventually the more numerous and better-supplied Americans drove off the Indians, who lost perhaps 50 dead. Harrison's force held the field but took a far worse beating. The officers sustained especially high casualties. Joseph Hamilton Daveiss, his friend Isaac White, militia Captains Spier Spencer and Jacob Warwick, and Colonel Owen all died. Harrison's good friend Thomas Randolph (who was serving as his acting aide-de-camp) was also killed, and Judge Luke Decker, another close friend of the governor's, was among the many wounded. Harrison escaped without a scratch. His overall casualties were 188—worse than literal decimation—including 68 killed or mortally wounded.[19]

The army spent the rest of the day bracing for an attack that did not come. The next day they cautiously advanced into Prophetstown and pillaged what utensils and corn they needed. According to at least one of Harrison's officers, they also found British-made muskets. Harrison ordered the town and the remaining grain stores torched.[20] They encountered no resistance. The Prophet and his followers had long since fled.

While they held the field and might have technically claimed a victory, Harrison's army was in mourning. On the outside of his Tippecanoe campaign journal, John Tipton scrawled this verse:

> Young Mayjr Dark Recd a wound
> Just By his fathers Side
> Those feeble hands shall bee Revengd
> For my Sons Death he Cryd
> And like a man Destracted out
> Of the lines he flew and
> Like a bold verginion [Virginian] a
> Savag there he Slew[.][21]

Not long after Tippecanoe, Harrison wrote to his favorite physician, Dr. John Scott of Frankfort, Kentucky. The governor reflected on just how lucky he had been to make it through the battle. He attributed the fact that he had escaped harm to *"providential* interferrence [sic]." Not only had he mounted a different horse, but he had also survived an assassination attempt led by a black wagon driver, Ben, who had deserted from the army. Ben was to lead several warriors to Harrison's tent but was apprehended by one of the officers while scouting the scene late on the night of November 6. Ben was bound spread-eagle, tried for treason shortly after the battle, and sentenced to death. But Harrison took pity on Ben, who was taken back to Vincennes and pardoned. The governor still seemed to prefer to "err in favor of life."[22]

Harrison was correct in assuming that Tecumseh and the Prophet were mobilizing for war against the United States. But the governor was badly mistaken in thinking his preemptive strike would avoid a wider conflict. Still, the Prophet suffered a serious blow to his prestige after he failed to safeguard his warriors in the battle. He lost about fifty men killed, with an unknown number of wounded. And he had to know that Tecumseh would not be pleased when he returned.[23]

Still, despite the legend that arose of the Prophet being stripped of power in the wake of Tippecanoe, American correspondence (and Tecumseh's speeches) in the weeks and months afterward suggests otherwise. Indians opposed to American expansionism soon regrouped near Prophetstown, and Tenskwatawa still seems to have had a number of adherents. Further, Tecumseh's speeches after Tippecanoe blame American aggression, not his brother, for the battle.[24]

William Henry Harrison also had some explaining to do after Tippecanoe.[25] Why was he not better prepared for an attack? Why had he not fortified his camp? In October 1810, the governor specifically mentioned the purchase of forty axes to Secretary Eustis. They were not only used to build fixed fortifications, but "it was also my intent to have placed the troops each night under the cover of a breastwork of trees after the example of general Wayne." In the intervening year of increasing tensions, had the Prophet's force suddenly become less formidable? Harrison later explained why he had not placed even simple abatis to protect his camp—he felt his troops would have such an advantage in a night action that he never seriously considered suffering a night attack. However, he told Kentucky governor Charles Scott that the only reason he had not fortified the camp with felled trees was because he did not have enough axes to do so. (John Tipton noted that after the action on the 7th ceased, the men built breastworks around the camp.)[26] As demonstrated by the shifting and wholly unsatisfying explanations for this failure, Harrison was painfully aware that by not fortifying his camp he had committed a horrible blunder, one General Wayne never would have made.

While the justification for the campaign was, in hindsight, ripe for inquiry, only a few people questioned its necessity at the time, and they did so from suspect motives. But the death of so many prominent frontier citizens, especially Joseph Daveiss, led many to criticize Harrison's tactics in the campaign. The *Western Courier*, as reprinted in the December 5, 1811, *Washington Intelligencer*, described Daveiss as "this pre-eminent son of Kentucky" who, when informed that the Indians had been beaten, replied, "I have done my duty, I am satisfied, my country is victorious." He died a few hours later. The battle never even made the front page of the *Vincennes Western Sun*, but Ohio and Kentucky newspapers did break from the usual pattern of leading with news of the Napoleonic Wars. One Ohio paper, the *Supporter* (Chillicothe), printed dispatches from Louisville, Kentucky, asserting that the battle had been a failure. Casualties, the columnist noted (erroneously), had been about equal in number, "tho' our loss is men of merit." The next week featured a front-page, poetic lament over the death of Daveiss, and one anonymous Kentuckian offered, "In the fall of col. Daveiss, the nation has sustained an irreparable loss."[27]

While Harrison never publicly admitted his mistakes, his defensive statements after the battle suggest he knew he had bungled parts of the campaign. Further, he probably felt some guilt and tried to assuage it with an old pattern of behavior for him—seeking pensions and employment for the wounded veterans of the service. In February 1812, for example, he sought to get a job at the land office for Capt. Samuel White of Kentucky, formerly a gunsmith, who took a bullet in the shoulder at Tippecanoe and could no longer use his arm.[28]

Indiana's legislature passed a resolution honoring the regular troops and the army as a whole, but the governor was conspicuously absent from the praise. Colonel John Boyd, who had commanded the regular troops under Harrison, spread the word back East that he, rather than the governor, had been the real hero of the battle. Although his son Albert survived, John Badollet nevertheless had harsh words for Harrison's campaign. Some Kentuckians felt Harrison had sacrificed others, particularly Daveiss, to safeguard himself. The fact that Daveiss was a Federalist and Harrison (by now) an avowed Republican fueled the unfair accusation that Harrison had protected himself while letting Daveiss charge and die. Charges of military incompetence, even cowardice, wounded Harrison deeply, partially explaining why the former captain's excuses, such as those he offered Secretary Eustis and Governor Scott, were sometimes lame and contradictory.[29]

Harrison weathered this storm because he eventually received support from his Knox County base, as well as the praise of officials in Washington who had only scattered reports of what had transpired. One of the nation's most important newspapers, the *Washington Intelligencer*, for example, seemed loath to criticize Harrison after the action. One editorialist identified as "T," on December 3, 1811, did allow that perhaps Harrison should have fortified his camp. Yet T added, "'Tis said and truly, that emergencies discover the man. And surely emergencies have discovered Gov. Harrison to possess presence of mind, valor and military skill, qualities which need the experience of a few battles only to make an able military commander." The December 5 issue erroneously listed Harrison's casualties as only twenty killed and fifty-seven wounded, less than half the actual number.[30]

Most westerners did not wait for a more objective assessment of the events before adding their two cents. General Andrew Jackson of the Tennessee militia swiftly offered his moral and military support for Harrison's invasion. The Indians, Jackson asserted, were "deceitful," "barbarians," and a "banditti," "excited . . . by secret agents of great Britain." They had to be destroyed, and "*our murdered Countrymen must be revenged.*" Jackson notified Harrison that he was holding his troops on alert and could march with a thousand men at a day's notice. (Given that he had made a similar offer to Aaron Burr a few years before, that was probably the least he could do.) A week later Governor Willie Blount of Tennessee praised Jackson for his offer to help and endorsed the spirit of Harrison's campaign by hoping that, if Jackson marched, he would "purge the camps of the Indians of every Englishmen to be found there in opposition to the forces of the U.S. and also bring the Indians to their proper senses."[31]

Harrison's militia officers passed their own resolutions in favor of his conduct, and as the months passed it seemed increasingly tactless to criticize the governor while he was engaged in an Indian war. On December 19, 1811, the *Washington Intelligencer* printed (on the front page) Harrison's explanatory (and defensive) address to his legislature and its statement of thanks to him. Two days later the *Intelligencer* published President Madison's address to Congress on the matter. The president declared:

> While it is deeply lamented that so many valuable lives have been lost in the action which took place on the 7th ult. Congress will see with satisfaction the dauntless spirit and fortitude victoriously displayed by every description of the troops engaged, as well as the collected firmness which distinguished their commander on an occasion requiring the utmost exertions of valor and discipline. It may reasonably be expected that the good effects of this critical defeat and dispersion of a combination of savages which appears to have been spreading to a greater extent, will be experienced not only in a cessation of the murders and depredations committed on our frontier, but in the prevention of any hostile incursions otherwise to have been apprehended.

Before long, the Battle of Tippecanoe came to be seen as a great victory that had staved off disaster on the frontier. Apparently, someone forgot to tell the Indians.[32]

In the months after Tippecanoe, incensed warriors, no longer concentrated at Prophetstown and with no reason to even feign peaceful designs, lashed out at isolated settlements throughout Illinois and Indiana. In cleaving the hornet's nest with his sword, Harrison had simply loosed enraged hornets. Although most American officials had assumed one fight would extinguish the Indian threat, at least one of Harrison's Tippecanoe comrades had recognized ominous portents in the immediate aftermath. As Baronet Vasquez, who had served as a translator for Zebulon Pike in 1806–1807, wrote to his brother, "[T]he danger is past; the Indians have crossed the river and have abandoned all their booty, but actually the settlers should beware—that threatens war."[33]

The attacks of the Winnebago, Potawatomi, and Kickapoo followers of the Prophet demonstrated that, regardless of spin, the Tippecanoe campaign had been fruitless and even counterproductive. When Tecumseh returned in the spring of 1812, a de facto frontier war had already broken out. Later that summer, the issue of America's maritime rights and the slow pace of trans-Atlantic communications led the United States to declare war on Britain. Canada was now fair game, and the United States sought to quickly mobilize an army and invade. In the spring of 1812, William Henry sent Anna and the children off to Kentucky and ultimately to Cincinnati for their safety.[34] He made sure John Vanderlyn would not be painting any scenes involving his family.

Harrison stopped being the active governor of Indiana in 1812, with Secretary Gibson taking over the duties. Harrison continued to draw his governor's salary until 1813, however, which rankled some politicians. He never officially resigned as governor, although he had secured other employment. If Americans had to fight the Revolution all over again, against evil Britain and its dastardly Indian allies, then who better to lead them than a son of a signer of the Declaration of Independence? A patriotic dinner in Vincennes on December 27, 1811, had featured this toast: "May the 7th of Nov. [i.e., the Battle of Tippecanoe] prove to our enemies that the spark of '76 is not yet extinguished," accompanied by nine cheers.[35]

Lingering questions remained about Harrison's fitness to hold high rank, largely the result of Colonel Boyd's criticisms after Tippecanoe. But Harrison was still very popular in the West. Kentucky had initially blamed Harrison for bungling Tippecanoe and mourned the death of Daveiss. The increased Indian raids and declaration of war against Britain, however, retroactively justified Harrison's campaign. Governor Scott of Kentucky made him a general in the Kentucky militia, and President Madison soon topped that by making him a major general in the U.S. Army, charged with command in the West and the invasion of Canada. With confirmation of Harrison's commission, President Madison appointed another Virginian, Thomas Posey, as Indiana Territory's new governor.[36]

Harrison's 1812–13 campaign delivered mixed results. In December 1812 he unleashed the dogs of war on his old friends the Miamis, even though few had taken part in the attacks on Americans. To safeguard his supply line while American troops marched north, Harrison sent Colonel John Campbell to destroy the Mississinewa villages. It was the kind of

ruthlessly practical decision Caesar would have made. Robert Breckenridge McAfee, a soldier in the Mississinewa campaign, noted in his journal
that the log and bark homes of the Miamis were "burnt by Order of Genl
Harrison." The troops also discovered and broke into the tomb of a
Miami chief there. Harrison then sent a detachment to burn the town of
the recently deceased Little Turtle, despite the chief's many efforts on
the governor's behalf. McAfee later published a version of his journal as
the *History of the Late War in the Western Country* (1816)—the first book
published in Lexington, Kentucky. Interestingly, neither Harrison's order
to burn the villages nor the desecration of the chief's tomb made it into
the published version. The Americans were mindful of grave desecration,
however. The Pittsburgh *Gazette* printed an account of the campaign,
describing how the American dead were buried in Indian homes, which
were then torn down and burned "to prevent any trace of their deposit
being discovered by the Indians."[37]

Even in turning on the Miamis, however, Harrison's orders to Colonel
Campbell displayed the many layers of the Jeffersonian mind. "Indian
hating" was always a complex phenomenon. Most Delaware Indians
adhered to the United States, and Campbell's route of march was to avoid
them if possible. Harrison did not want any indiscriminate attacks on
them. The Mississinewas, however, occupied more strategic ground.

Still, while he ordered the destruction of the villages, he also called for
protecting chiefs who had been friendly to the United States—sort of. He
mentioned Richardville, White Loon, Silver Heels, Pacane, and Charley,
who had "undeviatingly exerted themselves" to keep the peace with the
United States. "It is not my wish that you should run any risk in saving
those people," he wrote, but if they and the relatives of the late Chief
Little Turtle could be spared, it would please both Harrison and the president. (In fact, it was the late war chief's nephew, Little Thunder, who
skillfully led the Miami resistance to the assault.) Further, Campbell's
"character as a soldier" would protect the women and children, who
were to be captured but not harmed.[38] Harrison knew American warriors
sometimes got out of hand—in truth, as much as Indian warriors did—
and he wanted to preclude any stain on his or the national honor.

When he received reports of the Mississinewa campaign, Harrison was
ecstatic. Not only had it succeeded—despite Campbell's ten killed and

forty-six wounded—but the army had shown considerable restraint. The general—who was not informed of the desecration of Miami graves—praised the men for their gallantry. They had fought well, but, what is more, they had spared women, children, and even warriors who surrendered. "The general believes that humanity and true bravery are inseparable," his general orders noted. While "severe retaliation" might have its place, the gain from such was "very uncertain." Much more reliable were the "blessings which providence" secured to soldiers who fought hard but exhibited mercy toward the vanquished. (Harrison did not learn that from Caesar.) As a gentleman from Virginia rather than a tyrant from imperial Rome, Harrison intoned, "Let an account of the murdered innocence be opened in the records of Heaven against our enemies alone." Americans would not strike the helpless or fallen or pay "for the scalp of a massacred enemy."[39]

Still, Harrison's remarks were part praise and part plea. The fact that he felt compelled to mention the need for mercy suggests that it was not second nature to his men. Harrison wanted the success but not the mess of winning a frontier war against Indians. He was asking a lot, and he knew it. The British in Canada had similar feelings about the unpleasant methods so common in frontier combat, but they were so short of men that they could not afford to be as high-minded or high-handed as Harrison. Pragmatism trumped principle. Less than two weeks after Harrison praised his troops for being "in battle a lion, but, the battle once ended, in mercay [sic] a lamb,"[40] the British handed the United States another propaganda victory.

In January 1813, General James Winchester, against Harrison's orders, advanced north to the River Raisin and defeated British forces at Frenchtown. He was extremely negligent in laying out his perimeter defense, however, and a British-Indian counterattack routed him and captured most of his men. When the British commander, Colonel Henry Procter, moved out, he refused to assign any regular troops to guard the eighty wounded Americans left in Frenchtown. Instead, fifty Indian allies watched the prisoners. After breaking into a cache of liquor, the warriors murdered about thirty of them. Some died by tomahawk and knife, others perished helpless in buildings set afire. Several of the corpses were thrown into the street to be eaten by foraging pigs. For Americans, the

"Massacre on the River Raisin" was yet another British-Indian atrocity. "Remember the Raisin" became a battle cry.[41]

For most American Indian warriors, the idea that killing prisoners was inherently wrong was literally a foreign concept. Sometimes captives, particularly women and children, were adopted to replenish a village's population. But the way individual warriors disposed of their own captives was their business—an idea long and widely accepted by practically all the tribes. War chiefs or British officers accompanying war parties had little, if any, coercive authority to stop captors bent on bloody retribution. Besides, without prisons or the resources to keep prisoners for an extended time, the only practical options were adoption or execution. Otherwise, they might have to fight the same men yet again. Finally, the vast majority of Indians recognized the right of grieving relatives to exact revenge on an enemy—whether directly involved or not. As General Procter acknowledged, "[I]t is almost impossible to save any prisoner . . . where the Indians have lost lives."[42]

Americans found such explanations unsatisfying. Reports of the River Raisin affair sickened General Harrison. Wildly exaggerated tales of barbarity did nothing to calm him. In a letter to Acting Secretary of War James Monroe, he passed on allegations (which later proved false) that General Winchester himself had been scalped and disemboweled by the Indians: "Such are the allies of a power which boasts its attainments in every art and science and such the war associates of British officers who claim distinction for their nice feelings and delicate sense of honor." Two days later he wrote Monroe again, this time making a point to mention that Winchester had advanced against his orders.[43]

As military commander, General Harrison was far more cautious in the years after Tippecanoe.[44] His criticism of Winchester's impetuous moves toward the River Raisin came from genuine disapproval, as well as a desire to shield himself from blame. It had been difficult enough to secure his appointment with the army, and Harrison, still stinging from the period of rebuke following the Tippecanoe campaign, was eager to burnish his reputation through military achievement. He now realized what he should already have known from serving under Wayne: rash action against Indians in battle was often disastrous.

In the spring of 1813, General Procter and almost a thousand men invaded northern Ohio. With them were hundreds of warriors led by Tecumseh. Their first target would be Fort Meigs, outside what is now Perrysburg, Ohio. Tecumseh and his Indians probably had mixed feelings about the area—it was near Fort Miami, where they had been denied their British father's protection years before in the aftermath of Fallen Timbers. However, they were also eager to attack Fort Meigs, for they knew that behind its walls was "a man widely regarded as a major author of their misfortunes: William Henry Harrison." Harrison no doubt had happier thoughts about being near the site of his first great military triumph, but his situation carried a psychological burden as well. Aside from his own life, the lives of many Ohioans were in jeopardy if Fort Meigs fell to the enemy. To protect his country as well as his own family, Harrison had to stop them. Fort Meigs would be held at all costs.[45]

Harrison had about twelve hundred men, half of them Ohio and Kentucky militia. More Kentuckians were also en route under Brigadier General Green Clay. Harrison had ordered extensive earthworks inside the fort, which, thanks to his brilliant engineer Eleazor Wood, rendered the British barrage largely ineffective. After a week of enduring British siege guns, on May 5 Harrison's reinforcements arrived. He had formulated a plan not only to receive the new men but also to coordinate their arrival with sorties to disable the British siege batteries. It was a clever plan, but it required strict discipline to carry out. Harrison had long maintained that militias were unruly, but he issued his orders and hoped for the best.[46]

At first, the American maneuvers caught Tecumseh and the British off guard, spiking cannon and driving off smaller British and Indian parties. But Lieutenant Colonel William Dudley, who led his Kentuckians with bravery and stupidity, ignored Harrison's warning not to chase the enemy too far from the safety of Fort Meigs. Harrison made repeated attempts to signal them, to no avail. Tecumseh led a furious counterattack that killed Dudley and dozens of his men. A number of Kentuckians were captured, having sought out British soldiers to surrender to in the hopes of avoiding Indian vengeance. General Procter had them placed under a detail of Redcoats and taken to Fort Miami.[47]

The Redcoats intended to protect the prisoners there and made some attempts to do so. Once the Americans were herded into the fort, however, warriors who had missed the action against Dudley, mainly Ojibwas and Potawatomis, forced them to run a gauntlet. The warriors did not fancy the idea of returning home without scalps or plunder, and they menaced the prisoners. When a British soldier protested, they shot him dead. Soon a massacre was in the making.[48]

Word of the slayings reached Tecumseh and Matthew Elliott, a long-time employee of the British Indian Department. They galloped to the scene and put an end to the carnage, but not before a dozen or more prisoners lay dead. One Tecumseh biographer argues that politics rather than humanity may have been his primary motive: the chief needed British aid to fight the Americans and knew that the murdering of prisoners was a key source of tension between the allies. Reportedly, Tecumseh castigated Procter publicly for failing to prevent the killings. Revealingly, official British dispatches neglected to mention that only Tecumseh, not their own troops, had been able to end the slaughter. Only when the Kentuckians were later paroled did the word spread.[49] But whatever his motivations, Tecumseh's efforts to spare prisoners' lives were not psychologically dissected by the grateful Americans he saved. Stopping the massacre became one of the central features of the great chief's legend—after the war was over.[50]

For the second time that year, Harrison had issued perfectly sound orders that were not obeyed, resulting in disaster. Harrison's General Orders of May 9, 1813, noted that while "it rarely occurs that a General has to complain of the excessive ardour of his men," it seemed always to be the case with the Kentucky militia. Such impetuous bravery was "scarcely less fatal than cowardice." Dudley paid the ultimate price for his Kentucky zeal, and his foolhardy charge had allowed Procter's Indian allies to score an impressive victory. Tactically, the campaign had not been pretty for the United States. General Harrison lost about three hundred total casualties and about six hundred captured. But most of those losses were not his fault, and he had performed his duties capably. More important, Procter abandoned the siege a few days later. Strategically, the battle for Fort Meigs proved an American victory.[51]

The highlight of Harrison's campaign came in the fall of 1813, not long after Oliver Hazard Perry's great naval victory on Lake Erie sent the British army scurrying north to reestablish its supply lines. On October 5, near Moravian Town in Upper Canada, Harrison's army—led by mounted Kentucky riflemen—charged the outnumbered British and their Indian allies at the Battle of the Thames. Henry Procter had been promoted to general, but his martial skills seem to have declined in inverse proportion to his rank. The demoralized British behaved shamefully and ran off in the first moments of the attack.[52] (Like Harrison at Tippecanoe, Procter had misplaced his entrenching equipment, leaving his men exposed.)

Their Native allies, hoping to buy time for their retreating women and children, elected to stay and fight. It was in this action that Tecumseh died. No one ever established who killed him. Richard Mentor Johnson, a U.S. senator from Kentucky and leader of Kentucky mounted volunteers, was nevertheless hailed as the man who shot Tecumseh.[53]

Part of the reason it was difficult to identify just who had killed the great chief was because Johnson's Kentuckians—no doubt remembering "the Raisin" and Dudley's defeat at Fort Meigs—mutilated what was reputed to be his corpse, taking skin home as souvenir razor strops. For Harrison at least, identifying the flayed corpse as Tecumseh proved as impossible as it was sickening. While the general eagerly reported his great victory to his superiors, the letters made no mention of Tecumseh. Nor did he relate the Kentuckians' post-battle behavior. Twenty-one years after the event, Harrison still could not bear to mention directly that American soldiers had desecrated the body of Tecumseh. He was so "greatly vexed & mortified" by the act, he noted, that he had refused to let any of the captured British attempt to identify the chief. Perhaps he did not care to have his prisoners call him a hypocrite.[54]

Harrison later explained that he had been "desirous that it [the desecration of the corpse] should be attributed to our Indians who would I knew suffer no loss of honour by it." Still, he knew that his countrymen, not his supposedly savage allies, had committed the deed. His friend Henry Clay displayed one of the strops in Washington that winter, and Kentuckians continued to brandish and brag about such trophies for years afterward. When General Harrison visited Washington that December, he was one of Henry Clay's dinner guests. Surely, he must have seen or heard about Clay's souvenir. We can only speculate what the scion of Berkeley's response was, for he never wrote it down.[55]

The Kentucky volunteers had fought bravely, yet some inhumanity was apparently inseparable from that bravery. For the self-conscious gentleman from Berkeley, his greatest military triumph had been, for the moment, tarnished by his inability to keep his men civilized around his fallen savage foes. While Tecumseh was later perversely incorporated into the pantheon of American legend,[56] his demise generated no inflammatory Jane McCrea–type portrait.

Harrison was buoyed by the victory but felt tainted by its celebration. So when his invasion gave him the opportunity to display his honor by keeping an old promise, he leaped at the chance. Amid the chaos of the war, a Canadian militia officer had the apparent gall to ask Harrison for a personal guarantee of protection. Given the state of affairs and the fact that the Canadian's sons and grandsons were serving the Crown, he should not have expected sympathy from a bristling American patriot like General Harrison. However, this particular Canadian militia officer was the old fur trade magnate John Askin, who had moved north from Detroit in 1802. Harrison had not forgotten his vow to repay Askin for the trader's leniency in handling Francis Vigo's debts. No self-respecting Virginia gentleman would go back on his word, at least his word to another white man. Ten days after Tecumseh's death, Harrison unhesitatingly ordered that Askin and his household be left unmolested "during his good behaviour." Although not entirely neutral in the conflict, Askin remained remarkably inactive during the war.[57]

While not positive that Tecumseh was dead, the general knew he had delivered a body blow to the British-Indian alliance. The Redcoats' poor showing, he realized, would sap much of the Indians' enthusiasm. In the weeks after the Battle of the Thames, he was confident, even cocky, about detaching the Crown's Native allies. Five days after the battle, Harrison recommended that clemency be granted to the Ottawas and Wyandots, despite their having fought alongside the British. He did so because the people of the Michigan Territory felt this policy would quickly bring peace to their quarter. As a father angered by wayward children, the general entertained harder sentiments toward other tribes: "The Miamies and Potawatimies deserve no mercy, they were the tribes most favored by us." The Potawatomis in particular had been "cruel and inveterate enemies."[58]

Nevertheless, Harrison suggested extending an armistice to them as well. He did not want to drive them deeper into Canada or into the arms of the British. Instead, he hoped to lure them back to American soil, "where they will be perfectly in our power." Diplomacy would be cheaper than bullets: "Indeed I believe the Indian War may be terminated with a little management without any further bloodshed." Harrison extended the offer of an armistice to the "Miamis, Potawatomis, Wyandots, Weas, Eel River Miamies [sic], Ottawas, and Chippewas." He then concluded that they were sincere in their desire for peace, with the possible exception of the Potawatomi chief Main Poc. General Harrison promised loyal tribes that their treaty annuities would be delivered, and he even promised his recent enemies that they would receive some food as well. Harrison did not like making the latter promise, but he decided that "[u]nless this is done they must plunder the inhabitants which will again produce hostilities."[59]

With the Indians momentarily quieted, the general could address their erstwhile allies. General Procter, in a move displaying that his tact was the equal of his tactics, had written the American commander asking if the rights and property of captured British officers would be observed. The response fairly exploded from Harrison's pen.

Harrison held Procter in such contempt by this point that he would have lowered his own social status by responding to him. Instead, he directed these queries to Procter's superior officer, General John Vincent. The son of a Signer stated that he had been safeguarding the rights of his prisoners, which was far more than could be said for those captured by General Procter: "The unhappy persons of that description who have escaped from the tomahawks of the savages in the employment of the British Government, under the immediate orders of that Officer, have suffered all the indignities and deprivations which human nature is capable of supporting." Harrison had a question of his own, for which he wanted "an explicit declaration." Would the Indians allied with the British be allowed to continue "that horrible species of warfare" they had long practiced on American troops and civilians alike? He mentioned the River

Raisin and several other instances where not only prisoners of war but also American women and children had been murdered and mutilated "under the very eyes of the British Commander and the Head of the Indian Department."[60]

Harrison wrote Vincent: "You are a soldier Sir, and as I sincerely believe possess all those honorable sentiments which ought always to be found in men who follow the profession of arms." He urged Vincent to stop using Indian allies. Their methods, Harrison argued, were not only horrifying and destined to breed animosity for generations but also futile in the greater war. Further, he asserted, if the king's Native allies committed more depredations, Harrison would unleash his own Indian auxiliaries against Canada "and direct them to carry on the war in their own way."[61]

Britain had never offered any excuse for utilizing Indian warriors, he continued, "unless we can credit the story of some British Officer who dared to assert that 'as we employed the Kentuckians you had a right to make use of the Indians.' If such injurious sentiments have really prevailed to the prejudice of a brave, well informed and virtuous people, it will be removed by the representations of your officers, who were lately taken upon the River Thames."[62] That would explain why, five weeks prior to writing these words, Harrison had refused to let any British officers examine the skinned corpse that was presumably Tecumseh. The American narrative for wars with Britain made no room for morally complicated characters.

General Vincent was taken aback by Harrison's charges, and his response was rather weak. He thanked the American for treating British prisoners decently and assured him that the Indians under his direct observation had always been well behaved.[63] As the Canadian winter set in, such sparring by courier was preferable to moving the armies.

As it turned out, the Battle of the Thames was William Henry's last hurrah as a fighting man. In November he headed east, to report on his activities in person and perhaps to brag a bit too. He attended public dinners in his honor in New York City and Philadelphia. He then traveled to Washington, with the choicest pieces of General Procter's captured correspondence in tow, to rub elbows and politic a bit, and he was making plans for a major campaign in the spring of 1814.[64] Generally, he was quite popular with troops from the Ohio Valley, but the opinion was not unanimous. A Kentuckian (and Federalist) in his army, Samuel McDowell, Jr., wrote to a friend in the spring of 1814:

> Genl. Harrison has (his officers say) unnecessarily harassed the army, that at least 1700 men have been buried at Fort Meggs [sic] (including what was killed at Dudlay defeat) [.] We have lost some of our best men & I fear will lose a great many more before we take Canada if Genl. Harrison commands he will kill more men by unnecissary fatigue than ever the British or Indians will[.] Officers that are friendly to him as a man dispise him as a General/ they say he is for ever busy something brewing nothing doing[.] I fear War conducted by such a Genl. will for ever be unsuccessful[.] I wish an honourable peace but fear we will not soon get it.[65]

The "unnecessary harassment" was likely the result of strenuous efforts by the general to avoid being caught by surprise as he had been outside Prophetstown or to avoid costly mistakes such as those made by Winchester and Dudley. Harrison was a brave officer, but at Tippecanoe and during the War of 1812, it seems he did his best when his enemies were either outnumbered or very poorly led. As with his political battles in Indiana, it does not appear that Harrison ever won a fair fight.

In the aftermath of the Thames, Harrison's main battles were bickering over his record keeping for supplies and a quarrel with Secretary of War John Armstrong over the proper chain of command in the western army. (No doubt Harrison soon wished for the undisputed command Anthony Wayne had enjoyed with the Legion.) It appears that Secretary Armstrong was looking to force the removal or resignation of general officers so he might promote some of his favorites. He set about trying to annoy Harrison by sending orders directly to officers under the general's command and directing him to send full accounts of all his dealings with contractors— essentially an audit of Harrison's activities. The key dispute was with the firm of (Benjamin) Orr and (Aaron) Greely, who had supplied rations to Harrison's army in the fall of 1813. The case was convoluted, but the weight of the evidence and subsequent congressional investigation indicated that Orr and Greely were war profiteers and were angry with Harrison for cutting into their enormous profits by denying them undeserved transportation fees.[66] Initially, in the spring of 1814 Harrison refused to quit, sending an open letter to Congress defending one of his Cincinnati

contractors, John Piatt, against charges of price gouging. He also forwarded relevant documents to the War Department.[67]

The last thing Harrison needed was another headache. His father-in-
law, Judge Symmes, had died that February, and aside from his wife's grief,
he had to manage the judge's unruly estate. Two weeks before the judge's
death, Harrison had indicated to the secretary of war that only his patriotism kept him from retiring. Up through May 10, 1814, Harrison behaved
as if he had no intention of leaving the army. On May 11, 1814, Harrison
wrote Armstrong to ask that the president accept his resignation.[68]

Harrison noted that even before his appointment, he had suffered
"Most Malicious insinuations" against his character—a reference to Colonel
Boyd's criticisms after Tippecanoe. He also offered that he no longer felt a
court-martial was necessary to clear his name and had no desire to subject
his reputation to "to the Suggestions of Malice & Envy."[69] The letter was
cordial but cold. He wrote a far different letter to the president.

He explained to Madison that he felt the current war was "just and
necessary" and that normally a citizen should set aside all private considerations at such a time. However, he had concluded that resigning now
would be "as compatible with the claims of patriotism, as it is with those
of my family, and a proper regard for my own feelings and honor." He
further asserted that he continued to wish the best for Madison's administration and that he would not forget the "favors that it is out of [my]
power to repay."[70]

Yet Harrison did not really want to quit. His resignation was merely an
extension of a political culture wherein public officers had to feign a
complete lack of personal ambition, to acknowledge that they served only
as a sacrifice to the public good. He was actually appealing to Madison,
one Virginia gentleman to another, to refuse the resignation and soothe
his bruised honor. Given the trust Madison put in Harrison immediately
after this incident, it is plausible that the president would have done just
that. But what Harrison thought would be a ritual cleansing of his reputation backfired because Madison was then home in Virginia. Armstrong
seized the opportunity to pull a fast one—rather than forwarding the
resignation letter to Madison, he accepted it himself, noting, "[y]our resignation has been communicated to the President."[71] General Harrison
had been outflanked.

He was too proud to beg the president for reinstatement, which would likely have been granted. It was more than a gentleman could bear. He had other concerns, like Anna and the children. And Judge Symmes's estate needed attention. But he had not resigned simply because of family, fear, or finances. His was the burning rage of an aristocrat whose honor had been repeatedly and wantonly slighted. It was probably best for Armstrong that the general did not believe in dueling. Harrison no doubt could recall instances of other men from Virginia's leading families who had received grievous insults while suffering in the service of their country. A young George Washington had doggedly sought an officer's commission in the British Army, and after being repeatedly spurned, he chose to retire in the midst of the Seven Years' War. George Rogers Clark had faced embarrassing questions about his supply requisitions during wartime and been unfairly ruined. Unlike Clark, he quit early enough to preserve his reputation.[72]

Harrison's staff wrote him a thoughtful adieu, noting that he was "a disciple of Wayne . . . who emulated the Virtues of the immortal Washington." It was the highest compliment anyone could have paid him. Harrison had already retired to North Bend, Ohio, by the time the letter arrived. He was touched by the gesture and wrote a nice thank-you note to his former comrades.[73]

Although he had left the army, William Henry Harrison's experience with Ohio Valley Indians, and his voluminous record of land cessions acquired, led to his appointment as treaty commissioner once again in 1814. The day after Harrison officially resigned his commission in the army, President Madison was signing one for him to treat with Indians. Clearly, Madison had not lost any confidence in Harrison. The commission's wording seemed calculated to salve Harrison's raw feelings. "Know ye, That reposing special Trust and Confidence in the Abilities, Prudence and Fidelity of William H. Harrison, late a Major General in the Service of the U States," it began. That July, Harrison and Governor Lewis Cass of Michigan Territory negotiated a "treaty of peace and friendship" with the Miamis, as well as some Potawatomis, Ottawas, and Kickapoos. The treaty was held at Greenville, Ohio. Peace was given not just by the United States but also by its allies, the Wyandots, Delawares, Senecas, and Shawnees—Tecumseh and the Prophet had never held sway with the majority of their own nation.[74]

Some aspects of the treaty council differed from Harrison's previous efforts, particularly the fact that a war still raged on the frontier. Secretary of War Armstrong had originally included a demand for more land cessions as a condition of peace. However, perhaps following previous advice from General Harrison and others, that demand was dropped. Harrison had noted that, on the question of land cessions, the hostile tribes should be "made easy." Prolonging the war would be expensive, but once peace was restored, additional territory could be had "for a consideration so trifling that it ought not to be regarded." The two goals of the negotiations would be to secure peace with the hostile tribes and to have them turn their warriors against Britain.[75]

Other aspects of the council must have seemed very familiar. The negotiations were to have begun on July 5, but Harrison insisted on having the council house moved 30 rods (about 500 feet) to the northeast so it might rest on the exact spot on which Wayne's council house had stood during the Treaty of Greenville nearly twenty years earlier. No doubt Harrison remembered the spot well. So did one of the Miami chiefs, Katunga, or Charley.[76] Another old tactic was the inclusion of tribes already allied to the Americans, who might be used as leverage against the others.

Harrison presented the Wyandots, Shawnees, and Delawares—three tribes that, as a whole, had adhered to the United States—with elaborately ornamented silver pipes, each engraved with symbolic images of American benevolence. Harrison spoke first, stating that while Britain had been successful in driving a wedge between the United States and its Indian children, he hoped that "neither the Devil nor his friends the British" would be able to separate them again. He insisted that the Prophet was a tool of Britain and that Tecumseh had never had the right to question the Fort Wayne treaties of 1809. Then he launched into a fairly lengthy defense of his Tippecanoe campaign, arguing that the Prophet's men had been the first to shed blood.[77]

When Katunga rose to give the Miami answer, he offered that his people had long been loyal to the Americans, even after the Mississinewa campaign had destroyed many of their homes. The Miamis had sided with Britain only with great reluctance, and only then because they were unable to restrain their younger men. Harrison blanched at the reference to

Mississinewa. Perhaps the decision still troubled him. He testily responded that while he had made a point of trying not to insult anyone at the council, Katunga had taken a different course. He then defended the burning of the Mississinewa villages, insisting that because of their strategic location, even "had they been whites and in the strictest alliance with the United States—good policy required that their corn should be destroyed to prevent its supplying the Hostile tribes with food."[78] Harrison should have mentioned that he had given specific orders to spare Katunga's life if possible. But he did not, and the Miamis found Harrison's explanation insultingly implausible.

While all the tribes present professed a desire for peace with the United States, the demand that they also send war parties against the British proved a major sticking point. Katunga spoke again, noting that in previous conflicts the United States had merely asked the Indians to remain neutral. He stated that the Miamis had not shed first blood in this war. That assertion drew an emotional interjection from John Johnston. The Indian agent at Fort Wayne indignantly proclaimed Katunga a liar and recounted that the Miamis had killed his own brother. Harrison took this opportunity to address the Miamis separately and admonished their chiefs to disavow Katunga's speech.[79]

Harrison again addressed the assembled Indians and claimed that the expedition against the Mississinewa towns had been directed at Tecumseh, whom Harrison thought was hiding there, and some of his adherents. (The surviving orders to Campbell make no mention of Tecumseh, the Prophet, or their followers.)[80] He lamely added that the only way to prevent such unpleasant incidents in the future was for friendly Indians to completely separate themselves from hostile ones, something Harrison knew was impossible.[81]

Katunga reiterated that the Miamis merely wanted to be neutral in the conflict. He was answered by General Cass, who insisted that because they had sided with Britain, neutrality was no longer an option. The United States, Cass continued, had "thrown the British on their backs" thirty years before, when the country was "in a State of infancy." Now the United States had achieved "Manhood" and needed no help to defeat the British. But the Miamis had to wage war on the British, he added, because their young men could not be trusted to sit still during a war. They needed to have their aggression channeled against Britain.[82]

After the venerable Crane, or Tarhe, stated that his Wyandots would fight the British, Pacane and some of his Miamis also agreed to fight. Harrison offered a war belt, which was greeted enthusiastically by the Wyandots, Shawnees, Delawares, Kickapoos, Potawatomis, Ottawas, and some of the Miamis. The Indian agents were then instructed to provide whiskey for the Indians, many of whom danced their war dances.[83]

At the treaty itself, the Miamis and others pledged to provide warriors to fight against Britain, their quotas to be determined by the president. The Wyandots, Senecas, Delawares, and Shawnees, "who have preserved their fidelity to the United States throughout the war," restated their commitment to the United States and promised to make no separate peace.

Among the dozens of chiefs who marked the treaty were the old Chiefs Tarhe of the Wyandots and Black Hoof of the Shawnees, both of whom had resented and resisted the efforts of the upstarts Tecumseh and the Prophet to claim authority. Katunga, however, did not mark the treaty.[84] Tarhe had spoken of his gratitude for Harrison's having stated "that our Lands should be secured to us, so long as the Sun shone on them." The treaty journal does not quote Harrison as saying any such thing, only that the United States was not seeking additional land cessions at the time.[85]

Harrison had previously assessed Tarhe as "a venerable, intelligent, and upright man." Black Hoof and fellow Shawnee chiefs Wolf and Lewis were "attached to us from principles as well as interest—they are honest men." In marking the treaty with General Harrison (on July 22) they received another affirmation of protection from the United States. The treaty did not include a formal land cession to the United States or any annuities. It did continue the trend of rapidly eroding the tribes' sovereignty, however, by stating that the United States would establish the boundaries between them.[86]

Harrison and Cass wrote a report to Armstrong, with some surprising suggestions. They noted that "[o]ur Indian Department is better organized for peace than War" and suggested that it be reformed along British lines. Specifically, they stated that having agents living in closer proximity to the Indians would be especially valuable for both gathering and disseminating information. Alexander McKee and Matthew Elliott, two of the men frontier Americans hated most, were offered as examples of effective Indian agents.[87] Harrison's suggestions were perfectly sound, although one suspects he also took some pleasure in asserting his superior knowledge of Indian affairs to the man who had driven him from the army.

Conclusion

The Grandee of North Bend

Although William Henry Harrison had not really wanted to retire from public life in 1814, he needed a break from the manifold pressures of service. He began to settle in to life as a civilian again and sought to consolidate and improve his property. Part of that task was making sure he had enough laborers to work his new land.

While the Harrisons were still living in Indiana, one of their black "indentured servants," Betty, had run off to Ohio. With the old planter's mentality but a practiced ability to skirt the finer points of law north of the Ohio, Harrison had Betty's two sons "apprenticed" to him by the Hamilton County (Ohio) overseers of the poor. The boys, James and John, were to learn "farming," which sounds rather like assigning them to basic manual labor in Harrison's fields, until each had reached age twenty-one. At that time each would receive three nice suits of clothes, one for holidays and two for everyday wear, as well as a Bible. At the time they were apprenticed, James was fifteen months old and John only six months old.[1]

In November the former governor wrote to a friend that "I am Settled here I believe for life—With as Good a prospect of Happiness as any person Can have." He had replaced much of the overused cornfields with six hundred acres of clover and other grasses to support his Merino sheep and cattle. He hoped to soon have an additional seven hundred acres under cultivation. Such improvements were not cheap, but he was managing by selling off small parcels of land. He was also pleased to report the birth of yet another child, his ninth, daughter Anna Tuthill Harrison. Despite an arthritic knee, he seemed to be enjoying his semiretirement, pawning off some of the day-to-day tasks of managing his holdings to his nephew and son-in-law John Cleves Short and shooting partridges with abandon.[2]

The Americans never did take Canada. But Tecumseh's death knocked the wind out of militant pan-Indianism, and although the Prophet tried to step in as a war leader, his brother's moccasins were far too big to fill. The death of other prominent warriors, such as Main Poc, further deflated Indian resistance north of the Ohio River. In the South, Tecumseh's allies among the Creeks, the Red Stick faction, waged an exceptionally bloody campaign against American settlers. They were put down in even more brutal fashion by Tennessean Andrew Jackson's army at the Battle of Horseshoe Bend in 1814. The Battle of New Orleans the following January made Jackson a national hero, but Horseshoe Bend was arguably the more crucial battle. It broke the last large pocket of Indian militancy east of the Mississippi River. Britain, at the 1814 peace negotiations in Ghent, tried to insist on an Indian buffer state in the Northwest as a condition for peace. The Americans refused, the British relented, and Tecumseh's dream truly died.[3]

In the aftermath of Jackson's great victory, Harrison took the opportunity to congratulate him. Although the two had yet to meet, Harrison wrote, he well remembered how Jackson had offered to send ready aid after the Battle of Tippecanoe—"at a Most Critical period of my life." He asserted that he had made a similar offer to Jackson as he was preparing to defend New Orleans—if so, the document has been lost—and how happy he would have been to serve under Old Hickory, even if only at the head of a regiment. He added, "My adverse fortune did not however permit this but Condemned me to a life of ease & retirement when my whole Soul was devoted to the profession which I had been Compelled to abandon."[4] Despite what seemed like an idyllic life, Harrison was growing restless. His poor treatment by Armstrong still rankled. Like his father before him, he needed public duties and the public laurels they bestowed.

A few months after he sent the wistful missive to Jackson, the patriarch of North Bend received an urgent letter from Alexander J. Dallas, the acting secretary of war.[5] Although the Peace Treaty at Ghent had ended the war with Britain, some Indian allies of both parties in the Great Lakes region seemed bent on continuing the contest. And there was some question of whether the treaty technically applied to the Wyandots, Delawares, Shawnees, Senecas, and Miamis, who were already under treaty with the United States. President Madison wanted Harrison and several other trusted Indian agents to head off further troubles. Some depredations had already occurred in the Detroit area, and Madison did not trust the British to stop influencing Indians living within the bounds of the United States. President Madison soon issued the commissions.[6]

Harrison replied that "[t]he business of treating with the Indians [is] at all times disagreeable," particularly now because of the intense mutual hostility between whites and Indians on the frontier. White settlers spoke of little but exterminating all Indians, even the faithful ones who had inflicted far fewer injuries to their white neighbors than they had received. Although he had made a career out of aggressive land acquisition, Harrison (noting that he had not yet seen the actual instructions) again stated his hope that the president was not seeking additional lands, which would be impossible and disastrous in the current climate. He mentioned that a cession treaty by Gen. William Hull of Michigan Territory (with the Chippewas, 1808) was still causing irritation.

Although Harrison offered that charges of improper treaty negotiating were often false, in this case he believed Hull truly had "grossly imposed" on them. (Tecumseh would have chuckled at that.) Harrison also described the untenable position of the loyal tribes, many of whom had fled their brethren to escape attack, only to be assaulted in the white settlements. The Miami chief Owl had been shot at while visiting Vincennes after the war, and others had been murdered. Harrison stated emphatically: "From the experience of fifteen years in the management of Indian affairs I have no hesitation in saying that it will be useless to call the Indians to General Council until their resentment for the injuries they have received be in Some measure assuaged."[7]

He was familiar with injuries of another kind, but the commission from the president was helping to assuage them considerably. The additional vote of confidence from Madison confirmed, Harrison said, what he had been telling himself. The "outrage to my feelings which I experienced in the manner in which my resignation of my commission in the army was accepted, is to be attributed to the minister [Armstrong] who, not contented with the success of his schemes to force me from the service, had determined also that I should quit it with the impression that it was viewed by the Government as a happy riddance of an officer who had no pretensions on the score of merit or service." In Harrison's view, Armstrong had not only stabbed him in the back but had then poured salt over the wound. So cleansing was Madison's approval, however, that even though accepting the commission would prove arduous and detrimental to his private pursuits, he would answer the call.[8]

It was, Harrison asserted, a perilous hour. He summed up America's choices if continued land acquisition from the Indians were to be pursued: (1) commit immediate genocide, or (2) follow the tried-and-true Jeffersonian policy of "justice & humanity" toward the Indians, gaining their confidence and slowly convincing them that their only hope was to accept American annuities. Fortunately, Madison understood that seeking additional cessions at the time was absurd, and the commissioners (as Harrison later learned) were expressly ordered to assure the Indians that they were not seeking more land.[9]

Although he complained about the taxing nature of Indian councils, in truth the reaffirmation of the government's favor energized Harrison. He quickly fell back into his old patterns, including writing on behalf of wounded veterans who could benefit from government jobs. He also attempted to safeguard his war record against detractors, asking fellow war hero Oliver Hazard Perry to help him correct a newspaper piece that had accused Harrison of sloth in moving his army across Lake Erie in 1813.[10]

In August 1815, Harrison and the commissioners were in Detroit to meet with the Wyandots, Ottawas, Potawatomis, Chippewas, and as many of their former Native enemies still in Canada as would attend the council. They even invited Tenskwatawa, the Shawnee Prophet. They tried to start in earnest on August 22 but found it difficult to gather enough of the affected Indians to make talks worthwhile. After several abortive attempts because of sparse attendance, on August 31 Tarhe of the Wyandots, "the eldest son" of the Great Father, was given the honor of lighting the council fire. Predictably, he spoke in favor of remaining attached to the United States and took steps to ritually cover the dead. The next day, General Harrison recounted the history of the late war, diplomatically citing the courage of the British troops with whom so many Indians had been recently allied. He described Andrew Jackson's great victory over the

British at New Orleans but omitted mentioning Jackson's earlier victory over the Creeks at Horseshoe Bend or his own triumph on the Thames.[11] President Madison, Harrison asserted, only wanted a cessation of hostilities, fulfillment of previous treaties, and a promise not to molest surveyors on lands already purchased by the United States.

The most noteworthy event of the council was an appearance by the Prophet, who spoke on September 4. His speech, while not recorded in exact detail, was described as pacific and conciliatory in tone. The mood was slightly dampened the next day, however, when the commissioners found that he had left the council suddenly, causing some to feel uneasy about his intentions. He had in fact returned to Canada, where he felt far more secure. On September 8 those still present marked the treaty, although a Potawatomi chief lamented that he agreed to the former land cessions with a heavy heart. His ancestors had agreed to them, he opined, perhaps because they were "Less enlightened."[12]

This last Indian treaty negotiated by William Henry Harrison, although he claimed to dislike the work, was a much-needed boost to his reputation and his ego. By any reasonable measure, Harrison and the commissioners achieved the president's objectives, and they did so without wasting public monies. It was good that Harrison could point to such an accomplishment because an old enemy was on the offensive.

Jonathan Jennings, as Indiana Territory's delegate to Congress, was still after his former governor. Specifically, he had introduced a number of resolutions before Congress questioning Harrison's use of public funds while he was Indiana's chief executive. The resolution Harrison now responded to concerned his use of funds as Indian affairs plenipotentiary. He first stated that although exact figures eluded him, he was reasonably certain that his treaties over seven years had secured title to about 50 million acres of land, at a cost of a little under two cents per acre.[13]

He also suggested that the fact that he was the only Indian superintendent under investigation and the resolution was clearly from Jennings constituted "sufficient evidence of its being intended as a personal attack." Two could play that game. Harrison offered that one of the closest friends of the source of this personal attack was a "Scotch tory" "whose brothers reside in Upper Canada, and are largely concerned in the Indian trade." Lest there be any doubt that he was referring to William

McIntosh, he recounted how he had won a defamation lawsuit against the said Tory.[14] Jennings's attacks never led to anything substantive, but they grieved Harrison, which was probably the primary intent. There was nothing laudable in the effort, but one might argue that Harrison had a right to expect some retribution for his territorial political shenanigans.

Shortly before Christmas, Harrison fired off a massive packet of letters and documents to Henry Clay, the speaker of the House, with the ultimate goal of finally resolving the dispute with Orr and Greely. The packet contained numerous depositions, which consistently indicated that the contractors were making huge profits and that their complaint with Harrison was based on his denying them even more. Congress would eventually reach the same conclusion, but not until 1817, after Harrison had spent the better part of three years worrying about the issue.[15]

As 1815 drew to a close, the transplanted scion of Berkeley was nursing a wounded ego and trying to remove the recent smudges from his family's coat of arms. Although he remained seemingly indispensable to Ohio Valley Indian affairs and was proud of his contributions, he nevertheless felt self-pity because of the host of calumnies cast his way. With the outcome of the contractor investigation still very much in doubt, he poured out some of his grief to John McClean, chair of the House Committee on Accounts and Harrison's congressman. Some men had, he allowed, performed greater service to their country, but none had exceeded him in "zeal and fidelity." He insisted that he sought no award and would be content with anonymity, but he simply could not allow the unwarranted violence to his character to go unchallenged.

In a maudlin comparison, he referenced the man whose defeat had been his greatest triumph: "I see that my old opponent (Proctor) [sic] has been severely reprimanded by the Prince Regent. My fate has been more hard than his. He had (I presume) a fair trial, I have been condemned unheard. His crime was the loss of an army and a province; mine of having incurred (in what way I know not) the hatred of a minister [Armstrong], and forcing a contractor to do his duty."[16] These were dark days for Harrison, but eventually the skies, like his reputation, would brighten considerably.

The War of 1812 had been a strange one. Most of the battles had gone poorly for the Americans. Once news of Jackson's victory at New Orleans arrived, however, the War of 1812 suddenly became hugely popular in the United States. Excepting pockets of die-hard New England Federalists, most Americans now saw the war as glorious and retroactively justified. As with the battle of Tippecanoe, the facts of the matter proved far less important than the subsequent reaction of the American public. Both contemporaries and historians noted that Americans saw the War of 1812 as a second war for American independence. The Revolutionary analogy was fitting, in that the second American Revolution left as many glaringly unanswered questions as the first.[17] None of the quarrels with Britain were resolved at the Treaty of Ghent.

As John Sugden stated in the epilogue to *Tecumseh: A Life,* an entire generation of American politicians based their careers largely on the role they played in fighting against Tecumseh and his allies. Andrew Jackson negotiated treaty cessions with the Indians of the Southeast in the aftermath of the war. He was able to build on Harrison's precedents, although by comparison William Henry's councils were subtle and genteel affairs. Jackson began blurring the line between the heavy-handed acculturation President Jefferson and Governor Harrison had implemented and the outright exclusion of Indians from American society he would pursue during his presidency (1829–37).[18]

Congress's "War Hawks," most notably Kentuckian Henry Clay and South Carolinian John C. Calhoun, went on to long and extraordinary careers. Richard Mentor Johnson became Martin Van Buren's vice president in 1836 with the slogan "Rumpsey-dumpsey, rumpsey-dumpsey, Col. Johnson killed Tecumsey," although he was careful never to make the claim himself. Johnson was nearly dumped from the Democrats' 1840 ticket, although not for his political philosophy. The Democrats saw him as a liability in part because Johnson, instead of just keeping a female slave as a concubine, had the effrontery to live with her as his common-law wife. They kept him for the campaign, though, because they needed a bona fide war hero. Johnson had been severely wounded at the Battle of the Thames, and his battle scars were necessary to counter the Whig candidate for president.[19]

Van Buren's presidency (1837–41) had seen the final removal of the eastern Indian tribes, sent west to Kansas and later Oklahoma. He fulfilled the movement begun by his predecessor, Andrew Jackson. Mercifully, many of those chiefs who had tried to accommodate the United States in the hope of maintaining their lands were long since dead. Jean Baptiste Ducoigne had died in April 1811 and was interred at the Kaskaskia mission, where the local militia saw that he was buried with military honors. Little Turtle, struggling to the last to maintain some autonomy for the Miamis, died in July 1812 and also received the rights of war. In death these chiefs gained the acceptance and protection of their father that had often eluded them in life. Americans could not resist trying to acculturate Indian chiefs, even in death. Little Turtle's son-in-law William Wells died a heroic and gruesome death one month later while trying to protect the Americans in the Fort Dearborn Massacre. Wells fought bravely, and the vengeful Potawatomis who slew him cut out his heart and divided it among themselves.[20] The Americans were not the only ones who liked to posthumously incorporate people.

The Shawnee chief Black Hoof died in Ohio in 1832, reportedly at age 107, with his tribe's removal imminent. Jean Baptiste Richardville ascended to Miami prominence but had to watch as a series of treaties further dissected his tribe's holdings in the 1820s and 1830s. Richardville, a trilingual, educated, and acculturated métis, was a shrewd negotiator, however. He secured enough inalienable, privately owned land that when he died in 1841 he left acreage for about half the Miami tribe to live on. Miamis still live on those lands today. Saddest of all was the case of Tenskwatawa, the fallen Shawnee Prophet. Unpopular with the British in Canada and largely disgraced within his own tribe, he eventually settled in Kansas, having returned to the bottle as well as to the United States. He occasionally sat for portraits and regaled visitors with stories about his increasingly venerated brother, dying in 1836.[21]

Indiana became a state in 1816, with Jonathan Jennings as its first governor. Although he had criticized William Henry Harrison's rapacity regarding Indian land treaties, he himself negotiated large cessions in 1818 and 1832. He resigned as governor in 1822 and became Indiana's U.S. congressman for the period 1822–31. He smoothed his relationship with Harrison long enough to share the stump with the former governor when they both campaigned for Henry Clay in 1826. Unfortunately for Jennings, he never did shake one behavior of which Harrison disapproved—excessive drinking. Jennings's life was cut short by a sudden heart attack in 1834. He was fifty years old. At his death Jennings was so destitute that, despite his years in public service, he lay in an unmarked grave until Indiana's state legislature provided a monument in 1892.

Such was not the fate of Thomas Jefferson, whose presidency did so much to establish Indian policy precedents and who went on to found the University of Virginia. He died on July 4, 1826, exactly fifty years after his Declaration of Independence was first signed. His old friend, rival, and the man who had appointed the first governor of the Indiana Territory, John Adams, died within hours of him.[22]

William Henry Harrison somehow survived, with public honor intact, all the political and military scandals that had plagued him from 1805 to 1815. He went on to become a U.S. senator from Ohio and resigned that office to become U.S. minister to Colombia. He was the Whigs' losing presidential candidate in 1836. The 1840 presidential election featured the "Log Cabin Campaign," which built on Harrison's record as an Indian fighter and emblem of the frontier common man. The Whigs took the scion of an elite Virginia family, who had suffered repeated attacks because of his aristocratic, even autocratic tendencies and weathered charges of fraud and land jobbing, and passed him off as a simple, cabin-dwelling frontiersman who drank hard cider. Aside from not seeming rustic enough, his opponent, Martin Van Buren also labored under the Panic of 1837, which was partially his predecessor's fault. The Whigs staged great rallies at the Tippecanoe battlefield in 1836 and 1840 to capitalize on their candidate's fame as an Indian fighter. The depression their wagons made in the ground there is still faintly visible. With running mate John Tyler of Virginia, Harrison ran under the slogan "Tippecanoe and Tyler, Too" and crushed Van Buren in the electoral college.[23]

President Harrison died after only thirty-one days in office, having contracted pneumonia after delivering his two-hour inaugural address in a cold wind.[24] He was the first president to die in office, and numerous funeral orations asserted that the death of a sitting president was a punishment from God for the nation's sins. He rests just outside Cincinnati, entombed under a large obelisk inscribed with a list of his public services. The monument is grand, conveying unmistakably that therein lies a man of considerable worth and repute within his community. It is greater than most Virginia plantation grandees could have hoped for—not bad for a man whose first real job paid twenty-four dollars a month. The tomb sits on a hill, facing the Ohio River as it slowly and inexorably rolls west. One suspects Old Tippecanoe would have approved.

Harrison's sudden death left both his Whig Party and the country in something of a lurch, as the Whigs were as unprepared for a John Tyler presidency—he was on old Democrat—as was Tyler himself. Tyler would sign the bill annexing Texas in one of his final presidential acts, something Harrison's old compatriot Andrew Jackson heartily approved of. Harrison's wife, Anna, despite reservations about her own health, lived until 1864. Her grandson Benjamin Harrison was elected president in 1888.[25]

The issue of slavery, both north and south of the Ohio River, remained largely unresolved. The growing profitability of cotton agriculture, thanks to Eli Whitney's cotton gin, would in subsequent years solidify slavery's hold on the antebellum South.[26]

The anti-slavery Article VI of the Northwest Ordinance, however, belatedly did its job; by discouraging slave owners from settling in the Ohio Valley for fear of eventual emancipation, it helped ensure a strong anti-slavery voting bloc in the Midwest. Yet the Illinois and Indiana state constitutions, which did ban slavery, did not extinguish existing human bondage in their states. Slavery continued there into the 1830s and 1840s. Further, midwestern states in general adopted numerous codes, such as poll taxes, designed specifically to discourage free blacks from settling there.[27]

American women remained largely trapped in the Republican Mother's role and only gradually, through innovations like the factory system, began to acquire any economic independence. While the national government saw black male suffrage as imperative at the end of the Civil War, the suffragettes' calls for political equality were not answered until the twentieth century. The War of 1812 had been waged against Britain, not paternalism or patriarchy.

William Henry Harrison and his Indiana neighbors were products of their time. They promoted Indiana's statehood in an effort to spread the American Revolution westward, as did Thomas Jefferson. In turn, the quest for land ownership sprang from the English gentleman's ideal of financial and social independence through acquiring real estate. Indiana's story from territory to state exemplifies the possibilities and limitations of Revolutionary ideology on the frontier. Harrison's Indiana made tentative steps to at least acknowledge its responsibilities to, if not equality for, black servants, Indians, women, and poor white men. It was the best that paternalism had to offer. Fighting the Second War for Independence was psychologically important for Americans of Harrison's generation and let them feel that they were continuing a righteous cause. The degree to which Anglophobia permeated, even saturated, all manner of issues—such as divorce, slavery, Indian policy, trade—strongly suggests that the fear and hatred of Britain was often heartfelt, if not always perceptive.[28]

What are we to make of William Henry Harrison and his generation of Americans? How should we view these people who so strongly championed the great ideals of the American Revolution yet exemplified so many of its flaws as well? It would seem overly harsh, not to mention ahistorical, to criticize them too deeply for commonly held ideas about race and society that we find repugnant today. And yet those views cannot but tarnish the lustrous vision of them we once held. The student of history's challenge, it seems, is to neither praise nor bury Caesar but simply to try to understand him. It is hoped that these pages have shown that, despite what most of his biographers have asserted, Harrison was no saint, no unalloyed knight defending democracy. Nor was he a purely malevolent force who trod upon the rights of nonwhites and commoners out of malice and simple greed. As governor of Indiana Territory, as a soldier, and as a man, he saw his own interests and those of his country as one and the same, and he tried to advance them as best he could.

William Henry Harrison was a son of Virginia.

Notes

INTRODUCTION

1. For the *Chesapeake-Leopard* Affair, see Tucker and Reuter, *Injured Honor.*

2. WHH to General Assembly, August 18, 1807, in Clanin, ed., *Papers of William Henry Harrison.*

3. Anderson, *Crucible of War,* 745.

4. For example, as recently as 2000 the Miami Indians of Oklahoma sued the state of Illinois, arguing that Harrison's Treaty of Grouseland (1805) had given them rights to the Vermillion River watershed lands in east-central Illinois. The suit was later dropped.

5. Onuf and Sadosky, *Jeffersonian America,* 4–5.

6. See Warren, *History of the Rise, Progress, and Termination of the American Revolution.*

7. For example, see Quimby, *U.S. Army in the War of 1812;* Gunderson, *Log-Cabin Campaign.*

8. Hagan in *Journal of Interdisciplinary History* 5, 4 (Spring 1975): 756–58.

CHAPTER 1

1. See Horsman, "William Henry Harrison," 125–49.

2. Sydnor, *American Revolutionaries in the Making,* 89.

3. Isaac, *Transformation of Virginia,* 320.

4. See Brown, *Good Wives, Nasty Wenches;* Fischer and Kelly, *Bound Away,* 134.

5. Breen, *Tobacco Culture,* 8.

6. For the linking of solvency and honor in the Chesapeake, see Norton, "Gender and Defamation in Seventeenth-Century Maryland," 3–39.

7. Breen, *Tobacco Culture,* 86; Brown, *Good Wives, Nasty Wenches,* 250.

8. Isaac, *Landon Carter's Uneasy Kingdom,* 174.

9. Breen, *Tobacco Culture*, 8; Morgan, *American Slavery, American Freedom*, 380–83.

10. Young, *Fathers of American Presidents*, 43.

11. Smith, *Benjamin Harrison*, 23–55; Fischer and Kelly, *Bound Away*, 134. The *Virginia Gazette* (microfilm), October 11, 1776, noted, "We hear that Benjamin Harrison, Esq., of Berkeley, is chosen a Delegate in Congress, in the room of Thomas Jefferson, Esq., resigned."

12. Smith, *Benjamin Harrison*, 10, 22.

13. Boyd, *The Declaration of Independence*, 83; Maier, *American Scripture*, 119–21.

14. See Isaac, *Landon Carter's Uneasy Kingdom*, 138–41, and Isaac, *Transformation of Virginia*, 311.

15. Fischer and Kelly, *Bound Away*, 164–67.

16. Ibid., 153–54.

17. Paine, under the pseudonym "The Forester," to "Cato" (William Smith) in series of jousting editorials in the *Pennsylvania Gazette*, 1776. Quote from second letter to Cato, April 10, 1776, reproduced in Paine's *Common Sense*, 202.

18. Harrison quoted in Calloway, *American Revolution in Indian Country*, 281.

19. Daniel K. Richter, "Onas, the Long Knife: Pennsylvanians and Indians 1783–1794," in Hoxie, Hoffman, and Albert, eds., *Native Americans and the Early Republic*, 126.

20. Fischer, *Paul Revere's Ride*, 25. British nationalism had been built largely on seeing France as the "other," but Americans would use Britain for that role. See Colley, *Britons*, 5.

21. Colley, *Captives*, 225–26. The conundrum did not, however, prevent British forces from trying to introduce smallpox among the Americans later in the war; see Fenn, *Pox Americana*.

22. Colley, *Captives*, 228.

23. See Axtell, "The White Indians of Colonial America," 55–88, 67–68; Heard, *White into Red*, 98; Person, "The American Eve," 668–85, 675–76.

24. Colley, *Captives*, 230. For reasons mentioned earlier, British propagandists were never able to fully capitalize on American atrocities, like the murder of dozens of Christian Delaware Indians by Pennsylvania militia at Gnaddenhutten in 1782. For the American atrocity at Concord, see Fischer, *Paul Revere's Ride*, 218.

25. Smith, *Benjamin Harrison*, 55; Cleaves, *Old Tippecanoe*, 4; Ward, *The American Revolution*, 151.

26. Quoted in Young, *Fathers of American Presidents*, 41.

27. Quoted in Smith, *Benjamin Harrison*, 70.

28. Harrison to Campbell, March 6, 1783, in the Papers of Arthur Campbell, Filson Historical Society.

29. Young, *Fathers of American Presidents*, 43.

30. Fischer and Kelly, *Bound Away*, 129, 202.

31. Ibid., 132, 136–37.

32. Smith, *Benjamin Harrison*, 78–80.

33. See WHH's letter to Charles de Hault Delassuss, written in French in his hand, in Clanin, ed., *Papers of WHH*.

34. Cleaves, *Old Tippecanoe*, 5–7; Goebel, *Harrison*, 16–18. The Virginia gentry and evangelicalism are discussed in detail in Isaac, *Transformation of Virginia*.

35. Quote in Goebel, *Harrison*, 18. Now obsolete in the army, an ensign was the most junior rank of commissioned officer, just above master sergeant. Gunderson, "Apprentice in Arms," 3–29.

36. Goebel, *Harrison*, 19.

37. Quote in Gunderson, "Apprentice in Arms," 3.

38. White, *Middle Ground*, 369–78.

39. Holton, *Forced Founders*, quote on 211.

40. Carter, ed., *Territorial Papers vol. 2*, 12–18, 39–50.

41. Combs, *The Jay Treaty*, 10–12.

42. The standard military account of this time is Sword, *Washington's War*. See also Gaff, *Bayonets in the Wilderness*.

43. Gunderson, "Apprentice in Arms," 4; Jones, *Fort Washington at Cincinnati*, 17–18, quote on 17.

44. Gunderson, "Apprentice in Arms," 5.

45. See Report of a Special Committee of the House of Representatives on the Failure of the Expedition against the Indians, March 27, 1792, in Smith, ed., *The St. Clair Papers*, vol. 2, 286–99.

46. Wilkinson's career is covered in Jacobs, *Tarnished Warrior*; for his attack on Clark, see Van Every, *Ark of Empire*, 101, 107–108, and Jones, *William Clark*, 54, 73.

47. Gunderson, "Apprentice in Arms," 8.

48. An eighteenth-century gentleman, and Harrison certainly considered himself one, took great pride in controlling his passions and appetites, including drinking. See Brown, *Good Wives, Nasty Wenches*, 324–27.

49. Quotes in Gunderson, "Apprentice in Arms," 8. See also Winthrop Sargent to Secretary of War, June 9, 1792, and Judge Symmes to Sargent, June 30, 1792, both in Carter, ed., *Territorial Papers vol. 2*, 400–403, and Sargent to Symmes, June 4, 1792, and June 13, 1792, both in Carter, ed., *Territorial Papers vol. 3*, 377–80.

50. Gunderson, "Apprentice in Arms," 8.

51. Ibid., 9; Hawkins to the President, February 10, 1792, in Carter, ed., *Territorial Papers vol. 2*, 367; Knopf, "Anthony Wayne," 37.

52. Steele to Campbell, January 29, 1792, in Papers of Arthur Campbell, Filson Historical Society.

53. George Rogers Clark Papers, Mss C CGRC, Clark in Beargrass (Kentucky) to his brother Col. Jonathan Clark in Spotsylvania, Virginia, 1792 [no month], Filson Historical Society.

54. Rohrbough, *Land Office Business,* 65–72; Fischer and Kelly, *Bound Away,* 168–71; Cayton, *The Frontier Republic,* 2.

55. Knopf, "Anthony Wayne," 35–42, quote on 37.

56. Ibid., 38.

57. Putnam to Secretary of War, August 16, 1792, in *American State Papers, Class II Indian Affairs,* vol. 1, 240; Sword, *Washington's War,* 211–13, 346, 363–65. The treaty is covered in Edmunds, "'Nothing Has Been Effected,'" 23–35.

58. Sword, *Washington's War,* 215–17; Hutton, "William Wells: Frontier Scout and Indian Agent," 184–95.

59. Quoted in Calloway, ed., *The World Turned Upside Down,* 181–83; see also, Linklater, *Measuring America,* 60.

60. Knopf, "Anthony Wayne," 39; order against firing guns in camp mentioned October 29, 1793, in copy of the army's General Orders, found in the back of an anonymous journal of Wayne's campaign, Filson Historical Society; Gunderson, "Apprentice in Arms," 9; for Knox's christening of the Legion, see Sword, *Washington's War,* 234; *The Centinel of the North-Western Territory* (microfilm), Ohio State Library. Andrew R.L. Cayton also discusses discipline in the Legion in "'Noble Actors' upon 'the Theatre of Honour': Power and Civility in the Treaty of Grenville," in Cayton and Teute, eds., *Contact Points,* 235–69.

61. Wayne Orderly Books, Book 4, 143–45, quotes on 144; Book 6, 61, Filson Historical Society; Gunderson, "Apprentice in Arms," 11.

62. Inflation conversion factors are not meant to be exact, but they offer a rough estimation. This text uses the tables available from Oregon State University, http://oregonstate.edu/dept/pol_sci/fac/sahr.htm, accessed August 12, 2005.

63. Gunderson, "Apprentice in Arms," 13–14. For Harrison's complaining, see WHH to John Tipton, December 6, 1833, in Esarey, ed., *Messages and Letters* 2, 746–47. The Filson Historical Library, Special Collections, Mss C W ov32 [oversize], has an Anthony Wayne payroll document for the General Staff, May–July 1793, noting the salaries of Harrison and the other four aides. General Wayne got $166 a month plus forage.

64. Nelson, "'Never Have They Done So Little,'" 43–55, citation on 46.

65. Gunderson, "Apprentice in Arms," 18–19.

66. James Wilkinson from Camp Ouiatenon, report to Gen. Charles Scott, June 3, 1795, in Thomas Bodley Correspondence (photostats of originals held by Bodley family), Mss A. B668a, Filson Historical Society; Jones, *William Clark,* 54, 64.

67. As late as July 25 of the next year, the wary *Centinel of the North-Western Territory* noted, "It seems, however, to be the general opinion of those who are best acquainted with the Indian character, that a peace at this time, grounded as it would be, on no decisive action, can hardly be expected to be coupled with duration"

(microfilm, Ohio State Library). This is not to say that forty deaths were inconsequential, as, depending on the number of warriors, this might have approached 10 percent killed, that is, literal decimation. But given the confederacy's peak numbers of just a few weeks before and the long-term significance of the defeat, the number seems surprisingly low. The answer may lie partially in Lawrence H. Keeley's observation that in nonstate societies, warfare tends to be more frequent than in large civilizations; thus even small casualty figures can add up to disaster over several years. See Keeley, *War Before Civilization,* 88–94.

68. For troop numbers and casualty counts, see Van Every, *Ark of Empire,* 324; Sword, *Washington's War,* 306, 312; Sugden, *Blue Jacket,* 176.

69. Sugden, *Blue Jacket,* 179. R. David Edmunds, *Tecumseh and the Quest for Indian Leadership,* 40–42, notes that Tecumseh and his younger brother Lalawethika [later the Prophet], also present, had lost an older brother, Sauwauseekau, in the battle, which added to their bitterness toward both the Americans and the British.

70. Quoted in Cleaves, *Old Tippecanoe,* 21.

71. Harrison at Fort Greeneville to Carter Harrison, November 27, 1794, William Henry Harrison Papers (microfilm), Series 1, reel 1, Library of Congress.

72. For Ducoigne as informant, see Wayne to Secretary of War Knox, October 17, 1794, in Knopf, ed., *Anthony Wayne: A Name in Arms,* 157; Knopf, "Anthony Wayne," 40; Calloway, *Crown and Calumet,* 225.

73. In the Illinois State Historical Library manuscripts, OC 229, see Arthur St. Clair in Cincinnati to Anthony Wayne [at Greenville], May 30, 1795, wherein St. Clair notes that Indians were still stealing horses from the Mingo Bottom in Ohio in March and May and that killings continued in the Illinois country, forty miles above Kaskaskia.

74. Pickering quoted in Sword, *Washington's War,* 325; see also, Horsman, *Expansion,* 89.

75. Horsman, *Expansion,* 101.

76. William Henry Harrison Papers, M O364, Indiana Historical Society Library; Sword, *Washington's War,* 325–27; quote from Rev. David Barrow (1753–1819) diary (typescript of original held by Barrow family), 1795, June 24–25, 12, Mss A. B278, Filson Historical Society.

77. Roughly $362,000 in 2004 dollars, using the Oregon State University Inflation Conversion Factors.

78. Sword, *Washington's War,* 325–27.

79. Quotes from Barrow diary, 1795, June 24–25, 12, Filson Historical Society.

80. Quoted in Sword, *Washington's War,* 328.

81. Ibid.

82. Sugden, *Tecumseh: A Life,* 181; Sword, *Washington's War,* 329; Carter, *Little Turtle,* 75–77.

83. Sword, *Washington's War,* 328–30; Carter, *Little Turtle,* 152–53.

84. Sword, *Washington's War,* 329–30; Kappler, ed., *Indian Treaties,* 42.

85. White, *Middle Ground,* 494, notes that while civil chiefs normally handled diplomacy, the long period of warfare in the region had made war chiefs far more prominent. See also, Kappler, ed., *Indian Treaties,* 44; Sugden, *Tecumseh: A Life,* 79–80; Edmunds, *Shawnee Prophet,* 16–18.

86. Wayne quoted in White, *Middle Ground,* 472.

87. Quote in ibid.

88. Quotes in Cayton, "'Noble Actors' upon 'the Theatre of Honour,'" in Cayton and Teute, eds., *Contact Points,* 258. According to David B. Stout, "The Piankashaw and Kaskaskia and the Treaty of Greene Ville," 360–63, neither the Kaskaskias nor the Piankashaws apparently attended Greenville or signed for themselves and were only added later, probably by General Wayne.

89. Dowd, *A Spirited Resistance,* 114; for the needs of chiefs and post-Greenville plague, see White, *Middle Ground,* 494–96.

90. Cayton, "'Noble Actors' upon 'the Theatre of Honour,'" in Cayton and Teute, eds., *Contact Points,* 266.

91. Gunderson, "Apprentice in Arms," 23; for proclamation submitted by WHH, see *Centinel of the North-Western Territory* (microfilm), March 14, 1794.

92. *Centinel of the North-Western Territory,* May 17, 1794.

93. Ibid., May 24, 1794.

94. Ibid., September 13, 1795.

95. Ibid., March 26, 1796.

96. Calloway, "Beyond the Vortex of Violence," 16–26. On page 16 he notes, "'Indian' and 'white' were major criteria in determining the relations between peoples, but they were not the only criteria."

97. Gunderson, "Apprentice in Arms," and Goebel, *Harrison,* discuss Harrison as a student of Wayne's. Harrison's brother officers William Clark and Meriwether Lewis were also present at Greenville, which no doubt influenced Clark when he was governor of the Missouri Territory. See Jones, *William Clark,* 82–86.

CHAPTER 2

1. Quotes in WHH to Carter Harrison, November 27, 1794, William Henry Harrison (WHH) Papers, Library of Congress.

2. Ibid.

3. Cleaves, *Old Tippecanoe,* 23; all quotes in ibid.

4. Cleaves, *Old Tippecanoe,* 23–24; Gunderson, "Apprentice in Arms," 7. The August 31, 1795, receipt for the three hundred dollar loan is in the WHH Papers.

5. Bond, ed., *Intimate Letters of John Cleves Symmes,* xvii.

6. Quote in WHH to Carter Harrison, November 27, 1794, WHH Papers; Gunderson, "Apprentice in Arms," 12–13.

7. Cayton, *Frontier Indiana*, 174–75; Cleaves, *Old Tippecanoe*, 24–25.

8. Cayton, *Frontier Indiana*, 174–75; Cleaves, *Old Tippecanoe*, including Harrison quote, 25–27.

9. Knopf, *Wayne: A Name in Arms*, 478.

10. For frontier army woes, see Major Hamtramck to Secretary of War, March 3, 1797, in John Francis Hamtramck Papers, Filson Historical Society; Cayton, *Frontier Indiana*, 167, 175; Cleaves, *Old Tippecanoe*, 26–27.

11. Cayton, *Frontier Indiana*, 174–75; Sargent quote in Sargent to Pickering, May 21, 1798, in Rowland, ed., *Mississippi Territorial Archives vol. 1*, 16.

12. Harrison quote in Cleaves, *Old Tippecanoe*, 27.

13. Isaac, *Transformation of Virginia*, 131; Brown, *Good Wives, Nasty Wenches*, 344.

14. Isaac, *Transformation of Virginia*, 131. Edmund Morgan first made this point in *American Slavery, American Freedom*.

15. Isaac, *Transformation of Virginia*, 131–32, quote on 131.

16. For Harrison and Vincennes University, see Esarey, *History of Indiana*, 176–77; Constantine, ed., "Minutes of the Board of Trustees for Vincennes University," 313–64; and Philbrick, ed., *Laws of Indiana Territory*, 532–39; for agricultural society, see *Vincennes Western Sun* (microfilm), May 9, 1810; for War of 1812 orphans, see Goebel, *Harrison*, 125–26.

17. For Virginia gentlemen and horse culture, see Brown, *Good Wives, Nasty Wenches*, 277–79, and Aron, *How the West Was Lost*, 127; see also, *Freeman's Journal*, Tuesday, March 5, 1799; *Freeman's Journal* (newspaper ads) and other early Ohio newspapers, March 4, 1796–February 23, 1813 (microfilm), Ohio Historical Society.

18. Isaac, *Landon Carter's Uneasy Kingdom*, 139–41.

19. Inflation Conversion Factors, Oregon State University.

20. Onuf, *Statehood and Union*, 60–64; Eric Hinderaker, "Liberty and Power in the Old Northwest, 1763–1800," in Skaggs and Nelson, eds., *The Sixty Years' War for the Great Lakes*, quote on 236.

21. Pease, ed., *Laws of the Northwest Territory*, 129.

22. Rohrbough, *Land Office Business*, 22.

23. Cayton, *Frontier Indiana*, 175; quote in Carter, ed., *Territorial Papers vol. 3*, 519. As Andrew Cayton noted in *The Frontier Republic*, 45, many of the Northwest's appointed officials preferred the more refined East to their rustic posts, and absenteeism was chronic.

24. Goebel, *Harrison*, 34.

25. Goebel, *Harrison*, 42, 45; *Western Spy and Hamilton Gazette* (microfilm), October 29, 1799; Webster, *William Henry Harrison's Administration of Indiana Territory*, 184; Fischer and Kelly, *Bound Away*, 171–72.

26. See Horsman, "Virginia Gentleman in the Old Northwest," 128–29.

27. Ca. December 2, 1799–May 14, 1800, in Clanin, ed., *Papers of WHH.*

28. Ibid., January 9, March 28, 1800.

29. Harrison quote in his speech to the House, May 3, 1800, in ibid.

30. Andrew R.L. Cayton covers the struggle between Jeffersonians and Federalists for the Ohio Valley in *The Frontier Republic.*

31. McCoy, *The Elusive Republic,* 9–14. McCoy, *The Elusive Republic,* 68, notes that in 1776, John Adams, later a Federalist, felt individual land ownership was essential to liberty and virtue. See also, Owsley and Smith, *Filibusters and Expansionists,* 2, 11, quote on 1.

32. Clanin, ed., *Papers of WHH,* February 18, 1800; Rohrbough, *Land Office Business,* 23.

33. Clanin, ed., *Papers of WHH,* Harrison quote, March 31, 1800. For opposition to Harrison's measures, see WHH to Worthington, in Clanin, ed., *Papers of WHH,* April 25, 1800.

34. Ibid., April 8, 1800.

35. Ibid., February 21, March 5, 1800.

36. Elliot's troubles did not end with his death. The wagon returning his body to Cincinnati was ambushed and stolen by Indians, his servant killed, and the coffin unceremoniously dumped out. A later party had to retrieve the coffin for burial in Cincinnati. See *Virginia Herald and Fredericksburg Advertiser* (microfilm), November 13, 1794.

37. Ibid., May 7, 1800; *Annals of Congress, 8th Congress, 2nd Session, 1804–1805, vol. 14,* 69, 1002. For Elliot's death and memorial, see *Centinel of the North-Western Territory* (microfilm), October 11, October 25, 1794. When Harrison's grandson became president, a major plank in his platform was to institute bonuses for veterans. See Socolofsky and Spetter, *The Presidency of Benjamin Harrison,* 34–36.

38. *Western Spy and Hamilton Gazette* (microfilm), March 5, 1800; Cayton, *Frontier Indiana,* 169.

39. WHH to Worthington, April 25, 1800, in Clanin, ed., *Papers of WHH.*

40. Esarey, ed., *Messages and Letters 1,* 18. Also in ibid., and *Western Spy and Hamilton Gazette* (microfilm), June 11, 1800.

41. Goebel, *Harrison,* 51.

42. Clanin, ed., *Papers of WHH,* May 12–13, and WHH to Thomas Willing, June 10, 1801, in Clanin, ed., *Papers of WHH;* Esarey, ed., *Messages and Letters 1,* 5; Smith, *Benjamin Harrison,* 78; Goebel, *Harrison,* 53–54, 18; Cleaves, *Old Tippecanoe,* 32.

43. Cleaves, *Old Tippecanoe,* 32.

44. Ibid., ix.

45. Gunderson, "Apprentice in Arms," 12–13; Harrison, "Proprietors of the Northern Neck," 413–15.

46. Morgan, *American Slavery, American Freedom,* 383.

47. Cayton, *Frontier Indiana*, 167.

48. WHH to Massie, January 17, 1800, in Clanin, ed., *Papers of WHH*.

49. WHH to Worthington, April 25, 1800, in ibid.; Cayton, *Frontier Indiana*, 176.

50. Esarey, *History of Indiana*, 155; Symmes in Vincennes to Judge Robert Morris in New Jersey, June 22, 1790, in Bond, ed., *Correspondence of John Cleves Symmes*, 287–90.

51. Cleaves, *Old Tippecanoe*, 32.

52. Goebel, *Harrison*, 56–59; Webster, *Harrison's Administration*, 187–88.

53. Gibson's brother George died at St. Clair's defeat in 1791; Woollen, *Biographical and Historical Sketches*, 11–14.

54. Clanin, ed., *Papers of WHH*, January 10, 1801.

55. Philbrick, ed., *Laws of Indiana Territory*, xv–xvi, ccxxxv, quotes on xvi.

56. Ibid., 1–29, quote on 3.

57. Barnhart and Riker, *Indiana to 1816*, 321; Green, *William Henry Harrison: His Life and Times*, 93–95; WHH to Findlay, October 15, 1801, in Clanin, ed., *Papers of WHH*.

58. JCS to WHH, March 30, 1801, and WHH to McIntosh, April 3, 1801, both in Clanin, ed., *Papers of WHH*.

59. Cayton, *Frontier Indiana*, 176–77; Cleaves, *Old Tippecanoe*, ix–x.

60. Cayton, *Frontier Indiana*, 181.

61. Now run by the Grouseland Foundation, Inc.

62. Isaac, *Transformation of Virginia*, 74–79, 351–54.

63. Cleaves, *Old Tippecanoe*, 45.

64. Ibid., 55; Breen, *Tobacco Culture*, quote on 86.

65. WHH to Findlay, October 15, 1801, and WHH to Dayton, November 30, 1801, both in Clanin, ed., *Papers of WHH*.

66. Erney, *The Public Life of Henry Dearborn*, 1–3.

67. HD to WHH, February 23, 1802, in Clanin, ed., *Papers of WHH*.

68. For quote, see Wallace, *Jefferson and the Indians*, 277. Early national attitudes toward Indians and expansion have fostered considerable debate and literature. For the standard interpretations, see Horsman, *Expansion and American Indian Policy;* Sheehan, *Seeds of Extinction;* Prucha, *Great Father;* as well as Wallace, *Jefferson and the Indians*.

69. Prucha, *Great Father,* 42; Goebel, *Harrison*, 89–90; Hutton, "William Wells," 183–222.

70. WHH to HD, July 15, 1801, in Clanin, ed., *Papers of WHH*.

71. Harrison proclamations of July 20, 1801, and August 31, 1801, both in ibid. For Gibson's botching, see WHH to Charles Jouett, February 2, 1803, in ibid. For Harrison's distillery failure, see note in Esarey, ed., *Messages and Letters 1*, 35.

72. White, *Middle Ground*, 499; Gipson, ed., *Moravian Indian Mission*, 315; quotes in WHH to HD, July 15, 1801, in Clanin, ed., *Papers of WHH*.

73. WHH to Jonathan Dayton, November 30, 1801, in Clanin, ed., *Papers of WHH.*

74. HD to WHH, December 22, 1801, in ibid.; White, *Middle Ground,* 203–205.

75. WHH to HD, July 15, 1801; HD to WHH, December 22, 1801, both in Clanin, ed., *Papers of WHH.*

76. Appointment of Davis Floyd, February 23, 1802, WHH to HD, April 26, 1802, Proclamation offering a reward to a jailbreaker, May 5, 1802, and Judge Harry Innes to WHH, July 22, 1802, all in Clanin, ed., *Papers of WHH.*

77. WHH to HD, December 3, 1801, and HD to WHH, December 30, 1801, both in ibid.

78. Quote in WHH to HD, February 26, 1802, HD to WHH, June 17, 1802, and HD to WHH, June 18, 1803, all in ibid.

79. Rafert, *Miami Indians,* 66–68. In fact, these purchases had never been recognized by Britain prior to the Revolution either. See Barnhart and Riker, *Indiana to 1816,* 175; quotes in WHH to HD, February 26, 1802, in ibid. For more on the Illinois and Wabash Company, see Robertson, *Conquest by Law.*

80. WHH to HD, February 26, 1802, in Clanin, ed., *Papers of WHH;* HD to Daniel Vertmer, August 6, 1802, in Record Group 107, Miscellaneous Letters Sent by the Secretary of War, 1800–1809 (microfilm), National Archives; Dearborn quote in HD to WHH, July 29, 1802, in Clanin, ed., *Papers of WHH.*

81. This seems odd because Tanner, ed., *Atlas of Great Lakes Indians,* 48, suggests the area around Vincennes was predominately Piankeshaw in the second half of the eighteenth century. By Harrison's own estimation, WHH to HD, February 26, 1802, in Clanin, ed., *Papers of WHH,* however, the Piankeshaws were reduced to perhaps twenty-five–thirty warriors. Negotiations at an Indian Council, September 12–17, 1802, in Clanin, ed., *Papers of WHH;* Goebel, *Harrison,* 104.

82. Carter, *Little Turtle,* 39; Rafert, *Miami Indians,* 38. John Sugden, *Blue Jacket,* asserts that Blue Jacket, not Little Turtle, was the primary leader in the victory over St. Clair; see also Hutton, "William Wells," 203. Hutton, "William Wells," 191, 205, further notes that although he had fought against the United States through 1791, Wells became "the agent of expansionists" from 1792 on. However, his loyalty to the Miamis clashed with Harrison's zeal for land cessions and strained the friendship the two men had formed while working for General Wayne.

83. Anson, *Miami Indians,* 14.

84. See Owens, "Jean Baptiste Ducoigne"; quote in September 15, 1802, Speech of Lapoussier, in Clanin, ed., *Papers of WHH.*

85. R. David Edmunds, *The Potawatomis,* 161, writes, "By 1802 the Potawatomis and Miamis so dominated Indian affairs in Indiana that the lower Wabash tribes sought their approval before taking any action," although his only source for this is Governor Harrison. Goebel, *Harrison,* 102; HD to WHH, February 21, 1803, in Carter, ed., *Territorial Papers vol. 7,* 86.

86. Wallace, *Jefferson and the Indians,* 225.

87. Jefferson to HD, August 12, 1802, in Carter, ed., *Territorial Papers vol. 7,* 68.

CHAPTER 3

1. "Report of Committee," in Carter, ed., *Territorial Papers vol. 2,* 149. Report also cited in Berwanger, *Frontier against Slavery,* 9; Finkelman, *Slavery and the Founders,* 54. See also *The St. Clair Papers vol. 2,* 342. Turner ruffled local feathers on other issues as well, such as Indian affairs and local jurisdiction, as noted by Alvord, *Illinois Country,* 404–405. See also, Hammes, ed., *Cahokia, St. Clair County Record Book B 1800–1813,* 13.

2. Cayton, *Frontier Indiana,* 187–88. In addition to Harrison's own land speculation, the Northwest Ordinance allotted one thousand acres to territorial governors. See Pease, ed., *Laws of the Northwest Territory 1788–1800,* 124; Goebel, *Harrison,* 76.

3. Isaac, *Transformation of Virginia,* 132.

4. "Note on the Government of Indiana Territory [January 1, 1803]," in Carter, ed., *Territorial Papers vol. 7,* 138; "Report of Committee," in Carter, ed., *Territorial Papers vol. 2,* 149; also cited in Berwanger, *Frontier against Slavery,* 9; Esarey, ed., *Messages and Letters 1,* 60–62.

5. Petition of December 28, 1802, in Clanin, ed., *Papers of WHH*; Smith, *Benjamin Harrison,* 10, 22.

6. Petition of December 28, 1802, in Clanin, ed., *Papers of WHH.*

7. Esarey, ed., *Messages and Letters 1,* 73, note 1. See Malone, ed., *Dictionary of American Biography,* vol. 15, 363–65; Malone, ed., *Dictionary of American Biography,* vol. 8, 10; *Biographical Dictionary of the U.S. Congress,* 2060, 1536; committee quoted in Adams, *History of the United States,* vol. 6, 76.

8. Philbrick, ed., *Laws of Indiana Territory,* 40.

9. Ibid., 42.

10. Ibid., 40, 42, quote on 40.

11. WHH to Worthington, October 26, 1803, in Clanin, ed., *Papers of WHH*; Fischer and Kelly, *Bound Away,* 171.

12. WHH to Worthington, October 26, 1803, in Clanin, ed., *Papers of WHH.*

13. *Biographical Dictionary of the U.S. Congress,* 655, 1709, 1734. Territorial delegates could debate and make suggestions to the Congress but had no vote.

14. Dunn, "Slavery Petitions and Papers," 468; Esarey, ed., *Messages and Letters 1,* 61, note 1, 93; Parke quote in John Rice Jones to Judge Davis, January 21, 1804, in Carter, ed., *Territorial Papers vol. 7,* 169.

15. April 1, 1804, surety bond from WHH and JRJ, re: a Mulatto man, and Proclamation, April 6, 1804, both in Clanin, ed., *Papers of WHH.*

16. September 25, 1804, WHH, Gen. Washington Johnson, and John Johnston, surety bonds, in ibid.; Esarey, ed., *Messages and Letters 1,* 94, 95, note 1. According to Jacob Piatt Dunn, *Indiana,* 237, the legal battle ensued because the Kuykendalls had not been in "compliance with the formalities of the indenture laws" concerning George and Peggy.

17. Charge in Barnhart, ed., "The Letters of Decius," 263–96, quote on 282; see also chapter 4 in this volume.

18. Esarey, ed., *Messages and Letters 1,* 95, note 1; quote in Dunn, *Indiana,* 238.

19. Breen, *Tobacco Culture,* 90; Aron, *How the West Was Lost,* 194; Morgan, *American Slavery,* 383.

20. Clanin, ed., *Papers of WHH,* no exact date given.

21. Ibid.; Cayton, *Frontier Indiana,* 175–76; quote in Rohrbough, *Land Office Business,* 18, 29.

22. Known as Shadrach "Sr." and "Jr.," they were in fact uncle and nephew.

23. TJ to WHH, February 27, 1803, in Clanin, ed., *Papers of WHH.* In Peterson, ed., *Thomas Jefferson: Writings,* 1117, Peterson entitles the letter "Machiavellian Benevolence and the Indians."

24. Onuf, *Jefferson's Empire,* 49.

25. Appleby, *Inheriting the Revolution,* 4.

26. Ibid., 4–5.

27. Goebel, *Harrison,* 103, refers to the preliminary council as a "quasi-treaty." WHH to HD, March 26, 1803, nomination for governor and commission of Governor Harrison to treat with the Indians, February 8, 1803, and quote in HD to WHH, April 15, 1803, all in Clanin, ed., *Papers of WHH.*

28. Goebel, *Harrison,* 103; White, *Middle Ground,* 496, 501–502.

29. Potawatomis' quote in Dawson, *Historical Narrative,* 49–50; Kappler, ed., *Indian Treaties,* 65; second quote in Goebel, *Harrison,* 104.

30. Dowd, *Spirited Resistance,* 131.

31. Goebel, *Harrison,* 104–105; quote in Kappler, ed., *Indian Treaties,* 65; Horsman, *Expansion,* 143. For size of cession, see Royce, *Indian Land Cessions,* part 2, tract 26.

32. While Jefferson had professed, and would continue to profess, friendship with Ducoigne, in his instructions to Harrison he nevertheless suggested sending a spy to the chief's village to determine his willingness to cede lands; Wallace, *Jefferson and the Indians,* 223–27.

33. Goebel, *Harrison,* 105–106. The cession originally comprised the southern Illinois country from the Ohio to the watersheds of the Kaskaskia and Wabash rivers. However, it was considerably extended in 1818, as seen in Royce, *Indian Land Cessions,* part 2, tract 48.

34. Esarey, ed., *Messages and Letters 1,* 78. This refers to the western Potawatomis, led by war chiefs like Main Poc and Turkey Foot, rather than the St.

Joseph River or Chicago-area Potawatomis, who had strong ties to the United States. For differences among the Potawatomis, see Edmunds, *Potawatomis,* 156.

35. Actually getting the church was a different story. According to Carter, ed., *Territorial Papers vol. 16: Illinois Territory 1809–1814,* 75, Gov. Ninian Edwards to Secretary of War Eustis, February 24, 1810, almost seven years after the treaty the Kaskaskias still had not received the funds to erect their church.

36. Kappler, ed., *Indian Treaties,* 67–68.

37. HD to WHH, June 27, 1804, in Clanin, ed., *Papers of WHH;* Kappler, ed., *Indian Treaties,* 67–68. Joseph Jablow, *Indians of Illinois and Indiana,* 338, notes that "[a]ccording to a petition submitted on Oct. 1, 1800 to the Government by inhabitants of what is now southern Illinois (Randolph and St. Clair counties of Indiana Territory) the Kaskaskia Tribe of Indians, who alone can claim the Country in their neighborhood, do not exceed fifteen in number." Among the difficulties in determining the Kaskaskias' number are the fact that observers could not consistently distinguish between the Kaskaskias and other members of the Illinois confederacy, such as the Peorias, and the uncertainty as to whether the accounts list their numbers in terms of merely warriors or the entire population.

38. HD to WHH, June 27, 1804, and HD to TJ, January 8, 1805, both in Clanin, ed., *Papers of WHH;* quote in Horsman, *Expansion,* 147.

39. Jefferson wrote a letter of introduction for Constantin Francois Volney to Ducoigne, June 21, 1796. Apparently, though, Volney was too frightened of Indian attacks to venture west of Vincennes to deliver it. The letter is reproduced in Chinard, ed., *Volney et L'Amerique,* 41; TJ to WHH, February 27, 1803, and WHH to HD, both in Clanin, ed., *Papers of WHH.*

40. WHH to Jouett, June 8, 1803, in Clanin, ed., *Papers of WHH.*

41. Ibid.

42. Patterson, Clifford, and Hagan, *American Foreign Relations,* 62–64; Horsman, *Expansion,* 147.

43. WHH to Clark or Lewis, November 13, 1803, in Clanin, ed., *Papers of WHH.*

44. WHH to Delassus, March 6, 1803, in ibid.

45. Quotes in WHH to TJ, June 24, 1804; also TJ to WHH, July 14, 1804, both in ibid.

46. See Royce, *Indian Land Cessions,* part 2, tract 49; quote in Kappler, ed., *Indian Treaties,* 71; WHH to Jefferson, May 12, 1804, in Clanin, ed., *Papers of WHH.*

47. Royce, *Indian Land Cessions,* part 2, tract 49; Kappler, ed., *Indian Treaties,* 72. Tanner, ed., *Atlas of Great Lakes Indians,* 58–59, supports Miami ownership of this tract by previous occupation from at least the mid-eighteenth century.

48. WHH to James Findlay, September 22, 1804, in Clanin, ed., *Papers of WHH.*

49. Quotes in July 2, 1805, resolution from citizens of St. Louis, in ibid.; for fear of anti-slavery clause, see Webster, *Harrison's Administration,* 200.

50. Speech of Buckongahelas, April 9, 1804, in Clanin, ed., *Papers of WHH.*

51. Quote in WHH to HD, February 26, 1802, in ibid. A reasonable estimation of their combined population would be 3,000–5,000 people, 2/3 of whom would have been Sauks, according to Wallace, *Prelude to Disaster,* 11–12.

52. WHH to HD, February 26, 1802, in Clanin, ed., *Papers of WHH.*

53. The Americans were not singling out the Sauks and Foxes. Even before the United States took over Louisiana, colonial policy had been to try to discourage tribal warfare during times of general peace. In ibid., Dearborn wrote to Harrison on April 23, 1802, telling him to send "suitable characters," such as William Wells and Little Turtle, to the Potawatomis and Kickapoos to reconcile them to each other. See Trader Manuel Lisa in St. Louis to Charles Dehault Delassus, Lt. Gov of Louisiana, March 14, 1803, in Nasatir, ed., *Before Lewis and Clark vol. 2,* 717: "It is also well known that our good intentions are well proven in dividing by our efforts a party of 60 warriors of the Kickapoo nations, who lately were going out upon a war against the Osages with the intention of surprising and attacking them, and in order to please them we were obliged to make them presents of goods and merchandise watching that they did not capture and destroy (if they had carried out their intended end) many white men who might have been victims of their voracity."

54. In *Before Lewis and Clark vol. 2,* 741, Captain Amos Stoddard to HD, June 3, 1804, mentioned a Sauk attack on the Osages, noting, "The Saucks are the implacable enemies of the Osages, and I suspect it will be difficult to reconcile them."

55. Wallace, *Prelude to Disaster,* 4–5, 17–18.

56. Ibid., 19.

57. HD to WHH, June 27, 1804, in Clanin, ed., *Papers of WHH;* also ibid., 20.

58. Kappler, ed., *Indian Treaties,* 74–77; Wallace, *Prelude to Disaster,* 20.

59. Kappler, ed., *Indian Treaties,* 74, 76.

60. Quote in Wallace, *Prelude to Disaster,* 21. The *Western Spy and Hamilton Gazette* of December 26, 1804, noted that Harrison had "purchased from the Saix & Fox Indians 51,200,000 acres of land containing 80,000 square miles, extending about 600 miles along the Mississippi. It is said, the purchase of this extensive body of land cost the United States only 2200 dollars in goods and an annual payment of 1000 dollars. This purchase is of much importance, not only from its intrinsic value, but as it consolidates our [holdings on the Mississippi River]."

61. Black Hawk's quotes in Jackson, ed., *Black Hawk: An Autobiography,* 54, 51.

62. Wallace, *Prelude to Disaster,* 16, 20.

63. Jackson, ed., *Black Hawk: An Autobiography,* 54; quote in ibid., 21.

64. Wallace, *Prelude to Disaster,* 6–7, 21; HD to WHH, June 27, 1804, in Clanin, ed., *Papers of WHH.*

65. Jefferson's letter in Clanin, ed., *Papers of WHH;* Royce, *Indian Land Cessions,* part 2, tract 50.

66. Wallace, *Prelude to Disaster,* 22.

67. See Bruff to Wilkinson, November 5, 1804, in Carter, ed., *Territorial Papers vol. 13,* 76–77; Pierre Chouteau to WHH, May 5, May 8, May 10, 1805, and Benjamin Parke to WHH, May 8, 1805, all in Clanin, ed., *Papers of WHH.*

68. Wilkinson to HD, July 27, 1805, and Wilkinson to Sauks, December 10, 1805, both in Carter, ed., *Territorial Papers vol. 13,* 165, 300–302, respectively.

69. Webster, *Harrison's Administration,* 202–203.

70. The exclusion of Wayne County was perhaps prescient. As seen in ibid., 202, on June 30, 1805, Wayne County was officially detached from Indiana, becoming Michigan Territory.

71. Ibid., 204–206.

72. Ibid; quotes in TJ to WHH, April 28, 1805, in Clanin, ed., *Papers of WHH.*

73. Esarey, *History of Indiana,* 173.

74. Quote in Robert Morrison to Joseph Morrison, December 31, 1805, Manuscripts, Robert Morrison Papers, SC1079, Illinois State Historical Library.

75. WHH to TJ, November 12, 1805, in Clanin, ed., *Papers of WHH.*

76. Robert Morrison to Joseph Morrison, December 31, 1805, Manuscripts, Robert Morrison Papers, SC1079, Illinois State Historical Library. Morrison is likely referring to William Biggs, who was initially pro-slavery but also in favor of dividing Indiana Territory. The other representative from Clark County was Davis Floyd, an ally of Harrison's. See Phibrick, ed., *Laws of Indiana Territory,* ccxlix–ccl.

77. As opposed to a court of common law, a court of chancery wields jurisdiction over equity and can override statute law. See Black, *Black's Law Dictionary,* 356. Morrison, as a trader in a cash-poor environment, probably feared such a court might confiscate his property if suits were brought against him.

78. Letters in Manuscripts, Robert Morrison Papers, SC1079, Illinois State Historical Library. Esarey, *History of Indiana,* 173, estimates that Illinoisans were being asked to pay 2/5 of the taxes for a territorial government that could do little or nothing for them.

79. The Illinoisans were correct in prophesying a land tax. See Phibrick, ed., *Laws of Indiana Territory,* 147–53, 171–74; WHH to TJ, November 20, 1805, in Clanin, ed., *Papers of WHH.*

80. Carter, ed., *Territorial Papers vol. 7,* 218, 220.

81. *Indiana Gazette* in Indiana State Library, Indianapolis (microfilm).

82. Ibid. As seen in Miller, ed., *Indiana Newspaper Bibliography,* 213–14, the *Sun* continues to this day as the *Vincennes Sun-Commercial.* While Stout did print plenty of editorials that criticized Harrison, he was definitely in favor of the governor's policies. The *Western Sun* was the only newspaper printed in Indiana until after the War of 1812.

83. WHH to Worthington, December 25, 1804, in Clanin, ed., *Papers of WHH.*

CHAPTER 4

1. WHH to HD, August 26, 1805, and TJ to WHH, February 27, 1803, both in Clanin, ed., *Papers of WHH*.

2. HD to WHH, quote in Horsman, *Expansion*, 147; Jefferson quote in TJ to WHH, May 1, 1805, in ibid.

3. Delawares to Wells, March 30, 1805, in Clanin, ed., *Papers of WHH*.

4. First quote in ibid., and Patterson to Wells quote in April 5, 1805, letter, both in Clanin, ed., *Papers of WHH*; Sugden, *Tecumseh*, 106–107; Gipson, ed., *Moravian Mission*, 328–29; for Patterson's murder, see Thompson, *Sons of the Wilderness*, 45–46.

5. Quote and Wells letter in Carter, *Little Turtle*, 173. Hutton, in "William Wells," 208, note 55, observes, "It is interesting . . . that Wells' counterpart in the British Indian service, Matthew Elliot, was also distrusted by his superiors because of his marriage to an Indian and sympathies for the Indians' plight."

6. TJ to WHH, May 1, 1805, in Clanin, ed., *Papers of WHH*.

7. First quote in HD to WHH, May 24, 1805; second quote in HD to WHH, June 20, 1805, both in ibid.

8. For two interpretations of this broader issue, see Sheehan, *Seeds of Extinction;* Wallace, *Jefferson and the Indians*.

9. Thornbrough and Riker, eds., *Journals of the General Assembly*, 39.

10. Ibid., 39–40.

11. Ibid., 41.

12. Royce, *Indian Land Cessions*, tract 56; Kappler, ed., *Indian Treaties*, 80–81.

13. For relative location of tribes involved, see Tanner, ed., *Atlas of Great Lakes Indians*, 40–41, 58–59, 93, 98–99; for 1809 treaty threats, see Rafert, *Miami Indians*, 71–72; Edmunds, *Potawatomis*, 163; quote in HD to WHH, August 18, 1806, in Clanin, ed., *Papers of WHH*.

14. Like other treaties Harrison negotiated, the Treaty of Grouseland also led to contention years afterward. In 2000, members of the Miami tribe tried to lay claim to the Wabash watershed lands in Illinois, specifically the Vermillion River Valley. See Tanner, ed., *Atlas of Great Lakes Indians*, 58, 93, 98; Kappler, ed., *Indian Treaties*, 81.

15. In Clanin, ed., *Papers of WHH*, see WHH's letters to HD from April 26, May 27, July 10, August 10, and August 26, 1805, and WHH to HD, March 3, 1805.

16. Goebel, *Harrison*, 115. Gipson, ed., *Moravian Mission*, 365, 414–15, reveals that in July 1805 the Delawares dismissed Tedepachsit as chief, in part because he had signed the 1804 treaty, and in 1806 he was among those executed for witchcraft at the behest of the Shawnee Prophet. See also WHH to HD, April 26, 1805, in ibid.

17. WHH to HD, August 26, 1805, and WHH to TJ, August 29, 1805, both in Clanin, ed., *Papers of WHH*.

18. WHH to HD, November 29, 1805, in ibid.

19. Quote in WHH to HD, January 1, 1806, in ibid.

20. "Traditional" is a nebulous term for the Ohio Valley, given the great shifts in populations and cultures in the region in the seventeenth, eighteenth, and nineteenth centuries. Some of Tenskwatawa's religious teachings seemed influenced by Christianity, for example. See Edmunds, *Tecumseh* and *Shawnee Prophet*. See also Sugden, *Tecumseh;* Dowd, *Spirited Resistance;* White, *Middle Ground*, 503–10.

21. WHH to Jared Mansfield, August 8, 1806, in Clanin, ed., *Papers of WHH*.

22. HD to WHH and William Hull, June 17, 1806, and William Wells to WHH, June 19, 1806, both in ibid.; for *Chesapeake-Leopard* Affair, see Tucker and Reuter, *Injured Honor*.

23. Thornbrough, ed., *Correspondence of John Badollet*, 9–11, 18.

24. Ibid., 10–13, quote on 44.

25. Ibid., 21; quote in Badollet to Gallatin, January 1, 1806, ibid., 62.

26. Ibid., 21; quote in Badollet to Gallatin, December 16, 1804, ibid., 40.

27. Quote in WHH to TJ, June 18, 1805, in Clanin, ed., *Papers of WHH*; Philbrick, ed., *Laws of Indiana Territory*, 136.

28. Philbrick, ed., *Laws of Indiana Territory*, 136.

29. Until recently this document, as well as the Knox County Court Files from the territorial period, was housed in the Knox County Records Library.

30. Register of Negro Slaves, 1805–1807, McGrady-Brockman House, 2, 8.

31. According to Henry Scofield Cooley, "A Study of Slavery in New Jersey," in *Early Studies of Slavery by States vol. 1*, 28–29, while New Jersey officially began a program of "gradual" emancipation in 1804, in reality slaves were simply "apprenticed" for long terms under conditions not unlike slavery.

32. "An Act respecting Apprentices," in Philbrick, ed., *Laws of Indiana Territory*, 500.

33. Ibid., 95, 136, quote on 43.

34. Ann was also referred to as a mulatto. Minutes of the Court of Common Pleas, 1807–1810, Knox County Court Files, 1796–1820, in McGrady-Brockman House. In Thornbrough, *Negro in Indiana*, 17, note 1, she mentions this case as the only instance in Indiana where an indentured servant managed to get a restraining order against her master, although the order was really intended to restrain the master's wife.

35. Minutes of the Court of Common Pleas, 1807–1810, Knox County Court Files; *Common Pleas Court Minutes 1807–1810 Knox County Indiana*, vol. 1, transcribed and typed by the Indiana Historical Records Survey (1941), 76.

36. Hames, ed., *Cahokia, St. Clair County Record Book B 1800–1813*, 57, notes that "[a]fter 3 publications on 3 consecutive Sundays without opposition," Joseph Henry Richard and Mary Louis Lafleur, "a free Negro and Negress, natives of the Indies, residing in this parish," were married, April 28, 1800. Faribault-Beauregard,

ed., *La population des forts français d'Amérique* (two volumes), lists numerous black marriages and baptisms from the colonial period.

37. Thornbrough, *Negro in Indiana*, 3.

38. In the early territorial days, some in the Illinois country may have wanted slaves for the saltworks in what is now Gallatin County, but the first concrete evidence for this comes only in 1814. See "An Act concerning negroes and Mulattoes" (approved December 22, 1814), which stated in part that "experience has proved that the manufacture of salt in particular, at the United States Saline cannot be successfully carried on by white laborers." In Philbrick, ed., *Laws of Illinois Territory 1809–1818*, 157–58. (Thanks to Dr. James Cornelius for this reference.)

39. "Act concerning the Introduction," in Philbrick, ed., *Laws of Indiana Territory*, 136.

40. For quotes, see "Petition to Congress by the People of the Illinois Country," April 6, 1808, in Carter, ed., *Territorial Papers vol. 7*, 547, and Thornbrough, *Negro in Indiana*, 9, respectively.

41. Register of Negro Slaves 1805–1807, McGrady-Brockman House, 14.

42. Cleaves, *Old Tippecanoe*, 351, note 40; WHH to Henry, May 10, 1806, and WHH to Ridgely, May 24, 1807, both in Clanin, ed., *Papers of WHH*; William Henry Harrison Papers M 0364, Indiana Historical Society Library; Thornbrough, *Negro in Indiana*, 12.

43. Badollet to Gallatin, August 31, 1805, in Thornbrough, ed., *Correspondence of John Badollet*, 49.

44. Dunn, "Slavery Petitions," 504.

45. Ibid.

46. Eighteenth- and nineteenth-century political writings typically utilized aliases, and often they were names from the Classical world. Decius seems an odd choice, however. Emperor Decius (A.D. 249–51) is best remembered for organizing the persecution of Christians and insisting upon a loyalty oath to Rome's traditional gods; see Lewis and Reynolds, eds., *Roman Civilization Selected Readings vol. 2: The Empire*, 550, 566. (Thanks to Dr. Ariel Loftus for this source.) However, as Bernard Bailyn pointed out, it was not uncommon for Revolutionary-era Americans to reference classical authors without knowing what they were talking about; see Bailyn, *Ideological Origins of the American Revolution*, 23–26.

47. Originals of the pamphlet are housed in the Library of Congress. The most user-friendly format, which I use, is the reprint edited by John D. Barnhart in the *Indiana Magazine of History*, vol. 43, no. 3 (September 1947): 263–96.

48. Ibid., 264; February 14, 1795, *Centinel* acronym on microfilm, Illinois Historical Survey, University of Illinois Library.

49. Philbrick, ed., *Laws of Indiana Territory*, ccxlii–ccxliv, lxxx–lxxxvi.

50. Barnhard, ed., "The Letters of Decius," 282.

51. Ibid.; quote in Jones to WHH, January 5, 1806, in Clanin, ed., *Papers of WHH*.

52. Barnhard, ed., "The Letters of Decius," 263; Goebel, *Harrison*, 63–64; WHH to TJ, July 5, 1806, in Clanin, ed., *Papers of WHH.*

53. Unrau, *White Man's Wicked Water,* 2.

54. Mancall, *Deadly Medicine,* 5–7.

55. Rorabaugh, *The Alcoholic Republic,* 125, 146, 156.

56. Edmunds, *Tecumseh,* 65.

57. Mancall, *Deadly Medicine,* 7–8; Unrau, *White Man's Wicked Water,* 17–18; White, *Middle Ground,* 499.

58. Gipson, ed., *Moravian Indian Mission,* 3–12; Nelson, *A Man of Distinction among Them,* 145. See also Leonard Sadosky, "Rethinking the Gnadenhutten Massacre: The Contest for Power in the Public World of the Revolutionary Pennsylvania Frontier," in Skaggs and Nelson, eds., *The Sixty Years' War,* 187–213.

59. Gipson, ed., *Moravian Indian Mission,* 13–15.

60. Wallace discusses the difficulty in convincing Indians to adopt American gender norms and culture in *Jefferson and the Indians,* 297–98; for execution of accused witches, see ibid., 194–95, quote on 194.

61. For repeated references to Gnadenhütten over the course of five years, see Gipson, ed., *Moravian Indian Mission,* 141, 155, 436; for "gindower," see 275; for Mary, see 346, 356, quote on 346. Mary died May 21, 1805.

62. Ibid., 262, 333, quote on 334.

63. Ibid., 339–40, quote on 354.

64. The importance of the communal menstrual hut was immeasurably clarified for me during a public lecture by Shawnee author Dark Rain Thom at the Watseka (Illinois) Public Library, March 14, 2002; for Richardville's mother, see Carter, *Little Turtle,* 76; for trade reinforcing gender roles, see Wallace, *Jefferson and the Indians,* 298.

65. My account follows Edmunds, *Shawnee Prophet,* 28–31.

66. Ibid., 28, 34.

67. Ibid., 34. Compare Tenskwatawa's teachings with those of Beata—whose first vision predated his by several months at least—in Gipson, ed., *Moravian Indian Mission,* 333, 335, 339–40, 354–55, 402.

68. Edmunds, *Shawnee Prophet,* 34–36, quote on 35. Howard, *Shawnee,* 104, describes how Shawnee men sometimes struck their wives for "correction" and how wives typically pulled and twisted their husbands' testicles in retaliation.

69. Edmunds, *Shawnee Prophet,* 38.

70. Ibid., 40.

71. Aron, *How the West Was Lost,* 197.

72. Dawson, *Historical Narrative,* 49–50; Gipson, ed., *Moravian Indian Mission,* 357–58, 358, note 7.

73. Gipson, ed., *Moravian Indian Mission,* 365, 369, note 12, quote on 402; Edmunds, *Shawnee Prophet,* 42.

74. Gipson, ed., *Moravian Indian Mission,* 414–15; Edmunds, *Shawnee Prophet,* quote on 43–44.

75. Gipson, ed., *Moravian Indian Mission,* 415–16, quote on 415; Edmunds, *Shawnee Prophet,* 45.

76. Edmunds, *Shawnee Prophet,* quotes on 46; for Patterson's protest, see Esarey, ed., *Messages and Letters 1,* 121–23.

77. Edmunds, *Shawnee Prophet,* 46–47; Dowd, *Spirited Resistance,* 131.

78. WHH to the Delawares, pre-April 12, 1806, in Clanin, ed., *Papers of WHH*; Edmunds, *Shawnee Prophet,* 47–49.

79. WHH's address to Indiana General Assembly, July 29, 1805, in Clanin, ed., *Papers of WHH.*

80. Gregory Dowd, in *Spirited Resistance,* 119, describes Harrison's Anglophobic arguments as having a "dense redundancy."

CHAPTER 5

1. WHH to Dayton, January 12, 1803; second quote in WHH to Auguste Chouteau, April 7, 1805, both in Clanin, ed., *Papers of WHH.*

2. Floyd to WHH, May 22, 1805, in ibid.

3. For the Burr conspiracy, see Chidsey, *Aaron Burr;* Melton, *Aaron Burr.*

4. WHH to Wilkinson, June 7, 1805, in Clanin, ed., *Papers of WHH.*

5. Burr apparently stayed at Harrison's home on this visit, as mentioned by Francis Vigo in a letter on October 18, 1807, in Francis Vigo Papers, M 0289, Indiana Historical Society Library. See also, Wilkinson to WHH, September 19, 1805 [extract], in Clanin, ed., *Papers of WHH.*

6. Goebel, *Harrison,* 73; for Burr as WHH's guest, see Vigo to the editor of the *Aurora*[?], October 18, 1807, in Francis Vigo Papers M 0289, Indiana Historical Society Library.

7. Chidsey, *Aaron Burr,* 59; quotes in Burr to Harrison, October 24, 1806, in Clanin, ed., *Papers of WHH.*

8. Chidsey, *Aaron Burr,* 59, 72; quotes from address to the General Assembly, November 4, 1806, in Clanin, ed., *Papers of WHH.*

9. Burr to WHH, November 27, 1806, and Madison to WHH et al., November 28, 1806, both in Clanin, ed., *Papers of WHH.* See Jefferson's Special Message to Congress, January 22, 1807, in Washington, ed., *Writings of Thomas Jefferson,* vol. 3, 71–78.

10. Andrew Cayton, in *The Frontier Republic,* 91–92, notes that many political leaders in Ohio were appalled when they learned belatedly how many Ohioans had sympathized with Burr.

11. Carter, ed., *Territorial Papers vol. 7,* 552.

12. Chidsey, *Aaron Burr,* 131–32; Taylor to WHH, January 12, 1807, in Clanin, ed., *Papers of WHH.*

13. Quotes in WHH to Williams, April 3, 1807, in Esarey, ed., *Messages and Letters 1*, 205–207, 205, note 1; quote about Davis and Taylor in Thornbrough and Riker, eds., *Journals of the General Assembly*, 974.

14. Thornbrough and Riker, eds., *Journals of the General Assembly*, 974–75, Johnston and Decker quote on 974; "Blunderbuss," in *Vincennes Western Sun*, November 17 and November 25, 1807; WHH to TJ, July 16, 1808, in Clanin, ed., *Papers of WHH.*

15. Carter, ed., *Territorial Papers vol. 7*, 511–14.

16. Formerly appointed by the president—something that rankled frontier Democrats—seats on the Legislative Council became elected positions by an act of Congress in February 1809; see Thornbrough and Riker, eds., *Journals of the General Assembly*, 10.

17. Ibid., 975, 1006–1007, quote on 1006.

18. For *Chesapeake-Leopard* Affair, see Tucker and Reuter, *Injured Honor.*

19. WW to WHH, June 19, 1807, in Clanin, ed., *Papers of WHH.*

20. Appleby, *Inheriting the Revolution*, 3.

21. Colley, *Captives*, 228–29.

22. Three volumes, quote in vol. 2, 26.

23. Discussed in Namias, *White Captives*, 132–33.

24. Quotes in ibid., 144.

25. Ibid.

26. White, *Middle Ground*, 376–77.

27. WHH August 18, 1807, speech in Clanin, ed., *Papers of WHH.*

28. WHH quote to HD, July 11, 1807, in ibid. Dowd, *Spirited Resistance*, 119, notes that Harrison never equated his bribing of compliant Indian chiefs with mirror efforts by the British.

29. Calloway, *American Revolution in Indian Country*, 231–32; Tecumseh's speech to Harrison at the Vincennes Council, August 20, 1810, in Clanin, ed., *Papers of WHH.*

30. Wallace, *Jefferson and the Indians*, 310–12; Dowd, *Spirited Resistance*, 118–19.

31. For Dearborn's spying, see HD to William Hull, July 30, 1807, and HD to Peter Sailly, November 27, 1807, both in Miscellaneous Letters Sent by the Secretary of War, 1800–09 (microfilm), Record Group 107, National Archives.

32. Wells to WHH, August 20, 1807, and WHH to Assembly, September 8, 1807, in Clanin, ed., *Papers of WHH.*

33. Webster, *Harrison's Administration*, 229, 231; quote in Carter, ed., *Territorial Papers vol. 7*, 367; for Red's jailbreak, see Esarey, ed., *Messages and Letters 1*, 190; also WHH to Assembly, August 17, 1807, in Clanin, ed., *Papers of WHH;* Wallace, *Jefferson and the Indians*, 312.

34. HD to WHH, Hull, and Kirker, September 17, 1807, and John Smith to WHH and Hull, September 27, 1807, both in Clanin, ed., *Papers of WHH.*

35. Sugden, *Tecumseh,* 187; quote in WHH to Assembly, September 27, 1808, in ibid.

36. Woollen, *Biographical Sketches,* 378–79; court information in Clanin, ed., *Papers of WHH,* March 16, 1807. The Harrison-McIntosh feud began shortly before the rift between Harrison and John Rice Jones, Harrison's defense counsel. Angus McIntosh was one of John Askin's partners in the Miamis Trading Company, to which Vigo was indebted. See McIntosh's brother Angus's suit against Harrison, March 16, 1807, in Clanin, ed., *Papers of WHH.* For Vigo quotes, see Vigo to John Askin, June 9, 1804, translation, in Quaife, ed., *John Askin Papers vol. 2,* 419–20.

37. WHH to TJ, October 10, 1807, in Clanin, ed., *Papers of WHH.*

38. *Vincennes Western Sun,* September 12, 1807; *Western World,* March 3, 1808, excerpts in Woollen, *Biographical Sketches,* 378–79; land claims in Philbrick, ed., *Laws of Indiana Territory,* lxxxiv–lxxxvi. Ford (comp.), *British Officers Serving in the American Revolution,* 118, lists one William McIntosh as an ensign in the 71st (Highland) Regiment of Foot, November 3, 1777.

39. *Vincennes Western Sun,* September 26, 1807.

40. Resolutions adopted at a meeting of the French inhabitants of Vincennes, September 18–20, 1807, which WHH included with a letter to TJ, October 10, 1807, in Clanin, ed., *Papers of WHH.*

41. WHH to TJ, October 10, 1807, and TJ to McIntosh, January 30, 1808, both in ibid.

42. Sometimes seen as "Messenger."

43. WHH to Jonathan Dayton, January 12, 1803, in Clanin, ed., *Papers of WHH;* Philbrick, ed., *Laws of Indiana Territory,* ccl.

44. Letter from Messinger to Lyon, October 17, 1808, in John Messinger Papers, Illinois State Historical Library.

45. Etcheson, *Emerging Midwest,* 6.

46. Thornbrough, ed., *Correspondence of John Badollet,* 93; Berwanger, *Frontier against Slavery,* 11; Esarey, ed., *Messages and Letters 1,* 127, 230, note 2.

47. Goebel, *Harrison,* 82–83; Webster, *Harrison's Administration,* 220.

48. April 6, 1808, petition in Carter, ed., *Territorial Papers vol. 7,* 547.

49. For Illinois as a pro-slavery region, see Alvord, *The Illinois Country,* 422; Davis, *Frontier Illinois,* 116–17; "Deposition of Davis Waddell and Others, Oct. 12, 1808," in Carter, ed., *Territorial Papers vol. 7,* 602.

50. October 19, 1808, petition in Carter, ed., *Territorial Papers vol. 7,* 603–605.

51. Thornbrough, ed., *Correspondence of John Badollet,* 333–35 (Badollet included a copy of this petition in his November 13, 1809, letter to Gallatin).

52. Committee report, October 19, 1808, in Thornbrough and Riker, eds., *Journals of the General Assembly,* 232–38.

53. Dunn, "Slavery Petitions," 522–23.

54. See Jefferson's *Notes on the State of Virginia,* Query VIII, in Washington, ed., *The Writings of Thomas Jefferson vol. 7,* 404.

55. Dunn, "Slavery Petitions," 524–25.

56. Ibid., 526–27.

57. Thornbrough and Riker, eds., *Journals of the General Assembly,* 238; Berwanger, *Frontier against Slavery,* 12. The Legislative Council's actions on this bill appear to have been a major factor in the citizenry calling for their popular election.

58. Goebel, *Harrison,* 84.

59. Ibid., 63, shows, for example, that Harrison appointed friend and fellow Virginian Waller Taylor as chancellor of the territory, and Taylor later tried an important legal case for him. Harrison also appointed his closest political friend, Benjamin Parke, as a territorial judge. When Parke later resigned, Harrison appointed another Virginian friend, Thomas Randolph, to take his place.

60. According to Cayton, *Frontier Republic,* x–xi, an identical struggle was taking place in Ohio and elsewhere.

61. Harrison County petition in Carter, ed., *Territorial Papers vol. 7,* 703–704; see additional petitions on 705–706.

62. Dill editorial in *Vincennes Western Sun* (microfilm), Indiana State Library; Philbrick, ed., *Laws of Indiana Territory,* cclv; Webster, *Harrison's Administration,* 237–38.

63. Esarey, ed., *Messages and Letters 1,* 613; Goebel, *Harrison,* 59.

64. Thornbrough, ed., *Correspondence of John Badollet,* 133–34, 143; Webster, *Harrison's Administration,* 225.

65. Etcheson, *Emerging Midwest,* 42–43; quotes in *Vincennes Western Sun,* January 28, 1809, and February 11, 1809, respectively.

66. Referred December 12, 1809, in Carter, ed., *Territorial Papers vol. 7,* 687, 690.

67. Isaac, *Transformation of Virginia,* 104–105, 109.

68. Ibid., 109.

69. WHH to Assembly, July 29, 1805, in Clanin, ed., *Papers of WHH;* Philbrick, ed., *Laws of Indiana Territory,* 213–14.

70. WHH to Assembly, August 17, 1807, in Clanin, ed., *Papers of WHH.*

71. Legislature's reply to the governor, August 19, 1807, in ibid., 237; Philbrick, ed., *Laws of Indiana Territory,* 399–425, quote on 413. As seen in *Laws of Indiana Territory,* 424, in yet another homage to the Revolutionary generation, the law also stipulated that the militia utilize Baron von Steuben's drilling instructions.

72. WHH to Assembly, September 27, 1808, in Clanin, ed., *Papers of WHH.*

73. WHH to Assembly, September 27, 1808, and WHH to HD, September 1, 1808, both in ibid.

74. Petition to Congress by Citizens of Harrison County, referred December 12, 1809, in Carter, ed., *Territorial Papers vol. 7,* 693; quote in WHH to Wm. Eustis, April 26, 1809, also Knox County militia resolution, both in ibid.

75. Harrison's friends in Vincennes, in both the territorial legislature and the militia, came through in grand fashion in late 1809, managing to get their

memorials asking for his reappointment as governor printed in column one of the front page of the *Washington Intelligencer,* Washington, D.C., December 8, 1809.

CHAPTER 6

1. Esarey, *History of Indiana,* 155, 179. Determining the Indian population for this era remains frustrating: Tanner, ed., *Atlas of Great Lakes Indians,* 70, states that ca. 1790, the entire Great Lakes–Ohio Valley region probably contained a little more than 30,000 Indians. Sugden, *Tecumseh,* 187, contends that in Ohio, Indiana, Illinois, Michigan, and Wisconsin in 1810, there were perhaps 70,000 Indians—as opposed to 270,000 whites in the same area. Davis, *Frontier Illinois,* 116, asserts an 1800 Indian population of 100,000 in Indiana Territory.

2. Esarey, *History of Indiana,* 179–80, 203–204; Esarey, ed., *Messages and Letters 1,* 51, note 1, 70.

3. Miller, *Indiana Newspaper Bibliography,* 211, 213; quote in *Indiana Gazette,* August 7, 1804 (microfilm), Indiana State Library.

4. *Indiana Gazette,* August 7, August 14, 1805.

5. Miller, *Indiana Newspaper Bibliography,* 211, 213.

6. *Vincennes Western Sun,* March 23, 1808.

7. Ibid., July 11, 1807, July 8, 1809.

8. Appleby, *Inheriting the Revolution,* 4.

9. *Vincennes Western Sun,* November 25, 1809.

10. Ibid.

11. Esarey, *History of Indiana,* 176–77, quote on 176; Philbrick, ed., *Laws of Indiana Territory,* 532–39, 202–203.

12. For legislation and references to wolf bounties, see Philbrick, ed., *Laws of Indiana Territory,* 30, 562–63; Philbrick, ed., *Laws of Illinois Territory 1809–1818,* 47, 159, 191, 233; Lathrop Sapp, comp., *Randolph County Illinois Orphans Court Records 1804–1809,* 22, 30, 31; Lathrop Sapp, comp., *Randolph County, Illinois Commissioners' Court Records 1802–1807,* 56, 103.

13. See Sleeper-Smith, *Indian Women and French Men.* For Mrs. Vigo, see Henry Cassidy to Mrs. Vigo, July 27, 1798, in Francis Vigo Papers, M 0289, Indiana Historical Society Library; for Lusk, see Lathrop Sapp, comp., *Randolph County, Illinois Commissioners' Court Records 1802–1807,* December 1804 session, 75.

14. Cayton, *Frontier Indiana,* 181; Harrison quote in WHH to James Findlay, receiver at the Cincinnati land office, September 22, 1804, in Clanin, ed., *Papers of WHH.*

15. Harrison's salary complaints of December 25, 1804, June 11, 1805, December 1, 1808, and August 30, 1809, all in Clanin, ed., *Papers of WHH;* see June 16, 1809, affidavit of James Morrison, Charles Wilkins, and Jonathan Taylor, in Mss A.T243j, Jonathan Taylor Papers, Filson Historical Society.

16. Inflation Conversion Factors, Oregon State University website.

17. *Vincennes Western Sun,* June 23, 1812. On the same list, Harrison's enemy John Rice Jones had thousands of acres sold.

18. Quote in McIntosh to WHH, February 8, 1806; also WHH to John Askin, Sr., February 9, 1806, and May 21, 1806, all in Clanin, ed., *Papers of WHH.* For Vigo's woeful financial situation, see John Askin to Vigo, May 12, 1804, and Pierre Chouteau to Vigo, March 15, 1805, both in Francis Vigo Papers, M 0289, Indiana Historical Society Library.

19. WHH to Mansfield, April 24, 1806, in Clanin, ed., *Papers of WHH;* for Easton, see Rufus Easton to WHH, November 29, 1806, in Clanin, ed., *Papers of WHH.* Easton was referring to a letter written by Harrison and Governor Wilkinson to Gallatin on October 19, 1805. The governors assured Gallatin that charges against Antoine Soulard of forging land claims were false. Apparently it was Easton who had made these charges, and he felt the two governors' defense of Soulard hurt his own prestige. See Easton to Jefferson, December 1, 1806, in Carter, ed., *Territorial Papers vol. 14,* 43–46.

20. Later that session the legislature did repeal the tax on milk cows, replacing it with a new land tax, as seen in Thornbrough and Riker, eds., *Journals of the General Assembly,* 164, note 8.

21. Ibid., 164, 265.

22. Will of Isaac White, May 23, 1811, reproduced in White, *Sketch of the Life of Colonel Isaac White,* 23. Special thanks to Dr. James Cornelius for this source.

23. Anna Harrison to John Cleves Short, July 10, 1808, in Bond, ed., *Intimate Letters of John Cleves Symmes,* 145.

24. The Knox County Court Files 1796–1820, formerly housed in the Knox County Records Library, are now located in the McGrady-Brockman House, 7th and Hart Streets, Vincennes, Indiana.

25. *Black's Law Dictionary,* 6th ed., 1503, defines trespass on the case as "[t]he form of action, at common law, adapted to the recovery of damages for some injury resulting to a party from the wrongful act of another, unaccompanied by direct or immediate force, or which is the indirect or secondary consequence of the defendant's act. Such action is the ancestor of the present day action for negligence where problems of legal and factual cause arise."

26. Norton, "Gender and Defamation," 3–39.

27. Knox County Court Files, Box 2, folder 139-2, Box 3, folders 269 and 284, Box 9, folder 679; *Common Pleas Court Minutes 1796–1799 Knox County, Indiana,* vol. 2, transcribed and typed by the Indiana Historical Records Survey, Indianapolis, 1941, 315; quote in *Minutes of Common Pleas Court Knox County 1801–1806,* transcribed and typed by the Indiana Historical Records Survey, 1940, 204.

28. Knox County Court Files, Box 10, folder 759.

29. Ibid., Box 16, folders 1069, 1069-2; *Common Pleas Court Minutes 1807–1810 Knox County Indiana Part Two,* transcribed and typed by the Indiana Historical Records Survey, Indianapolis, 1941, 325.

30. Knox County Court Files, Box 9, folder 703 (ca. 1805) (Chisley-Adams case), Box 17, folder 1187 (Catt-Decker case).

31. WHH to Assembly, August 18, 1807, in Thornbrough and Riker, eds., *Journals of the General Assembly,* 128; Philbrick, ed., *Laws of Indiana Territory,* 247–48; for rape statutes, see Thornbrough and Riker, eds., *Journals of the General Assembly,* 52–53, and Philbrick, ed., *Laws of Indiana Territory,* 247.

32. Hartog, *Man and Wife in America,* 70–71, 84, 87, quote on 71.

33. Basch, *Framing American Divorce,* 20–22; Marylynn Salmon, "Republican Sentiment, Economic Change, and the Property Rights of Women in American Law," in Hoffman and Albert, eds., *Women in the Age of the American Revolution,* 448.

34. Quote from *Centinel of the North-Western Territory,* April 25, 1795 (microfilm).

35. *Western Spy and Hamilton Gazette* (Cincinnati), December 7, 1811, (microfilm).

36. Basch, *Framing American Divorce,* quote on 99.

37. WHH to Assembly, in Thornbrough and Riker, eds., *Journals of the General Assembly,* 129. Harrison and the assembly were also generally in favor of the institution of marriage and subjected bachelors in the territory to a county tax, as they were seen as disruptive to society; mentioned in Philbrick, ed., *Laws of Indiana Territory,* cxxviii. Allusions to the Roman Republic and the Roman Empire, and their alleged American and British counterparts, were fairly common among the eighteenth-century Virginia gentry. See Isaac, *Transformation of Virginia,* 109.

38. See Brown, *Good Wives, Nasty Wenches,* especially 191–96.

39. WHH to Assembly, in Thornbrough and Riker, eds., *Journals of the General Assembly,* 129.

40. Cited in Basch, *Framing American Divorce,* 35.

41. Harrison quote in Thornbrough and Riker, eds., *Journals of the General Assembly,* 129–30, 130, note 11, quote on 130.

42. Basch, *Framing American Divorce,* quote on 37.

43. Act in Philbrick, ed., *Laws of Indiana Territory,* 648; see also Thornbrough and Riker, eds., *Journals of the General Assembly,* 287.

44. Philbrick, ed., *Laws of Indiana Territory,* cxxviii; Morgan, *American Slavery,* 235–36; Carole Shammas, "Early American Women and Control over Capital," in Hoffman and Albert, eds., *Women in the Age of the American Revolution,* 152.

45. Cayton, *Frontier Indiana,* 167–69.

46. Anna Harrison to John Cleves Symmes, February 7, 1811, in Bond, ed., *Intimate Letters of John Cleves Symmes,* 147; see also Cayton, *Frontier Indiana,* 167–68.

47. John Cleves Symmes at Cleves to Anna Harrison at Vincennes, March 7, 1808, in Bond, ed., *Intimate Letters of John Cleves Symmes,* 144.

48. McCoy, *Elusive Republic,* 7.

49. November 4, 1806 address to the Assembly, in Clanin, ed., *Papers of WHH.*

50. Rorabaugh, *Alcoholic Republic,* 6–8. Quotes in Philbrick, ed., *Laws of Indiana Territory,* "An Act for the Prevention of Vice and Immorality," 367–75, and

"Crimes and Punishments," 247. Philbrick, cxxiv, asserts that such laws were generally ineffective.

51. Appleby, *Inheriting the Revolution*, 4.

52. Ayers, *Vengeance and Justice*, 9–33, quotes on 13.

53. Ibid., 14–16.

54. Ibid., 19, 17.

55. *Vincennes Western Sun*, September 30, 1809.

56. Ibid.

57. White, *Sketch of the Life of Colonel Isaac White*, 12–13.

58. *The Argus of Western America* (Frankfort), January 28, 1809. [Bound collection, Filson Historical Society Library, Louisville, Kentucky.]

59. Philbrick, ed., *Laws of Indiana Territory*, 372–73; *Vincennes Western Sun*, October 1809.

60. Freeman, *Affairs of Honor;* Monroe, *Republican Vision.*

61. *Vincennes Western Sun*, October 1, 1808.

62. Philbrick, ed., *Laws of Indiana Territory*, ccliii–ccliv; Alvord, *Illinois Country*, 426.

63. Alvord, *Illinois Country*, 426–27.

64. For McNamee and Randolph, see *Vincennes Western Sun*, June 10 and July 1, 1809; for Randolph's pistol practice and the McIntosh attack, see Badollet to Gallatin, November 13, 1809, in Thornbrough, ed., *Correspondence of John Badollet*, 119–20; for gentry daggers, see ibid., 143; Mills, *Jonathan Jennings*, 116.

CHAPTER 7

1. Quote from Gallatin to Badollet, May 12, 1809, 117, also Badollet to Gallatin, March 27, 1809, both in Thornbrough, ed., *Correspondence of John Badollet*, 105.

2. Ibid., 335-49; WHH to Gallatin, August 29, 1809, and WHH to Ewing, December 1, 1808, both in Clanin, ed., *Papers of WHH.*

3. All in Thornbrough, ed., *Correspondence of John Badollet:* Gallatin quotes in Gallatin to WHH, September 27, 1809, 113; Badollet quotes in Badollet to Gallatin, August 8, 1808, 102; also Badollet to Gallatin, March 27, 1809, 105.

4. McNamee to Pres. of Senate, December 12, 1809, in Carter, ed., *Territorial Papers vol. 7*, 683–84.

5. Anti-slavery editorial of "A Citizen of Vincennes," January 28, 1809; anti-slavery editorial of "An Enemy to Tyranny," November 19, 1808; pro-slavery editorial of "An Enemy to Scoundrels," November 19, 1808; "Slim Simon's" editorial countering "A Citizen of Vincennes," February 11, 1809, all in *Vincennes Western Sun.*

6. Harrison to Gallatin, August 29, 1809, in Clanin, ed., *Papers of WHH.*

7. Badollet to Gallatin, November 13, 1809, in Thornbrough, ed., *Correspondence of John Badollet*, 116–18.

8. Ibid., 121–22.

9. Ibid., 109–10, 126–28, quote on 128.

10. Ewing letter in Carter, ed., *Territorial Papers vol. 8,* 26.

11. Ewbank and Riker, eds., *Laws of Indiana Territory,* 22, 138. In Philbrick, ed., *Laws of Indiana Territory,* 463, the 1807 act does not say "of color" but merely "servants." Only in the repeal is "of color" used. Thornbrough, *Negro in Indiana,* 23–25.

12. Ewbank and Riker, eds., *Laws of Indiana Territory,* 226, 485; petition quoted in Carter, ed., *Territorial Papers vol. 8,* 235; Berwanger, *Frontier against Slavery,* 4, 22–23.

13. Davis to Breckenridge, January 16, 1806, in Carter, ed., *Territorial Papers vol. 7,* 355.

14. *Vincennes Western Sun,* May 20, 1809, August 11, 1809, and April 14, 1810; Litwack, *North of Slavery,* 31.

15. Finkleman, ed., *Slavery in the North and the West,* xii; Litwack, *North of Slavery,* 3.

16. Woolen, Howe, and Piatt Dunn, eds., *Executive Journal of Indiana Territory,* 83; Thornbrough, *Negro in Indiana,* 22; Berwanger, *Frontier against Slavery,* 11; Pease, ed., *Laws of the Northwest Territory 1788–1800,* 129.

17. Berwanger, *Frontier against Slavery,* 11.

18. Quote in Dunn, *Indiana,* 311–12; Goebel, *Harrison,* 372.

19. Aron, *How the West Was Lost,* 146.

20. Woollen, *Biographical Sketches,* 29–31; Miller, *Indiana Newspaper Bibliography,* 213; Mills, *Jonathan Jennings,* 85.

21. Woollen, *Biographical Sketches,* 30–31; Goebel, *Harrison,* 64, 85; Webster, *Harrison's Administration,* 225; Thornbrough, ed., *Correspondence of John Badollet,* 127; Carter, ed., *Territorial Papers vol. 7,* 654. In a letter to John Messinger in Cahokia, September 7, 1808, John Messinger Papers, Illinois State Historical Library, Badollet offered that "[a]ll thinking men in the Territory are now uniting in the honest and patriotic endeavours to avert the mighty and lamentable evils of Slavery" and recommended Jennings as the assembly's clerk on those grounds. Also WHH to Gallatin, August 29, 1809, in Carter, ed., *Territorial Papers vol. 7,* 665–68.

22. Quotes in *Vincennes Western Sun,* March 11, 1809. Also see Mills, *Jonathan Jennings,* 109.

23. Goebel, *Harrison,* 61–62, 86.

24. Quotes in Jesse B. Thomas to John Messinger, December 12, 1808, John Messinger Papers, Illinois State Historical Library; Poindexter quote in *Annals of Congress vol. 19, 10th Congress, 2nd Session 1808–1809,* 493.

25. Carter, ed., *Territorial Papers vol. 8,* 142–45, quotes 142–44.

26. Thornbrough, ed., *Correspondence of John Badollet,* 126–28; Goebel, *Harrison,* 65. Goebel suggests, "[I]t may be hazarded that much of the outcry against [Harrison's] appointments arose from the bitterness of the 'outs' against the 'ins,' rather than because he had made appointments that were intrinsically bad."

27. Few in Indiana showed an inclination to push for emancipation within their borders, so the repeal of the Act concerning Introduction largely ended the debate until after the War of 1812.

28. Etcheson, *Emerging Midwest,* 22–23, quote on 42–43.

29. Quote from Message of the Governor, November 4, 1806, in Thornbrough and Riker, eds., *Journals of the General Assembly,* 111.

30. WHH to HD, November 9, 1808, and TJ to WHH, December 22, 1808, both in Clanin, ed., *Papers of WHH;* quotes in Wallace, *Jefferson and the Indians,* 317.

31. Aron, *How the West Was Lost.*

32. Esarey, *History of Indiana,* 179; quotes in WHH to Eustis, August 29, 1809, in Carter, ed., *Territorial Papers vol. 7,* 670–71; WHH to HD, September 16, 1805, and Eustis to WHH, July 15, 1809, in Clanin, ed., *Papers of WHH;* Sugden, *Tecumseh,* 183.

33. While Harrison's bitter detractor John Badollet stated that Harrison took a circuitous route to Fort Wayne as a public relations tour to build support for himself, it seems the governor's primary activity in the week preceding the council was a social call on his father-in-law in Ohio, spending most of the time drinking tea with Judge Symmes and neighbor ladies and accepting a saddle and mare for his wife. See Thornbrough, ed., *Correspondence of John Badollet,* 131; John Cleves Symmes to Mrs. William Henry Harrison, September 11, 1809, in Bond, ed., *Correspondence of John Cleves Symmes,* 297–99.

34. Clanin, ed., *Papers of WHH.* As seen in Thornbrough, ed., *Letter Book of Fort Wayne,* 67, WHH wrote to Secretary of War Eustis that "more than half of all the Indians at the Treaty were Putawatamies [sic] part from the Agency of Chicago & others from Detroit attracted by the novelty [?] of the Treaty."

35. Thornbrough, ed., *Letter Book of Fort Wayne,* 60, 69, 74.

36. Edmunds, *Potawatomis,* 164; Rafert, *Miami Indians,* 71–72.

37. Clanin, ed., *Papers of WHH.*

38. Ibid.; for Britain's influence on Indians, see Horsman, *Matthew Elliot,* 158–66, and Calloway, *Crown and Calumet,* 196–202, 228–30.

39. Dawson, *Historical Narrative,* 52; Harrison's speech in Esarey, ed., *Messages and Letters 1,* 369–73; for Potawatomis' poverty, see Edmunds, *Potawatomis,* 169.

40. Carter, *Little Turtle,* 145, 178; Esarey, ed., *Messages and Letters 1,* 373–76 (quote on 375). Debate exists among historians as to whether Little Turtle was a Miami proper or an Eel River. For interpretations, see Rafert, *Miami Indians,*

71–72, and Carter, *Little Turtle*, 47. Little Turtle himself is quoted as saying, at a June 21, 1805, Indian council held at Fort Wayne, "I am no Miami. I am only their interpreter," in Esarey, ed., *Messages and Letters 1*, 138.

41. Kappler, ed., *Indian Treaties*, 101–102.

42. Royce, *Indian Land Cessions*, tracts 71–73; ibid., 103–104.

43. Journal of Treaty Negotiations with the Wea at Vincennes, October 24–26, 1809, in Clanin, ed., *Papers of WHH*.

44. In Esarey, ed., *Messages and Letters 1*, 178–79, Pawatomo, chief of the Illinois Kickapoos, Oulawau, chief of the Wabash Kickapoos, and a Kickapoo chief named Chasso made a speech to Harrison on December 16, 1805, complaining that their American father treated them poorly, unlike previous European fathers. According to Kappler, ed., *Indian Treaties*, 105, none of these men marked the treaty. R. David Edmunds, "A History of the Kickapoo Indians," unpublished master's thesis, Illinois State University, 82, notes that the other tribes marking the treaty feared Kickapoo vengeance for ceding lands the Kickapoos used and that Harrison only succeeded by bribing a small minority of the Kickapoos into sanctioning the cessions; also Royce, tracts 73–74; Kappler, ed., *Indian Treaties*, 104; first quote in WHH to Eustis, November 3, 1809, in Clanin, ed., *Papers of WHH;* second quote in Edmunds, "History of the Kickapoo Indians," 83.

45. In 1796 a St. Joseph Potawatomi chief stated, "[L]ast summer I ordered my people from the Wabash, but they were deaf to me . . . not an Inch of Land of that Country belongs to us, and those obstinate intruders who now hunt there— are dependent upon their Wabash Brethren [the Miamis] for permission"; Jablow, *Indians of Illinois and Indiana*, 333.

46. *Vincennes Western Sun*, November 18, 1809.

47. WHH to Eustis, November 3, 1809, in Clanin, ed., *Papers of WHH;* Sugden, *Tecumseh*, 184.

48. WHH to Eustis, November 3, 1809, in Clanin, ed., *Papers of WHH*.

49. WHH to Eustis, October 3 and November 3, 1809, both in ibid.; Rafert, *Miami Indians*, 71–72; Sugden, *Tecumseh*, 184; Carter, ed., *Territorial Papers vol. 7*, 671; Thornbrough, ed., *Letter Book of Fort Wayne*, 68.

50. Goebel, *Harrison*, 115; Sugden, *Tecumseh*, 187; Wilson, "Early Indiana," 427.

51. WHH to Eustis, November 3, 1809, in Clanin, ed., *Papers of WHH;* Horsman, *Expansion*, 154; other quotes in *Vincennes Western Sun*, December 9 and December 16, 1809. The *Scioto Gazette* of Chillicothe, Ohio, November 6, 1809 (microfilm) printed the following: "This treaty, formed under the most inauspicious circumstances, upon satisfactory terms, should put a seal upon the slanderous tongue of faction, whose opposition to its formation, aided by British influence, has been rendered abortive by the superior wisdom of its patriotic negociator. The information of the acquisition of a country so much desired, and promising such advantages, must be highly gratifying to every well wisher to his country."

52. *Vincennes Western Sun*, November 18, 1809.

53. Badollet to Gallatin, November 13, 1809, in Thornbrough, ed., *Correspondence of John Badollet*, 132–33.

54. Quote in General Court of the Indiana Territory, September Term, 1810, in Clanin, ed., *Papers of WHH, Harrison v. McIntosh*.

55. See Goebel, *Harrison*, 125–26; *Harrison v. McIntosh*, the General Court of Indiana Territory, summonses, January 10, 1811, and Taylor's finding for Harrison, April 12, 1811, in Clanin, ed., *Papers of WHH*. Etcheson, *Emerging Midwest*, 42–43, and Aron, *How the West Was Lost*, 101, both make the point that politicians like Harrison were wary of the need to appear proper so their constituents would submit to the rule of law.

56. Goebel, *Harrison*, 57; Harrison's quote in WHH to Eustis, December 24, 1810, in Clanin, ed., *Papers of WHH*.

57. Eustis to WHH, March 7, 1811, in Carter, ed., *Territorial Papers vol. 8*, 113; Goebel, *Harrison*, 115-17; Sugden, *Tecumseh*, 187.

58. For examples of this "Harrison as Machiavel" theory, see Dangerfield, *Era of Good Feelings*, 26, and Adams, *History of the United States*, vol. 6, 77–89.

59. Clanin, ed., *Papers of WHH*, January 16, 1809. That same day he also freed a white man jailed for the same offense; Philbrick, ed., *Laws of Indiana Territory*, 667.

60. Legislative Council to WHH, October 5, 1808, in Clanin, ed., *Papers of WHH*.

61. Journal of the Treaty Negotiations with the Delawares et al., Fort Wayne to Vincennes, October 5, 1809, in ibid.

62. Apparently, Dearborn's anger at Wells did not solely arise from Harrison's criticisms. The secretary also blamed Wells for the failure of Rev. William Kirk's "civilizing" mission among the Indians; see John Smith to Wells, July 9, 1807, HD to Wells, August 5, 1807, HD to William Kirk, August 5, 1807, and HD to Charles Jouett, August 6, 1807, all in Records of the Office of the Secretary of War Letters Sent, Correspondence of the War Department Relating to Indian Affairs, vol. B, April 23, 1804–July 5, 1809, National Archives (microfilm). Harrison quote re Wells in WHH to Eustis, December 3, 1809, and WHH to Dearborn, July 10, 1805, both in Clanin, ed., *Papers of WHH*.

63. Hutton, "William Wells," 213–15, quotes on 213; WHH to Eustis, December 3, 1809, and WHH to TJ, October 3, 1809, both in Clanin, ed., *Papers of WHH*.

CHAPTER 8

1. Harrison got actual proof of this after the fact and failed to note that it was only after the Fort Wayne treaties that bloodshed took place. See WHH to James Monroe, December 18, 1813, in Clanin, ed., *Papers of WHH*.

2. Sugden, *Tecumseh*, 187. Linda Colley, in *Captives*, 9, makes the argument that Britain's relatively small standing army combined with imperial ambitions (in an odd way) to hold the nation captive to the interests of its desperately needed foreign allies, like American Indians.

3. Johnston to WHH, June 24, 1810, in Clanin, ed., *Papers of WHH*; Sugden, *Tecumseh*, 387–401. Sugden and also Edmunds, *Tecumseh*, cover Tecumseh's life in detail.

4. WHH to Eustis, August 7, 1811, in Clanin, ed., *Papers of WHH*.

5. Dowd, "Thinking and Believing," 309–35; Tanner, ed., *Atlas of Great Lakes Indians*, 104.

6. Edmunds, *Shawnee Prophet*, 90–91, Tecumseh quote on 91.

7. Ibid., 102–105.

8. Sugden, *Tecumseh*, 167; for number of warriors, see ibid., 86.

9. Asperheim, "Double Characters," Ph.D. diss., University of Illinois; Hammack, *Kentucky and the Second American Revolution*, 4–11, Johnson quote on 10.

10. For troop figures, see Sugden, *Tecumseh*, 228, 231–32; White, *Sketch of the Life of Colonel Isaac White*, 14–15.

11. This view was adopted by Henry Adams in his *History of the United States*, vol. 7, 77–89, and Dangerfield, *Era of Good Feelings*, 26, among others.

12. Wm. Clark to his brother Jonathan, August 17, 1811, in Holmberg, ed., *Dear Brother*, 259; see also Jones, *William Clark*, 197–201; Terry to brother Joseph Terry, November 23, 1811, in Joseph Terry Papers, Duke University Rare Book and Special Collections Library.

13. Resolutions concerning Indians, July 11, 1811, in Clanin, ed., *Papers of WHH*; John D. Drummens Letters, October 14, 1811, Mss C D, Filson Historical Society. John died at Tippecanoe, and Rebeca later applied for a pension from the government.

14. Badollet to Gallatin, October 26, 1811, and November 19, 1811, both in Thornbrough, ed., *Correspondence of John Badollet*, 200, 206.

15. Crawford, ed., "Mrs. Lydia B. Bacon's Journal" [part 1 of 2], 367-86, quotes on 383.

16. Harrison had sent Delaware and Miami deputations to Prophetstown to seek Tenskwatawa's compliance and to warn other Indians not to join him. They had failed. See Edmunds, *Shawnee Prophet*, 105–108.

17. Ibid., 110.

18. Sugden, *Tecumseh*, 231–32.

19. Ibid., 234–235; Edmunds, *Shawnee Prophet*, 112; Tipton quote of November 7, 1811, from Journal of John Tipton, in Robertson and Riker, eds., *John Tipton Papers vol. 1*, 78.

20. Extr. from an army officer on the Wabash to his friend, *Western Spy and Miami Gazette*, December 7, 1811.

21. Robertson and Riker, eds., *John Tipton Papers*, 83. This may have been a reference to Lt. Col. William Darke, who fought with St. Clair in 1791 and had two sons wounded in the campaign. See Sword, *Washington's War*, 193.

22. WHH to Scott, sometime after November 11, 1811, in Clanin, ed., *Papers of WHH*.

23. Supposedly, Tecumseh was so angry with his brother that he seized him by the hair and shook his head violently, repeatedly threatening him with death. See Sugden, *Tecumseh*, 235–36; Edmunds, *Shawnee Prophet*, 117–19.

24. Dowd, "Thinking and Believing," 322–27; WHH to Christopher Greenup of Lexington, May 29–30, 1812, and Tecumseh in Amherstburg to British Indian Agent Matthew Elliott, June 8, 1812, both in Clanin, ed., *Papers of WHH*.

25. Sugden, *Tecumseh*, 259.

26. Quote in WHH to Eustis, October 24, 1810, WHH to Eustis, December 24, 1811, and WHH to Scott, December 13, 1811, all in Clanin, ed., *Papers of WHH*; Robertson and Riker, eds., *John Tipton Papers*, 79.

27. First quotes in *Washington Intelligencer*, December 4, 1811 (microfilm); "tho' our loss" and "In the full of" quotes in *Supporter*, November 23 and November 30, 1811, respectively (microfilm).

28. WHH to Gallatin, February 4, 1812, in Clanin, ed., *Papers of WHH*.

29. December 4, 1811 resolution, in Esarey, ed., *Messages and Letters 1*, 655; Quimby, *U.S. Army in the War of 1812 vol. 1*, 176; Thornbrough, ed., *Correspondence of John Badollet*, 206–24; Goebel, *Harrison*, 124.

30. See *Washington Intelligencer*, December 3, December 5, December 19, December 21, 1811.

31. Jackson to WHH, November 28, 1811, and Blount to Jackson, December 4, 1811, both in Moser and Macpherson, eds., *Papers of Andrew Jackson vol. 2*, 270, 272, respectively.

32. Resolutions of December 7–27, 1811, in Clanin, ed., *Papers of WHH*.

33. Baronet Vasquez in *Village of the Prophet*, November 9, 1811, to Benito Vasquez, St. Louis, Louisiana Territory, Vasquez Family Collection, Missouri Historical Society, St. Louis.

34. Cleaves, *Old Tippecanoe*, 111.

35. Esarey, ed., *Messages and Letters 1*, 678–81.

36. Quimby, *U.S. Army in the War of 1812 vol. 1*, 176; Goebel, *Harrison*, 164–65. Goebel asserts that Harrison's political friends in Washington, most notably Congressman Henry Clay of Kentucky and Senator Thomas Worthington of Ohio, helped secure his appointment as major general.

37. McAfee journal in Filson Historical Society's Mss A M113 3, Robert Breckenridge McAfee Papers; *Gazette* quote in Esarey, ed., *Messages and Letters 2*, 273.

38. Quimby, *U.S. Army in the War of 1812 vol. 1*, 115–18; WHH to Campbell, November 25, 1812, in Clanin, ed., *Papers of WHH*.

39. General Orders, January 2, 1813, in Clanin, ed., *Papers of WHH*.

40. Ibid.

41. Quimby, *U.S. Army in the War of 1812 vol. 1*, 134–38; Sugden, *Tecumseh*, 322–23.

42. Procter quoted in Sugden, *Tecumseh*, 326.

43. WHH to Monroe, January 24 and January 26, 1813, both in Clanin, ed., *Papers of WHH*.

44. Kentuckian Richard M. Johnson, briefly on leave from military duties, took his seat in Congress in November 1813 and proposed a campaign of mounted volunteers (like himself) to campaign against the hostile Indians that winter. When the War Department asked Harrison his opinion, he urged caution, stating that a few raids against certain villages were all that should be attempted. Johnson's bold plan was rejected. See Hopkins, ed., *Papers of Henry Clay vol. 1*, 750, note 1.

45. Sugden, *Tecumseh*, 328. After the battle Harrison mentioned the "situation of [his] family" and his "feelings of a husband and a Father" in his May 13, 1813, letter to the secretary of war, in Clanin, ed., *Papers of WHH*.

46. Sugden, *Tecumseh*, 329–31; Quimby, *U.S. Army in the War of 1812 vol. 1*, 190–94; WHH to Secretary of War, April 28, 1813, in Clanin, ed., *Papers of WHH*.

47. WHH to Secretary of War Armstrong, May 5, 1813, in Clanin, ed., *Papers of WHH*; Sugden, *Tecumseh*, 331–33; Quimby, *U.S. Army in the War of 1812 vol. 1*, 194.

48. Sugden, *Tecumseh*, 336.

49. Ibid., 335–38; Quimby, *U.S. Army in the War of 1812 vol. 1*, 195.

50. Sugden, *Tecumseh*, 338.

51. General Orders in Clanin, ed., *Papers of WHH*; Quimby, *U.S. Army in the War of 1812 vol. 1*, 196–97.

52. WHH to Armstrong, October 9, 1813, in Clanin, ed., *Papers of WHH*.

53. For Tecumseh's death, see Sugden, *Tecumseh*, 374–80.

54. WHH to John Tipton, May 2, 1834, in Esarey, ed., *Messages and Letters 2*, 750–54, quote on 751.

55. Quote in ibid.; see also Sugden, *Tecumseh*, 379; Clay to Thomas Bodley, December 18, 1813, in Hopkins, ed., *Papers of Henry Clay vol. 1*, 842.

56. See Sugden's epilogue to *Tecumseh*.

57. Clanin, ed., *Papers of WHH*, Protection Granted John Askin, October 15, 1813; see also editor's notes in same.

58. WHH to Armstrong, October 10, 1813, in ibid.

59. WHH to Armstrong, October 10 (first two quotes) and October 16 (last quote), 1813, both in ibid.

60. WHH to Gen. Vincent, November 3, 1813, in ibid.

61. Ibid.

62. Ibid.

63. Vincent to WHH, November 10, 1813, in ibid.

64. WHH toasts in NYC (December 1), Philadelphia (December 9), and WHH to Monroe, December 18, 1813, all in ibid.

65. Samuel McDowell, Jr., to Andrew Reid, April 7, 1814, Mss A M138, Samuel McDowell Papers, 1735–1817, Filson Historical Society.

66. See WHH to Henry Clay, December 20, 1815, and WHH to John McClean (chairman of the House Committee on Accounts), December 29, 1815, both in Clanin, ed., *Papers of WHH.*

67. Armstrong to WHH, April 29, 1814, and WHH to Armstrong, May 10, 1814, both in ibid.; Cleaves, *Old Tippecanoe,* 218–21.

68. WHH to Armstrong, February 13, 1814, and WHH to Armstrong, May 11, 1814, both in Clanin, ed., *Papers of WHH;* Bond, ed., *Intimate Letters of John Cleves Symmes,* 148, note 6.

69. WHH to Armstrong, May 11, 1814, in ibid.

70. WHH to Madison, May 11, 1814, in ibid.

71. Armstrong to WHH, May 24, 1814, in ibid.

72. Cleaves, *Old Tippecanoe,* 216–23; Jones, *William Clark,* 94.

73. Charles S. Todd et al., to WHH, June 3, 1814, and WHH to Todd et al., June 6, 1814, both in Clanin, ed., *Papers of WHH.*

74. Kappler, ed., *Indian Treaties,* 105–107; quote in Commissions for WHH et al., June 1, 1814, in ibid.

75. WHH to Armstrong, December 21, 1813, and Armstrong to WHH et al., June 11, 1814, both in Clanin, ed., *Papers of WHH.*

76. Journal of the Treaty Negotiations with the Wyandots, etc., July 1814, in ibid.

77. Ibid., July 8.

78. Ibid., July 10.

79. Ibid., July 15.

80. WHH to Campbell, November 25, 1812, in ibid.

81. Journal of the Treaty Negotiations with the Wyandots, etc., July 15, 1814, in ibid.

82. Ibid.

83. Ibid., July 16.

84. In WHH and Cass to Armstrong, July 23, 1814, in ibid. They stated that the treaty was satisfactory for almost all: "two or three of the Miami chiefs only refuse to sign—of all that were present—one of them is a half Frenchman whom We know to have been in British pay—with the rank of captain in the Indian Department—His objection was that he wished to remain Neutral—We gave them all distinctly to understand that No Neutrals would be permitted unless they would remove within the settlements—if they object to this it is our decided opinion that they ought to be seized and taken to a place where they can do no injury."

85. Journal of the Treaty Negotiations with the Wyandots, etc., July 21, 1814, in ibid.

86. Kappler, *Indian Treaties,* 105–107; quotes in WHH to Armstrong, March 22, 1814, in ibid.

87. WHH and Cass to Armstrong, July 17, 1814, in ibid.

CONCLUSION

1. John Williamson and Elmore Williams assign apprentice to WHH, September 22, 1814, and WHH's Deposition to Griffin Yeatman, October 20, 1814, both in Clanin, ed., *Papers of WHH.*

2. WHH to James Henry, November 10, 1814, WHH to John Cleves Short, November 17 and November 24, 1814, all in ibid.

3. Sugden, *Tecumseh,* 387–401; Brands, *Andrew Jackson,* 174–283.

4. WHH to Jackson, April 20, 1815, in Clanin, ed., *Papers of WHH.*

5. During and shortly after the War of 1812, the post of War Department head was an unsettling revolving door, much to the detriment of the armed services.

6. Dallas to WHH et al., June 9, 1815, and Madison to WHH, Duncan McArthur, and John Graham, June 13, 1815, both in Clanin, ed., *Papers of WHH.*

7. WHH to Dallas, June 26, 1815, in ibid.

8. Ibid.

9. Ibid.; Dallas to WHH et al., June 9, 1815, in ibid.

10. See WHH, James Taylor, and James Findlay to Dallas, re: retaining Major Thomas Martin, a veteran of the Revolution, as arms keeper at the Federal Arsenal in Newport, Kentucky, July 18, 1815, and WHH to Perry, July 31, 1815, both in ibid.

11. Journal of the Treaty Negotiations with the Wyandots, etc., August 31 and September 1, 1815, in ibid.

12. Ibid., Sept. 4, 5, and 8.

13. The problem with trying to be exact about these matters is that it is impossible to know just how much money would have been paid had the treaties been honored as written. If the promised annuities had been paid in perpetuity, the cost of such lands would eventually add up to far more than two cents per acre. Still, there was no denying that both Harrison's friends and his detractors felt he was buying lands cheaply.

14. WHH to Secretary of War George Graham, November 25, 1815, in Clanin, ed., *Papers of WHH.* Unbeknownst to WHH, by this time Graham was out, and William Crawford was the new secretary of war.

15. WHH to Clay, December 20, 1815, in ibid.; Cleaves, *Old Tippecanoe,* 240.

16. WHH to McClean, December 29, 1815, in Clanin, ed., *Papers of WHH.* For Procter's actual fate, see Antal, *Wampum Denied,* and Sugden, *Tecumseh's Last Stand.*

17. As Peter S. Onuf and Leonard J. Sadosky put it in *Jeffersonian America*, 24, "This 'Second War for Independence' was, after all, not so different from the first: nearly disastrous in fact, but increasingly glorious in retrospect."

18. Sugden, *Tecumseh*, 387–401; McCoy, "Democracy in Print," Ph.D. diss., University of Illinois, 73–118.

19. Peterson, *The Great Triumvirate;* Gunderson, *Log Cabin Campaign,* 79–81, 241–46.

20. A handful of Seminoles, relatives of the Red Stick Creeks, held out in the Florida Everglades and were never completely removed. See Dowd, *Spirited Resistance,* 172; Owens, "Ducoigne," 109–36, quote on 133; Carter, *Little Turtle,* 227–33; Hutton, "William Wells," 221–22.

21. Cayton, *Frontier Indiana,* 263; Rafert, *Miami Indians,* 286–87; Edmunds, *Shawnee Prophet,* 184–90; Sugden, *Tecumseh,* 386–88.

22. *Biographical Directory of the United States Congress,* 1260; Malone, ed., *Dictionary of American Biography vol. 10,* 32–34; Mills, *Jonathan Jennings,* 213, 228–29.

23. Harrison soundly defeated Van Buren in the electoral college, 234 to 60, but the popular vote was close, with Van Buren losing by only 150,000 ballots. See Gunderson, *Log Cabin Campaign,* 118, 140, 254; Goebel, *Harrison,* 233–35, 242–43, 253–60, 312–20, 342–65.

24. Harrison's was the longest inaugural address to that time. When his grandson Benjamin spoke at his own inauguration, he spoke only half as long and wore heavy long underwear to protect himself from the weather. See Socolofsky and Spetter, *Presidency of Benjamin Harrison,* 2.

25. Gunderson, *Log Cabin Campaign,* 273–74; Bond, ed., *Intimate Letters of John Cleves Symmes,* 166, note 17.

26. Aron, *How the West Was Lost,* 146–47.

27. Thornbrough, *Negro in Indiana,* 23–25.

28. Paul Finkelman, "Slavery and Bondage in the 'Empire of Liberty,'" in Williams, ed., *Northwest Ordinance,* 61–88; Berwanger, *Frontier against Slavery,* 26–30; Onuf, *Jefferson's Empire,* 49.

Bibliography

ARCHIVAL SOURCES

Duke University Rare Book and Special Collections Library, Durham, North
  Carolina
    Joseph Terry Papers
Filson Historical Society, Louisville, Kentucky
    Rev. David Barrow Diary
    Thomas Bodley Correspondence
    Papers of Arthur Campbell
    George Rogers Clark Papers
    John Drummens Letters
    John Francis Hamtramck Papers
    Robert Breckenridge McAfee Papers
    Samuel McDowell Papers
    Jonathan Taylor Papers
    Anthony Wayne Orderly Books
Illinois State Historical Library (now the Abraham Lincoln Presidential
  Library), Springfield
    John Messinger Papers
    Robert Morrison Papers
    Anthony Wayne Manuscripts
Indiana Historical Society Library, Indianapolis
    William Henry Harrison Papers
    Francis Vigo Papers
Library of Congress, Washington, D.C.
    William Henry Harrison Papers (microfilm)
The McGrady-Brockman House, Vincennes, Indiana
    Knox County Court Files, 1796–1820
    Register of Negro Slaves, 1805–1807

Missouri Historical Society, St. Louis
    Vasquez Family Collection
National Archives, Washington, D.C.
    Correspondence of the War Department Relating to Indian Affairs, Military
    Pensions, and Fortifications 1791–97 (microfilm)
    Record Group 107, Correspondence from the Secretary of War (microfilm);
    includes
Miscellaneous Letters Sent by the Secretary of War, 1800–1809 (microfilm)

PUBLISHED PRIMARY SOURCES

American State Papers, Class II, Indian Affairs, vol. 1. Washington, D.C.: Gales and
    Seaton, 1831.
Annals of Congress, vols. 4–24. Washington, D.C.: Gales and Seaton, 1851–53.
Axtell, James, ed. *The Indian Peoples of Eastern North America: A Documentary History
    of the Sexes.* New York: Oxford University Press, 1981.
Bond, Beverley W., Jr., ed. *The Correspondence of John Cleves Symmes: Founder of the
    Miami Purchase.* New York: Macmillan, 1926.
————. *The Intimate Letters of John Cleves Symmes and His Family.* Cincinnati: His-
    torical and Philosophical Society of Ohio, 1956.
Boyd, Julian P., ed. *The Papers of Thomas Jefferson,* 20 vols. Princeton: Princeton
    University Press, 1952.
Buell, Rowena, ed. *The Memoirs of Rufus Putnam and Certain Official Papers and
    Correspondence.* Boston: Houghton Mifflin, for National Society of the Colonial
    Dames of America in the State of Ohio, 1903.
Calloway, Colin G., ed. *The World Turned Upside Down: Indian Voices from Early
    America.* Boston: Bedford Books, 1994.
Carter, Clarence Edwin, ed. *Territorial Papers of the United States.* Washington, D.C.:
    U.S. Government Printing Office, 1934–1962.
    Vol. 2: The Territory Northwest of the River Ohio, 1787–1803, 1934.
    Vol. 3: The Territory Northwest of the River Ohio, 1787–1803 cont. 1934.
    Vol. 7: Indiana Territory, 1800–1810, 1936.
    Vol. 8: Indiana Territory, 1800–1810 cont., 1939.
    Vol. 13: The Louisiana-Missouri Territory, 1803–1805, 1949.
    Vol. 14: The Louisiana-Missouri Territory 1806–1814, cont. 1949.
    Vol. 16: Illinois Territory, 1809–1814, 1948.
Chinard, Gilbert, ed. *Volney Et L'Amerique: D'Apres Des Documents Inedits et Sa Cor-
    respondence avec Jefferson.* Baltimore: Johns Hopkins University Press, 1923.
Clanin, Douglas E., ed. *The Papers of William Henry Harrison, 1800–1815* (micro-
    film). Indianapolis: Indiana Historical Society, 1999.

Clark, William. "A Journal of Major-General Anthony Wayne's Campaign against the Shawnee Indians in Ohio 1794–1795," R. C. McGrane, ed. *Mississippi Valley Historical Review* 1, no. 3 (December 1914): 418–44.

Common Pleas Court Minutes 1796–1799 Knox County, Indiana, 2 vols. Transcribed and typed by the Indiana Historical Records Survey, Indianapolis, 1941.

Common Pleas Court Minutes 1807–1810 Knox County, Indiana, 2 vols. Transcribed and typed by the Indiana Historical Records Survey, sponsored by the Indiana Historical Bureau, Indianapolis, 1941.

Dunn, Jacob Piatt, Jr., ed. "Slavery Petitions and Papers." *Indiana Historical Society Publications* 3, no. 12. Indianapolis: Indiana Historical Bureau, 1895.

Esarey, Logan, ed. *The Messages and Letters of William Henry Harrison, 1800–1816* (2 vols.). New York: Arno, 1975 [reprint of the 1922 Indiana Historical Commission ed.].

Ewbank, Louis B., and Dorothy L. Riker, eds. *Laws of Indiana Territory 1809–1816.* Indianapolis: Indiana Historical Bureau, 1934.

Faribault-Beauregard, Marthe, ed. *La population des forts français d'Amérique (XVIIIe siècle)* (2 vols.). Montréal: Éditions Bergeron, 1982, 1984.

Ford, Worthington Chauncey, comp. *British Officers Serving in the American Revolution 1774–1783.* New York: Historical Printing Club, 1897.

Gipson, Lawrence Henry, ed. *The Moravian Indian Mission on White River: Diaries and Letters May 5, 1799, to November 12, 1806* (trans. from original German). Indianapolis: Indiana Historical Bureau, 1938.

Hammes, Raymond H., ed. *Cahokia, St. Clair County Record Book B 1800–1813.* Springfield: Illinois Research Center for Colonial and Territorial Studies, 1982.

Holmberg, James J., ed. *Dear Brother: Letters of William Clark to Jonathan Clark.* New Haven: Yale University Press, 2002.

Hopkins, James F., ed.; Mary W.M. Hargreaves, associate editor. *The Papers of Henry Clay [10 vols.] vol. 1: The Rising Statesman 1797–1814.* Lexington: University of Kentucky Press, 1959.

Houck, Louis, ed. *The Spanish Regime in Missouri.* Chicago: R. R. Donnelley & Sons, 1909.

Jackson, Donald, ed. *Black Hawk: An Autobiography.* Urbana: University of Illinois Press 1987.

James, James Alton, ed. *George Rogers Clark Papers 1778–1781.* Springfield: Illinois State Historical Library, 1912.

Kappler, Charles J., ed. *Indian Treaties 1778–1883.* New York: Interland, 1972.

Knopf, Richard C., ed. *Anthony Wayne: A Name in Arms.* Pittsburgh: University of Pittsburgh Press, 1960.

"The Letters of Decius," John D. Barnhart, ed. *Indiana Magazine of History* 43, no. 3 (September 1947): 263–96.

Minutes of Common Pleas Court Knox County 1801–1806. Transcribed and typed by the Indiana Historical Records Survey, Indianapolis, 1940.

"Minutes of the Board of Trustees for Vincennes University" (December 6, 1806–September 12, 1807) [part 1 of 2], Robert Constantine, ed. *Indiana Magazine of History* 54, no. 4 (December 1958): 313–64.

"Minutes of the Board of Trustees for Vincennes University" (October 16, 1807–December 11, 1811) [part 2 of 2], Robert Constantine, ed. *Indiana Magazine of History* 55, no. 3 (September 1959): 247–93.

Moser, Harold D., and Sharon Macpherson, eds. *The Papers of Andrew Jackson vol. 2, 1804–1813.* Knoxville: University of Tennessee Press, 1984.

"Mrs. Lydia B. Bacon's Journal, 1811–1812" [part 1 of 2], Mary M. Crawford, ed. *Indiana Magazine of History* 40, no. 4 (December 1944): 367–86.

Nasatir, A. P., ed. *Before Lewis and Clark: Documents Illustrating the History of Missouri 1785–1804,* 2 vols. St. Louis: St. Louis Historical Documents Foundation, 1952.

Padover, Saul K., ed. *The Complete Jefferson.* Freeport, N.Y.: Books for Libraries, 1969.

Pease, Theodore Calvin, ed. *Laws of the Northwest Territory 1788–1800.* Springfield: Illinois State Historical Library, 1925.

Peterson, Merril D., ed. *Thomas Jefferson: Writings.* New York: Literary Classics of the United States, 1984.

Philbrick, Francis S., ed. *Laws of Illinois Territory 1809–1818.* Springfield: Illinois State Historical Library, 1950.

———. *Laws of Indiana Territory 1801–1809.* Springfield: Illinois State Historical Library, 1930.

Quaife, Milo M., ed. *The John Askin Papers 1747–1820* (2 vols.). Detroit: Detroit Library Commission, 1928–31.

Robertson, Nellie Armstrong, and Dorothy L. Riker, eds. *The John Tipton Papers, 1809–1839* (3 vols.). Indianapolis: Indiana Historical Bureau, 1942.

Rowland, Duncan, ed. *The Mississippi Territorial Archives 1798–1803: Executive Journals of Governor Winthrop Sargent and Governor William Charles Cole Claiborne vol. 1.* Nashville: Brandon, 1905.

Sapp, Peggy Lathrop, comp. *Randolph County Illinois Commissioners' Court Records 1802–1807.* Springfield: Wanda Warkins Allers and Eileen Lynch Gochanour, 1986.

———. *Randolph County Illinois Orphans Court Records 1804–1809.* Springfield: Wanda Warkins Allers and Eileen Lynch Gochanour, 1986.

Smith, William Henry, ed. *The St. Clair Papers: The Life and Public Services of Arthur St. Clair,* 2 vols. Cincinnati: Robert Clarke, 1882.

Thornbrough, Gayle, ed. *The Correspondence of John Badollet and Albert Gallatin 1804–1836.* Indianapolis: Indiana Historical Society, 1963.

————. *Letter Book of the Indian Agency at Fort Wayne, 1809–1815*. Indianapolis: Indiana Historical Society, 1961.

Thornbrough, Gayle, and Dorothy L. Riker, eds. *Journals of the General Assembly of Indiana Territory 1805–1815*. Indianapolis: Indiana Historical Bureau, 1950.

Volney, Constantin François. *View of the Climate and Soil of the United States of America: To Which Are Annexed Some Accounts of Florida, the French Colony on the Scioto, Certain Canadian Colonies, and the Savages or Natives* (translated). London: J. Johnson, 1804.

Washington, H. A., ed. *The Writings of Thomas Jefferson*, 9 vols. Washington, D.C.: Taylor & Maury, 1854.

Woollen, William Wesley, Daniel Wait Howe, and Jacob Piatt Dunn, eds. "Executive Journal of Indiana Territory 1800–1816." *Indiana Historical Society Publications* 3, no. 3 (1900).

PERIOD NEWSPAPERS

The Argus of Western America (Frankfort), January 28, 1809. Bound collection, Filson Historical Society Library, Louisville, Kentucky.

The Centinel of the North-Western Territory (Cincinnati), November 9, 1793–June 4, 1796. Illinois Historical Survey, University of Illinois Library, Urbana (microfilm).

Freeman's Journal (Cincinnati) and other early Ohio newspapers, March 4, 1796–February 23, 1813. Ohio Historical Society, Cincinnati (microfilm).

Indiana Gazette (Vincennes), August 7, 1804–August 14, 1806. Indiana State Library, Indianapolis (microfilm).

Scioto Gazette (Chillicothe, Ohio), December 24, 1804–November 27, 1811. University of Illinois Newspaper Library, Urbana (microfilm).

Supporter (Chillicothe, Ohio), November 25, 1809–November 30, 1811. University of Illinois Newspaper Library, Urbana (microfilm).

Vincennes Western Sun, July 11, 1807–February 14, 1813. Indiana State Library, Indianapolis (microfilm).

Virginia Gazette (Richmond), 1776. University of North Carolina Library, Chapel Hill (microfilm).

Virginia Herald and Fredericksburg Advertiser, 1792–1795. University of North Carolina Library, Chapel Hill (microfilm).

Washington Intelligencer (Washington, D.C.), December 3, 1809–December 21, 1811. University of Illinois Newspaper Library, Urbana (microfilm).

The Western Spy and Hamilton Gazette (Cincinnati), August 6, 1799–November 23, 1811. Indiana State Library, Indianapolis (microfilm).

The Western Spy and Miami Gazette (Cincinnati), Cincinnati, Ohio Historical Society, Cincinnati (microfilm).

DISSERTATIONS AND THESES

Asperheim, Stephen. "Double Characters: The Making of American Nationalism in Kentucky, 1792–1833." Ph.D. dissertation, University of Illinois, 2003.

Edmunds, R. David. "A History of the Kickapoo Indians in Illinois from 1750–1834." Unpublished master's thesis, Illinois State University, 1966.

McCoy, Colin. "Democracy in Print: The Literature of Persuasion in Jacksonian America, 1815–1840." Ph.D. dissertation, University of Illinois, 2001.

Tevebaugh, John Leslie. "Merchant on the Western Frontier: William Morrison of Kaskaskia, 1790–1837." Ph.D. dissertation, University of Illinois, 1962.

SECONDARY SOURCES

Adams, Henry. *History of the United States of America,* 9 vols. New York: Antiquarian, 1962.

Allen, Robert S. *His Majesty's Indian Allies: British Indian Policy in the Defence of Canada, 1774–1815.* Toronto: Durndun, 1992.

Alvord, Clarence Walworth. *The Illinois Country 1673–1818.* Chicago: A. C. McClurg, 1922.

Anderson, Fred. *Crucible of War: The Seven Years' War and the Fate of Empire in British North America, 1754–1766.* New York: Alfred A. Knopf, 2000.

Anson, Bert. *The Miami Indians.* Norman: University of Oklahoma Press, 1970.

Antal, Sandy. *A Wampum Denied: Procter's War of 1812.* Ottawa: Carleton University Press, 1997.

Appleby, Joyce. *Inheriting the Revolution: The First Generation of Americans.* Cambridge: Harvard University Press, 2000.

Aron, Stephen. *How the West Was Lost: The Transformation of Kentucky from Daniel Boone to Henry Clay.* Baltimore: Johns Hopkins University Press, 1996.

Axtell, James. "The White Indians of Colonial America." *William and Mary Quarterly* 32, no. 1 (January 1975): 55–88.

Ayers, Edward L. *Vengeance and Justice: Crime and Punishment in the 19th-Century American South.* New York: Oxford University Press, 1984.

Bailyn, Bernard. *The Ideological Origins of the American Revolution,* 25th Anniversary ed. Cambridge: Harvard University Press, 1992.

Barnhart, John D. *Valley of Democracy: The Frontier versus the Plantation in the Ohio Valley, 1775–1818.* Bloomington: Indiana University Press, 1953.

Barnhart, John D., and Dorothy L. Riker. *Indiana to 1816: The Colonial Period.* Indianapolis: Indiana Historical Society, 1971.

Barr, Daniel P., ed. *The Boundaries between Us: Natives and Newcomers along the Frontiers of the Old Northwest Territory, 1750–1850.* Kent, Ohio: Kent State University Press, 2006.

Basch, Norma. *Framing American Divorce: From the Revolutionary Generation to the Victorians.* Berkeley: University of California Press, 1999.

Bernstein, R. B. *Thomas Jefferson.* New York: Oxford University Press, 2003.

Berry, Thomas Senior. *Western Prices before 1861: A Study of the Cincinnati Market.* Cambridge: Harvard University Press, 1943.

Berwanger, Eugene H. *The Frontier against Slavery: Western Anti-Negro Prejudice and the Slavery Extension Controversy.* Urbana: University of Illinois Press, 1967.

Biographical Directory of the United States Congress 1774–1989. Washington, D.C.: U.S. Government Printing Office, 1989.

Black, Henry Campbell. *Black's Law Dictionary: Definitions of the Terms and Phrases of American and English Jurisprudence, Ancient and Modern,* 6th ed. St. Paul, Minn.: West, 1990.

Boyd, Julian P. *The Declaration of Independence: The Evolution of the Text,* Gerard W. Gawalt, ed. Hanover: University Press of New England, 1999.

Brands, H. W. *Andrew Jackson: His Life and Times.* New York: Doubleday, 2005.

Breen, T. H. *Tobacco Culture: The Mentality of the Great Tidewater Planters on the Eve of Revolution.* Princeton: Princeton University Press, 1985.

Brown, Kathleen M. *Good Wives, Nasty Wenches, and Anxious Patriarchs: Gender, Race, and Power in Colonial Virginia.* Chapel Hill: University of North Carolina Press, 1996.

Calloway, Colin G. *The American Revolution in Indian Country: Crisis and Diversity in Native American Communities.* New York: Cambridge University Press, 1995.

———. "Beyond the Vortex of Violence: Indian-White Relations in the Ohio Country 1783–1815." *Northwest Ohio Quarterly* 64, no. 1 (Winter 1992): 16–26.

———. *Crown and Calumet: British-Indian Relations, 1783–1815.* Norman: University of Oklahoma Press, 1987.

———. "'We Have Always Been the Frontier': The American Revolution in Shawnee Country." *American Indian Quarterly* 16, no. 1 (Winter 1992): 39–52.

Carter, Harvey Lewis. *The Life and Times of Little Turtle: First Sagamore of the Wabash.* Urbana: University of Illinois Press, 1987.

Cayton, Andrew R.L. *Frontier Indiana.* Bloomington: Indiana University Press, 1996.

———. *The Frontier Republic: Ideology and Politics in the Ohio Country, 1780–1825.* Kent, Ohio: Kent State University Press, 1986.

Cayton, Andrew R.L., and Fredrika J. Teute, eds. *Contact Points: American Frontiers from the Mohawk Valley to the Mississippi, 1750–1830.* Chapel Hill: University of North Carolina Press, 1998.

Chidsey, Donald Barr. *Aaron Burr and His Strange Doings in the West.* New York: Crown, 1967.

Clark, Jerry E. *The Shawnee.* Lexington: University Press of Kentucky, 1993.

Cleaves, Freeman. *Old Tippecanoe: William Henry Harrison and His Time.* New York: Charles Scribner's Sons, 1939.

Colley, Linda. *Britons: Forging the Nation 1707–1837.* New Haven: Yale University Press, 1992.

————. *Captives*. New York: Pantheon Books, 2002.

Combs, Jerald A. *The Jay Treaty: Political Battleground of the Founding Fathers*. Berkeley: University of California Press, 1970.

Dangerfield, George. *The Era of Good Feelings*. New York: Harcourt, Brace, 1952.

Davis, James E. *Frontier Illinois*. Bloomington: Indiana University Press, 1998.

Dawson, Moses. *A Historical Narrative of the Civil and Military Services of Major-General William Henry Harrison, and a Vindication of His Character and Conduct as a Statesman, a Citizen, and a Soldier*. Cincinnati: Cincinnati Advertiser, 1824.

Dowd, Gregory Evans. *A Spirited Resistance: The North American Indian Struggle for Unity, 1745–1815*. Baltimore: Johns Hopkins University Press, 1992.

————. "Thinking and Believing: Nativism and Unity in the Ages of Tecumseh and Pontiac." *American Indian Quarterly* 16, no. 3 (Summer 1992): 309–35.

Drimmer, Melvin, ed. *Black History: A Reappraisal*. Garden City, N.Y.: Doubleday, 1968.

Dunn, Jacob Piatt, Jr. *Indiana: A Redemption from Slavery*. Boston: Houghton Mifflin, 1888.

Early Studies of Slavery by States vol. 1. Northbrook: Metro Books, 1972.

Edmunds, R. David. "'Nothing Has Been Effected': The Vincennes Treaty of 1792." *Indiana Magazine of History* 74, no. 1 (March 1978): 23–35.

————. *The Potawatomis: Keepers of the Fire*. Norman: University of Oklahoma Press, 1978.

————. *The Shawnee Prophet*. Lincoln: University of Nebraska Press, 1983.

————. *Tecumseh and the Quest for Indian Leadership*. New York: Little, Brown, 1984.

Edwards, Ninian W. *History of Illinois from 1778 to 1883; and Life and Times of Ninian Edwards*. Springfield: Illinois State Journal Company, 1870.

Elkins, Stanley, and Eric McKitrick. *The Age of Federalism*. New York: Oxford University Press, 1993.

Erney, Richard Alton. *The Public Life of Henry Dearborn*. New York: Arno, 1979.

Esarey, Logan. *A History of Indiana: From Its Exploration to 1850*. Indianapolis: W. K. Stewart, 1915.

Etcheson, Nicole. *The Emerging Midwest: Upland Southerners and the Political Culture of the Old Northwest, 1787–1861*. Bloomington: Indiana University Press, 1996.

Faye, Stanley. "Illinois Indians on the Lower Mississippi 1771–1781." *Illinois State Historical Society Journal* 35, no.1 (March 1942): 57–72.

Ferling, John. *A Leap in the Dark: The Struggle to Create the American Republic*. New York: Oxford University Press, 2003.

Finkelman, Paul. *Slavery and the Founders: Race and Liberty in the Age of Jefferson*. Armonk, N.Y.: M. E. Sharpe, 1996.

————, ed. *Slavery in the North and the West*. New York: Garland, 1989.

Fischer, David Hackett. *Albion's Seed: Four British Folkways in America*. New York: Oxford University Press, 1989.

———. *Paul Revere's Ride.* New York: Oxford University Press, 1994.

Fischer, David Hackett, and James C. Kelly. *Bound Away: Virginia and the Westward Movement.* Charlottesville: University Press of Virginia, 2000.

Franklin, John Hope, and Loren Schweninger. *Runaway Slaves: Rebels on the Plantation.* New York: Oxford University Press, 1999.

Freeman, Joanne B. *Affairs of Honor: National Politics in the New Republic.* New Haven: Yale University Press, 2002.

Gaff, Alan D. *Bayonets in the Wilderness: Anthony Wayne's Legion in the Old Northwest.* Norman: University of Oklahoma Press, 2004.

Goebel, Dorothy Burne. *William Henry Harrison: A Political Biography.* Indianapolis: Historical Bureau of the Indiana State Library and Historical Department, 1926.

Green, James A. *William Henry Harrison: His Life and Times.* Richmond: Garret and Massie, 1941.

Grenier, John. *The First Way of War: American War Making on the Frontier.* New York: Cambridge University Press, 2005.

Gunderson, Robert Gray. *The Log-Cabin Campaign.* Lexington: University Press of Kentucky, 1957.

———. "William Henry Harrison: Apprentice in Arms." *Northwest Ohio Quarterly* 65 (Winter 1993): 3–29.

Hammack, James Wallace, Jr. *Kentucky and the Second American Revolution: The War of 1812.* Lexington: University Press of Kentucky, 1976.

Harrison, Fairfax. "The Proprietors of the Northern Neck: Chapters of Culpepper Genealogy." *Virginia Magazine of History and Biography* 33, no. 4 (October 1925): 413–15.

Hartog, Hendrik. *Man and Wife in America: A History.* Cambridge: Harvard University Press, 2000.

Hauser, Raymond E. "The Illinois Indian Tribe: From Autonomy and Self-Sufficiency to Dependency and Depopulation." *Illinois State Historical Society Journal* 69, no. 2 (May 1976): 127–38.

Heard, J. Norman. *White into Red: A Study of the Assimilation of White Persons Captured by Indians.* Meutchen, N.J.: Scarecrow, 1973.

Hickey, Donald R. *The War of 1812: A Forgotten Conflict.* Urbana: University of Illinois Press, 1989.

Hinderaker, Eric. *Elusive Empires: Constructing Colonialism in the Ohio Valley, 1673–1800.* New York: Cambridge University Press, 1997.

Hoffman, Ronald, and Peter J. Albert, eds. *Women in the Age of the American Revolution.* Charlottesville: University of Virginia Press, 1988.

Holton, Woody. *Forced Founders: Indians, Debtors, Slaves, and the Making of the American Revolution in Virginia.* Chapel Hill: University of North Carolina Press, 1999.

Horsman, Reginald. *Expansion and American Indian Policy, 1783–1812.* East Lansing: Michigan State University Press, 1967.

———. *The Frontier in the Formative Years, 1783–1815.* Albuquerque: University of New Mexico Press, 1975.

———. *Matthew Elliott, British Indian Agent.* Detroit: Wayne State University Press, 1964.

———. "William Henry Harrison: Virginia Gentleman in the Old Northwest." *Indiana Magazine of History* 96, no. 2 (June 2000): 125–49.

Howard, James H. *Shawnee! The Ceremonialism of a Native American Tribe and Its Cultural Background.* Athens: Ohio University Press, 1981.

Hoxie, Frederick E., Ronald Hoffman, and Peter J. Albert, eds. *Native Americans and the Early Republic.* Charlottesville: University Press of Virginia, 1999.

Hurt, R. Douglas. *The Indian Frontier 1763–1846.* Albuquerque: University of New Mexico Press, 2002.

Hutton, Paul S. "William Wells: Frontier Scout and Indian Agent." *Indiana Magazine of History* 74 (September 1978): 183–222.

Indians of Ohio and Indiana Prior to 1795, 2 vols. New York: Garland, 1974.

Isaac, Rhys. *Landon Carter's Uneasy Kingdom: Revolution and Rebellion on a Virginia Plantation.* New York: Oxford University Press, 2004.

———. *The Transformation of Virginia 1740–1790.* Chapel Hill: University of North Carolina Press, 1982.

Jablow, Joseph. *Indians of Illinois and Indiana: Illinois, Kickapoo, and Potawatomi Indians.* New York: Garland, 1974.

Jacobs, James Ripley. *Tarnished Warrior: Major-General James Wilkinson.* New York: Macmillan, 1938.

Jones, Landon Y. *William Clark and the Shaping of the West.* New York: Hill and Wang, 2004.

Jones, Robert Ralston. *Fort Washington at Cincinnati.* Cincinnati: Ohio Society of Colonial Wars, 1902.

Jordan, Winthrop D. *White over Black: American Attitudes toward the Negro, 1550–1812.* New York: W. W. Norton, 1968.

Keeley, Lawrence H. *War Before Civilization: The Myth of the Peaceful Savage.* New York: Oxford University Press, 1996.

Kerber, Linda K. "The Paradox of Women's Citizenship in the Early Republic: The Case of Martin vs. Massachusetts, 1805." *American Historical Review* 97, no. 2 (April 1992): 349–78.

———. *Women of the Republic: Intellect and Ideology in Revolutionary America.* Chapel Hill: University of North Carolina Press, 1980.

Knopf, Richard C. "Anthony Wayne: The Man and the Myth." *Northwest Ohio Quarterly* 64, no. 2 (Spring 1992): 35–42.

Kurlansky, Mark. *Salt: A World History.* New York: Walker, 2002.

Linklater, Andro. *Measuring America: How an Untamed Wilderness Shaped the United States and Fulfilled the Promise of Democracy.* New York: Walker, 2002.

Littlefield, Daniel C. "John Jay, the Revolutionary Generation, and Slavery." *New York History* 81, no. 1 (January 2000): 91–132.

Litwack, Leon F. *North of Slavery: The Negro in the Free States 1790–1860.* Chicago: University of Chicago Press, 1961.

Maier, Pauline. *American Scripture: Making the Declaration of Independence.* New York: Alfred A. Knopf, 1997.

Mallet, Edmond. "Sieur De Vincennes, Founder of Indiana's Oldest Town." *Indiana Historical Society Publications* 3, no. 2. Indianapolis: Bowen Merrill, 1897, 41–62.

Malone, Dumas, ed. *Dictionary of American Biography,* 21 vols. New York: Charles Scribner's Sons, 1932–36.

———. *Jefferson and His Time* (6 vols.). New York: Little, Brown, 1948–81 [second printing].

Mancall, Peter C. *Deadly Medicine: Indians and Alcohol in Early America.* Ithaca: Cornell University Press, 1995.

McCoy, Drew R. *The Elusive Republic: Political Economy in Jeffersonian America.* Chapel Hill: University of North Carolina Press, 1980.

Melton, Buckner F., Jr. *Aaron Burr: Conspiracy to Treason.* New York: John Wiley & Sons, 2002.

Miller, John W. *Indiana Newspaper Bibliography.* Indianapolis: Indiana Historical Society, 1982.

Mills, Randy K. *Jonathan Jennings: Indiana's First Governor.* Indianapolis: Indiana Historical Society, 2005.

Monroe, Dan. *The Republican Vision of John Tyler.* College Station: Texas A&M University Press, 2003.

Morgan, Edmund. *American Slavery, American Freedom: The Ordeal of Colonial Virginia.* New York: W. W. Norton, 1975.

Morris, Richard B. *Government and Labor in Early America.* New York: Columbia University Press, 1956.

Namias, June. *White Captives: Gender and Ethnicity on the American Frontier.* Chapel Hill: University of North Carolina Press, 1993.

Nelson, Larry L. *A Man of Distinction among Them: Alexander McKee and the Ohio Country Frontier, 1754–1799.* Kent, Ohio: Kent State University Press, 1999.

———. "'Never Have They Done So Little': The Battle of Fort Recovery and the Collapse of the Miami Confederacy." *Northwest Ohio Quarterly* 64, no. 2 (1992): 43–55.

Norton, Mary Beth. "Gender and Defamation in Seventeenth-Century Maryland." *William and Mary Quarterly* 44, no. 1 (January 1987): 3–39.

———. *Liberty's Daughters: The Revolutionary Experience of American Women, 1750–1800.* Boston: Little, Brown, 1980.

Onuf, Peter S. *Jefferson's Empire: The Language of American Nationhood.* Charlottesville: University Press of Virginia, 2000.

―――. *Statehood and Union: A History of the Northwest Ordinance.* Bloomington: Indiana University Press, 1987.

Onuf, Peter S., and Leonard J. Sadosky. *Jeffersonian America.* Malden, Mass.: Blackwell, 2002.

Owens, Robert M. "Jean Baptiste Ducoigne, the Kaskaskias, and the Limits of Thomas Jefferson's Friendship." *Journal of Illinois History* 5, no. 2 (Summer 2002): 109–36.

―――. "Jeffersonian Benevolence on the Ground: The Indian Land Cession Treaties of William Henry Harrison." *Journal of the Early Republic* 22, no. 3 (Fall 2002): 405–35.

Owsley, Frank Lawrence, Jr., and Gene A. Smith. *Filibusters and Expansionists: Jeffersonian Manifest Destiny, 1800–1821.* Tuscaloosa: University of Alabama Press, 1997.

Paine, Thomas. *Common Sense,* Edward Larkin, ed. Toronto: Broadview, 2004.

Patterson, Thomas G., J. Garry Clifford, and Kenneth J. Hagan. *American Foreign Relations: A History to 1920.* Lexington: University of Kentucky Press, 1995.

Pence, George C., and Nellie C. Armstrong. *Indiana Boundaries: Territory, State, and County.* Indianapolis: Indiana Historical Bureau, 1967.

Person, Leland S. "The American Eve: Miscegenation and a Feminist Frontier Fiction." *American Quarterly* 37, no. 5 (Winter 1985): 665–85.

Pestana, Carla Gardina, and Sharon V. Salinger, eds. *Inequality in Early America.* Hanover, N.H.: University Press of New England, 1999.

Peterson, Merril D. *The Great Triumvirate: Webster, Clay, and Calhoun.* New York: Oxford University Press, 1987.

Prucha, Francis Paul. *The Great Father: The United States Government and the American Indians.* Lincoln: University of Nebraska Press, 1984.

Quimby, Robert S. *The U.S. Army in the War of 1812: An Operational and Command Study,* 2 vols. East Lansing: Michigan State University Press, 1997.

Rafert, Stewart W. *The Miami Indians of Indiana: A Persistent People 1654–1994.* Indianapolis: Indiana Historical Society, 1996.

Remini, Robert V. *Andrew Jackson and the Course of American Empire, 1767–1821.* New York: Harper & Row, 1977.

Roberts, Robert B. *Encyclopedia of Historic Forts: The Military, Pioneer, and Trading Posts of the United States.* New York: Macmillan, 1988.

Robertson, Lindsay G. *Conquest by Law: How the Discovery of America Dispossessed Indigenous Peoples of Their Lands.* New York: Oxford University Press, 2005.

Rogin, Michael Paul. *Fathers and Children: Andrew Jackson and the Subjugation of the American Indian.* New York: Alfred A. Knopf, 1975.

Rohr, Martha E. *Historical Sketch of Fort Recovery.* Portland, Ind.: Fort Recovery Historical Society, 1991.

Rohrbough, Malcolm J. *The Land Office Business: The Settlement and Administration of American Public Lands, 1789–1837.* Belmont, Calif.: Wadsworth, 1990.

Rorabaugh, W. J. *The Alcoholic Republic: An American Tradition.* New York: Oxford University Press, 1979.

Royce, Charles C. *Indian Land Cessions in the United States: Eighteenth Annual Report of the Bureau of American Ethnology, 1896–97 part 2.* Washington, D.C.: U.S. Government Printing Press, 1899.

Sheehan, Bernard. *Seeds of Extinction: Jeffersonian Philanthropy and the American Indian.* Chapel Hill: University of North Carolina Press, 1973.

Skaggs, David Curtis, and Larry L. Nelson, eds. *The Sixty Years' War for the Great Lakes, 1754–1814.* East Lansing: Michigan State University Press, 2001.

Sleeper-Smith, Susan. *Indian Women and French Men: Rethinking Cultural Encounter in the Western Great Lakes.* Amherst: University of Massachusetts Press, 2001.

Smith, Howard W. *Benjamin Harrison and the American Revolution.* Williamsburg: Virginia Independence Bicentennial Commission, 1976.

Socolofsky, Homer E., and Allan B. Spetter. *The Presidency of Benjamin Harrison.* Lawrence: University Press of Kansas, 1987.

Stevens, Frank E. "Illinois in the War of 1812." *Transactions of the Illinois State Historical Society for 1904,* no. 9. Springfield, 1904, 62–197.

Stout, David B. *Piankashaw and Kaskaskia Indians.* New York: Garland, 1974.

Sugden, John. *Blue Jacket: Warrior of the Shawnees.* Lincoln: University of Nebraska Press, 2000.

———. *Tecumseh: A Life.* New York: Henry Holt, 1997.

———. *Tecumseh's Last Stand.* Norman: University of Oklahoma Press, 1985.

Sword, Wiley. *President Washington's War: The Struggle for the Old Northwest, 1790–1795.* Norman: University of Oklahoma Press, 1985.

Sydnor, Charles S. *American Revolutionaries in the Making: Political Practices in Washington's Virginia* [orig. published as *Gentlemen Freeholders,* 1952]. New York: Free Press, 1965.

Tanner, Helen Hornbeck. "The Glaize in 1792: A Composite Indian Community." *Ethnohistory* 25, no. 1 (1978): 15–39.

———, ed. *Atlas of Great Lakes Indian History.* Norman: University of Oklahoma Press, 1987.

Taylor, Alan. *The Divided Ground: Indians, Settlers, and the Northern Borderland of the American Revolution.* New York: Alfred A. Knopf, 2006.

Thompson, Charles N. *Sons of the Wilderness: John and William Connor.* Indianapolis: Indiana Historical Society, 1937.

Thornbrough, Emma Lou. *The Negro in Indiana: A Study of a Minority.* Indianapolis: Indiana Historical Society, 1957.

Tucker, Robert W., and David C. Hendrickson. *Empire of Liberty: The Statecraft of Thomas Jefferson.* New York: Oxford University Press, 1990.

Tucker, Spencer C., and Frank T. Reuter. *Injured Honor: The Chesapeake-Leopard Affair, June 22, 1807.* Annapolis: Naval Institute Press, 1996.

Unrau, William E. *White Man's Wicked Water: The Alcohol Trade and Prohibition in Indian Country, 1802–1892.* Lawrence: University of Kansas Press, 1996.

Van Every, Dale. *Ark of Empire: The American Frontier 1784–1803.* New York: William Morrow, 1963.

Wallace, Anthony F.C. *Jefferson and the Indians: The Tragic Fate of the First Americans.* Cambridge: Harvard University Press, 1999.

———. *Prelude to Disaster: The Course of Indian-White Relations Which Led to the Black Hawk War of 1832.* Springfield: Illinois State Historical Library, 1970.

Ward, Harry M. *The American Revolution: Nationhood Achieved, 1763–1788.* New York: St. Martin's, 1995.

———. *The Department of War, 1781–1795.* New York: Greenwood, 1981.

Warren, Mercy Otis. *History of the Rise, Progress, and Termination of the American Revolution. Interspersed with Biographical, Political, and Moral Observations,* 3 vols. New York: AMS, 1970 [reprint of the 1805 Boston edition].

Webster, Homer J. *William Henry Harrison's Administration of Indiana Territory.* Indianapolis: Indiana Historical Bureau, 1907.

White, George Fauntleroy. *Sketch of the Life of Colonel Isaac White of Vincennes, Indiana.* Washington, D.C.: Gibson Bros., 1889.

White, Richard. *The Middle Ground: Indians, Empires, and Republics in the Great Lakes Region, 1650–1815.* New York: Cambridge University Press, 1991.

Williams, Frederick D., ed. *The Northwest Ordinance: Essays on Its Formulation, Provisions, and Legacy.* East Lansing: Michigan State University Press, 1987.

Williams, Gary S. *The Forts of Ohio: A Guide to Military Stockades.* Caldwell, Ohio: Buckeye Book Press, 2003.

Wilson, George R. "Early Indiana: Trails and Surveys." *Indiana Historical Society Publications* 6, no. 3. Indianapolis, 1919, 349–457.

Woehrman, Paul. *At the Headwaters of the Maumee: A History of the Forts of Fort Wayne.* Indianapolis: Indiana Historical Society, 1971.

Woollen, William Wesley. *Biographical and Historical Sketches of Early Indiana.* Indianapolis: Hammond, 1883.

Young, Jeff C. *The Fathers of American Presidents.* Jefferson, N.C.: McFarland, 1997.

Zitomersky, Joseph. *French Americans–Native Americans in Eighteenth-Century French Colonial Louisiana.* Lund, Sweden: Lund University Press, 1994.

Index

CPSIA information can be obtained at www.ICGtesting.com
Printed in the USA
LVOW081853300112

266004LV00005B/3/P

9 780806 141985